LEARNING TO TEACH
ENGLISH
IN THE
SECONDARY SCHOOL

This forward-looking book combines theory and practice to present a broad introduction to the opportunities and challenges of teaching English in secondary school classrooms. Each chapter explains the background to current debates about teaching the subject and provides tasks, teaching ideas and further reading to explore issues and ideas in relation to school experience.

With reference to new legislation, the chapters suggest a range of approaches to the teaching of reading, writing, speaking and listening, drama, media study, information technology, language study, grammar, poetry, Shakespeare, GNVQ and A Level English Language and Literature. *Learning to Teach English in the Secondary School* offers principles and practical examples of teaching and learning in the context of the end of the twentieth century when new notions of literacy compete with the demands of national assessment.

Taking as its starting point the changing ideologies of English as a subject, the text addresses questions about the nature of teacher education. It raises issues concerning competence-based courses, working with a mentor in school and monitoring the development of a student teacher.

Jon Davison teaches at Canterbury Christ Church College.
Jane Dowson teaches at De Montfort University, Bedford.

D1438177

Learning to Teach Subjects in the Secondary School Series

Series Editors
Tony Turner, Institute of Education, University of London; Sue Capel, Canterbury Christ Church College; and Marilyn Leask, De Montfort University, Bedford.

Designed for all students learning to teach in secondary schools, and particularly those on school based initial teacher training courses, the books in this series complement *Learning to Teach in the Secondary School* and its companion, *Starting to Teach in the Secondary School*. Each book in the series applies underpinning theory and addresses practical issues to support students in school and in the training institution in learning how to teach a particular subject.

Learning to Teach English in the Secondary School
Jon Davison and Jane Dowson

Learning to Teach Modern Foreign Languages in the Secondary School
Norbert Pachler and Kit Field

Learning to Teach History in the Secondary School
Terry Haydn, James Arthur and Martin Hunt

Learning to Teach Physical Education in the Secondary School
Susan Capel

LEARNING TO TEACH
ENGLISH
IN THE
SECONDARY
SCHOOL

A companion to school experience

Jon Davison and Jane Dowson

London and New York

First published in 1998
by Routledge
11 New Fetter Lane, London EC4P 4EE

Simultaneously published in the USA and Canada
by Routledge
29 West 35th Street, New York, NY 10001

Reprinted 2000

Reprinted 2001, 2002 (three times), 2003 by RoutledgeFalmer

RoutledgeFalmer is an imprint of the Taylor & Francis Group

Selection and editorial matter © 1998 Jon Davison and Jane Dowson;
individual chapters © their authors

Typset in Ehrhardt by
J&L Composition Ltd, Filey, North Yorkshire

Printed and bound in Great Britain by
TJ International Ltd, Padstow, Cornwall

British Library Cataloguing in Publication Data

A catalogue record for this book is available from the British Library

Library of Congress Cataloging in Publication Data

Learning to teach English in the secondary school / edited by Jon
  Davison and Jane Dowson.
    p.   cm.—(Learning to teach subjects in the secondary
school)
  Includes bibliographical references (p.   )
  1. English language—Study and teaching (Secondary)—Great
Britain.   2. English literature—Study and teaching (Secondary)—
Great Britain.   3. English teachers—Training of—Great Britain.
I. Davison, Jon.   II. Dowson, Jane.   III. Series.
LB1631.L333   1997
428'.0071'241—dc21   97-15889
                                                                      CIP

ISBN 0–415–15677–7

Contents

Introduction to the series

This book, *Learning to Teach English in the Secondary School*, is one of a series of books entitled *Learning to Teach Subjects in the Secondary School: A Companion to School Experience*, covering most subjects in the secondary school curriculum. The books in this series support and complement *Learning to Teach in the Secondary School: A Companion to School Experience* (Capel, Leask and Turner, 1995), which addresses issues relevant to secondary teachers. These books are designed for student teachers learning to teach on different types of initial teacher education courses and in different places. However, it is hoped that they will be equally useful to tutors and mentors in their work with student teachers. In 1997 a complementary book was published entitled *Starting to Teach in the Secondary School: A Companion for the Newly Qualified Teacher* (Capel, Leask and Turner, 1997). That second book was designed to support newly qualified teachers in their first post and covered aspects of teaching which are likely to be of concern in the first year of teaching.

The information in the subject books does not repeat that in *Learning to Teach*, rather, the content of that book is adapted and extended to address the needs of student teachers learning to teach a specific subject. In each of the subject books, therefore, reference is made to *Learning to Teach*, where appropriate. It is recommended that you have both books so that you can cross-reference when needed.

The positive feedback on *Learning to Teach*, particularly the way it has supported the learning of student teachers in their development into effective, reflective teachers, has encouraged us to retain the main features of that book in the subject series. Thus, the subject books are designed so that elements of appropriate theory introduce each behaviour or issue. Recent research into teaching and learning is incorporated into this. This material is interwoven with tasks designed to help you identify key features of the behaviour or issue and apply these to your own practice.

Although the basic content of each subject book is similar, each book is designed to address the unique nature of the subject. In this book, for example, the centrality of language to learning and pupil development, and the debates relating to culture and correctness are highlighted.

We, as editors, have found this project to be exciting. We hope that, whatever the type of initial teacher education course you are following and wherever you may be following that course, you find that this book is useful and supports your development into an effective, reflective English teacher.

Susan Capel, Marilyn Leask and Tony Turner
January 1997

Illustrations

FIGURES

TABLES

TASKS

Contributors

Richard Bain is vice-principal at Norham Community Technology College in North Tyneside. He has worked as a consortium co-ordinator with the Language in the National Curriculum project (LINC), as English adviser for Gateshead LEA and as an Ofsted inspector. Publications include: *Talking to Learn* (Macmillan, 1988), *Take Any Book* (Macmillan, 1990), *Reflections: Talking about Language* (Hodder, 1991), *Looking into Language*, ed. (Hodder, 1992), *Exploring Letters* (Cambridge, 1993), *Exploring Language and Power* (Cambridge, 1993), *The Grammar Book* (NATE, 1997), *Pride and Prejudice*, ed., (Cambridge, 1996).

Gabrielle Cliff Hodges is a senior lecturer in English at Homerton College, Cambridge, where she jointly co-ordinates the secondary English and Drama PGCE course. She was formerly Head of English in a Cambridgeshire comprehensive school. Previous publications include chapters and articles about writing and reading development within the secondary age range and the teaching of poetry. She is currently Chair of the National Association for the Teaching of English.

Caroline Daly is involved with several aspects of initial and ongoing teacher education; she currently lectures on the PGCE Secondary English course at London University Institute of Education and on the PGCE and B.Ed. Secondary English courses at De Montfort University, Bedford. She works with the LEA and London University INSET for serving teachers. She taught English in secondary schools for eleven years, five of them as a Head of Department. Having completed an MA at the London University Institute of Education, she is continuing her research interests in literacy, reading and gender.

Jon Davison is principal lecturer and Director of Secondary Initial Teacher Education at Canterbury Christ Church College. Formerly Head of English and Media Studies in a London comprehensive school, he became an advisory teacher at the English and Media Centre, London, where he contributed to the *Advertising* pack, winner of the 1994 British Film Institue's Paddy Whannel Award for media education. During the 1980s he was a member of the ILEA English and the Micro development group and ran INSET courses on English and IT. He is a member of the National Association for the Teaching of English publications committee. He contributed chapters to *Learning to Teach in the Secondary School* and to its companion volume for NQTs *Starting to Teach in the Secondary School*. He is co-author of *Subject Mentoring in the Secondary School* (Routledge, 1997).

Jane Dowson is a senior lecturer in English and Cultural Studies; she co-ordinates the PGCE and B.Ed. Secondary English courses at De Montfort University, Bedford. She spent ten years teaching English in an upper school and was a member of the Northamptonshire and East Midlands Flexible Learning Working Parties. She was a member of the National Shakespeare in Schools Project, 1992/3, sponsored by RSA and RSC. She contributed chapters on the School Curriculum and the National Curriculum to *Learning to Teach in the Secondary School* (Routledge, 1995). Publications on Women's Poetry include *Women's Poetry of the 1930s: a critical anthology*, ed. (Routledge, 1995) and *Selected Poems of Frances Cornford*, ed. (Enitharmon, 1996).

Peter Gilbert has taught English in an upper school for nineteen years. He has been involved in various aspects of sixth form English; he is a qualified verifier for GNVQ, is currently responsible for Key Stage 4 English Language and is an external examiner for English Language with MEG.

John Moss is a senior lecturer in English at Canterbury Christ Church College. A former Head of English, Drama and Media Studies in a large comprehensive school, he has taught PGCE Secondary English courses for five years. He is the Research Officer for the National Association for the Teaching of English and has published the results of various investigations of the English curriculum in *NATE News*. He is co-author of *Subject Mentoring in the Secondary School* (Routledge, 1997).

Veronica Raybould has taught English for several years in three different schools; she is a sixth form tutor and co-ordinates A Level English Literature in an upper school. She has a particular interest in teaching and learning strategies and is involved in staff training for developing flexible learning throughout the curriculum.

Elaine Scarratt is Head of Media Studies at Christ the King VIth Form College, London. Previously she taught English, Media Studies and Drama in large London comprehensive schools. She has run INSET as part of the BFI's annual Media Studies conference. She contributed to *Dialogue and Difference: English into the 1990s* (Routledge, 1989) and co-authored *After the Bomb*, which won the TES Schoolbook Award in 1991.

Acknowledgements

We would like to thank the series editors of *Learning to Teach Subjects in the Secondary School*, particularly Sue Capel and, at Routledge, Helen Fairlie for their guidance and support.

Permission to use materials has been granted as follows:

The chart Figure 4.1. Sample English Syllabus for Years 8 and 9 by Sally Carter-Tabasso, PGCE Secondary English, De Montfort University, Bedford, 1995/6, taken from 'An Investigation into the level of implementation of the National Curriculum at a secondary school during 1996 for Key Stages 3 and 4' and by the English Department at The Radcliffe School, Wolverton.

'GCSE '98: What's the Difference?' (*English and Media Magazine*, 34, Summer 1996, pp. 21–26), by the English and Media Centre.

'GCSE English: The Background to the Current Concerns' (*NATE News*, Spring 1994, p. 9), by NATE.

The article 'Was Shakespeare a Tory?' by David Lister, printed in *Independent on Sunday*, January 1993, by *Independent on Sunday*.

Figure 13.1: 'Marking grid: AEB GCE A Level Literature', the extract from the AEB 1996 Examiners' Report, and the 'standard' Shakespeare Question on Paper 1 by the AEB. The AEB point out that any answers or hints on answers are the sole responsibility of the author and have not been provided or approved by the Board.

Figure 13.3: 'English Language Marking Grid', by the Cambridge Examining Board.

Permission to print 'The Writer', by Sujata Bhatt, from *Jumping Across Worlds* (Bhinda, ed., 1994, NATE), originally published in *Brunizem* (Bloom, Carcanet) has been given by Carcanet Press.

Permission to print 'Don' Go Ova Dere' by Valerie Bloom from *Duppy Jamboree* (Bloom, 1992, Cambridge University Press) has been given by Valerie Bloom and Cambridge University Press.

Permission to print 'Youth and Age' from *Catching the Spider* by John Mole (Mole, 1990, Blackie) has been given by John Mole.

'Skills', by Anne Stevenson, from *Four and a Half Dancing Men* (Stevenson, 1993, Oxford University Press) has been printed by permission of Oxford University Press.

'The Fair' by Vernon Scannell was taken from Vernon Scannell's *Selected Poems* (Allison and Busby) and has been reproduced by permission of the author.

'Swan Killed in Savage Attack' by Suzanna Chambers, taken from *Cambridge Evening News* (3/12/97) has been printed courtesy of *Cambridge Evening News* Material quoted from the National Curriculum in Chapter 3 is Crown copyright and is reproduced by permission of the Controller of HMSO.

Note

Many teacher education courses have their own nomenclature to describe various participants in the programme. Those studying to become teachers are variously described as interns, students, student teachers, trainee teachers and so on. For the purposes of clarity, we have used the following terms in this book:

- **pupils** – children and young adults in school;
- **student teachers** – participants in the teacher education programme;
- **tutors** – staff of university departments or colleges of education;
- **mentors** – staff in school.

Introduction

What is expected of a would-be teacher of English and what does the student teacher expect from a teacher education course? DES Circular 9/92 heralded the era of competence-based teacher education with a requirement for substantial elements of Initial Teacher Education (ITE) courses to be based in school. Two-thirds of Secondary PGCE courses are spent in school; therefore, during those 120 days, much of the responsibility for the development of student teachers now rests with mentors working in partnership with Higher Education Institutions (HEIs). Therefore, much of the time on your course will be spent working with your mentor and departmental colleagues in school, not only to develop your classroom skills, but also to develop you in the widest sense as a subject specialist. In recent years, the terms 'reflection' and the development of the student teacher as a 'reflective practitioner' (Schön, 1983; Calderhead, 1989; Lucas, 1991; Rudduck, 1991) have become central to ITE programmes run by HEIs. Indeed, it would appear that the reflective practitioner is now 'the dominant model of professional in teacher education' (Whiting *et al.*, 1996). The aim of this book, therefore, is to promote a coherent approach to school experience which will help you to draw together and investigate what you read, what you have experienced during your own education, and your school experience as an English specialist. More general approaches to school experience can be found in the companion volume *Learning to Teach in the Secondary School* (Capel, Leask and Turner, 1995).

Learning to Teach in the Secondary School is a valuable introduction to issues which concern every student and new teacher; *Learning to Teach English in the Secondary School* is complementary in looking at aspects like assessment or being a 'professional' in the context of becoming a subject specialist in English. The chapters introduce issues concerning the teaching of English which particularly relate to current developments such as competence-based and competence-assessed courses; working with a mentor; working with the National Curriculum; using IT in English lessons; understanding GNVQ. In addition, we are introducing aspects of English teaching which sound familiar, such as Speaking and Listening, Reading, Writing, teaching Shakespeare.

How might you use this book? It is intended to be sufficiently flexible to suit different stages of initial teacher education and different contexts. It is assumed that the book can be read in its entirety as a course text and also be used as a reference book, particularly on school experience. For example, you may be teaching a scheme of work on poetry or be involved in assessing speaking and listening for the first time: you would then consult the relevant chapters for principles and ideas which would aid your planning and your evaluation of your lessons. Some tasks are more suited to your university or college sessions, and may be directed by the tutor; others are clearly school-based. It is unlikely that you will undertake all the tasks but you may wish to try some out on your own or with a partner. Above all, the tasks are designed to guide your thinking and enquiry about *why* teachers do what they do and *why* you will make the decisions that you do. What is important, however, is that you consider and apply the principles to your particular context.

In the following chapters, the point is made several times that, just as when you are teaching, aspects of English are integrated, so, although these chapters are separated into activities like 'Writing', 'Drama' or 'Knowledge about Language and Grammar' for the purposes of investigation, it is recognised that they are all interdependent and interactive. You will be able to transfer principles raised in one area to their significance in another area; this is particularly true, of course, with media and information technology education.

It is usual for student teachers to begin a course with a fairly clear idea about what 'being an English teacher' is like; their reading and observations in school soon illustrate that there are many models of English teacher and that there are competing ideas about the aims of English teaching; they may be surprised to realise the extent to which English is perceived as 'political' by politicians, journalists and teachers. The lack of clarity and lack of consensus about the nature and aims of English teaching can be unsettling, but also exciting as the English teacher appreciates the significance of their role; because of the relationship between language and power, English teaching, which is based on a notion of literacy, is inherently political. As Burgess puts it, 'the connections between language, education and full participation in a political democracy have lain behind debates round English throughout two centuries.' (Burgess, 1996, p. 67).

It is in the context of encouraging new teachers to participate in the debates about language, education and power, that the first three chapters outline the 'battles' for English; they examine the changing ideas about the nature of English and their implications for the perceived roles of the English teacher. The background to current legislation demonstrates that a concept of what constitutes 'good practice' in English teaching is not fixed and never has been. English teachers may argue fiercely about whether to set their groups, whether drama should be used by all teachers, whether all pupils should take literature exams or how best to teach a child to spell or recognise a sentence.

Debates about the relative importance of grammar and spelling, language and literature, drama and media studies are longstanding and continuing. If you are coming to this book hoping for 'answers' you may be disappointed. We cannot reduce complicated processes concerning the relationship between language, thinking and identity into simple guidelines; we cannot resolve the questions about the proper nature of language study or how to teach someone to read or spell. These debates, along with 'what constitutes a text', and more precisely what constitutes a 'good text', or 'major author' are the bread and butter of English and Cultural Studies; these debates keep English as a dynamic subject which interacts with social trends.

The chapters consciously combine the critical issues surrounding each aspect of English teaching with ideas for classroom practice in order to encourage individual critical thinking. Many of the tasks are exploratory in nature and aim to provide opportunities to develop principles by which to make decisions concerning what and how to teach a text or an oral lesson or GCE A level; they are not offering blueprints. There are, however, some common approaches to the discussions and tasks; most signifcantly, there is a consensus that the job of the English teacher is to enable each child to become more literate. Although there is disagreement about what constitutes literacy, the current thinking is that we should speak of 'literacies' as incorporating the range of texts which people read; this version of literacy is not as radical as it might sound to conservative thinkers. The development of literacy has always been based upon available reading material; available reading material now encompasses all kinds of fiction and non-fiction, media and technological sources.

Many applicants to teacher education declare a love of 'literature', 'reading' or 'books' as their reason for wanting to teach English. Once on the course, they find themselves being asked to question the definition of 'book', the terms of describing a 'text' and the notion of reading. In schools they find that teaching a literary work is a small part of what English teachers do. The skills of critical analysis, however, which they have developed during their degree, are central to all areas of English teaching. *Learning to Teach English in the Secondary School* offers opportunities to work through the transition from previous engagement with English or cultural studies to the school curriculum; with its emphasis on 'critical practice', it suggests that it is not only possible but essential to retain a critical perspective on your reading and school experience, and on your model of initial teacher education. It is intended that, from an understanding of historical changes in the subject from the more remote and recent past, you will develop alternative ways of seeing the present conditions in education. We are also concerned that you will be a participant in setting the agenda for English teaching in the future.

It is a truism that what is most up-to-date is quickly dated. This is particularly applicable to the English curriculum which is subject to frequent changes in statutory requirements. We have had to make reference to current orders, particularly reference to the National Curriculum, but realise that these may change. At all times, it is acknowledged that it is the *principles* of suggested teaching ideas which are important and that these would have to be implemented with reference to current syllabuses and resources.

1 Which English?

INTRODUCTION

Where are you coming from?

As you begin your secondary English ITE course, you will bring to it a perception of what English teaching is about which has been formed from a combination of: your own school experience of being taught English; your undergraduate studies in English, and perhaps other subjects; information you have gleaned from sources such as the Press, observation visits to schools, and conversations with teachers you know; and, in some cases, work experience which is related to your planned career, such as TEFL teaching or running a youth club drama group.

Any analysis you have undertaken of these experiences may have engaged you in thinking about one or more of three different approaches to defining what English is: the identity of English as an academic subject, its scope and limits; the effective teaching and learning of English in schools; the English curriculum as it is defined by the National Curriculum and its assessment mechanisms.

If you were asked what English is during an undergraduate literature or language seminar, you would probably have concentrated on the first of these matters, and it is also likely that you would feel more confident about it than the others. You will, therefore, expect your ITE course to require you to explore ideas about the teaching and learning of English and the relationship between these ideas and the statutory curriculum. You may not realise at this point that these explorations are likely to challenge you to re-evaluate your understanding of what English as an academic subject is.

OBJECTIVES

By the end of this chapter you should:

- be aware of the major versions of English available to you and their implications for your work;
- be aware of the complexity of the debates about English;

- be able to place your own past, present and future experiences of English in the context of these debates.

THE DIVERSITY OF ENGLISH

Your re-evaluation of English may well begin as soon as you meet the other members of your ITE English method group. You will find that the ideas of your fellow student teachers have been influenced by a wide range of different academic experiences of English. You may find, in a single ITE English group, student teachers who have experienced:

- A Levels in English which explored English Literature, the English language, or both, in varying combinations;
- chronologically structured English Literature degrees, whose over-arching questions and concerns were with the relationships between literary tradition and originality or issues of canonicity;
- degrees in English Language, in which they have explored historical and geographical variations in English and learned to use sophisticated tools for analysing spoken and written language;
- degrees in English Language and Literature, in which studying the history of the language and stylistics has given them a perception of the significance of language change and writers' language choices to the analysis of literature;
- degrees centred on current debates about the value of different kinds of literary theory and the ways in which they can inform reading practices, which have been explored by reference to a range of literary and non-literary texts;
- joint honours degrees in which the study of philosophy, history or art has given them particular perspectives on ways in which the study of literature can be enriched by a knowledge of one or more types of social, historical or cultural context;
- joint honours degrees in English and Drama in which, among other things, they have experienced the value of practical drama methods in interpreting texts;
- joint honours degrees in English and Education in which they have explored issues such as language development which have a direct bearing on the teaching they will undertake in school.

You may value highly the approaches to English you have experienced, or you may have developed a critical distance from them. In either case, you will expect the school English curriculum to be underpinned by theoretical positions about the subject which you can compare with those which have influenced your own educational experiences to date. However, the variety of ideas about 'what English is' is represented in an ongoing debate about the school English curriculum which is complicated by further debates about how children learn.

TASK 1.1   THE EDUCATIONAL PURPOSES OF ENGLISH

Write a fifty-word statement defining the educational purposes of English as you understand them from your own educational experience at A Level and/or degree level. Exchange your statement with another student teacher and write a fifty-word commentary on his or her statement. In a group discuss the statements and commentaries you have produced, identifying repeated words and ideas and any contradictions. Try to achieve a consensus statement, and consider the reasons for your ability or inability to do this.

The Cox Report views of English

The debates about English are particularly clearly illustrated by the problem that faced Brian Cox's committee when it was appointed to draw up the first National Curriculum for English in the late 1980s. The Cox Report's authors pointed out:

> Throughout our work we were acutely aware of the differing opinions that are held on a number of issues that lie at the heart of the English curriculum and its teaching. Our Report would not be credible if it did not acknowledge these differences and explain our response to them.
>
> (DES, 1989, para. 1.17)

The Report went on, famously, to define the different views of English its writers found in the teaching profession:

> 2.21   A 'personal growth' view focuses on the child: it emphasises the relationship between language and learning in the individual child, and the role of literature in developing children's imaginative and aesthetic lives.

This view is associated with a child-centred approach to learning in English and language development experiences such as creative writing, talk and improvised drama. A particularly influential book promoting this view is Dixon's *Growth Through English*, first published in 1967.

> 2.22   A 'cross-curricular' view focuses on the school: it emphasises that all teachers (of English and of other subjects) have a responsibility to help children with the language demands of different subjects on the school curriculum: otherwise areas of the curriculum may be closed to them.

This view is associated with Chapter 12 of the Bullock Report, *A Language for Life* (DES, 1975) which was influenced by the work of Barnes, Britton and Rosen (1969) in *Language, the Learner and the School*. These writers placed a new emphasis on the role of speaking and listening in learning, which also figures in the 'personal growth' view of English. They also recognised that, since language is the medium through which most teaching and learning takes place, language development in all the processes of speaking and listening, reading and writing must be a whole school responsibility. Their arguments led to the introduction of language across the curriculum policies in many schools.

> 2.23 An 'adult needs' view focuses on communication outside the school: it emphasises the responsibility of English teachers to prepare children for the language demands of adult life, including the workplace, in a fast-changing world. Children need to learn to deal with the day-to-day demands of spoken language and of print; they also need to be able to write clearly, appropriately and effectively.

This view is associated with the expectations of school leavers which are expressed by employers' groups such as the CBI. Some other commentators who are concerned with the ways in which education prepares pupils for citizenship may also regard themselves as holding an 'adult needs' view of English, which may incorporate aspects of one or more of the other Cox views.

> 2.24 A 'cultural heritage' view emphasises the responsibility of schools to lead children to an appreciation of those works of literature that have been widely regarded as amongst the finest in the language.

This view is associated with schools of literary criticism which claim to be able to determine which books are most worth reading. A leading figure in the promotion of the idea of cultural heritage is F.R. Leavis, who, for example, in his book on the novel, *The Great Tradition* (1948), argued that the great novelists can be identified because 'they are all distinguished by a vital capacity for experience, a kind of reverent openness before life, and a marked moral intensity.'

> 2.25 A 'cultural analysis' view emphasises the role of English in helping children towards a critical understanding of the world and cultural environment in which they live. Children should know about the processes by which meanings are conveyed, and about the ways in which print and other media carry values.

This view is associated with forms of criticism which acknowledge that interactions between writers, readers and texts are influenced by a range of social, cultural and historical factors. Holders of this view may believe that the investigation of these interactions in relation to any text, literary or non-literary, print or non-print, written or spoken, is potentially of equal value, since the merit of a text is not absolute but culturally determined. They may also believe that it would be appropriate for the teaching of literature to be subsumed into 'cultural studies', or that this subject should replace English in the curriculum. (All quotations are from DES 1989, para. 2.21–2.25; commentary added.)

These views of English have been the subject of much discussion and research, both by those who have attempted to find out to what extent each view is represented in the teaching profession (e.g. Goodwyn, 1992), and by those who have questioned the validity of the categories or their definitions, or suggested other ways of defining viewpoints in the debate about what English is. You may be particularly interested in a contribution to this debate, made shortly after the Cox Report was published, by a group of student teachers (Daly, Mathews, Middleton, Parker, Prior and Waters, 1989). The historical context of the debate among views of English which Cox identified is explored further in Chapters 2 and 3.

CONSENSUS OR COMPROMISE?

What has become most clear from this debate is that many teachers cannot accept the position Cox took, that the different views 'are not sharply distinguishable, and ... certainly not mutually exclusive.' (paragraph 2.20). Reading between the lines of the definitions of the 'cultural heritage' view and the 'cultural analysis' view, for example, it is not difficult to find a sharp distinction between the 'appreciation of those works of literature that have been widely regarded as amongst the finest', and 'critical understanding of the ... cultural environment.' (paragraphs 2.24–2.25). The distinction is between being taught a taste for what a particular group in society, whose identity is hidden by the passive construction, wishes to have culturally transmitted, and learning to make an active analytical response to all the signs and sign systems of all the cultural products available to that analysis.

You may find this distinction reflected in positions held in your ITE English group, which may include those whose ambition as teachers is 'to pass on' something, a love of a particular kind of literature, for example, and those who seek 'to change' something, perhaps their pupils' sense of their own power to influence the development of society. Daly *et al.* provide an important statement of one version of the second position: 'we must develop goals, classroom approaches and materials which will transform "English" into the study of how and why our entire culture is produced, sustained, challenged, remade' (1989, p. 16). The distinction between 'cultural heritage' and 'cultural analysis' is both profound and political. Cox produced a compromise, rather than a consensus, English curriculum, perhaps in an attempt to steer a course between the Scylla and Charybdis of extreme views. However, any coherent rationale for English must confront the political issues, at the very least by acknowledging their existence.

Critical literacy in practice

One particularly valuable attempt at achieving a coherent radical vision of English which nevertheless acknowledges the complexity of the arguments about it can be found in West and Dickey's *Redbridge High School English Department Handbook* (1990). This book draws on a range of ideas about language, learning and literacy to formulate a theoretical position which might drive the work of a secondary English department in a typical urban high school: a multifaceted statement of departmental philosophy introduces detailed suggestions for teaching. A key text for the authors is Freire's *Literacy: Reading the Word and the World* (1987) from which they derive a view of English as 'critical literacy':

> English is concerned with the processes of language and with all aspects of the making of meaning. Its business is the production, reproduction and critical interpretation of texts, both verbal and visual, spoken and written.
>
> Its aim is to help [pupils] achieve critical literacy. To do this it seeks to:
>
> - enable [pupils] to make meaning
> - develop their understanding of the processes whereby meanings are made
> - develop [pupils'] understanding of the processes whereby meanings conflict and change.
>
> (West and Dickey, 1990, pp. 10, 23)

The authors note that this definition is intended to encompass 'aspects of Media Education and Drama that are undertaken by the English department'. They state that they see the definition as building on Cox's description of 'cultural analysis' by emphasising the social dimension of literacy: in a democratic society, pupils have the right to *make* and *contest* meanings as well as to understand how they are made. This definition of critical literacy informs the practical details of the schemes of work suggested in the book, and, in doing so, illustrates how the way teachers think about what English is influences their planning models and classroom practice.

All the schemes of work include sections headed: starting point, exploration, reshaping, presentation and opportunities for reflection/evaluation. For example, in a unit of work called 'Introduction to Media Education' pupils work on a photographic project. Among other things, the pupils are asked to:

- start by discussing the statement: 'The Camera Never Lies. . .' and by creating a display about this idea;
- explore a range of magazine photographs in a sequence of work which draws attention to issues of authorship, intention, technique and representation;
- 'reshape' a collection of photographs of their school which they take themselves into sets of six frame sequences, some negative, some positive, some balanced;
- present a selection of the photographs to an audience either within the class or outside it;
- reflect on the presentations in oral and written responses which may cover issues such as: the way the project has affected their view of the school; their understanding of the relationship between selectivity and representation.

(Selected and adapted from West and Dickey, 1990, pp. 151–152)

This unit of work shows how pupils who are studying the ways in which texts (here, primarily visual texts) are created, can extend their learning in important ways by participating in the processes by which similar texts are shaped and reshaped. Above all, pupils following this unit of work will learn about the power of makers of texts to make meaning consciously, deliberately and persuasively, and to contest meanings constructed by other makers of texts.

LINC'S FUNCTIONAL MODEL OF LANGUAGE

While learning about and through textual construction is at the heart of the model of critical literacy proposed by West and Dickey, their definition begins by identifying 'the processes of language' as the primary concern of English. The unpublished materials produced by the LINC (Language in the National Curriculum) project offered a model of language which could provide a coherent rationale for the English curriculum, and which complements West's and Dickey's work through its comparable emphasis on meaning-making. The authors of the materials see their work as an attempt to form a synthesis of the language theories of Britton and Halliday. Britton's importance is that his work, centred in language in education, 'clearly demonstrated the centrality of context, purpose and audience in language use [and is] grounded in fundamental consideration of the relationship between language and thought.' Halliday's work complemented this by offering 'functional theories of language [which] placed meaning at the centre' (LINC, 1992, 2). The authors define the theories of language implicit in the materials as follows:

1 As humans we use language primarily for social reasons, and for a multiplicity of purposes.

2 Language is dynamic. It varies from one context to another and from one set of users to another. Language also changes over time.
3 Language embodies social and cultural values and also carries meanings related to each user's unique identity.
4 Language reveals and conceals much about human relationships. There are intimate connections, for example, between language and social power, language and culture and language and gender.
5 Language is a system and is systematically organised.
6 Meanings created in and through language can constrain us as well as liberate us. Language users must constantly negotiate and renegotiate meanings.

(LINC, 1992, pp. 1–2)

The practical implications of the LINC view of language for teaching are best indicated in *Knowledge about Language and the Curriculum: the LINC Reader* (Carter, 1990). In particular, George Keith, in Chapter 4, outlines a scheme of work for Key Stage 3 which any English department could usefully consider using as the basis of a coherent and systematic approach to language teaching. The integrity of the scheme of work derives from the centrality accorded to work on Language and Society and the investigation of talk. The following practical suggestions for exploring this topic demonstrate how the LINC theories of language recorded above can be translated into schemes of work:

● using questionnaires and interviews to find out information about people's attitudes, beliefs, opinions: vox populi – getting people talking (will involve reflection on method of enquiry as well as on content of data);
● 'they don't speak our language' – enquiries into occupational dialects;
● jargon; officialese; slang; codes accents; Received Pronunciation; talking 'posh'; talking 'dead common'; regional stereotypes and foreign accent; stereotypes – use BBC tapes, *English with an Accent*, *English Dialects*;
● 'the language of situations' (pragmatics) – having an argument; being questioned or interviewed; threatening, bullying; embarrassing situations;
● euphemisms and taboo subjects in conversation;
● ways people talk to each other (gender, age, social class, social power);
● the speech of young children as a source of knowledge about language;

(Carter, 1990, pp. 90–91)

The LINC Project and its materials are discussed further in Chapter 3.

Transforming society?

Taken together, West's and Dickey's text-centred interpretation of critical literacy and LINC's functional model of language could be seen as providing the basis of a departmental rationale for English teaching which would assert the capacity of English to extend democracy by teaching pupils how language use is related to power and how they can access power through language. However, it is important to recognise that the adoption and translation of critical literacy into schemes of work and lesson plans can be seen as the appropriation of a potentially radical and democratising idea by an inherently divisive education system. Some commentators would see the entire history of English teaching in schools and universities as a warning about this. Similarly, although LINC addresses some aspects of the relationship between language and society, Peim (1992, p. 39), for one, has argued that its materials do nothing to counteract 'the deeply scandalous fact that the constitution of English, the core of the National Curriculum, remains structured to maintain inequality'. Peim argues that few steps can be made towards democratising society through language education until it is recognised that: 'Institutional definitions of literacy need to be seriously reconstructed, redefined or de-defined so that one limited notion of literacy can no longer serve as a mark of social superiority' (1992, p. 37). We will consider some ways in which the redefinition of literacy is currently absolutely inevitable later in this chapter.

TASK 1.2   VIEWS OF ENGLISH IN THE CLASSROOM

Observe three English lessons at your placement school with the intention of determining what view of English is being communicated to pupils or constructed by them. Make notes on matters such as: the choice of material; statements made by the teacher about the purpose of the work; the kinds of questions the teacher asks; the sequence of activities pupils engage in. You may find evidence of more than one view of English in a single lesson, or that one teacher teaches lessons which seem to offer very different views of English on the same day. Discuss your findings with the teachers and/or your fellow student teachers.

ENGLISH IN THE NATIONAL CURRICULUM (1995)

While critical literacy and functional approaches to language teaching have offered teachers a coherent development of Cox's cultural analysis view of English, the statutory English curriculum has become increasingly isolated from any kind of explicitly stated rationale, radical or otherwise, during the 1990s.

As Cox points out in his book *Cox on Cox* (1991), it was against his wishes that his Report was published with the chapters (1–14) describing its rationale *following* those (15–17) which defined what became the statutory English curriculum in *English in the National Curriculum* (DES 1990). The statutory Orders did not include this rationale at all, but teachers could at least turn to the Cox Report to help them understand the thinking behind the requirements placed upon them. In *English in the National Curriculum* (1995), two pages of General Requirements offer the only overview, which is more concerned with stressing the importance of Standard English than defining the whole English curriculum. Moreover, the content of those pages shows that, at sentence level, the 1995 document is a heavily redrafted revision of earlier documents, in which meaning has been lost as the result of battles between various interest groups to control the definition of the curriculum.

There is only scope in this chapter to illustrate this point with one example, so a statement about a particularly controversial issue, the place of Standard English in the curriculum, has been chosen. According to *English in the National Curriculum* (DFE 1995):

> The richness of dialects and other languages can make an important contribution to pupils' knowledge and understanding of standard English.
>
> (DFE, 1995, p. 2, para. 2)

The first thing to notice about this sentence is that it is ungrammatical. It needs to be prefaced by 'Learning about . . .' or 'Experience of . . .' to make sense. Secondly, the sentence makes an absurd and dangerous claim. This becomes quite apparent as soon as we construct a logically analogous sentence:

> [Experience of] the richness of a wide range of regional and world cultural behaviours can make an important contribution to pupils' knowledge and understanding of one particular form of English cultural behaviour.

The analogy exposes the original sentence as a transparent example of nonsensical cultural imperialism: one form of English cultural behaviour is said to feed off the spice island 'richness' of all other forms.

If we go back one stage in the public history of the development of the 1995 English curriculum, to *English in the National Curriculum (Draft Proposals, May 1994)*, we can establish precisely how the 1995 statement has come about. The equivalent sentence in this document reads:

> The richness of other languages and dialects can make an important contribution to pupils' knowledge and understanding of language.
>
> (SCAA, 1994, p. 1, para. 4)

This sentence has nothing to do with Standard English, and makes a more logical statement about the relationship between the study of examples of kinds of language and the development of an understanding of language principles. In the 1995 document, an act of imperialist linguistic vandalism has eradicated the logic of a Standard English sentence, by replacing *language* with *standard English*. This has clearly been done because of the concern to beef up the English curriculum's emphasis on Standard English which is apparent throughout the document. In this case it has been done at the expense of sense and logic.

In fact, the version of the sentence in SCAA, 1994, is close in meaning to Attainment Targets at age 16, number 13 in the *Report of the Committee of Enquiry into the Teaching of English Language* (The Kingman Report, 1988a), which states that:

> all pupils should be given the opportunity to . . . Make some systematic comparisons [of English] with other languages learned or used in school and in present day British society, so that an interest in linguistic diversity might be encouraged.

> Understand that: all languages are rule-governed systems; the status accorded to different languages used in any community is determined by social rather than linguistic factors.
>
> (DES, 1988a, p. 53)

However, despite the shared emphasis of these documents on a learning process through which principles are derived from the comparison of examples, there are at least two important differences. One assumption in Kingman appears to be that comparisons lead to the discovery of the principles of language and finally to an interest in linguistic diversity. SCAA appears to suggest that the interest in linguistic diversity must come first. Secondly, whereas Kingman makes an explicit statement about the need for pupils to understand that the status of particular languages is socially determined, SCAA avoids this issue.

The clearest statements about these matters in the history of government-sponsored documents on the topic come in the introductions to the chapters on accent, dialect and Standard English and multilingualism in *Language in the National Curriculum: Materials for Professional Development* (1992), introduced earlier in this chapter:

> Children have the potential to gain a confident control of a repertoire of language, including Standard English, as long as the school values the diversity of language competence, including that of accent and dialect, which children bring to it.
>
> (LINC, 1992, p. 276)

> multilingual language learning is not subtractive ('more of one language equals less of another') but mutually additive, whereby the growth of competence in one language enhances that in another through constant comparison of the ways that the two languages achieve – or sometimes fail to achieve – identical or similar meanings.
>
> (LINC, 1992, p. 300)

In this second statement multilingual pupils are given an active role in language learning which does not involve any language in having a higher status than another, and, interestingly, the route of comparison is not via principles but meanings, which, as we indicated earlier, are at the core of LINC's functional model of language.

This discussion has suggested that *English in the National Curriculum* (1995) is unreliable as a guide because it was written by groups who were competing to impose their views of English on the curriculum. The document has neither of the two kinds of integrity which are available to English teachers: neither a coherent theoretical rationale whose practical application is demonstrated, nor an acknowledgement that any statement about the English curriculum is made in the context of a complex and unresolved debate, in which contributors have political, as well as educational objectives. This lack of integrity in the statutory curriculum has made it increasingly possible for English teaching in schools to be controlled by new assessment mechanisms such as those which have been introduced in the GCSE syllabuses for 1998 examination, or the Key Stage 3 grammar tests under pilot at the time of writing, which drive teaching in directions which bear very little relationship to what most English teachers believe to be good practice.

The implications of this situation for you as a student teacher are very serious. It will be vital for you to discover where the tutors responsible for your ITE course and the teachers in the schools in which you are asked to work stand in relation to the various debates which have been described. Some of the questions you should ask tutors, Heads of English departments and mentors include the following:

- does your English teaching aim to reflect the complexity of the debates about what English is, or to promote a particular view of the subject?
- how is that aim realised at the practical level of planning?
- do you expect me to teach as if I share your aims in my teaching?
- how does your aim relate to the educational principles which determine the character of national assessments, and what do you do about this in practice?
- in what ways does the National Curriculum influence your practice, and how should it influence mine?
- how as a student teacher can I experiment in order to begin to formulate my own view of English?

TASK 1.3   EXPLORING LANGUAGE DEBATES IN OFFICIAL DOCUMENTS

Identify a language issue, such as multilingualism, drafting, dialect, discourse structure, grammar, literary English, language

variety, Spoken Standard English. Either on your own or in a
group of student teachers, find and compare statements about this
issue in *English for Ages 5–16* (1989), *Language in the National
Curriculum: Materials for Professional Development* (1992), *English
in the National Curriculum* (1995). What similarities and
differences, emphases and omissions do you notice in the
documents? Where does *English in the National Curriculum* stand
on this issue in relation to the ongoing debates about language
represented in the documents collectively?

FUTURES

So far, this chapter has asked you to consider ideas about English which
are derived from your own educational experience, from recently formulated but established views of the subject, and from debates which have
contributed to the introduction and revision of the National Curriculum.
The last part of the chapter will focus on some developments which are
currently transforming teachers' perceptions of what school curriculum
English is or can be. Three central threads in these developments concern: ideas about the importance of genre and rhetoric; the impact of new
technologies on speaking, reading and writing and the relationships
between them; the regionalisation and globalisation of English.

Postmodern textuality: genre and rhetoric

One way in which the 'personal growth' and 'cultural analysis' views of
English may form a new synthesis is through an adjustment of the ideas
about the self which are associated with the former, in the light of ideas
about genre and rhetoric which are associated with the latter. The discussion of 'critical literacy' earlier in this chapter drew attention to the
value of examining the ways in which meanings are constructed in texts.
Pupils who are to be politically empowered by the English curriculum
need to understand both how different genres work and how to select and
adapt the genre which is most appropriate to their purpose when they
seek to use spoken or written texts to exert influence on society. This
understanding must be partly based on consideration of the conventions
used in different genres. Some of these conventions are major and structural, but others operate at the level of syntax and vocabulary. For example, science fiction often translates familiar social and ethical problems to
unfamiliar narrative contexts, but also makes use of specialised vocabulary to define the technological capabilities of its characters.

The art of rhetoric was historically concerned with using language to
exert influence, or to persuade, and in particular with the careful selection

of figures of speech, the arrangement of language features in a spoken or written text, and with oratorical delivery. It offers us insights into the constructedness of texts at the level of language detail, and promotes the view that effective oral communication is founded on technique rather than on personality traits. Thinking about rhetoric and genre together can help us to see that the composition of a text in a particular genre and using particular rhetorical devices has something of the nature of a scientific experiment about it, since it involves throwing one of a number of available frameworks over reality. It may even suggest that meaning only exists in the constructs of different generic and rhetorical procedures. Another way of putting this is to say that rhetoric and genre provide the kind of real or imaginary theatrical masks which actors use to establish character and to make the communication of dramatic meaning possible.

This view of textual construction has something in common with postmodern views of the fragmentation and constructedness of the self, which in some versions would suggest that the self is only identifiable and definable in terms of the language or conventions through which it is expressed at particular times. Personal growth may then be about the taking on of new selves *through* the taking on of new rhetorical and generic conventions. Teaching in a way which draws attention to rhetoric and genre may then make an important contribution to the personal growth of those who experience it. In practical terms this may mean placing greater emphasis on allowing pupils to experiment with the conventions of genres, by providing them with opportunities for parody, to transpose texts from one genre to another, and to create new genres or texts which, like a considerable number of postmodern 'literary' texts, make use of a number of different genres.

Literacies and new technologies

New technologies are having an accelerating impact on our understanding of what it is to be literate, and how literacy is achieved. At the core of *English in the National Curriculum* (1995) is the statement that stands at the head of the Programmes of Study for each Key Stage: 'Pupils' abilities should be developed within an integrated programme of speaking and listening, reading and writing.' It is widely recognised that a fifth term 'viewing' needs to be inserted into this list of processes, to reflect the media literacy which plays such an important role in pupils' lives and their language development. However, we must now also acknowledge the relevance to language development of Websites, CD-ROMs, multimedia texts, hypertext and e-mail, and that these technologies challenge the ways in which we understand both the individual processes of reading, writing, speaking and listening, and the relationships between them.

For example, reading texts on computers, and especially Web pages with 'hot words', draws attention to the multidimensionality of reading, which has never been so apparent before. We know that we are not obliged just to read in a sequential way across and down a two–dimensional page, but nor are we limited to exploring the two-dimensional architecture of that page as we do when, for example, we look at a footnote. Reading a Website is more like playing three-dimensional chess: one move through a 'hot word' can completely redirect our attention, and even if we do choose to return to our earlier preoccupations it may be with an entirely new perspective on them. This experience modifies our understanding of what reading is. Some other experiences of using the Internet challenge our conceptions of the boundaries between the different language processes. For example, discussion pages on which ephemeral comments about a topic can be recorded and responded to, and which are periodically cleared by whoever maintains the site, are redefining the boundaries between speech and writing.

New technologies can also cause us to rethink our positions in relation to the established views of English discussed earlier in this chapter. For example, the Internet may affect the extent to which we tend towards 'cultural heritage' or 'cultural analysis' views. It is making available a wide range of texts which it was previously difficult to access. A substantial number of pre-twentieth-century literary texts by women which are out of print are available on the Internet. This makes it much easier than it has been before to demonstrate that the male white literary canon promoted in the 'cultural heritage' view of English is a construct. For some time, word processing has made texts available to readers in many different states and drafts in a way that shows us that meanings are not fixed.

The discussion of the different versions of the Revised National Curriculum earlier in this chapter illustrates how access to such drafts can affect our understanding of material we are presented with, and allow us to recognise how the possibility of shifting meaning in particular directions is related to power. The easy links between pages and sites on the Internet make readers very aware of the intertextual context of texts, and draw attention to the ways in which many apparently coherent and complete texts both contain gaps and draw, in different ways, on the work of a multiplicity of authors. Indeed, readers using the Internet have to learn to recognise and accommodate the fact that what they experience as a single reading event consists of texts produced by many different authors. These processes promote modes of reading which are linked with the 'cultural analysis' view of English.

Regionalisation and globalisation

At exactly the time at which *English in the National Curriculum* is promoting a view of English centred on the importance of Standard English, students of language are gaining more access to other systematic, rule-governed and dynamic versions of English than has ever been available before. Academic studies have long drawn attention to differences such as those between American Standard English and English Standard English to explode the myth that there is one Standard English which should be developed and used for global communication, and they have also demonstrated the systematic, rule-governed character of all dialects. However, in the last ten years, recognition of the value of regional and international varieties of English in the media, in film and in literature has reoriented the way many readers of visual and print texts perceive their relationship to speakers and writers who use dialects other than those with which they are most familiar. We place more value on the global diversity of Englishes than on the dominance of one English, and recognise that the high status accorded to particular versions of English has been culturally determined.

In this context, it is apparent that *English in the National Curriculum*'s category of 'texts from other cultures' should be more properly called 'texts from different cultures' and that the notion of a monolithic 'cultural heritage' is less rich than the idea of belonging to a global language culture, in which our own version of English, whatever that may be, exists as one regional variety of language which twentieth-century communications technology makes globally available alongside many others.

TASK 1.4   THE TEXTUAL REPRESENTATION OF THE DIVERSITY OF ENGLISH

What all three sections of the preceding discussion of 'futures' for English have in common is a sense of a need to develop approaches to teaching which promote and celebrate diversity and flexibility in language use, a moving in and out of and between genres, language modes, texts and/or cultural perspectives.

Find a literary or non-literary text or group of texts in which the writer or producer encourages the reader or viewer to experience shifts in meaning or a multiplicity of meanings, and write a commentary in which you either describe your response to the material or suggest ways in which you could use it in the classroom.

SUMMARY AND KEY POINTS

The claims that can be made for the possible effect of centring teaching on the developments in English discussed in the last part of this chapter may be large or small. There is no doubt that developments in each area are giving teachers new insights into literacy and into the ways in which language works. However, it is important to remain cautious about the extent to which any of these developments will transform the educational experience or lives of pupils. Centring the writing curriculum on genre and rhetoric will not in itself give pupils access to the audiences they need to begin to influence society; battles are currently taking place to achieve structural control of the Internet which may limit the access to it of many less privileged groups in global culture; there are questions to ask about the domination of global language culture by particular Englishes and by Englishes collectively.

Many of the formulations of English discussed in this chapter can be interpreted as serving the interests of particular privileged groups rather than as genuinely offering pupils the empowerment which can be stated as at least one justification for even those versions of English which may now strike us as most reactionary. As you begin your development as an English teacher, one question which you should keep firmly at the centre of your thinking, despite the temptation to abandon it which may result from your having to address more immediate issues, concerns your pupils more than English. What futures do you imagine for them, and how can your English teaching contribute to their development towards those futures?

FURTHER READING

Thought-provoking brief discussions of the current directions of developments in English teaching can be found in 'Beliefs about English', *English in Education* (1995) 29 (3), pp. 38–49, by Robin Peel and Sandra Hargreaves and a collection of short articles by various authors grouped under the heading 'The Future of English' (1996) in the *English and Media Magazine*, 34, pp. 4–20. *Writing the Future: English and the Making of a Culture of Innovation* (NATE, 1995) by Gunther Kress challenges us to develop a curriculum for English to meet the needs of the social individual in the twenty-first century.

Goodman, S. and Graddol, D. (1997) *Redesigning English: New Texts, New Identities*, London: Routledge.

Mercer, N. and Swann, J. (1997) *Learning English: Development and Diversity*, London: Routledge.
Both books form part of the series of four (the other two cover *English: History, Diversity and Change* and *Using English: From Conversation to Canon*) which support the Open University course U210. The first book considers what kind of language English has become and addresses issues related to the cultural, political and economic implications of the globalisation of English via printed and electronic media. The second book contains a section which explores the issues in English teaching. All four books will provide you with a wealth of thought-provoking material to reflect upon as you study to become a teacher of English.

2 Battles for English 1: 1870–1980

English is a subject suitable for women and the second- and third-rate men who are to become schoolmasters.

(Professor Sanday, 1893)

INTRODUCTION

Because of the way in which English Literature is often presented as a body of historical texts, there is a notion that English as a subject spreads back into the mists of time. English as a recognisable school subject has existed only since the beginning of the twentieth century and the category of English Literature as we know it is little more than a hundred years old (Gossman, 1981, p. 341). The Oxford School of English was not established until 1894 in the face of strong opposition from the Classicists as the quotation which opens this chapter indicates (Palmer, 1965 , pp. 104–117). Nevertheless, within this century the centrality of English to the education of children has been recognised and the subject now exists as part of the 'core' of the National Curriculum. However, the progress from new to established subject has not been a smooth journey and, at times, the conflicting beliefs about the nature and purpose of English have caused fierce debate, not least during the late 1980s and the first half of the 1990s, when there were two national reports on the teaching of English – Kingman and Cox – and the National Curriculum Order for English, produced in 1990, was revised twice in 1993 and 1994. This chapter explores the roots of the views about English teaching which underpinned the recent debates.

TASK 2.1 WHY ENGLISH?

Before you read any further, answer this question: 'Why should it be mandatory for every child in this country to study English in school as part of a core of the National Curriculum?'

Either by yourself or with a partner, brainstorm all the reasons you would give for studying English. Then list your reasons in order of importance. If possible, discuss them with another student teacher/pair and be prepared to justify your list and the relative importance of your reasons. Then as you read this chapter, look for the connections between your reasons and the reasons others have given during the last one hundred years.

OBJECTIVES

By the end of this chapter you should:

- have some knowledge of the key reports which determined the shape of English as a subject;
- be aware of philosophies and attitudes to culture and social class which underpinned the establishment of English on the curriculum;
- understand the importance to the subject that has been placed upon the literary 'canon';
- be aware of the reasons why notions of 'correctness' have been seen as central to English;
- begin to understand that different and conflicting paradigms of English teaching have existed;
- become aware of the philosophies which underpinned the ways in which you were taught English.

THE NINETEENTH CENTURY

> I would give unusual weight to the teaching of English language, literature, and history, to attempt to humanise and refine a boy's mind by trying to familiarise him with English poetry, and to inspire him with the best authors whom I could place before him.
> (Rev. G.G. Bradley, Headmaster, Marlborough School, cited in the Schools Inquiry Commission, 1868, p. 420)

A question of power

Before the turn of this century, English did not exist as a separate school subject (Ball, 1985, p. 53). Not until 1904 did the Board of Education *Regulations* require all elementary and secondary schools to offer courses in English Language and Literature. The reasons for the subject's inclusion in the curriculum of State schools were not necessarily ones that teachers today might deem educational. Indeed, some commentators (for example, Eagleton, 1983, p. 23ff) believe that the need for State education and the importance of English was 'advocated in a hard-headed way as a means of social control' (Gossman, 1981, p. 82). There is not space in a chapter of this length fully to detail the growth of the subject; however, the main strands of development are worth exploration, as many of the earlier beliefs and opinions about the subject can be found to underpin much of what happens in the name of English today. Although the Cox Report notes that 'views about English teaching have changed in the last twenty years and will continue to do so' (DES and Welsh Office, 1989, para. 2.4), it is possible to trace the differing views of English teaching back to the origins of State education in this country.

With the growth of Victorian technology there was an obvious need for a workforce trained 'in terms of future adult work': a workforce comprising adults who could read simple instructions; understand verbal commands; give and receive information and who exhibited 'habits of regularity, "self discipline", obedience and trained effort' (Williams, 1961, p. 62). Broadly, this utilitarian approach to education was dealt with in terms of 'Reading' and 'Writing' lessons. The overall aims of such an approach were to be articulated later in the Board of Education *Elementary Code* (1904, p. viii). Teachers should give pupils:

> some power over language as an instrument of thought and expression, and while making them conscious of the limitations of their own knowledge, to develop in them [such] a taste for good reading and thoughtful study . . . to implant in the children habits of industry, self control and courageous perseverance in the face of difficulties.

For Matthew Arnold, poet and HMI, writing in 1871, English Literature was 'the greatest power available in education'. Earlier, in *Culture and Anarchy* (1869), he writes 'the working class which, raw and half developed, has long been hidden amidst poverty and squalor and is now issuing from its hiding place to assert an Englishman's heaven born privilege of doing as he likes' (p. 105). Arnold was not alone in expressing concern about the working class and the growth of organised labour movements. It needs to be remembered that those drafting educational documents at the turn of the century would have clear memories of the turbulent times which characterised life in Europe in the nineteenth century: just over a hundred years since the French Revolution; less since the Paris communes; the rise of the working movement with the foundation of the Labour Party in 1893; left-wing philosophies emerging, and the Russian Revolution just around the corner. At a time of great social change policy makers believed that what was needed was a force for cohesion and social unity. For Arnold it lay in education. Arnold was much influenced in his thinking by Wordsworth. As a child he spent holidays in the cottage neighbouring the poet's own cottage, and as he grew up he developed a belief in the power of poetry to act as 'an excellent social cement' (Eagleton, 1983, p. 23).

The power of poetry

In the Preface to his *Lyrical Ballads* (1800), Wordsworth argues:

> Poetry is the first and last of all knowledge – it is as immortal as the heart of man . . . The Poet binds together by passion and knowledge the vast empire of human society, as it is spread over the whole earth, and over all time.

Elsewhere, in *A Defense of Poetry* (1840) Shelley regards poetry as 'something divine', because 'it is not like reasoning . . . It is as it were the interpretation of a diviner nature through our own.' To inhabit the realm of literature is somehow to transcend the quotidian; to be at one with a diviner nature; to be at one with the 'vast empire of human society.' That its nature could not be debated, rather its truths could only be 'felt' or 'experienced', is significant, because this view gave rise to the development of poetry 'appreciation' rather than 'criticism' in the school curriculum for much of the first half of the twentieth century. As Palmer (1965, p. 39), in his excellent history of the subject, puts it 'The main emphasis in the moral evangelical approach to literature is upon reading, upon the value of making contact with the great imaginations of the past.'

ENGLISH AND THE BOARD OF EDUCATION

> The present is an age of educational reform. The methods of teaching most of the subjects in the curriculum have undergone considerable changes and been vastly improved, during the last decade.
> (Roberts and Barter, 1908)

Good taste v. slang

The reader might be forgiven for thinking that this quotation from *The Teaching of English* had been written in the 1990s. However, the first twenty years of the twentieth century saw an outpouring of publications from the Board of Education which might almost match the National Curriculum Council (NCC) documentation were it not for the fact that the plethora of NCC documentation was produced in just four years. A series of Circulars were produced which attempted to define and structure the curriculum in elementary and secondary schools. Board of Education (1910) *Circular 753* was instrumental in establishing the nature of English as it came to be in school. It shows clearly the underlying philosophies mentioned earlier:

> instruction in English in the secondary school aims at training the mind to appreciate English Literature and at cultivating the power of using the English Language in speech and writing . . . Literature

supplies the enlarged vocabulary which is the mechanism of enlarged thought, and for want of which people fall helplessly back on slang, the base coin of the language. Pure English is not merely an accomplishment, but an index to and a formative influence over character.

(para. 2)

Clearly, the approach is a high cultural, pure-English-as-civilising-agent approach advocated in the previous century by Matthew Arnold. The Circular envisages its own literary canon: a body of great literary works to which pupils need to be introduced. Pupils 'should be taught to understand, not to criticise or judge' the great works (para. 36). Texts recommended include *Hiawatha*, *The Rime of the Ancient Mariner*, *Robinson Crusoe*, *Stories of Heroes*, *Patriotic Songs*, *Gulliver's Travels*, and the poetic works of Milton, Gray, Coleridge, Tennyson and Wordsworth. There is an obvious lack of Dickens, or any other novelist, who might venture into the realms of social realism; but stories of courage distanced in the realms of Romanticism were quite acceptable. Maybin (1996, p. 236) reminds us that canonical texts have always been important not only because they are regarded as the backbone of English Literature, but also in relation to the definition of Standard English. In compiling his English dictionary, Samuel Johnson based it upon the books he regarded as illustrating 'authoritative uses and meanings in the language'. Similarly, histories of English languages in the nineteenth century focused upon the written works, which were believed to be most important, rather than the spoken word. The importance of literature in relation to its 'divine' nature, in relation to notions of correctness and Standard English, and the subordinate status of the spoken word (particularly, perhaps, when spoken by a working-class child) fundamentally determined the nature of English in school throughout the twentieth century.

Literature was also to be used as a source of composition. *Circular 753* stated that pupils should be taught to write 'so as to satisfy the requirements of good sense and good taste' (para. 38). In a perplexing paragraph teachers are told 'Quality not fluency should be aimed at' (para. 42), which does not bear analysis. Perhaps the most damaging approach is the method by which this quality might be achieved. A composition should be set upon a subject 'which has been excellently handled by some competent writer'. Subsequently, the piece of literature is used for 'criticism and comparison with the pupils' attempts' (para. 40). One can only imagine the effect of seeing how pitifully short one's essay fell from the 'masterpieces' of the 'great writers'. To sum up, the document offered little opportunity for personal expression. A pupil was to be brought into the presence of the great minds to learn 'by heart copious extracts from the English classics' (para. 22) – of 'good prose' as well as poetry – and pupils' written work was to be compared with 'great literature'.

The unsuitability of novels

Startlingly perhaps for teachers today, the Circular has this to say: 'Novels, indeed, though occasionally points for discussion, are rarely suitable for reading in school' (para. 34) and 'Boys and girls will read of their own accord many books – chiefly fiction. These . . . are only of transitory interest, and involve little or no mental effort' (para. 17). Part of the explanation for the antipathy to novels lies in the growth of mass production. For at least twenty years, novels had been widely and cheaply available. This antipathy to the indulgence of children in popular culture can be traced to the present day in educational documents: from cinema through radio, television and video, to computer games. The *Times Educational Supplement* (1915) noted that:

> all headteachers who were consulted agreed that cinematograph shows were physically detrimental to scholars in consequence of the late hours, loss of sleep, and the bad atmosphere, and that the mental effect upon the children was to make them more fond of noise, ostentatious display, self-advertisement and change. The pictures excited their minds and created a love of pleasure and disinclination for steady work and effort.

A further explanation of this hostility to popular culture lies in the view of high culture which underpins *Circular 753*. The canon of 'great' literature must *per se* be fixed for all time and cannot admit works of popular cultural origin. 'Divine' works are inarguable and pupils must be taught to appreciate them, for 'the real teachers of Literature are the great writers themselves. . .the greater the work, the more it speaks for itself' (para. 21). However, rather bizarrely the Circular also asserts, 'all literature, prose as well as poetry, is a foreign language and requires to be learnt as such' (para. 26). How then can it 'speak for itself'? Undoubtedly, the writers are referring here to the 'base coin of language' indulged in by working-class children. Such an attitude to the difference between literary language and the spoken language of working-class children and the negative effects of popular culture is also in evidence in the Newbolt Report (Board of Education 1921):

> The great difficulty of teachers in elementary schools in many districts is that they have to fight against evil habits of speech contracted in home and street. The teacher's struggle is thus not with ignorance but with a perverted power.
>
> (para. 59)

Here again an official document displays a clear attitude to children from the working class, who in their culture of 'home and street' are believed to threaten established norms, not through ignorance, but by virtue of a 'perverted power'. Part of this power was, no doubt, located within developing popular culture. Therefore, the best thing an English teacher can do for a pupil is 'to keep him from the danger of the catchword and everyday claptrap' (Board of Education 1921, para. 81); 'to teach all pupils who either speak a definite dialect or whose speech is disfigured by vulgarisms, to speak Standard English' (para. 67) – there is no acknowledgement that Standard English is, in itself, a dialect. For working-class children, the Newbolt Report rather perplexingly believes that 'English may be a negative quantity' (para. 59).

TASK 2.2   CORRECTNESS AND CHARACTER

Look back over this chapter so far. Examine the language of the educational policy makers. Alone, or with a partner answer the following questions:

1. What recurring connotations do you notice in the language (for example the adjectives) used to describe the working class and children's spoken language? What attitudes does such language display?
2. How important do you believe is Standard English in written work?
3. How important do you believe is Standard English speaking?
4. Can great literature be inspirational and an influence over the formation of character?
5. Can/should English teaching be used as a form of *social engineering*?

   How do the reasons given in these early documents for the importance of studying English compare with your reasons produced in Task 2.1?

THE NEWBOLT REPORT

> The most formidable institution we had to fight in Germany was not the arsenals of the Krupps or the yards in which they turned out submarines, but the schools of Germany . . . An educated man is a better worker, a more formidable warrior, and a better citizen.
>
> (Lloyd George 1918, cited in Baldick, 1983)

Play up! and play the game!

It is significant that the first major evaluation of education after the First World War was carried out into *The Teaching of English in England*

(Board of Education, 1921) by what came to be known as the Newbolt Committee, which was appointed by the government in May 1919. The shock waves of the refusal of some working men to 'go over the top' in the trenches and the 1918 mutinies in the British army had rumbled through the military establishment to reach government level. If English had been introduced into the curriculum to 'gentle the masses' it was seen as failing, not solely because of the levels of illiteracy among young working men conscripted into the services in 1914. The Committee discovered that, in schools, 'English was often regarded as being inferior in importance, hardly worthy of any substantial place in the curriculum' (para. 6); while in boys' schools the study of English was 'almost entirely neglected' (para. 106). More worrying to the Committee was the attitude of the working class, 'especially those belonging to organised labour movements, [who] were antagonistic to, and contemptuous of literature . . . a subject to be despised by really virile men . . . to be classed by a large number of thinking working men with antimacassars, fish-knives and other unintelligible and futile trivialities of "middle-class culture" and "to side-track the working movement"' (para. 233).

The Committee sat on 42 days and its report was drawn up by a sub-committee in 18 days. The constitution of the Committee bears analysis, for its composition undoubtedly shaped the approach to English which underpinned, not only the Report, but also the teaching of English for the following thirty years. Sir Henry Newbolt chaired the Committee. Oxford-educated and Professor of Poetry from 1911 to 1921, Newbolt is, perhaps, now best remembered for his poem *Vitae Lampada*, which details the virtues of self-sacrifice for one's country and contains the refrain: 'Play up! play up! and play the game!' Other Oxford men on the Committee were John Bailey, F.S. Boas and Professor C.H. Firth. While from Cambridge came Sir Arthur Quiller-Couch and John Dover Wilson (critic and HMI). Other notable members included Professor Caroline Spurgeon, best known for her exhaustive work on Shakespeare's imagery; J.H. Fowler, of *English Usage* fame; and George Sampson (q.v.). With such luminaries on a committee of fourteen members, it is not surprising that notions of correctness, cultural heritage and a belief in the humanising nature of literature should hold sway.

Although the Report is lengthy (393 pages) it is 'seldom positive in its proposals' (Palmer, 1965, p. 82). Like all reports produced by a committee it is, on occasions, contradictory. English is asserted to be the 'basis of school life' (para. 61) and the Report coins a phrase which still has currency, 'every teacher is a teacher of English, because every teacher is a teacher in English' (para. 64). However, in a contradictory paragraph, it notes that good English teaching 'demands skill and resource, [and] is too often thought a task which any teacher can perform' (para. 116) – a problem which had been noted in *Circular 753*, ten years earlier.

Changing methodologies

Although the Report's central philosophy mirrors earlier Board of Education publications, its approach to methodology is different. The Report is critical of the approaches advocated in Circular 753. It is against 'giving the children a model essay by Lamb or Hazlitt' (para. 78): exactly what had been promoted in Board of Education documents of 1904, 1906, 1908 and 1910. Similarly, it deplores that there was often 'Too much emphasis on grammar and punctuation, spelling' (para. 79). And, correcting the strange, 'Quality, not fluency' statement, the Report maintains, 'until there is some fluency, highly critical methods will tend to repress the pupil into silence' (para. 80). Paragraph 81 lists eleven 'positive methods' for the improvement of English lessons. While most of them are fairly standard and had been proposed earlier – 'listening'; 'using the dictionary'; 'summarising' – three recommendations appear surprising:

> g) proposals from the children about the choice of subjects; class discussions, dramatic work;
> h) preparation in advance of the subject matter of composition . . .
> k) free and friendly criticism by the scholars of each other's work.

> All agree in emphasising the value of oral exercises.
> (Board of Education, 1921, para. 81.)

Such methodology would not seem out of place in an English department today. However, in the 1920s it is obvious that factors such as class size would have mitigated against the adoption of these recommendations, in the same way it did against the Report's belief in the value of discussion between small 'groups of children' (para. 74). It is clear that within its short existence as a curriculum subject, what we now believe to be 'traditional' methods were the backbone of English teaching, and the more progressive recommendations would not be adopted for approximately fifty years. Indeed, the Hadow Report (Board of Education, 1926, pp. 190–193) on *Education and the Adolescent* actively promoted the methodology of *Circular 753*, which the Newbolt Report had attempted to discourage.

English for the English

In the same year as the Newbolt Report appeared, a member of the Committee, George Sampson, published *English for the English* (1921), which contained 'A Plea' for, and a detailed 'Programme' of, English teaching. Sampson castigates 'the extravagant British workman' and his 'moral, intellectual and emotional level', whose habits lead him to 'the newest and nudest revues' and who ends by 'being divorced' (Sampson, 1921, pp.

104–105). Whereas he believes the schoolboy may be saved from the baser, corrupting influences in life, because 'English in the largest sense here used, is the one subject that will cover all aspects of education – intellectual, moral and emotional – and very especially it will cover all that we at present leave naked and barbarous' (p. 105). Sampson believes that the subject will not change the situation, rather it will 'cover' the glaring social inequalities in society. Such an attitude was to re-emerge in the *Report on Secondary Education*, the Spens Report, which proposed that, 'it should be possible for the spread of a common habit of English teaching to soften the distinctions which separate men and classes in later life' (Board of Education, 1938, p. 222). Some commentators have proposed that such statements from Newbolt, Sampson and Spens indicate a belief in the power of English to 'break down the barriers of social class' (Palmer, 1965, p. 180). However, on examination of these reports it is clear that the authors believe that the classes will still be 'separate', but the working class will identify with members of superior classes through the development of 'clearness and exactitude of expression' (Board of Education, 1938, para. 113) and by accepting the 'diviner' nature of great literature be at one 'with the vast empire of human society': it is unsurprising that both Wordsworth and Arnold are referred to, and quoted from, throughout the Spens Report.

THE 1930s

A civilisation in crisis

The 1920s and 1930s saw a rapid expansion in the production of the popular press and publishing houses, the arrival of television and a global expansion in the distribution of Hollywood films. Such expansion was, of course, happening against a background of the arrival (and engineered swift dismissal) of the first Labour government, the General Strike, the Great Depression, the continued rise of Communism, social unrest in Europe and the rise of Fascism. It is little wonder that educational legislators may have felt besieged. Writing in his introduction to a new edition of Arnold's *Culture and Anarchy*, former member of the Newbolt Committee John Dover Wilson observed:

> Though the shadows of domestic agony under which it was written have passed away, if it is not too bold to say this within five years of the General Strike, a huger shadow has taken its place, that of world anarchy which threatens to bring the whole structure of civilisation toppling to the ground.
>
> (Dover Wilson, 1932, p. 28)

For the authors of the Spens Report, hope lay in the great tradition and the values and higher moral code espoused by the great writers, 'it involves the submission of the pupil to the influences of the great tradition; it is his endeavour to learn to do fine things in a fine way' (Board of Education, 1938, p. 161). The study of literature was believed to exercise 'a wide influence upon the life and outlook of the adolescent, more general and long lasting in its effects than that normally exercised by any other subject in the curriculum' (p. 218). Teachers 'may yet succeed in making the normal citizen of this country conscious and proud of his unequalled literary heritage' (p. 228). Here again we are presented with a view of culture as complete: a legacy, an heirloom, which having been cherished, is to be handed down to the next generation. Presumably, any citizen not 'conscious and proud of his unequalled literary heritage' is perforce 'abnormal'.

More worrying for some was the standard of spoken English, which was seen (or heard?) as 'slovenly, ungrammatical, and often incomprehensible to a stranger' (p. 220), but which the 'common habit of English teaching' (p. 222) would cure. The textbook *Good and Bad English* (Whitten and Whittaker, 1938, p. 69–71) mirrors this attitude throughout: for example 'NEVER – *never* – write "alright". It is all wrong (not alwrong), and it stamps a person who uses it as uneducated'. Elsewhere, other errors are regarded as equally damning: 'this crude usage is found only among the uneducated' and 'this usage is now confined to illiterate people'. Similar attitudes can be found in the April 1993 draft proposals for National Curriculum *English 5–16 (1993)* (DES and Welsh Office, 1993a) in its regular restatement that, from Key Stage 1 pupils 'should speak clearly using Standard English' and 'should be taught to speak accurately, precisely, and with clear diction'. The draft proposals include a variety of 'Examples': 'We were (not was) late back from the trip'; 'We won (not winned) at cricket'; 'Pass me those (not them) books'; 'Clive and I (not me) are going to Wembley'; 'We haven't seen anybody (not nobody)' (pp. 9–23). (It is, perhaps, too uncharitable to believe that the authors included the errors in parentheses in case English teachers were unaware that such forms were wrong.)

If high culture was to be the saviour of working-class children, the Spens Report, like earlier documents, knew where to lay the blame for their slovenly language:

> Teachers everywhere are tackling this problem [of debased forms of English] though they are not to be envied in their struggle against the natural conservatism of childhood allied to the popularisation of the infectious accents of Hollywood. The pervading influences of the hoarding, the cinema, and a large section of the public press, are (in this respect as in others) subtly corrupting the taste and habits of the rising generation.
>
> (Board of Education, 1938, p. 222–223)

The burgeoning mass media, like some virulent disease ('infectious'), were portrayed as corrupting a whole generation. As in earlier documents, the language of disease, corruption and perversion links the mass media and the working class. Popular culture was seen as a threat because pupils needed no introduction to it – it was the stuff of their lives – whereas they needed to be 'brought into the presence' of great writers who would civilise them. Therefore, high culture and popular culture were seen as objects of opposition and popular culture was not worthy of study.

LEAVIS

> English students in England today are 'Leavisites' whether they know it or not.
>
> (Eagleton, 1983, p. 31)

The Great Tradition and practical criticism

Arguably, the major influence upon the development of teaching English Literature in this country was the launch of the critical journal *Scrutiny* in 1932. It is beyond the scope of this chapter to attempt a complete evaluation of the contribution of F.R. Leavis and the 'Cambridge School' to the development of English studies – that has been done elsewhere at length (see for example Baldick, 1983; Ball, 1985; Daiches, 1956; Eagleton, 1983; Maybin, 1996; Palmer, 1965; Protherough and King, 1995). The intention here is to refer to those elements of Leavisite critical theory which have directly impinged upon the teaching of English in schools.

Central to Leavisite critical theory is the notion of 'close reading' or 'practical criticism' (Richards, 1929) of texts, whereby the critic deals with 'an individual's work rather than a writer's achievements as a whole' (Daiches, 1956, p. 299). Unlike the vagaries of the Romantic appreciation promoted by Arnold and his descendants, which culminated in the Board of Education promoting a love of greatness in literature without judgement, practical criticism is 'unafraid to take the text apart' (Eagleton, 1983, p. 43). For Leavis, texts would be analysed in relation to the literary standards exemplified in the canon of great literature. It is this method which has come to be at the very core of the teaching of English Literature in universities and schools. However, while the Leavis's methodology may have differed from Newbolt's and Arnold's, his philosophy was strikingly similar. The Leavisite canon included *inter alia* Chaucer, Shakespeare, Jonson, Bunyan, Pope, Blake, Wordsworth, Keats, Austen and George Eliot. To be included in the canon a text had to 'display particular kinds of moral, aesthetic and "English" qualities which would arm readers against the moral, aesthetic and commercial degeneration of the age' (Maybin, 1996, p. 245).

It is clear that the belief in the humanising effects of great literature, produced in some past golden age, is central to the Leavisite view, as is a hostility to popular culture.

Leavis and Thompson's *Culture and Environment* (1933) is a study of contemporary industrial conditions, mass production, standardisation and advertising. Unquestionably, Leavis's purpose in the study of the media was, in the main, to inoculate us against the infectious corruption of their virulence. For Gossman (1981, p. 361), 'The Leavisites seem always to have been an embattled elite . . . bravely bearing witness to an ungodly age.' *Scrutiny* was published for twenty-one years. In 1948 Leavis published perhaps his best-known work, *The Great Tradition*. He lived until 1978 and without doubt influenced English teaching as it has come to be in schools (Mathieson, 1975). But as Eagleton (1983, p. 43) points out, in later years Leavis displayed 'a fierce hostility to popular education, an implacable opposition to the transistor radio and a dark suspicion [of] "telly addiction"'.

Practical criticism, however, found little support in the Board of Education's next major report on secondary schooling. In the Norwood Report (Board of Education, 1943) *Curriculum and Examinations in Secondary Schools* the authors not only criticise the notion of close reading, but also they reaffirm the power of literature proposed by Arnold and Newbolt. Paragraph 93 of the Report argues that 'too much attention has been paid to aspects [of great literature] which are of secondary importance and the higher values have been obscured.' It goes on to assert that these values are 'final and absolute: they cannot be broken down into constituent parts: they are beyond analysis and wait upon the appreciative powers of the pupil.' The paragraph concludes that the teaching of English Literature is concerned with that 'which is past analysis or explanation, and values which must be caught rather than taught.' 'Final and absolute' cultural values are fixed for all time. Values which are 'beyond analysis' are beyond question and therefore beyond discussion.

To sum up, in all educational documentation relating to the study of English which was produced before the Second World War, it is possible to identify a number of recurring themes. First, there is a belief that it is possible to identify a number of works from the past which stand the test of time because they exhibit certain values and qualities which are universal. Second, some believe that such works have a humanising effect on the lower classes and are, therefore, an aid to social stability. Third, pupils should be taught to appreciate great literature, not to criticise it. Fourth, the spoken and written language of working-class children is of extremely low quality. Fifth, the exposure of pupils to 'fine writing' will enable them to write and speak Standard English. Sixth, popular culture should be seen as a corrupting influence and an enemy to high culture.

ENGLISH TEACHING POST-WAR

From literature to language

Another report entitled *The Teaching of English* was published in 1952 by the Incorporated Association of Assistant Masters in Secondary Schools (IAAMSS). It is clearly anchored in 'traditional' views of the subject: 'The English continue to mishandle their language by slovenly pronunciation, by drab delivery, and by dull or tired writing; they tolerate too easily official jargon and advertisers' rhetoric; and they have little time or love for their own magnificent poetry' (IAAMSS, 1952, p. xv). Insisting on standards and correctness, the report promotes the virtues of 'speech training' (pp. 42–43) to remedy the problems it identified. It is interesting to note that the report was published by Cambridge University Press. But if the Oxford and Cambridge Schools were instrumental in shaping the 'English as literature' paradigm of the subject prior to the Second World War, arguably the most influential institution post-war has been the University of London Institute of Education (formerly the London Day Training College). Foremost among those associated with the Institute who have helped to shape the teaching of English in the last forty years are Britton, Barnes, Rosen and Martin. While the Cambridge School, for the most part, addressed itself to the teaching of the subject in grammar schools, the 'London School' was more associated with the spread of comprehensive education in the 1950s and 1960s. (The first purpose-built comprehensive, Kidbrooke School, opened in south-east London in 1954.) The difference between London and Cambridge in Britton's words was the difference 'between *using* the mother tongue and *studying* it' (Britton, 1973, p. 18). Ball (1985, p. 68) characterises the London approach as the 'English as language' paradigm of English teaching. Key texts which have underpinned the development of this paradigm are, among others, *Language and Learning* (Britton, 1970); *From Communication to Curriculum* (Barnes, 1976); *Language, the Learner and the School* (Barnes, Britton and Rosen 1969). Throughout the 1950s and up until the present day it is clear that both paradigms of English teaching have held sway, often to be found in the differing approaches of members of the same English department.

By 1947 the English Association, formed in 1906 to promote the development of the subject, had little influence. But in that year, the London Association for the Teaching of English (LATE) was founded by Britton and Gurrey. Although it is impossible to calculate direct influence accurately, it is possible that LATE, together with the National Association for the Teaching of English (NATE, formed in 1963), have done most to shape the teaching of English in the last forty years. The involvement in curriculum development projects, production of publications and participation in advisory work focused upon the needs and practices of classroom teachers have done much to develop the 'English as language' paradigm and to develop approaches to English Literature, which are far from 'traditional'.

If societal influences in Victorian times and in the 1920s and 1930s can be seen in some ways to have shaped the foundations of English teaching, the same may be said of the 1960s and 1970s. These two decades saw not only massive changes technologically in the 1960s and a crashing economic recession in the 1970s, but also radical changes in relation to State education. In terms of school examinations, Certificate of Secondary Education (CSE) English was introduced. It ran alongside O Level courses; but whereas O Level English examinations comprised 'Composition', 'Comprehension', 'Précis', 'Grammar/Vocabulary exercises', CSE was much less formal. Similarly, while O Level English Literature syllabuses focused, in the main, on writers drawn from the canon, CSE texts were more likely to be written by contemporary authors. Further, the introduction of CSE Mode 3 examinations – set and marked by teachers in school – and up to 100 per cent coursework elements, were regarded as 'soft options', open to cheating, by those who favoured the traditional 'terminal' O Level examination. Elsewhere, the restructuring of the teaching profession, the changes in teacher education, the spread of comprehensive schooling, the Raising of the School Leaving Age (RoSLA), the work of the Schools Council, all contributed to the conditions for curricular change.

However, the emergence of a language-based model of English teaching, which was not necessarily focused upon 'traditional' notions of grammatical correctness, of a model which some characterised as being in direct opposition to the 'traditional' literature-based model, caused genuine tensions – not only within the English department, but also in society at large. Subsequently, the publication of the *Black Papers*; concerns over 'falling standards' and 'progressive child-centred' education; the perceived threat to the eleven plus and grammar schools through comprehensive schooling, led to the establishment of another inquiry into all aspects of English teaching, chaired by Sir Alan Bullock.

A Language for Life

It is clear that the Report gathered evidence of a variety of practices in schools, which were both 'traditional' and 'progressive'. Reflecting the developments which had taken place since the 1950s, *A Language for Life* (DES, 1975) concludes 'The time has come to raise language as a high priority in the complex life of the secondary school'. However, Ball (1985, p. 75) notes that the Bullock Report attempts to steer 'a middle course'. It condemns the study of grammar in isolation, but asserts the traditional role of the teacher when it maintains the importance of teacher intervention in pupils' work. Both paradigms of English teaching – 'as language' and 'as literature' – are reinforced positively.

The Bullock Report, however, did little to allay fears articulated in right-wing sections of the Press about declining standards in schools. Similar fears were expressed about the 'secret garden' of education to which only educationalists had right of access. Whether he realised it or not, James Callaghan's launching of the 'Great Debate' in his speech at Ruskin College, Oxford, in 1976 led to increased direct government control of the teaching of subjects in schools, which was to culminate in the National Curriculum. The processes by which the first National Curriculum Order for English came to be established are discussed in the next chapter.

TASK 2.3   HOW WERE YOU TAUGHT ENGLISH?

Think back to your own school days. How were you taught English? What emphasis was placed upon the study of English Literature? Which texts were studied? How were they chosen? What part did 'appreciation' or 'criticism' play? What room was there for enjoyment? Did the teaching of grammar take place? Was this done in isolation, or in relation to literature, or your own writing? What emphasis was placed upon Standard English in writing and speaking? What strategies did your teachers use when correcting your work? What emphasis was placed upon discussion? Which paradigm of English do you feel characterised the way you were taught the subject? Did different teachers exemplify different models of the subject?

If possible, share your experiences with another student teacher. You might wish to discuss with your mentor, or another member of the English department in your placement school, the ways in which he or she was taught English and whether it has affected the beliefs they hold about the subject.

SUMMARY AND KEY POINTS

English is a relatively young subject. It has existed for less than one hundred years. Major reforms in the subject appear to take place in times of great social change. English in schools has been regarded as important for a variety of reasons – not least for the belief in the 'humanising' qualities of English Literature. A number of works from the past have been identified that are believed to exhibit certain values and qualities which are universal and which will stand the test of time. These texts have formed the literary canon. Authors included in the canon have been the bases for school examination syllabuses. The most fundamental change in relation to the study of literature has been the move from literary appreciation to literary criticism.

Notions of correctness and the importance of Standard English have been linked to a 'high culture' view of the subject, which have put it in opposition to popular cultural forms. Since the Second World War, the 'English as language' paradigm has placed greater emphasis upon using the language rather than studying the subject. Opposing models of English teaching have given rise to tensions within the school and in society at large.

FURTHER READING

Eagleton, T. (1983) *Literary Theory*, Oxford: Basil Blackwell.
Eagleton's book provides a comprehensive overview of literary theory. Chapter 1 'The Rise of English' charts in detail the development of approaches to English Literature which influenced the ways in which the subject has come to be taught in school.

3 Battles for English 2: English and the National Curriculum

English is not a means through which to educate children. Nor is it an independent and distinguished discipline in its own right. It must be, according to these trendies, a form of social engineering whose basic purpose is to instil in the minds of impressionable youngsters the self-evident virtues of socialist levelling down and the inevitability of minority politics . . . Standard English and its analysis is, according to these ideologue practitioners, a microcosm of the power struggle . . . The Government must halt the march of these trendy self-interested ideologues and sundry experts.

(*Daily Mail*, 26 June 1991)

INTRODUCTION

This chapter charts the development of the subject in the 1980s and aims to provide a summary of the processes by which the 1989 Cox Report's National Curriculum proposals and the 1990 Order for National Curriculum English were replaced by the 1995 (Dearing) Order: *English in the National Curriculum*. It sets out the main features of the Cox curriculum which have become the basis for the thinking about the direction of English teaching in England and Wales since its implementation in 1990: although it had certain limitations, it provided a consensus among English teachers concerning the nature of the subject. Consequently, teachers have tried to retain its principles while preparing their pupils for the examination requirements of the revised National Curriculum at 11, 14 and 16.

OBJECTIVES

By the end of this chapter you should:

- have some knowledge of the development of the National Curriculum;
- begin to understand that different and conflicting paradigms of English have influenced the National Curriculum Orders for English;
- have some knowledge of the key developments which determined the shape of English as a subject in the 1980s and 1990s.

ENGLISH FROM 5 TO 16

A question of standards

The decade of the 1980s was one which was as busy, in terms of the production of educational documentation, as the first twenty years of this century when English came into being as a school subject. The Great Debate initiated by James Callaghan was followed by a plethora of HMI reports on the curriculum in the late 1970s and resulted directly in the 1980 Education Act, which established the Parents' Charter. The 'secret garden' of education had been opened up to politicians and public alike, all of whom were to be regarded as having things to say about education which were as valid as educationists. The 1980 Act set in train the course of events which were to culminate in 1989, when the Cox National Curriculum Working Group for English published the report *English for Ages 5 to 16* (DES and Welsh Office, 1989).

Secretary of State, Sir Keith Joseph's speech to the North of England Education Conference on 6 January 1984 outlined the Government's intention to 'raise standards' through a move towards the establishment of agreed criteria for subjects and their assessment, which would lay the foundations of a national curriculum. His speech was followed swiftly by a series of HMI discussion documents 'intended as a contribution to the process of developing general agreement about curricular aims and objectives' (HMI, 1984b, p. 54). Significantly, *The Curriculum from 5 to 16* (HMI, 1984b) was the second document in the series: the first being *English from 5 to 16* (HMI, 1984a). English as a subject was still considered of special importance to HMI and policy-makers alike.

HMI recognised that *English from 5 to 16* 'was the most controversial publication in an HMI series' (HMI, 1986, p. 18). The document listed a number of age-related objectives for pupil development in the areas of Listening, Speaking, Reading, Writing and 'About language' – nomenclature developed, perhaps, to avoid the heated 'grammar' debate. The document contains all the beliefs about the purposes and nature of the subject described in the previous chapter: 'Speak clearly, audibly and pleasantly, in an accent intelligible to the listener(s)' (HMI, 1984a, p. 10); 'Creative uses of language may sometimes reject accepted usage . . . But such liberties with language need to be accompanied by clear awareness of how and why accepted usage is being rejected' (p. 22). Similarly, the seeds of National Curriculum English are also being sown: 'Have experienced some literature and drama of high quality, not limited to the twentieth century, including Shakespeare' and 'Read newspapers, magazines and advertising material critically . . . apply similar judgments to entertainment in other media – theatre, cinema or video films, television and radio' (p. 11).

Responses to the document were heated and many respondents expressed themselves in 'matters of belief, principle and practice which were close to their hearts' (HMI, 1986, p. 1). Responses were collated and discussed in *English from 5 to 16: The Responses to Curriculum Matters 1* (HMI, 1986). This report shows respondents to be 'anxious or angry' (p. 5) about the proposals in the earlier publication. Because the earlier document had been such a mixture of approaches to the subject, both 'traditional' and 'progressive', all parties felt dissatisfied – although 'Those who opposed objectives in any form were a very small minority' (p. 7). Elsewhere, 'There were widespread expressions of support for increased attention to the spoken word (speaking and listening)' (p. 18). Of course, those who responded to *Curriculum Matters 1* were a self-selecting group and may in no way be truly representative of the views of English teachers as a whole. Although many respondents were groups – schools, LEAs, HEIs and representative bodies – only 913 responses were received in total.

To some extent, *The Responses* document acknowledges that there are real differences in views held about, and approaches to teaching, English in schools and society – particularly in the area of what has come to be called 'Knowledge about Language'. Within the paper's 'Conclusions' HMI consider:

> It may be that a concentrated and thorough public discussion of the issues is needed; perhaps even a national enquiry is required to focus opinion and guide policy formation about what should be taught about our language and what needs to be known by teachers and pupils.
>
> (HMI, 1986, p. 19)

Within six months a Committee of Enquiry into the Teaching of English Language had been announced.

TASK 3.1   PRINCIPLES OF ENGLISH TEACHING

Obtain copies of *English from 5 to 16* (HMI, 1984) and *English from 5 to 16: The Responses to Curriculum Matters 1* (HMI, 1986).

First, examine 'Some Principles of English Teaching' (pp. 13–16) in *Curriculum Matters 1*. You may wish to discuss this section of the document with another student teacher or your mentor /tutor. What reservations or questions would you wish to raise with HMI about the beliefs expressed here? Second, read 'Matters Arising' (pp. 10–18) in *The Responses* document. How far are your own views represented in this section? Keep any notes you make and use them in any work you undertake on national curriculum English or which asks you to give an account of your own beliefs about the purposes of teaching English.

THE KINGMAN REPORT

> Baker asks poets' advice on English lessons.
>
> (*Independent*, 17 January 1987)
>
> Baker picks maths man to rescue grammar.
>
> (*Guardian*, 17 January 1987)

The return of grammar?

Secretary of State for Education, Kenneth Baker announced the forma-tion of the Kingman Committee which was to 'recommend benchmarks for what children should know about how the language works at ages 11 and 16' (*Independent*, 17 January 1987). He lamented the fact that schools no longer taught grammar and that little had been put in its place. Significantly, the first of the terms of reference for the Commit-tee was:

1. To recommend a model of the English language, whether spo-ken or written, which would:

    i) Serve as the basis of how teachers are trained to under-stand how the English language works.

    (DES, 1988a, p. 73)

   This statement signalled the Government's intention to control teacher education more tightly, particularly in the area of English: a stance which is apparent throughout the following decade. More cynical observers believed it to be significant that the Secretary of State had appointed an eminent mathematician and scientist, Sir John Kingman, to chair a committee on the teaching of English in that the committee might be more likely to expound 'traditional' views of the subject. Similarly, that the committee member who would chair the Working Group on English from 5 to 16 (DES and Welsh Office, 1989), which would lay the foundations of National Curriculum English, was Brian Cox, one of the authors of the right-wing *Black Papers* in the 1970s. *The Report of the Committee of Enquiry into the Teaching of English Language* (DES, 1988a) was published in March the following year and some readers were not heartened by the fact that its opening line was a quotation from the New-bolt Report (Board of Education, 1921). However, there was equal con-cern expressed in some quarters that the Report did not recommend a return to the formal teaching of grammar. For the purposes of this chap-ter it is worth noting that the Report did, indeed, make recommendations for the teaching of Knowledge about Language in teacher education pro-grammes and gave birth to the ill-fated Language in the National Cur-riculum (LINC) project which was set up to develop training materials to improve learning about language.

LANGUAGE IN THE NATIONAL CURRICULUM

The LINC Project (1989–1992) was just one of three major projects related to the teaching of English during the second half of the 1980s. The National Writing Project (1985–1989) and the National Oracy Project (1987–1993), were both controlled by the School Curriculum Development Committee (SCDC), which became the National Curriculum Council (NCC), the School Curriculum and Assessment Authority (SCAA) and is now called the Qualifications and Curriculum Authority (QCA). Both projects produced reports which were well received (see Further Reading at the end of this chapter). The LINC Project, however, was controlled directly by the DES, because the Kingman Report had 'failed to deliver the two simple, linked nostrums expected of it: that the most important thing teachers need to know about language concerns the grammar of sentences; and that children come to command language by being taught the grammar of sentences in advance' (Richmond, 1992, p. 14).

The LINC Project ran through its five stages of training of teachers, advisers and teacher educators throughout the country and appears to have been well received by the participants. However, because the package that had been developed still did not deliver the required approach to grammar, the Government not only refused to publish it, they maintained Crown copyright on the materials – thereby preventing anyone publishing them. Nevertheless, it is estimated (Richmond, 1992, p. 17) that at least 20,000 photocopied packages of the materials were in schools, LEAs and HEIs in 1992. It may be that the department in which you are working has a copy. The ban on the materials provoked the right-wing press to new heights of vitriol about progressive teaching methods in English. An ill-informed article, which referred to the *LINK* project throughout, in the *Daily Telegraph* (28 June 1992) is typical of the reaction:

> And although the DES will not publish the document, it is being distributed to teacher training institutions, where its voodoo theories about the nature of language will appeal to the impressionable mind of the young woman with low A Levels in 'soft' subjects who, statistically speaking, is the typical student in these establishments.

ENGLISH IN THE NATIONAL CURRICULUM

English under Orders

The Statutory Order: English in the National Curriculum (DES and Welsh Office, 1990) was issued in March 1990, and was intended to be phased into schools over four years, 1990–4. This report had to respond to not only the requirements of the Education Reform Act (1988) to establish a

National Curriculum, and the reports detailed above, but also it was informed by other documents: the recommendations of *The National Curriculum 5–16: A Consultation Document* (DES, 1987) which announced a 10-subject national curriculum for England and Wales, which was to be 'broad and balanced' with English, Maths and Science as core subjects; and the Task Group on Assessment and Testing's (TGAT) recommendations for assessment including a 10-level scale (DES, 1987).

The *Statutory Order* was prefaced with a letter from Duncan Graham, Chair of the National Curriculum Council, titled *English: Non-Statutory Guidance* (NCC, 1990). It made the point that the materials were devised by teachers and by advisers' groups along with the National Curriculum Council, and that it was a preliminary order; it promised more advice, particularly on KS4, literature and drama, at a later date.

The Cox Curriculum came in a loose-leaf A4 folder, divided into six sections. Section B introduced the concept of Programmes of Study into Practice – subdivided into the Attainment Targets: Speaking and Listening; Reading; Writing; and Spelling, Handwriting and Presentation. It was prefaced, however, with the recognition that although the curriculum had to be divided up for the purposes of assessment, in practice the aspects were integrated:

> The profile components are inter-related. For example, group discussion may precede and follow individual writing; writing may be collaborative; and listening to stories is often a preparation for reading ... Because of the inter-relationship between the language modes, in good classroom practice the programmes of study will necessarily and rightly be integrated.
>
> (DES and Welsh Office, 1989)

Other general guidance points were that teachers should plan to provide opportunities for pupils to use language in increasingly challenging ways, to take account of pupils' interests and maturity, and that the subsequent sections were illustrations of 'breadth and progression'. The requirement for each Attainment Target consistently emphasised that the curriculum should be broad and balanced and provide continuity and progression for all pupils. For example, the 'Requirement for Speaking and Listening' was as follows:

> **KS3 Breadth:** A wider range of contexts requiring individual contributions will be expected. Pupils should have opportunities for taking responsibility, such as making notes, or presenting findings on the group's behalf. In addition to a developing sensitivity to others, children take more formal individual roles such as giving a talk, or leading a group activity. They develop understanding of appropriate uses of varieties of English and of the social implications of inappropriate usage.

Progression: Children show increasing confidence and fluency, taking leading and discerning roles in discussion, encouraging others and responding with understanding and appreciation. They show rigour in their use of argument and evidence and take effective account of audience.

The *Implications for Teacher and Learning*, on the adjacent page, were:

At KS3 the teacher will need to help children extend their thinking and to reflect on their contribution. Activities will need to be increasingly varied, for example, the devising and production of drama where children make decisions, allocate responsibilities, conduct the rehearsal, present and evaluate it, giving reasons for their choice of setting, characterisation and event. In planning a poetry anthology, the children could discuss possible themes and layout, evaluate their reading and writing together, and use the anthology with their chosen audience to evaluate its success. Listening to different examples of dialect poetry, constructing them and devising and recording their own, will develop understanding of forms.

(NCC, 1990, B2, B3)

These examples illustrate the ways in which the English Orders built upon common good practice in English teaching; they gave practical illustrations which teachers found helpful and could adapt to their own contexts. They demonstrated ways in which the attainment targets are inter-related while identifying a specific focus for assessment. They stressed the importance of pupil progression through increasingly challenging tasks and the importance of developing language skills, including Standard English where appropriate, while appreciating language differences, such as dialect.

The 'Requirements of Reading' were similarly in tune with teacher philosophy and practice of combining cultural heritage with cultural analysis. At Key Stage 3 it required pupils to have the opportunity to read in a variety of ways and a variety of texts; these included, 'literature which is more distant in time from the pupils' immediate experience' and 'information texts of a highly specific kind', 'so that pupils could become versed in the interpretation of T.V., radio and the mass media'. At Key Stage 4, it stated that the range of texts 'will be largely determined by the level of difficulty which is appropriate'; the curriculum should include pre–twentieth century writing, Shakespeare and reference material of all kinds, as well as media texts.

Again, the requirements specified what was meant by 'broad and balanced' while allowing teachers to judge what was appropriate and to choose which pre–twentieth century, Shakespeare and media texts should be studied. In the 'implications', a 'wide range of writers' was emphasised in order to extend pupils' awareness of cultural contexts and their language competence. There was a balance between the historical signif-icance of texts and the importance of engaging with contemporary forms of information and reading.

Range and variety were also central to the Programmes of Study for KS3 Writing. The aim was to equip pupils to write in a variety of situa-tions with a variety of purposes. At Key Stage 3 they should be 'using more complex grammatical structures and more varied vocabulary' and at Key Stage 4, they should be able to 'understand stylistic effects' and be involved in evaluating the success of their writing. To this end, recipro-cal learning was recommended: 'The development of collaborative writ-ing and of the pupils as critical readers of each other's work will help understanding of layout, spelling and punctuation and grammar and the craft of writing' (B6 and B7).

The 'Requirement for Spelling, Handwriting (levels 1–4) and Presen-tation (levels 1–7)' gave constructive guidelines. For example, with spelling, it laid out that, 'A variety of techniques help children to master spelling conventions'. These included:

- reading with the teacher and referring to print such as captions and lists in the classroom;
- composing stories and poems and discussing the spelling of words and their patterns;
- grouping words and looking for common letter clusters in books and magazines;
- encouraging the development of visual memory;
- encouraging children to identify a word.

The Cox National Curriculum Order was influential upon the accep-tance and implementation of Schemes of Work which correlated to the Programmes of Study and clarified assessment objectives. It defined their nature and purpose:

> A scheme of work is a written practical guide to teaching and describes the work planned for pupils in a class or group over a specific period. It is an essential part of the school's responsibility. The scheme of work will include elements unique to English and will show where English work supports and is integrated with other subjects.
>
> (1.1, C1)

Furthermore, it advised that overall planning to implement the National Curriculum in English involves recognising and taking account of: the core and other foundation subjects of the National Curriculum; cross-curricular elements; the school's National Curriculum develop-ment plan; equal opportunities for all pupils. Other points were that:

- good practice begins with planning schemes of work which allow all children to take part (2.5, C2);

- if pupils' own interests provide the starting point for work, then writing, talk, mime or response in reading are more likely to be worthwhile (2.6, C2);
- teachers need to foster an atmosphere of encouragement, support and respect for the achievements of the pupil, as well as recognising that assessment will involve a range of ways of observing children and noting achievement (2.8, C2).

There was a section on Bilingual Children which gave guidance about building upon and making opportunities for using their first language while providing access to the curriculum and an enhancement of their learning of English. (2.9–2.14, C2–3). The first point under 'Organisation and Planning' was that 'Planning will need to be flexible in order to recognise the needs of individual children and to ensure progression, differentiation and relevance' (3.1, C4). There followed example tables of curriculum planning, and more detailed guidelines for Preparing a Scheme of Work and reviewing resources. These guidelines were the framework within which English departments adapted their syllabuses.

There were clear statements about the distinctive values of Literature, Language, Media Education, Drama, Information Technology and Information Retrieval. Each section was prefaced by a quotation, mostly from the Cox report, which, informed by research and experience, had worked through the issues of cultural change and of value in teaching knowledge about language and texts. The following statements are reproduced because they summarise the position of teachers concerning the respective areas of study.

> **Literature:** An active involvement with literature enables pupils to share the experience of others. They will encounter and come to understand a wide range of feelings and relationships by entering vicariously the worlds of others, and in consequence they are likely to understand more of themselves.
>
> (DES and Welsh Office, 1990, 1.0, D1)

> **Language:** Knowledge about Language would be an integral part of work in English, not a separate body of knowledge to be added on to the traditional English curriculum.
>
> (DES and Welsh Office, 1990, 2.0, D7)

> **Drama:** Drama is not simply a subject, but also a method, a learning tool. Furthermore, it is one of the key ways in which children can gain understanding of themselves and of others . . . Planning for Drama in the classroom requires a clear understanding of its nature and the contribution it can make to children's learning. Drama is not simply confined to one strand in the Statements of

Attainment which ceases after level 6. It is central in developing all major aspects of English.

(DES and Welsh Office, 1990, 3.0, D11)

Media Education: It aims to develop systematically children's critical and creative powers through analysis and production of media artefacts.

(DES and Welsh Office, 1990, 4.0, D16)

Media education in English was understood to contribute to most aspects of the English curriculum as well as across subjects. Guidance on planning recommended that teachers consider three approaches: media language; representation; producer and audiences. With reference to the last point, it recognised that pupils should be encouraged to produce, as well as analyse media texts.

IT: English teachers have much to contribute to children's familiarity with this technology and its uses, alongside the major aim of exploring it to promote language knowledge and skills in themselves.

(DES and Welsh Office, 1990, 5.0, D21)

Information retrieval

The section on information retrieval suggested ways in which the following statement could be implemented:

Good schools foster positive attitudes towards books and literature, encouraging pupils to become attentive listeners and reflective readers, library members both in and out of school, and book owners.

(DES and Welsh Office, 1990, 6.0, D22)

Although there was some disagreement about the emphasis on individual development in terms of personal relationships rather than of cultural identities, teachers were won over by the tone of the guidelines which respected their professional judgement while giving a clear rationale and useful examples. Even the guidelines on assessment were clear and acceptable:

Assessment: The assessment process should not determine what is to be taught and learned. It should be the servant, not the master of the curriculum. Yet it should not simply be a bolt-on addition at the end. Rather it should be an integral part of the educational process, providing both 'feedback' and 'feedforward'.

(*National Curriculum Task Group on Assessment and Testing: A Report*, 1988, 1.0, E1)

Section E, 'Gathering Evidence of Achievements', was informed by TGAT's advice that 'assessment should be integral to the curriculum'. It offered guidance about how it could be incorporated into everyday teaching. '*The guidance is by no means definitive, nor is it a requirement.* Teachers will want to adopt approaches to the gathering of evidence about their pupils' attainments which suit their own teaching style and which, at the end of the key stage, enable them to form a sound judgement of the level of each pupil's attainments in relation to the statutory attainment targets' (1.1, E1). The fact that the phrase '*by no means definitive*' was in italics emphasised the respect for a teacher's judgement.

The final section, 'Conclusion', looked at cross-curricular implications for teaching and learning, and recommended whole-school policies on matters such as 'information technology, the use of the spoken word, the reading and writing demands of all subject areas, drama, work with media, and study skills' (F1).

Generally, teachers were in sympathy with the Cox curriculum and were provided with time in order to rewrite their syllabuses in a way which accorded with the guidelines. Many departments found that this exercise was useful to their own professional development and in moderating their own practices. The process allowed them to share ideas and experiences, to reflect upon their aims and to evaluate their teaching against a common curriculum. The content of the curriculum was not threatening and did not interfere with preferred methods of arranging groups, of teaching or learning or of assessment strategies, although it did require more documentation to record pupil achievement. Teachers had to become familiar with the Orders and mark according to a ten-level scale. The ten levels were the most controversial and unsatisfactory aspect of the Orders because they required identification of one skill in a complex situation. As required, the National Curriculum was phased in at Key Stage 3 from 1990.

TASK 3.2 ASSESSING WRITING

In order to understand some of the concerns about assessment of English to levels, read the following extract from the Cox Report (DES and Welsh Office, 1989):

> The best writing is vigorous, committed, honest and interesting. We have not included these qualities in our statements of attainment because they cannot be mapped onto levels.
>
> (para. 17.31)

1. What do you think of this statement? Are there other elements of writing which display quality?
2. Do you believe it possible to assess how 'vigorous, committed, honest and interesting' is a piece of pupil's writing?

3. If you believe it is possible to do so – how would you go about it? What features would you look for?
4. If you believe it is not possible to do so, does this fact tell us more about:

    - the nature of the writing process;
    - the difficulties of defining quality in writing objectively;
    - the deficiency of a hierarchical model of assessment;
    - the belief that English teachers should only assess the assessible, such as correctness of spelling, grammar and punctuation?

    You might wish to discuss your responses with another student teacher or your mentor/tutor. Keep any notes you make and use them in your work on assessment in English.

REVISING THE NATIONAL CURRICULUM

> The 'revised' Order (DES, 1993) was far more than a revision of Cox's, it was actually grounded in a quite different philosophy from his and embodied different views of what talking, reading and writing actually mean.
>
> (Protherough and King, 1995, p. 1)

The furore that had surrounded the banning of the LINC materials was quickly taken up by Secretary of State, John Patten, at the Conservative Party Conference, 7 October 1992. He carefully positioned children and parents with the Government in wanting and needing 'the basics' of 'a good education', concerned with 'standards' – while the examination boards are lined up with '1960s theorists', 'the trendy left', and 'teachers' union bosses', who would destroy 'our great literary heritage'. He declared: 'They'd give us chips with Chaucer. Milton with mayonnaise. Mr Chairman, I want William Shakespeare in our classrooms, not Ronald MacDonald' (Patten, 1992).

As Brian Cox asks, 'For most teachers of English the NCC case for rewriting National Curriculum English seemed perverse. Why change a highly popular Order when the research into its implementation had only just begun?' (Cox, 1995, p. 47). Furthermore, John Patten, Secretary of State for Education from 1992, was advised by Civil Servants as well as by Brian Cox and the antagonism of teachers not to revise the curriculum for three good reasons:

- the English curriculum had proved popular, and there was as yet insufficient time since its inception to assess its strengths and weaknesses;

- a decision to revise the English curriculum would be extremely damaging to teacher morale, for teachers had expended great time and effort in implementing the 1989 programmes of study;
- in many cases teachers would immediately stop their work to implement the 1989 curriculum, and all good work to raise standards would be interrupted.

(Cox, 1995, p. 57)

NATE officers and officers of the National Association of Advisers in English set up a joint survey of 16 LEAs in order to investigate the implementation of the National Curriculum. The results were sent to NCC, DFE and HMI. The main findings were published in 'Made Tongue-tied by Authority' (Johnson, 1992). They reported improvements on all attainment targets, in the use of proper schemes of work and new systems for recording and assessing pupil progress. Overall, 'there was increased rigour, thoroughness and accountability in teachers' work in English. The survey concluded that a rewrite would have a devastating effect on teachers' morale and sense of professionalism, and would be more likely to lower standards than raise them' (Cox, 1995, p. 60).

Nevertheless, the NCC, now consisting of politicians rather than educationists, published *National Curriculum in English: The Case for Revising the Order*. The DFE issued proposals for the revision in April 1993, when Sir Ron Dearing was appointed as chair of the new School and Assessment Authority (SCAA); he was commissioned to review the National Curriculum and its assessment arrangements. He published an interim report in 1993, which was followed by a Consultation Report in September 1993. After a period of consultation, the final Dearing Report was published in 1993, as *English in the National Curriculum* (DFE, 1995) for implementation from September 1995. The Cox curriculum was therefore used in schools for six years, from 1989 to 1995, and had a huge impact on creating a consensus among English teachers and advisers about the nature, aims and practices of English teaching.

STANDARD ASSESSMENT TASKS

The School Examination and Assessment Council (SEAC) introduced pilot Standard Assessment Tasks (SATs) for Key Stage 1 in 1990. These were proved unsatisfactory and to impose too big a workload. They also went against the understanding that coursework would be the major means of assessment, allowing for assessment in various ways and which integrated with the programmes of study. The SATs were envisaged to interrupt continuity of curriculum experience and to run parallel to it. From October 1992 to March 1993, Tests for Key Stage 3 English were trialled in schools. The small number – thirty-two schools – and their opposition were suppressed, and, without consultation, the SATs were to be implemented in 1993. Teachers objected to the SATs on the grounds of uneducational methodology, insufficient piloting, inadequate time, resource implications (for example new Shakespeare texts for a whole year group) and the introduction of 'tiers'. Tiered examination papers would make mixed ability grouping difficult, when, for example, the bottom tier did not study a whole play and there were different texts for different tiers. The introduction of an anthology, with extracts from a narrow range of texts, as the basis for reading examination, was seen as impoverishing to students and contrary to the Cox orders which encouraged reference to a range of writers and texts.

Also of significance is that, subsequently, without discussion or consultation, Standard Assessment Tasks became Standard Assessment Tests – a move which further highlighted the Government's intention to develop 'simple pencil and paper tests' in its 'Back to Basics' campaign. Professor Paul Black had chaired the Task Group on Assessment and Testing (TGAT), which had recommended the introduction of Standard Assessment Tasks in the Working Group's report (DES, 1988b); he had also been Deputy Chair of the National Curriculum Council (1988–1991). He has been highly critical of the Government's 'superficial' approach to assessment:

> The development of the policy for national assessment seems to be a sadly typical example of the development of the National Curriculum. The government's own Task Group on Assessment and Testing (TGAT) produced recommendations which were welcomed widely and which the government broadly accepted. In subsequent development, most of the principles of TGAT have been abandoned.
>
> (Black, 1992, p. 7)

In many other ways, the SATs failed to assess the curriculum content, the programmes of study, and the philosophy of the new Orders. Brian Cox quotes from a letter in the *Guardian*:

> I chose to be a teacher because I love books and enjoy working with young people. I enjoy seeing youngsters involved in performing Shakespeare. I enjoy their pride in their writing. I'm pleased when we push up our exam success in competition with neighbour schools. I like to see pupils' success in public exams take them on to further study. Make no mistake about it, they worked harder under 100 per cent coursework than youngsters have ever worked.
>
> (Peter Thomas, Head of English, Wheatley Park School, Oxfordshire, the *Guardian*, 16 Feb. 1993. Cited in Cox, 1995, p. 110)

Other letters record the philosophical and practical objections to tests which disrupt whole schools, make demands on resources and staff time, and interfere with the continuity and progression of the curriculum. The boycott of the tests in 1993 was supported by the majority of state and independent schools, teachers, headteachers and parents. It was also ratified by the victory of the NAS/UWT in its appeal, on the grounds of intolerable workload, to the High Court. Consequently, Sir Ron Dearing's task was to 'slim down' the National Curriculum. This he did: it is shorter and there are fewer examinations. He did not, however, change the method of assessment or retain the successful aspects of the Cox National Curriculum. As reported in *The Real Cost of SATs* (1996), the Standard Assessment Tasks continued to drive the curriculum, cost unwarranted money on texts and administration, and take up curriculum time which would otherwise be spent on teaching and learning: 'The whole of the curriculum is now becoming SATs orientated' (LATE, 1996, p. 9).

ENGLISH IN THE NATIONAL CURRICULUM 1995

Sir Ron Dearing consulted with professionals over the revisions. In the final Orders, there was a response to a request for more emphasis on information technology, media and drama. English teachers and advisers were pleased that there was a simplification of the 10-level scale (to Level Descriptions) and of the testing arrangements, but were critical that certain aspects raised during the consultation process had been ignored, such as:

- the use of the term 'correct' in describing language use and the description of standard English;
- the reading lists included compulsory rather than exemplary authors. 'English' was understood to be the language the British speak in Britain and there was a clear bias against bilingualism.

The Dearing Curriculum appears to be acceptable because it has been drastically trimmed down to a basic summary for the programmes of study in each attainment target. Consequently, it is mechanistic and general; although it allows for some interpretation by teachers, it lacks vision and energy. Some of the Level Descriptions are so general that they are almost meaningless and the progression between them only nominal. Brian Cox's analysis is that 'This peculiar document opens doors. Most restrictions in the 1993 and 1994 drafts have been removed. What is left is often bare, boring and brief, but good teachers are allowed to develop their own initiatives' (Cox, 1995, p. 168.)

In *A Guide to the National Curriculum* the aims, called 'structure', of the Order are stated as:

> The overall aims in teaching English are to enable pupils to develop as effective speakers and listeners, readers and writers, and to use standard English fluently and accurately . . . In Wales, the linguistic

and cultural knowledge of Welsh-speaking pupils should be recognised and used when developing their competence in English.

(SCAA, 1996, p. 16)

KEY STAGE 4 AND GCSE

In 1989, the GCSE examination had been introduced in order to simplify and equalise assessment at 16, by providing one examination (instead of O Level and CSE) using, variously, numbers and grades. GCSE assessment was flexible between and within subjects, ranging from 100 per cent coursework (which had to include 20 per cent timed exercises under examination conditions) to 100 per cent 'open' or 'closed' book examinations, with differing proportions according to the examination board, and there were often options within the single syllabus. Boards developed syllabuses in English Language, English Literature and English (a combination of Language and Literature). They also developed possibilities for cross-over work between English Language and Literature, and with Humanities, such as the diary of a soldier in the First World War, but specified a maximum of two pieces of coursework. The GCSE examination proved to make demands on pupils in terms of workload and the pressure of continual assessment. The existing GCSE syllabuses were perceived as appropriate and successful ways of assessing the Brian Cox curriculum requirements at Key Stage 4; the only issue was over whether to mark and record by levels or grades and to streamline systems of recording. Since it had only just been introduced it was also considered needless to change it.

In 1992, legislation for GCSE was changed, making more examination compulsory and minimising the importance of Speaking and Listening. It introduced tiered examination papers. In the 1992 examination, there was a last-minute decision to award separate marks, worth 5 per cent, for accurate spelling, punctuation and grammar in terminal examination papers. The same requirements were also to be applied to coursework.

In 1994, requirements changed again and syllabuses had to come in line.

NEW REGULATIONS

In 1996, SCAA published new regulations for GCSE and all boards were required to rewrite their syllabuses and to produce specimen papers and mark schemes, and to be approved by SCAA, for implementation from September 1996, the first cohort therefore being examined in 1998.

Implications

- With tiered papers, there was pressure in English departments to question whether their current groupings were appropriate. The

Table 3.1 Summary of events: GCSE

1987		GCSE introduced – pilot run of GCSE with O Level/ CSE English.
1987	July	National Curriculum 5–16.
1987	December	TGAT.
1988	June	First examination of GCSE English syllabuses.
1989	June	National Curriculum Statutory Order; Key Stage 4 to be assessed through GCSE. Levels 1–3 not to be accredited.
1991	Spring	National Criteria for GCSE revised to reflect broader requirements of National Curriculum. 70% assessment through coursework and 30% through examination. Exam boards set up groups to produce new syllabuses accordingly.
1991	July	John Major publicly opposes 'too much coursework, project work and teacher assessment at GCSE'. No evidence to support the claim.
1991	Autumn	Syllabus development frozen. Coursework limited to 20%.
1992	January	National Criteria for GCSE rewritten: English – 60% examination; 40% coursework (including 20% Speaking and Listening). Literature – 70% examination; 30% coursework. Development of tasks for levels 1–3. Examination boards to rewrite syllabuses and produce specimen papers by April 1992.
1992	May	New syllabuses distributed to schools for implementation from September. Some amendments made into the autumn. Papers for levels 1–3 abandoned.
1992	September	Year 10 begins new GCSE courses.
1993	Spring	Decision that KS4 GCSE syllabuses and mark schemes, based on 10 levels, now to be certified with grades, not levels (no guidelines for levels 1–3).
1993	June	Last emendations of original GCSE syllabuses – steady improvements in results with 57% A–C grades.
1993	June	Last examination of original GCSE syllabuses (steady improvements of results, reaching 57% achieving A–C grades).
1993	Autumn	Revised specimen papers sent out by some, but not all, boards.
1994	January	Dearing's Final Report presents new timetable for the rewriting of GCSE criteria and new revised syllabuses.
1995		Publication of GCSE Regulation and Criteria, SCAA – set out new criteria for GCSE English Language and Literature.
1996	February	Approved syllabus for English and English Literature to be accompanied by specimen papers and mark schemes.
1996	September	Year 10 start new syllabuses (to be examined in 1998).

Source: Adapted from 'GCSE English: the background to the current concerns', *NATE News*, Spring 1994, p. 9.

content of the English syllabus was heavily literature-based and the requirement of each syllabus increased so that the nature and viability of English Literature were at stake. For schools, however, to lose dual entry would affect examination results, as pupils often gained high grades in both English Language and Literature.

• No roll up or down between tiers meant that departments would exercise caution over entering pupils for the Higher tier: pupils on the crucial C/D borderline may be entered for the foundation paper in order not to risk being Unclassified in case they did not achieve a D; this would be a process of lowering expectations and performance.

• Departments needed to revise their curriculum for years 10 and 11 to ensure that all aspects of the syllabuses could be incorporated and to look for units of work which could result in multiple assessment (e.g. work on examination text and coursework for English, including Speaking and Listening assessment pieces, and English Literature). They also needed to be wary of spending too long on coursework because of its diminished weighting (teachers accustomed to 100 per cent coursework GCSE were used to spending time on one piece in order to produce writing which was detailed and thorough, with perhaps several pieces from which the pupil could choose their best). To cover the requirements of Reading (English) and Literature (English Literature) it might be necessary to use short stories and extracts rather than whole novels. Media work need only include written forms, such as the language of newspapers and advertisements, so that other aspects which schools had developed would be minimal. Similarly, although in theory it should be possible to include new texts (often recently purchased) for wider reading and as a basis for language work, the content of the syllabuses had expanded so much that it would be difficult to do this in practice.

• The most consistent difference in performance between boys and girls is in GCSE English. Girls tend to be better at narrative and descriptive writing and in analysis of fictional texts. The added emphasis on responding to texts means that boys will be disadvantaged in both English and English Literature syllabuses.

SUMMARY AND KEY POINTS

The National Curriculum was born out of an almost unprecedented plethora of educational documentation produced by the Government and its agencies. For the first time in the history of state education, a curriculum for secondary schools was centrally imposed. English as a subject continued to be regarded as central to the politics of education. The opposing models of English identified in the previous chapter continued to create tensions for educationists and policy-makers. It would appear that for much of the latter half of the 1980s the Government sought to 'turn back the clock' in order to produce an English curriculum founded upon notions of correctness, Standard English and formal grammar, which culminated in the proposals for the Revised Orders for English (DES and Welsh Office, 1993). The next chapter discusses the ways in which teachers are working with the 1995 Orders.

FURTHER READING

Black, P., *et al.* (1992) *Education: Putting the Record Straight*, Stafford: Network Educational Press.
This collection of papers is written by many of the educationists who were at the heart of the development of the National Curriculum. It is a highly critical insider's view of the political machinations which influenced the development of education in this country in the 1980s and 1990s.

Cox, B. (1995) *The Battle for the National Curriculum*, London: Hodder & Stoughton.
This book gives an account of the implementation of the 1990 National Curriculum for English and the process by which it was replaced by the 1995 English in the National Curriculum. Although it pulls no punches in describing the political interference and shortcomings of the new Order, it recognises positive aspects in relation to the limits of the 1989 curriculum. Brian Cox suggests a way forward, rather than simply a nostalgic view of the current situation.

LATE (1996) *The Real Cost of SATs: A Report for the London Association for the Teaching of English*, London: LATE.
This report looks at the financial and educational costs of SATs, based on a questionnaire sent to schools after the 1995 tests. It reveals the amount of money and the cost of teaching time, workload and strain, and common objections such as the prevention of providing a broad and balanced English curriculum, inaccurate results, inappropriate means of testing the content of the National Curriculum, teacher morale, standards of achievement.

National Oracy Project (1991) *Teaching Talking and Learning at Key Stage 3*, London: NCC/NOP.

National Oracy Project (1993) *Teaching Talking and Learning at Key Stage 4*, London: NCC/NOP.
Together with the NOP's reports on Key Stages 1 and 2, these publications contain accounts of good practice within the English classroom, particularly in relation to equal opportunities, gender and bilingualism.

National Writing Project (1993) *Responding to and Assessing Writing*, London: Nelson.
This report considers key strategies for developing opportunities for a range of reponses to pupil writing in the classroom.

Richmond, J. (1992) 'Unstable Materials: The LINC Story' *English and Media Magazine*, Spring 1992, English and Media Centre/NATE.

John Richmond was joint leader of the North London Language Consortium, one of the consortia of LEAs which conducted the work of the LINC Project. His article describes in detail the conflict between the Government and those working on the Project.

4 Working with the National Curriculum

INTRODUCTION

This chapter follows on from Chapter 3 'Battles for English: The National Curriculum', by moving from an examination of how *English in the National Curriculum* (DFE, 1995) was eventually formulated and its implications for English teaching to how it works in practice. The 1995 (Dearing) National Curriculum was literally a 'slimmed down' version of the earlier model but it did not eliminate testing by examination or tiered papers and it prescribed reading lists of 'major authors'. It should, however, be remembered that one reason for the 'slimming down' was to reduce the content so that the programmes of study would not fill all the curriculum time and teachers could respond to the needs and interests of their pupils. In practice, the amount of prescribed reading, and the amount of time needed to prepare pupils for external examination and to complete coursework means that it is difficult to do anything else; in addition, it is difficult not to be driven by assessment. The return to timed examinations has meant a return to more whole-class teaching and 'cramming' for exams. At the same time, teachers are trying to hang on to the principles of 'active learning, critical thinking and cultural analysis' (Williamson and Woodall, 1996, p. 4) which are in danger of being ousted out by an assessment-driven curriculum. As a student teacher you need to work within the current National Curriculum Order while retaining a vision of the subject which is wider than the narrow focus on skills and cultural heritage and which sees beyond the demands of formal assessment.

The National Curriculum for English presents three major challenges for teachers: one is to plan their syllabuses and schemes of work so that all pupils have the best opportunities to perform to the best of their abilities in terms of the requirements of the programmes of study and of public examinations; the second is to plan for continuity and progression for all pupils in areas which are not assessed by examination at Key Stage 3 and Key Stage 4. For example, teachers want to introduce pupils to texts which are not prescribed, such as more non-British writers, more women writers and more media and information technology texts. All pupils should have opportunities to develop their own enthusiasms through individual wider reading and negotiated individual tasks. They will want them to take increasing responsibility for their learning through individual and group projects and by reflecting upon the learning processes. The third challenge is to the teacher's own subject knowledge; student teachers start their training with different experiences of studying English and have different strengths and gaps in terms of the school curriculum requirements. The importance of viewing the development of your own subject knowledge as part of your role as an English teacher is discussed in Chapter 14, 'Critical Practice'.

In this chapter, there is an emphasis on planning for working with the National Curriculum programmes of study. The sample lesson plan and scheme of work are designed to demonstrate ways of meeting the objectives in terms of Range, Key Skills and Standard English and Language Study; at the same time, they are designed to indicate that these need not preclude objectives which are not identified in the current National Curriculum Order. It is envisaged that this chapter will be read in conjunction with all the other chapters so that you will want to include the principles identified there in your planning.

OBJECTIVES

By the end of the chapter, you should:

- be able to have a working knowledge of the programmes of study for the National Curriculum and its assessment at Key Stages 3 and 4;
- consider ways of working with both the requirements of the National Curriculum and principles about the nature and aims of English teaching which are not explicit in the requirements;
- consider your own strengths and weaknesses in terms of subject knowledge.

NATIONAL CURRICULUM ENGLISH AT KEY STAGES 3 AND 4

English in the National Curriculum (DFE, 1995) sets out the requirements for pupils aged five to sixteen. It is organised into programmes of study (PoS) which set out the material to be covered and the opportunities which pupils must experience. Although you will be concentrating on the programmes of study for Key Stages 3 and 4, you should remember that there should be a continuum throughout all key stages; just as work at Key Stage 4 will be viewed as a development of Key Stage 3, Key Stage 3 should build upon pupils' learning at Key Stage 2. It is common for pupils entering secondary school at eleven or thirteen to find themselves 'out of their depth' or 'back-pedalling' because the teacher has not discovered where they have got to in their learning. At secondary level, the programmes of study for Key Stages 3 and 4 are combined, but specific knowledge and skills are identified for assessment at each stage: at Key Stage 3 through Standard Assessment Tests (SATs) and at Key Stage 4 by GCSE coursework and examination. The programmes of study are divided into three sections, Speaking and Listening, Reading, and Writing, but it is acknowledged that these will be integrated during any teaching and learning activity. Similarly, although the programmes of study are also divided into three sections, Range, Key Skills, and Standard English and Language Study, it is stated that pupils should be given opportunities that interrelate these requirements. (DFE, 1995, p. 4).

The main features of the programmes of study for English at Key Stages 3 and 4 are for pupils to have opportunities to/for:

Speaking and Listening
- talk for different purposes;
- participating in discussion and attentive listening;
- developing knowledge and use of standard English;
- active involvement in drama;
- critical engagement with media texts.

Reading
- read a wide range of high-quality poetry, prose and drama from the English literary heritage;
- read works from a range of cultures and traditions;
- read a range of non-fiction, media and IT-based texts;
- develop strategies for reading, information retrieval and application;
- develop personal and critical responses to reading.

Writing
- analyse a wide range of writing for knowledge about how language works;
- write in a variety of forms and genres;
- develop confidence as writers.

The three sections, Speaking and Listening, Reading, and Writing, are arranged under subheadings: Range, Key Skills and Standard English and Language Study. The 'Range' section, 'outlines the opportunities, contexts and experiences to be provided, to ensure breadth and rich-ness'. The work outlined in Range should provide the basis for the development of the more specific requirements under Key Skills, and Standard English and Language Study. Key Skills identify the compul-sory aspects of teaching to develop transferable skills in the three areas. The section on Standard English and Language Study, 'sets out the opportunities for learning about language, together with the require-ments for teaching those aspects of spoken and written language, which pupils must learn to be able to speak and write English effectively' (SCAA, 1996, pp. 17–18).

Achievement is measured by Attainment Targets for each section; progression is identified through Level Descriptions. It is important to remember that the Level Descriptions are deliberately placed after the programmes of study to endorse the principle that the programmes of study, not assessment, should guide teaching. The majority of pupils working at Key Stage 3 should be working within levels 3 to 7, and at Key Stage 4, between levels 4 and 8, with the brightest achieving 'Exceptional Performance'. The 'common requirements', as stated in *English in the National Curriculum* are to ensure access for 'the greatest majority of pupils' (DFE, 1995, p. 1). The requirements state that it should be made possible to select material from earlier or later Key Stages than that identified for the majority of pupils. The common requirements include that opportunities to develop and apply information technology should be available in English classes. Similarly, there should be appropriate provision, such as technological aids, signing or lip-reading, for pupils who need to use more non-visual or non-aural ways of acquiring information.

Teachers will want to follow these guidelines by developing a range of strategies so that all pupils have opportunities to participate in all activities. An inherent challenge of the National Curriculum, however, is the tension between a curriculum which aims at entitlement for all and one which uses levels of attainment and tiered assessment to separate pupils. In English, it is difficult to separate children by 'ability' because of the interrelationship of the three components, speaking and listening, reading and writing: one pupil may be better at listening or at contributing to discussion or at summarising key points but be weak at spelling. Consequently, English teachers often do not differentiate by setting groups; they sometimes differentiate by difficulty of text; more often they offer a range of activities and a choice of approaches and responses to a text, believing that 'differentiation by offering choice, negotiation and intervention at the individual level' (Daw, 1995, p. 12) is the most appropriate. This is particularly so since 'text' increasingly means media or information text as well as a written or more narrowly 'literary' text and since the meaning of 'literacy' has broadened to include the ability to read and write in several media.

WORKING WITH THE NATIONAL CURRICULUM AT KEY STAGE 3

Although the requirements of the National Curriculum are common to all maintained schools, they have to be 'translated' into a syllabus which is broken down into schemes of work. As a subject teacher, you have to follow the syllabus and schemes of work of your department but you are also responsible for designing them to fit the abilities of your particular class and for using the resources available, making your own if necessary. You therefore need to become familiar with the programmes of study and also the syllabus at your school; you should discuss with experienced teachers how they plan their schemes of work and lessons, and which resources are applicable to which units of the department's syllabus. This last point is important for two reasons: you may find that you are spending time developing worksheets or photocopying texts which already exist in the department or you may be using a text with Year 9 which the department usually reserves for Year 10. The following tables and tasks are designed to help you to get to know *English in the National Curriculum* and to see how it works in practice with reference to a school's syllabus and your lesson planning. It must be understood that the requirements here relate to the 1995 National Curriculum Order and the 1997 assessment tests; it is proposed to introduce a grammar test for 1998 and there may be other changes (there is a pressure from teachers to assess the Shakespeare play by coursework, for example). You will need to check out any new developments. Figure 4.1 outlines what has to be included at Key Stage 3.

For the sake of clarity, the list below of the requirements for the programmes of study is divided into sections, but in practice, English lessons will nearly always include elements of speaking and listening, reading, writing, and language study. Analysis of media texts is often integral to work on written texts or to writing activities (when a media text is the stimulus, for example). For this reason, it is not difficult for English teachers to identify elements of the programmes of study in their teaching. The difficulty is in identifying one or two elements which are the focus for progression and which are to be assessed. In reading and responding to a poem about a cat, such as 'A Case of Murder' by Vernon Scannell, for example, the teacher needs to decide whether she is going to concentrate on improving the pupils' abilities to discuss, in which case she will organise the class into small groups, give them questions about the subject matter and assess them by the Speaking and Listening Level Descriptions or whether they are to learn about the literary features of poetry and develop an informed response to their reading, in which case she may give them questions or set up activities on the poem which guide an exploration of the relationship between linguistic and formal features, such as vocabulary, rhythm and metaphor, and meaning; this work would be assessed by the Level Descriptions in Reading. This does not mean, of course, that because the focus is on oral activities, pupils are not improving their reading skills or because they are looking at features of poetry as genre, they are not speaking and listening, but that there are clear objectives to which the pupils can work and which are consistent with the criteria by which they will be assessed. The identification and communication of objectives and the criteria for assessment enables pupils to know for what they are aiming and teachers to fulfil the statutory requirements of keeping records of their own assessment of pupils' achievements.

Speaking and Listening	
The requirements for speaking and listening concern participation, range and accuracy in speech activities.	<ul><li>speak and listen in a range of contexts;</li><li>use standard English in talk;</li><li>participate in drama activities, e.g. role play.</li></ul>
Reading	
The requirements for reading are in terms of three genres of fiction, non-fiction, media texts and language study.	<ul><li>pre-C20 major poets from list;</li><li>C20 major poets</li><li>major playwrights, including Shakespeare – for the study of genre – e.g. comedy, tragedy, farce;</li><li>pre-C20 major authors (fiction) from reading list;</li><li>C20 major authors (fiction);</li><li>non-fiction (of quality): autobiography, biography, journals, diaries, letters, travel writing, leaflets;</li><li>independent wider reading (of increasing demand);</li><li>texts from other cultures and traditions;</li><li>analyse a range of forms of media text (of quality);</li><li>study language change;</li><li>study language varieties.</li></ul>
Writing	
The requirements for writing stress the importance of linking analysis with use and accuracy.	<ul><li>write a variety of forms: narrative, poetry, scripts and dialogue, non-fiction;</li><li>understand differences in writing;</li><li>planning, drafting, redrafting, proof-reading;</li><li>write in the vocabulary and grammar of Standard English;</li><li>improve spelling, punctuation and presentation;</li><li>increase vocabulary;</li><li>use more complex sentence structures;</li><li>take opportunities to develop and apply word processing skills.</li></ul>
Assessment Objectives – SATs	
Paper 1 (with optional Extension Paper for levels 7 and 8)	<ul><li>reading comprehension;</li><li>writing for different audiences: e.g. letters, diaries, reports, reviews;</li><li>creative writing;</li></ul>
Paper 2	<ul><li>Shakespeare play</li></ul>

Figure 4.1   *English in the National Curriculum*, Programmes of Study, Key Stage 3

In your planning, you should try to ensure that all the requirements of the programmes of study are fulfilled; you would also need to build in preparation for public examination, the Standard Assessment Tests (SATs). So far, SATs are taken in May of Year 9 and consist of two papers: paper 1 tests reading and comprehension and writing and paper 2 is a test on one scene from a Shakespeare play. There is an extension paper for paper 1 for pupils working at levels 7 and 8. Pupils working at levels 1 to 3 do not have to take the SAT papers and can be assessed by 'Optional Tasks' set by the teacher. SCAA produces a *Teacher's Handbook* with guidelines for setting and marking these tasks and a *Resource Booklet* with sample tasks. Schools have different policies about when the decision is made about which pupils should take the extension paper or the tasks. These decisions are accompanied by decisions over whether to set the groups to prepare them for the exams. For example, if levels 1 to 3 become a 'bottom set', how are they to study the Shakespeare play which is a requirement for all pupils, even though they will not be assessed on it?

To sum up so far, you need to ensure that all aspects of the programmes of study have been covered by all pupils and have records to prove it. Pupils need to be: prepared for the SATs; provided with extension work for the top levels; and provided with work for levels 1 to 3. In working with the requirements of the National Curriculum in conjunction with your school's syllabus, you need to ascertain what the syllabus includes, what it tells you and what it does not. The following table is an example of a syllabus for Key Stage 3 to cover years 8 and 9. The course comprises four compulsory units and one optional teacher-designed unit in each year. The compulsory units have been designed to cover the requirements of the National Curriculum, and include a range of tasks which are to be used in order to cover certain types of work, develop certain skills and further knowledge about language. The optional units recognise that the programmes of study are not intended to fill the whole of the curriculum.

This syllabus is designed to meet the requirements of Key Stage 3, and also to leave room for work which is not specified in the programmes of study, like creative writing, through the teacher-designed units. This model retains the principles of giving pupils opportunities to perform well in national assessment terms and also to be introduced to other work which is designed to meet their particular needs and interests and which allows the teacher some sense of autonomy.

In your planning and in keeping records, you have to monitor requirements which may be implicit, but not explicit in the syllabus. Looking at the requirements for 'Writing', for example, it is not specified in Table 4.1 where the following occur: the development of thinking through 'review, analysis, hypothesis, recollection and summary' (Range b); 'Pupils should be developing their competence in planning, drafting, redrafting and

Table 4.1 Sample English syllabus for Years 8 and 9

Year 8	Unit Title	Writing	Reading	Speaking and Listening
Autumn	School	Diaries. Poster. Newspaper articles. Personal and formal letters.	Short story/ novel about school. Poetry about school.	Drama: planning and consideration of effects. Explanation.
Spring 1	Animal project	Descriptions. Pamphlets. Poems.	Poetry. Media pamphlets.	Description. Argument. Debate. Persuasion. Development of thinking.
Spring 2	Class novel	Book review. Playscript. Stories. Comic script.	Novel.	Exploration. Narration. Development of thinking.
Summer 1	Teacher-designed unit (optional)	Project work – range of writing for different audiences. Presentation – including word processing	Non-fiction. Information retrieval.	
Summer 2	Short stories	Stories. Advertisements. Plans and diagrams.	Range of C20 and pre-C20 stories.	Narration.
Year 9				
Autumn	Pre-C20 fiction	Recreative narrative. Book review.	Book and film texts of pre-C20 fiction.	Narration.
Spring 1	*Across the Barricades*	Diaries. Chronological accounts. Editorial columns. Radio and TV scripts. Dialect guides. Lists. Greeting cards.	Novel.	Explanation. News report.
Spring 2	*Romeo and Juliet*	Essays. Invitations. Notes. Guides. Screenplay. Captions. Games. Poems.	Shakespeare play – book and film texts. Poetry.	As appropriate, e.g. hotseating, directing, improvisation and role play, debate.
Summer 1	Teacher-designed unit (optional)	Creative writing.	Individual wider reading. Poetry from a range of cultures.	Group discussion.
Summer 2	Media	Magazines. Advertisements. Newspapers. TV scripts.	Media – magazines, newspapers, radio, TV, film.	As appropriate: use Standard English in talk.

Source: Adapted from the scheme of work devised by the English Department at the Radcliffe School, Wolverton, used for 'An investigation into the level of implementation of the National Curriculum at Key Stages 3 and 4 by Sally Carter-Tabasso, PGCE Secondary English, De Montfort University, Bedford, 1995/6.

proofreading their work on paper and on screen' (Key Skills a); non-fiction writing; note-taking; learning about the components of words – 'including stem, prefix, suffix, inflection; grammatical functions of nouns, verbs, adjectives, adverbs, pronouns, prepositions, conjunctions and demonstratives' (Standard English and Language Study b). It must be stressed that this does not mean that these requirements are excluded but that they are not explicit in the syllabus. To demonstrate fulfilment of all the requirements of the National Curriculum Order, the relevant elements of Range and Key Skills need to be identified in lesson planning.

Lesson planning

Lesson planning also provides the means to identify the learning objectives in terms of pupils' progression which should be consistent with assessment objectives. With reference again to the poem 'A Case of Murder', it might seem like a good idea to ask pupils to rewrite the situation of the poem as a short story; it would be inappropriate, of course, to assess it on its demonstration of the features of a short story (surprise beginnings, twist in the tale and so on), if you had been talking about its poetry techniques or its treatment of fear or guilt. When beginning to teach, it is tempting to stick on a piece of writing at the end of an activity to give it value, but if it is an afterthought it may not be appropriate to the pupils' learning. You need to decide on your teaching and learning objectives and what you are assessing before you start; you will then be able to communicate these objectives to your pupils and give your lessons a sense of direction. In your summing up to pupils at the end of a lesson you can identify what has been achieved and in your own evaluation of the lesson, you should be able to ask yourself 'what has been learned and how?' in relation to your identified objectives. (See 'Schemes of Work and Lesson Planning', Unit 2.2 in Capel, Leask and Turner, 1995). Following the principle of working *with* but also *beyond* the National Curriculum, lesson plans can also identify objectives which are not specific requirements of the programmes of study; these may be procedural issues, such as ensuring that homework is understood and completed on time, cross-curricular issues, such as equal opportunities, or wider subject issues such as improving critical responses to film or television texts.

Figure 4.2 is a sample lesson plan which illustrates that any one lesson will include speaking, listening, reading, writing, and points about language, but that there is a clear aim in terms of what is to be learned and how that learning is to be measured.

It is only a skeleton of a plan. It can be a one-off lesson which you can use to record speaking and listening achievements, or it can be the start of

Class: 9   **Lesson Length**: 50 mins   **Levels**: 3–7
Date: June 4   **Position in scheme of work**: 1

Main Objective/s: Develop ability to narrate; understand the origins of fairy stories in oral and folk culture; compare C19 and C20 written versions; consider stereotyping; effective pair work.

Assessment: Confidence in speaking and listening.

National Curriculum Attainment Target(s):

1. Range	2. Key Skills	3. Language study

Speaking/Listening
  a) narration, develop
    thinking, analysis
  c) listening
	a) communicate in
	   speech
	c) listen attentively
		b) differences in speech
		   and writing; language
		   change

Writing		

Reading b) narrative structures,
      social significance
      of texts
	a) interpretation
	b) characterisation
		b) genre
		c) comparative analysis

Equipment/resources:
Worksheet 1 – Grimms' Stories, modern version
Worksheet 2 – chart of gender types in four stories

Lesson content and method		
Timing	Teacher activity	Pupil activity
15 mins	Introduce scheme of work and aims of lesson. Divide into pairs and instruct.	In pairs (A and B) retell story of *Cinderella* (A) and *Little Red Riding Hood* (B). Partner sums up and adds any omissions or differences.
10 mins	Draw out points about no 'fixed' version until C19 (Grimm and Anderson). Give out worksheets with C19 and modern versions (e.g. from *Inside Stories* 3 and 4)	Note differences between own version and C19. Read modern version.
15 mins	Give out worksheet 2 (chart of gender types – mother, daughter; other women, father, hero, other men – for *Cinderella, Little Red Riding Hood*, and two others of pupils' choice, e.g. *Hansel and Gretel, Snow White*)	Fill in worksheet. When finished or stuck join another pair.
10 mins	Feedback from groups to ensure understanding of stereotyping. Summing up, conclusions and follow up.	Feedback to whole group.

Figure 4.2 English lesson plan for Key Stage 3

a scheme of work which develops other objectives. For example, it could lead to the writing of a modern equivalent of a fairy story which would allow pupils to investigate the perceived 'authority' of received texts and to challenge gender stereotypes; their stories could be presented and assessed orally (to the class or read onto a tape recorder) or in writing. There are useful versions of fairy and folk tales from around the world in books such as *Changing Stories* (English and Media Centre, 1984) and *Inside Stories* 3 and 4 (Benton, 1991).

The lesson plan (Figure 4.2) illustrates that in any lesson there is an integration of activities but that there should be a focus on one (in this case, speaking and listening) for progression. It includes consideration of appropriate teaching strategies: pair and group work are best for speaking and listening to allow for maximum participation. Worksheets, such as a table to fill in on selected aspects of each story, are used to clarify instructions, to provide differentiation through allowing pupils to work at different paces and to release the teacher to support individuals. The plan is written with reference to the programmes of study but is also informed by wider theoretical principles. These principles include:

- the importance of understanding how stereotypes work;
- that written texts are not superior to oral texts;
- that texts are constructed for particular purposes and are value-laden (e.g. the teaching to nineteenth-century children that virtue and vice work meritoriously);
- developing powers of narrative are important because:

> Stories are a way in which we represent the world to ourselves and, in the stories we tell ourselves or others, stories also become a way in which we represent ourselves to the world. They also help us to understand experiences we may never have had personally – of another time, another place, another culture. Stories allow us to speculate about 'what if . . .?' Stories are the foundation of religions and of history. The culture and the beliefs of a society are deeply embedded in its stories. For both individuals and societies live by the stories they tell themselves.
>
> (Benton, 1991, pp. 9–10)

Consequently, studying folk, fairy and short stories from different traditions can be seen not just as fulfilling curriculum requirements but also as introducing pupils to alternative systems of government, family life and responses to experiences. Such experiences will enable pupils to develop greater powers of narrative discourse themselves which will empower them to question and resist oppressive systems: 'The less constrained the discourse, i.e. censored by power, the more it is likely to have recourse to narrative. Spontaneous speech narrative is the most difficult kind of language to censor . . . The narrative forms we master provide genres for thinking with' (Harold Rosen, in Prain, 1996, p. 10).

TASK 4.1   LESSON PLANNING FOR KEY STAGE 3

The aim of this task is to become familiar with *English in the National Curriculum* (DFE, 1995) and with your department's syllabus. With reference to your school's English syllabus for Key Stage 3, plan a lesson for a Year 8 or 9 mixed–ability class, using the outline above (Figure 4.2) or the one advised by your mentor or tutor. Identify your aims for the lesson and the relevant statements from Range, Key Skills and Standard English and Language Study. Teach the lesson plan and evaluate it with reference to your stated aims. After the lesson, discuss the suitability and success of your planning with your mentor.

SUMMARY OF WORKING WITH THE NATIONAL CURRICULUM AT KEY STAGE 3

So far, the principle of working with and beyond the National Curriculum programmes of study have been emphasised and illustrated. In practice, you may find that your planning is dominated by the demands to provide evidence of pupils' achievement in terms of the Attainment Targets and, in Year 9, by preparation for the SATs. In addition, Key Stage 3 needs to be understood in terms of continuity and progression throughout the curriculum phases. Whatever the activity may be, it should take into account the pupils' prior learning: in Year 8 (or Year 9 of an upper school) you need to consider continuity from work at Key Stage 3; you also need to perceive work at Key Stage 3 as preparation for Key Stage 4. In *English in the National Curriculum* (DFE, 1995) the programmes of study are combined for Key Stages 3 and 4; they are distinguished, however, in their assessment: SATs at Key Stage 3 and GCSE coursework and examinations at Key Stage 4.

ENGLISH IN THE NATIONAL CURRICULUM AT KEY STAGE 4: GCSE

The programmes of study and assessment requirements for Key Stage 4 have been adapted by SCAA into common requirements for all GCSE syllabuses for English with additional requirements being specified for English Literature. Consequently, all GCSE examining groups rewrote their syllabuses to conform to the new regulations for *English in the National Curriculum* (DFE, 1995). From September 1996, English

Speaking and Listening

For the purposes of assessment, the programmes of study are clustered into three categories:

- explain, describe, narrate;
- explore, analyse, imagine;
- discuss, argue, persuade.

Reading

There are nine categories of Reading, six of which are literature; they incorporate the writers prescribed in *English in the National Curriculum*:

- play by Shakespeare;
- range of drama;
- range of poetry;
- range of prose;
- work of pre-C20 author, from National Curriculum list;
- work of C20 writer;
- media;
- non-fiction;
- texts from other cultures and traditions.

Writing

For the purposes of assessment, the programmes of study are clustered into four categories (which are not the same as for Speaking and Listening) as follows:

- explore, imagine, entertain;
- inform, explain, describe;
- argue, persuade, instruct;
- analyse, review, comment.

Assessment

1. Examination (60%):
   Two x two-hour examinations consisting of two sections each (except SEG which has three sections).
   Section A – reading (including unseen reading test and non-fiction text – all boards).
   Section B – writing (including a test of 'argue, persuade, instruct' – all boards).
2. Coursework (40%):
   - 20% Speaking and Listening;
   - 20% Shakespeare play and pre-C20 prose – all boards;
   - three assessed assignments plus teacher's back-up record to be available for external moderator, if requested. (Oral assessment of Reading and of Literature texts allowed by some boards.)

Notes:

1. One text may cover several requirements: for example, coursework on Shakespeare and on Literature pre- and post-1900 can be cross-over pieces for English Literature coursework (although they may need to meet different objectives for the English or English Literature syllabus).
2. Boards differ over how each category of writing is examined. For example, 'explore, imagine entertain' and 'inform, explain, describe': exam (NEAB, ULEAC); exam and coursework (MEG and SEG); 'analyse, review, comment' is tied to other requirements, e.g. coursework literature (MEG); coursework media (NEAB); coursework literature from diverse cultures (SEG); examination and coursework literature from diverse cultures (ULEAC).
3. NEAB and ULEAC publish anthologies which meet many of the requirements of both their English and English Literature syllabuses, except a pre-1900 prose text (English) and a C20 drama text (Literature).
4. Most boards use pre-release material.
5. Grades are maintained but correspond to Level Descriptions.
6. Tiers of papers: foundation (F–C) and higher (D–A*) with no roll up or down: i.e. if a pupil fails to gain grade D at Higher, they are Unclassified.

The exam boards are as follows: Midland Examining Group (MEG); Northern Examinations and Assessment Board (NEAB); University of London Examinations and Assessment Council (ULEAC); Southern Examining Group (SEG).

Figure 4.3 GCSE English

The requirements of English Literature are demanding in terms of quantity and quality, the amount of content and the revised criteria:

Set texts

● evidence of the study of three genres;
● each genre to include a pre-C20 and C20 text.

Assessment

● coursework – 30%: three pieces;
● examination – 70% one paper (2hrs or 2hrs 30 mins) on specific set texts;
● (two tiers, as for GCSE English. Set texts common to both tiers.)

Figure 4.4 GCSE English Literature

Departments had to rethink their choice of examination board. Although there is, inevitably, much similarity in the content of syllabuses, there are differing priorities and philosophies implicit in the weighting, type of examination questions and choice of set texts. Some boards, for example, set different reading for each tier which is likely to preclude mixed-ability grouping. The requirements for GCSE English and GCSE English Literature are shown in Figures 4.3 and 4.4.

So far you have been given a summary of what is common in terms of content to syllabuses for English and English Literature. You have seen that you need to know how each aspect of the syllabus is to be assessed, whether by examination or coursework, and the skills which are the focus for assessment. Figure 4.5 shows in more detail what is required in terms of skills rather than content.

WORKING WITH GCSE ENGLISH AND ENGLISH LITERATURE

The following is an example of a scheme of work based on short stories. It deliberately connects with the sample lesson plan used in 'Working at Key Stage 3' (Figure 4.2) as a reminder that Key Stage 3 work is also preparation for Key Stage 4. It uses the same principles about narrative and therefore further illustrates the possibility of working both within and beyond the programmes of study. It meets the requirements of an English and/or English literature syllabus if you choose prescribed or recommended texts. With reference to the NEAB syllabuses for 1998, for example, you could use stories from *My Oedipus Complex and Other Stories* by Frank O'Connor, which are set for the English Literature examination, or choose stories for wider reading; the syllabus for 1998 suggests a comparison of stories by men and women, such as Thomas Hardy, Penelope Lively or Margaret Atwood.

The scheme of work is designed to meet the requirements of syllabuses for GCSE. It is also based upon principles which have long been common to English teachers, such as: the comparative analysis of texts sharpens critical awareness; a choice of tasks allows for differentiation; reading dif-

The statements refer to the opportunities which pupils should have.

Speaking and Listening
- Communicate clearly, structuring and organising their talk and adapting to different situations;
- use standard English;
- listen to and understand varied speech;
- participate in discussion, judging the nature and purposes of contributions and the roles of participants.

Reading
- Read with insight and engagement, making appropriate references to texts and developing and sustaining interpretations of them;
- distinguish between fact and opinion and evaluate how information is presented; follow an argument, identifying implications and recognising inconsistencies;
- select material appropriate to their purpose, collate material from different sources, and make cross-references;
- understand and evaluate how writers use linguistic, structural and presentational devices to achieve their effects and comment on ways language varies and changes.

Writing
- Communicate clearly, adapting their writing for a wide range of purposes and audiences;
- use and adapt forms and genres for specific purposes and effects;
- organise ideas into sentences, paragraphs and whole texts;
- use accurate spelling and punctuation, and present work neatly and clearly;
- use the grammatical structures of Standard English and a wide range of vocabulary to express meanings with clarity and precision.

Literature (separate syllabus)
- Respond to texts critically, sensitively and in detail, selecting appropriate ways to convey their response, using textual evidence as appropriate;
- explore how language, structure and forms contribute to the meanings of texts, considering different approaches to texts and alternative interpretations;
- explore relationships and comparisons between texts, selecting and evaluating relevant material;
- develop some understanding of literary tradition;
- appreciate the social and historical influences upon a writer.

Figure 4.5 Summary of Assessment Objectives for 1998: GCSE English and English Literature
Source: adapted from 'GCSE '98: What's the Difference?', *English and Media Magazine*, 34, Summer 1996, pp. 21–26.

ferent discourses enlarges pupils' own language use; telling and retelling develops thinking.

Therefore, although this scheme of work looks simple and clearly meets the requirements of the GCSE syllabus, it is also founded upon objectives which are not specified for assessment. It allows you to retain aims for your teaching which underpin the activities; these are to do with the development of pupils in terms of their language competence through cultural analysis and use of language. It is, nevertheless, only a basic framework for a scheme of work and you would need to spend sufficient time engaging with each of the three stories. Exploratory activities could include:

- comprehension questions;
- predictions;

Class: 10   **Syllabus**:
Title of scheme of work: Reading and Responding to Short Stories.
Main objective/s: to understand genre (short story); to develop ability
to write narrative.
Assessment:
Speaking/Listening –
Writing – write in a range of forms (short story); develop vocabulary,
  syntax, structure; use Standard English and accurate expression.
Reading – coursework essay for English Literature (understanding and
  response to structure, language and meaning in range of texts).

Equipment/resources: three texts, worksheets 1 and 2.

Sequence of lessons – showing continuity and progression
1. Read story 1. Complete chart (worksheet 1) to identify characteristics
   of short story – point of view, characterisation, treatment of time,
   surprise, social comment).
2. As for lesson 1 with story 2.
3. As for lesson 2 with story 3.
4. Develop thinking about short stories and the process of writing. Use
   supporting materials such as interviews with a short story writer.
   Clarify principles of planning and research before writing. Give out
   worksheet 1 and introduce choice of tasks (retelling a story provided,
   prequel or sequel of story provided, design own story, considering
   genre, e.g. romance; crime). Think about and make initial notes for
   homework.
5. Plan and draft story. Some pupils read out beginnings. Give out
   worksheet 2 which instructs (a) exchange story with partner and how
   to constructively criticise; (b) advice for redrafting.
6. As for 5. Complete for homework.

Figure 4.6 Scheme of work for Key Stage 4

- pupils devising questions for each other;
- role play or scripting for reading on the radio.

Worksheet 1 could be modelled on those provided in Heinemann *Core English* or *Contexts* folders. The point of worksheet 2 is to ensure that redrafting is a meaningful activity and not just a copying out. It will include guidance about checking spelling and punctuation, but should also provide guidance on experimenting with structure, syntax and vocabulary.

TASK 4.2   WORKING WITH A GCSE SYLLABUS

The aim of this task is for you to become familiar with a GCSE syllabus and supporting materials and to see how they work in practice. It is tempting to avoid the documentation provided by examining groups but their booklets are invaluable for giving guidance about what is to be taught, marking criteria and sample

---

examination materials. You should collect the syllabus materials and discuss them with your mentor.

1. Get a copy of the school's GCSE syllabus for English and English Literature. Discuss with the Head of English the reasons why this board was chosen. Read the syllabus and consider how it meets the common requirements for GCSE in terms of: reading, examination and coursework.
2. Look at sample materials provided by the examining group. Work out which knowledge and skills are tested in the examination.
3. Find out the departmental practice concerning teaching and assessing speaking and listening (e.g. are lessons specified for assessment? How are records kept?)
4. What is the marking and assessment policy for GCSE work (e.g. are grades put on pupils' work?)
5. Study the department's syllabus for years 10 and 11. Note how much time is allocated to each text or unit of work.
6. Plan your own scheme of work for a year 10 class in conjunction with their GCSE syllabus requirements for English and/or English Literature. Discuss it with your tutor.

AM I EQUIPPED TO TEACH THE NATIONAL CURRICULUM?

All teachers are likely to concentrate on the subject areas with which they are most confident and these are likely to correspond most closely to their own educational opportunities. Consequently, you may find yourself not only reproducing the attitudes and activities which you have experienced, but also avoiding the areas where you are less knowledgeable. Most experienced teachers have had to learn new curriculum requirements, like media studies, using information technology and knowledge about language. It is hoped that all teachers continue to see themselves as learners in their subject and to view new areas as welcome opportunities for personal development rather than as causes for resistance or anxiety. The final chapter in this book charts the curriculum requirements for English teachers in relation to their own educational opportunities. (See also Unit 1.1 and Task 1.1.2 in Capel, Leask and Turner, 1995.)

Curriculum resources

When you consider the demands in terms of the range of knowledge and approaches required to teach English, it can be reassuring to know that educational publishers always respond to the needs of teachers and excellent course texts and photocopiable folders, television programmes and

TASK 4.3   CHANGING HABITS

The aim of this task is to identify your own attitudes and insecurities when facing the requirements of the National Curriculum. In order to consider how your own experiences of English lessons at school may affect your approach to teaching, discuss the following questions with another student teacher, your mentor or tutor.

- **Reading**: were your progression and achievement measured by the number of classic writers? What part did television and film play in the classroom?
- **Speaking and listening**: were you actively encouraged to take a part in discussions? What were the places of debate, role play, small group discussion, producing media texts?
- **Writing**: what proportion of time was spent in creating poems, plays and narratives? How were they marked – by spelling, handwriting or the teacher's judgement? Did you know what she was looking for?
- **Language study**: to what extent were you taught grammar and to use standard English in writing or talk? Did you learn about language change and variety?
- **Methodology**: to what extent was teaching didactic or pupil-centred? How did you best learn? What motivated your learning?

educational software are produced. You will, of course, always need to know the resources well and adapt them for your class. Explore the resources in your school and training institution and ask colleagues in school for their recommendations. The following are particularly recommended to support your lesson planning with relation to the requirements of *English in the National Curriculum* (DFE, 1995):

Broadbent, S. (1995) *Key Stage 3 English Units*, London: The English and Media Centre.

Buckley, K. *et al.* (1995) *Exploring Pre-Twentieth-Century Fiction: A Language Approach*, Lancaster: Framework Press.

Little, R., Redsell, P. and Wilcock, E. (1986) *Contexts*, London and Oxford: Heinemann.

Shepherd, C. and White, C. (1991) *Novel Ideas*, Carlisle: Carel Press.

SUMMARY AND KEY POINTS

The requirements of the National Curriculum consist of programmes of study, which set out what is to be taught in Speaking and Listening, Reading and Writing. When planning lessons, you need to refer to the statements under Range, Key Skills, and Standard English and Language Study in order to identify learning objectives; you also need to refer to the Attainment Targets and adapt the Level Descriptions into criteria for assessment. An emphasis on assessment by examination at Key Stages 3 and 4 means that pupils need to be prepared for the skills demanded by timed examination as well as for coursework. Although you may believe that, 'archaic, limiting, timed end-of-Key-Stage exams have no place in the sort of wide-ranging assessment scheme that is necessary to reflect the complexities of the curriculum' (Hickman, 1995, p. 7) you will aim to enable all pupils to achieve their best in terms of national assessment, such as Level Descriptions, SATs, GCSE coursework and examination.

English teachers also aim to provide opportunities for all pupils to develop language awareness and use which are not explicitly identified in the programmes of study, or which may be identified but which are not assessed and therefore may lose significance, such as media analysis other than of newspapers. English teachers aim to underpin their adherence to the National Curriculum requirements with a rationale for the development of literacy in its broadest sense so that all pupils enjoy an enriching curriculum. As stated in the Introduction, the reason for this is the belief in 'the connections between language, education and full participation in a political democracy [which] have lain behind debates round English throughout two centuries' (Burgess, 1996, p. 67). The challenge for English teachers, therefore, is to work within and beyond the requirements of the National Curriculum.

The quantity and breadth of reading and other subject knowledge required to teach the full curriculum age and ability range means that you should be able to draw upon your strengths in the subject, but need to develop other areas: twentieth and pre-twentieth century literature in all genres; literature from a range of cultures; Shakespeare at all levels; media studies; drama approaches; formal and informal speaking and listening activities; language variety and language change; Standard English; information technology.

FURTHER READING

DES and Welsh Office (1995) *English in the National Curriculum*, London: HMSO.

Protherough, R. and King, P. (1995) *The Challenge of English in the National Curriculum*, London: Routledge.

This is an issue-based book which looks at working with *English in the*

National Curriculum without losing sight of the values and practices which English teachers have seen erased by a skills-based, pragmatic and over-prescriptive curriculum. It looks at the controversial questions involved in all areas of English teaching including grammar, assessment and pre-twentieth-century literature.

5 Speaking and listening

INTRODUCTION

Within the English curriculum the importance of reading and writing has always been uncontested, whereas the importance of speaking and listening has only recently been fully acknowledged. Before the 1960s oral work was very likely to consist of teacher-led question and answer sessions or formal activities such as reading aloud, debates, and prepared short talks. However, during the 1960s the influence of educators such as Andrew Wilkinson (cited in Howe, 1997, p. 6) and growing awareness of the work of psychologists such as Vygotsky led to more systematic studies of the role of classroom talk. New understandings about the relationship between language and learning emerged and led to significant changes in classroom practice. Speaking and listening were gradually afforded greater status and made a compulsory part of the assessment of English at GCSE. More recently 'Speaking and Listening' has become the first Attainment Target for English in the National Curriculum.

Vygotsky's theories are helpful to English teachers in a number of ways. First, he argues that children learn to think by talking with others, by engaging in a social process which enables them to 'grow into the intellectual life of those around them' (Vygotsky, 1978, p. 88). At a certain stage in the child's development, speech divides into two distinct kinds: 'communicative' speech to be used for communication with others and 'egocentric' speech or speech for oneself which will eventually turn inward to become 'inner' speech with its own idiosyncracies of grammar, for individual thinking. Inner speech has different rules from communicative speech: with inner speech, speaker and listener form the same consciousness so there is much that can be taken as read; with communicative speech the need is to be understood by another person so more must be made explicit. Inner speech is not, therefore, a mirror image of communicative speech. It is essentially different because it is serving a different purpose. The distinctive natures of inner and outer speech and the power of the dynamic relationship between them to enable intellectual development is vital to an understanding of how children become effective learners and the part that teachers have to play in that development.

In the late 1960s, with the aid of portable tape-recorders, researchers and teachers such as Douglas Barnes, James Britton and Harold Rosen were able to study much more systematically than ever before the kinds of spoken exchanges that took place between teacher and pupil, and between pupil and pupil in ordinary classrooms (Barnes, Britton and Rosen, 1969). They analysed how and when learning seemed to be taking place and the part played by home dialects, spoken Standard English, the task set, the formality of the context, and the authenticity of the problem to be solved. New understandings emerged about the role of exploratory talk in cognitive development, of how talk might be used to learn through speculating, hypothesising, arguing, negotiating, and so on. These understandings, in turn, led to new classroom practices. Teachers began to organise their classrooms for group work, to plan activities which involved solving problems, discussing texts, debating controversial issues more informally than hitherto. Time was also spent teaching *about* talk, making *explicit* what pupils knew *implicitly* about how, for example, spoken language is affected by the context and purpose of the communication and by the audience to whom it is addressed; about why and when people alternate between speaking in Standard English or their regional dialect. Whether pupils were learning *through* speaking and listening or learning *about* speaking and listening, silent classrooms were no longer prized once it was realised that talk might sometimes have a greater part to play in the development of learning than silence.

Gradually the move was towards recognising the centrality of speaking and listening and investigating how it might be assessed. Many felt that it never could be effectively assessed. Knowing that they were being assessed would affect how pupils performed and distort the outcome. Nevertheless, surveys into the development of oracy conducted by the Assessment of Performance Unit (APU) in the 1980s pointed the way to the development of assessment criteria and to exploring what constituted progression in speaking and listening (Johnson, in Norman, ed., 1992, p. 51).

The important point to remember, for those new to English teaching, is that speaking and listening in classrooms has not always been viewed the way it is now. It is worth familiarising yourself with how its current position has been arrived at (Howe, 1992, pp. 3–7; Johnson in Norman, ed., pp. 50–60), what some of the debates have been, and what theories have informed them so that you can begin to develop a rationale of your own for teaching and assessing speaking and listening. You may have vivid memories of what counted as speaking and listening when you were at school and strong feelings about it. But, however recently you were at school yourself, things will have changed. As a learner you need to trace for yourself the steps which will show you the moves from traditional patterns of speaking and listening in schools to new approaches adopted by many teachers nowadays. You have to make what is described in the

Bullock Report as 'a journey in thought' (DES, 1975, p. 141) about speaking and listening for yourself. This chapter is designed to help you map that journey.

It is worth bearing in mind, however, that although maps will take you a long way there may be value in sometimes deviating from marked routes. An account of where the origin of Virginia Woolf's experimental work may have lain buried is recounted in her biography by Lyndall Gordon. Like her father, Virginia loved,

> to step aside from the high road. . .to trust to innumerable footpaths, 'as thin as though trodden by rabbits', which led over the hill and moor in all directions. . .she followed natural paths which ignored artificial boundaries. The padlocked gates and farm walls were deceptive barriers for, when she climbed over, the path would continue quite happily.
>
> (Gordon, 1984, pp. 78–79)

Thus, in her novels, she was inclined to ignore the signposts of birth, marriage and death; instead she tended to focus on 'those unlooked-for moments that shape our lives'. With talk in classrooms it may be the same: although there is much to be gained from thoughtful and reflective planning and organisation, sometimes the best talk occurs when and where it is least expected, precisely in those unlooked-for moments. Be ready to listen for them.

OBJECTIVES

By the end of this chapter you should:

- be aware of some of the factors which contribute to or inhibit effective, purposeful speaking and listening in English;
- be aware of how teaching about the differences between spoken and written language and about different types of talk can assist pupils in their development as speakers and listeners;
- understand how planning and the organisation of classrooms can contribute to pupils' language, learning and cognition;
- begin to understand how to assess pupils' speaking and listening against given criteria and to link assessment with future planning.

OBSERVING SPEAKING AND LISTENING

In order to enable pupils to develop their ability in speaking and listening it is useful to consider the range of talk which may occur within the boundaries of the classroom. In order to evaluate pupils' speaking and listening (so that you can identify achievement and plan for progression) there has to be consideration of *audience*, *context* and *purpose*. It is also important to understand the role of the teacher in providing opportunities for all pupils to participate and achieve.

At the start of any initial teacher education course a great deal of time is spent by student teachers doing classroom observation. One of the best ways to begin thinking in depth about speaking and listening is to make diversity of talk and the range of classroom opportunities for speaking and listening key targets of that observation.

TASK 5.1   IDENTIFYING HELPS AND HINDRANCES

In order to gain a clearer picture of the variety and value of talk in the classroom, find as many opportunities as you can to observe pupils speaking and listening. Draw up a table like Table 5.1 and use it to jot down your observations. Compare your findings with those of other student teachers observing in different contexts and curriculum areas.

Contexts

While you are observing you will become increasingly aware of the difference made by the contexts in which speaking and listening are taking place. Small group discussions or question and answer sessions in English classrooms will involve pupils differently from drama lessons in which pupils are planning for performance or role playing. In library lessons, pupils engaged in research will talk and listen differently to each

Table 5.1 Observing speaking and listening

Factors contributing to effective, purposeful talk	Factors inhibiting effective, purposeful talk

other from how they will when working collaboratively on a computer screen in the computer suite.

Range, audience and purpose

You will begin to note the opportunities pupils are given to:

- talk formally/informally;
- talk in pairs/small groups/whole-class discussions;
- use talk to explore and develop ideas at length;
- use talk to express their feelings and opinions;
- use talk to question and challenge what they hear;
- use talk to negotiate;
- use talk to instruct/listen to, and act on, instructions;
- use talk to ask questions as well as answer them;
- use talk to plan, explore and evaluate other activities;
- talk to a specified audience;
- talk for a specified purpose;
- talk about speaking and listening;
- plan and evaluate their talk;
- discuss different types of talk being used in drama and role play.

The role of the teacher

The role of the teacher in developing pupils' speaking and listening is central. In terms of planning, organising, differentiating and so on, there is much to consider. In addition, however, teachers need to be conscious of how their own use of language affects the language used by pupils in their classes. It is, therefore, valuable to spend time in lessons observing teachers' as well as pupils' use of language.

A frequently used technique in many lessons across the curriculum, for example, is for teachers to ask questions of their pupils as a way of eliciting information, recapping on prior learning or checking instructions have been understood. It is worth considering, however, which are the pupils, in any one class, who are most likely to answer the teacher's questions? How long are pupils given to think before the chance to answer is passed on to someone else? Research reveals that:

> when questions are posed in everyday conversations, a response usually comes within less than a second of silence. This is also true of classroom questions. Teachers usually allow about a second for a reply and, if none is forthcoming, they take back the conversational floor. [But] where a longer silence was left – even one as short as three seconds – the quality and extent of pupils' responses improved dramatically.

> (Wood, in Norman, ed., 1992, pp. 204–213)

Wood goes on to suggest that particular types of teacher talk create a classroom climate which affects how pupils themselves will talk. For example, where closed questions are common and are not followed up by the teacher with open-ended questions, pupils' responses are often single words and under-developed. On the other hand, where teachers themselves speculate, surmise, listen and ask questions to which they do not already know the answers, pupils will often respond in kind, i.e. hypothesise in response to hypothesising, speculate in response to speculating. As part of your observations you may wish to note how teachers develop pupils' speaking and listening through the use of questioning and to evaluate your own success in using questions in lessons.

EXPLORING DIFFERENCES BETWEEN SPOKEN AND WRITTEN LANGUAGE

Speech is fundamentally different from writing. It has its own characteristic grammatical features and is greatly affected by the fact that it almost always takes place when speaker and listener are face to face. Despite this it is very easy to make quick and erroneous judgements about people based on the way in which they speak.

Examining your own knowledge and attitudes

As teachers it is vitally important that we understand clearly some of the differences between spoken and written language so that our judgements about pupils' achievements are not the result of ignorance or misconception. As Katharine Perera points out in *Understanding Language*:

> There are two important points to be made that concern the nature of speech on the one hand, and the nature of writing on the other. First, there is a fairly widely-held but mistaken view that speech is some kind of careless or sloppy version of writing. This view leads people to make judgements of speech that are inappropriate because they derive from the written standard . . .

> Secondly, it is necessary to realize that written language is not merely a transcription of speech; so learning to read and write means not just learning to make and decode letter shapes but also acquiring new forms of language. Some difficulties in reading spring from the language itself rather than from the written code, because there are some grammatical constructions which are common in writing but which occur very rarely in speech.
>
> (Perera, 1987, pp. 17–18)

Some characteristics of spoken language

Depending upon where, when, why and to whom they are talking, speakers will probably alter some or all of the following:

- their register (e.g. from formal to informal);
- their grammar (e.g. from clauses embedded in complex sentences to linked simple sentences peppered with gap-fillers, false starts and changes of direction);
- their dialect (e.g. from Standard English to regional);
- their accent (e.g. from a regional accent closer to Received Pronunciation);
- the paralinguistic features of their speech (e.g. gesture, body language);
- the prosodic features of their speech (e.g. tone, speed, rhythm).

Many of us find that when we explore our views about spoken language we unearth prejudices and misconceptions such as those described by Katharine Perera above. However, the more we investigate language, the more we see how complex speaking and listening can be and how significant the apparently ordinary spoken contributions of pupils often are.

Transcribing spoken language

Taping and transcribing pupils' talk can be a very helpful way for you to enlarge your understanding about their achievements. Finding time to listen to, and transcribe, what you have recorded can be very time-consuming. However, it is a very important thing to do from time to time, especially if you skim through what you have taped and only transcribe the key moments which are likely to be worth looking at in more detail.

The following example demonstrates what transcription can reveal. Both these transcripts record the words spoken by a pupil (D) in a piece of improvised drama. In the first transcript he is role playing a villager being asked by an interviewer (I) about a play to be performed by the village drama group.

Transcript 1: the interview

D: Well, I'm Tom Evans, and I'm sort of the narrator in these plays. We're sort of re-enacting the story of another legend which was about the two monsters that supposedly are buried in the mine . . . they're supposed to have thousands of years ago came and . . . well . . . arrived in Tallybont and murdered a few people . . . of the village and the people caught them, put them away, but they escaped again not long ago.

I: How did you find out about this story? How did you know it in the
     first place?
D: Well . . . I was down the mine and I was um hacking, hacking away um
     ready to push the cart away full of coal and um I sort of found this book.
     I don't know why there was a book down there. It was a sort of diary.

An analysis of the way pupil D speaks in role here shows that he employs
many of the features of spoken language. His speech includes examples
of hesitancies such as 'um' and 'sort of' which give him time to think
what comes next. His words are mostly a series of clauses linked by 'and',
for example 'and I was hacking', 'and I sort of found this book', 'and it
sort of told'. This is what Gunther Kress calls 'chaining' and it is characteristic of spoken as distinct from written language (Kress, 1992, p. 31).

In the second transcript the pupil is the same villager, now performing
in the play itself. The rest of the class, also in role as villagers, watch the
play being acted out. The performance begins with the sound of drilling
announcing that the characters are already down the mine. Pupil D then
begins to speak as Tom Evans, the narrator of the play's events. While he
narrates, the rest of his group mime the story. Putting down an imaginary
drill pupil D then picks up a fairly large, fat dictionary, the group's only
prop. His opening words explain what this dictionary is: it is an old diary,
the book which was found down the mine. Turning the pages of this
'diary' he then proceeds to 'read' from it.

Transcript 2: the performance

D : The story which I am about to tell is of one which I do not believe
     myself. Recently, in the village, it is said that two monsters suddenly
     came out of the cave and started murdering and killing the people of
     Tallybont. Several were killed. They were finally caught after a lot of
     effort. While they were trying to come out of the cave they were
     grabbed and seized by the people. They took them and put them in a
     cast iron coffin. The coffin was set in a hill and covered up. This is all
     I can say.
        A hundred years ago when the mine was opened for the first
     time it is said they did not like having a mine built on top of their
     grave and so they came out of the coffin to take revenge . . . there was
     a murder down the mine and it is not known if it was the monster but
     it could've been. The victim was found screaming and shouting,
     'Terror! Terror! It's coming!' He died of shock in hospital. They
     think it was the monsters that did it but that's only a legend.

The language of this second transcript is 'written' language even though
it has never been scripted. There is not a single example of hesitancy,
unlike the many which featured in the earlier 'spoken' version. Further-

more, the syntax shows all the signs of a 'hierarchical', embedded structuring which Kress says is distinctive of written language. Here we have relative clauses ('which I am about to tell') , adverbial phrases ('in the village'), use of the passive voice ('it is said') and so on.

These many distinctive features of pupil D's language, illuminated in the transcribing, suggest a highly sophisticated, internalised sense of the difference between spoken and written language. Because spoken language is ephemeral unless captured on tape or video, the achievements of many pupils are bound to pass us by. But two things can help to prevent us from underestimating what pupils can do: the first is to develop our own knowledge about language so that we may recognise more clearly what pupils' spoken language tells us about their learning and understanding; the

---

TASK 5.2 MAKING A TRANSCRIPT

If you have not had the opportunity to do so before (e.g. as part of your own schooling or university course), try making a transcript of a short piece of spoken language. The purpose of the task is to encourage you to focus your attention on some of the characteristic features of spoken language texts.

- Using a tape recorder, record someone, possibly another student teacher, talking about the school they used to go to. When you transcribe the tape you might end up with something like the following:

> Um I went to a quite a big private school and big red brick building with lots of very good facilities and swimming pool um and little well quite a big theatre as well where we put on quite a lot of shows and um I really liked doing English I had a really excellent English teacher who sort of inspired me um lots of poetry we did and also nineteenth century novels which I particularly enjoyed um what I liked about the school was that everyone was you could enjoy the work without feeling that you were um being boring in fact it had a very academic purpose to it um you weren't meant to it wasn't there weren't ideas about being cool um by not working or pretending that in fact for lots of people it the school was quite difficult there was a lot of pressure to do well to er produce things not just academic but also creatively um creative writing or drama um also suited me because sport was not at all emphasised um you could in fact it was quite looked down on if you enjoyed um playing sport against other teams um so in that respect it's quite unlike other private schools with the sort of play up and play the game ethos

- Ask other people to read the transcript. Before the tape is played to them, jot down under the heading 'Transcript' in a chart like the one below, what they predict about the speaker and how their words might sound.
- Play the tape. In the column headed 'Tape', jot down notes about what is actually heard.

(In this case the speaker is a young woman who sounds fluent and assured. The varied intonation and steady pacing of the spoken language mean that the whole hangs together and sounds more coherent than it appears when transcribed. The speaker does not have a regional accent, but certain features commonly associated with social class are prominent.)

Table 5.2 Analysing a transcript

	Transcript	Tape
accent		
tone		
pace		
fluency		
gender		

second is to spend time, now and then, analysing transcripts to remind ourselves of the complexities of what we are teaching and assessing.

Making transcripts with pupils

Transcribing tape-recorded speech is an activity which can be readily adapted for use in the classroom, with any age group, as long as there are

---

TASK 5.3 TRANSCRIBING ANECDOTES AND STORIES

The purpose of this task is to provide you with an activity, suitable for a year 8 or year 9 group, which you can use to discover how much pupils know or can learn explicitly about some of the characteristic features of spoken language texts.

- Equip yourself with a tape recorder and blank tape.
- Set the tape recorder running and ask each pupil in turn to recount a short anecdote about a topic such as the following:
  - How I got my scar
  - A time when I was really scared

– My earliest memory
– The most exciting time of my life

- Transcribe the anecdotes and make enough copies for pupils to have one each.
- Ask pupils to do some oral redrafting of their stories, shaping them as a practised storyteller might, drawing on some of the techniques of traditional storytelling. (You might wish to refer to a storyteller like Betty Rosen who, in her book *And None of It Was Nonsense* (1988), explains how certain aspects of storytelling may be taught.) When they are ready to do so, pupils retell their stories, perhaps being recorded this time on video so that facial gestures and body language can be discussed afterwards.
- Ask pupils to redraft their anecdotes using a deliberately literary style.
- Discuss with pupils some of the differences between their original anecdotes and their more crafted storytelling. They might, for example, notice differences between beginnings: impromptu anecdotes often begin with initiators such as 'right' or 'well' whereas a prepared story is more likely to start with a formulaic phrase such as 'A long time ago' or even possibly 'Once upon a time'.

sufficient tape recorders available to make it practicable. You may, however, wish to try the task out first with a small group of three or four pupils. Your planning will need to take account of the time needed between lessons for you (or the pupils) to transcribe their recordings.

EXPLORING VARIETY IN SPOKEN LANGUAGE

Having established, for yourself and with your pupils, some of the differences between spoken and written language, you might now wish to focus on variety in spoken language.

Formality and informality

An interesting area to investigate with pupils is how the context, audience and purpose for speaking and listening affect the formality or informality of the language used. A light-hearted piece of improvised role play such as the following can result in a serious consideration of language registers.

Pupils (perhaps in year 7 or year 8) read an article entitled 'Teachers in Detention' (Figure 5.1) and improvise a series of different conversations afterwards.

Teachers in Detention

By our Education Correspondent

There were red faces all round last night when two local teachers found themselves locked in school until the early hours of Saturday morning.

Working late

They had been working late in the workshops in the centre of the school campus. They did not realise that they had been locked in until they tried to get out at 9.30 p.m. last night.

999 call

But the most embarrassing moment was yet to come. The school caretaker, Mr Arnold Jones, was woken up in the middle of the night when he heard a noise of banging and clattering.
 'I thought it was vandals, so I dialled 999,' he said today. 'I can tell you, the police were not well pleased to be called out at two o'clock in the morning.'

Explanations

The teachers involved refused to comment – but they will certainly have some explaining to do on Monday!

Figure 5.1 'Teachers in Detention'

- In pairs, the two teachers talk to each other when they first realise what has happened.
- In threes, the two teachers explain/apologise tactfully to the Head on Monday morning.
- In fours, the teachers recount their experiences to two colleagues in the staffroom on Monday morning.
- In fours, one of the teachers explains to pupils in their form group on Monday morning (following the incident and the newspaper report) what has happened.

It is interesting to ask pupils to predict which of the four scenarios will result in the most formal or informal register and why. For example, will the conversation between the Head and the two teachers be more formal than the one which takes place in the form group? Afterwards pupils can discover whether their predictions were accurate and what factors contributed to the various registers being used.

Accent and dialect

Several of the activities described above may lead to discussions about accent and dialect and the use of Standard English. For example, pupils may discuss whether some of the roles in 'Teachers in Detention' are more likely than others to involve use of regional dialect words rather than their Standard English equivalents. In these circumstances it is important to be absolutely clear yourself about the concepts and knowledge involved, about what the differences are, for example, between accent and dialect or between Received Pronunciation and Standard English. Use of linguistic terminology, rather than labels from folk linguistics such as 'posh' or 'common', can help to move the discussion away from the stereotypical and towards a more precise knowledge and understanding of how spoken language works and is used.

PLANNING AND ORGANISING CLASSROOMS FOR SPEAKING AND LISTENING

Your observation of speaking and listening will have demonstrated to you how much talk goes on all the time in schools and how rich and varied it is. A good deal of what you have observed, however, will have been carefully planned for, with classrooms organised and tasks chosen to enhance opportunities for speaking and listening. Pupils need plenty of occasions to talk and listen informally and incidentally. They also need the chance to talk and listen in more formal and challenging contexts.

An important paragraph in the Bullock Report makes clear what the teacher's role must be:

> The teacher's role should be one of planned intervention, and his purposes and the means of fulfilling them must be clear in his mind. Important among these purposes should be the intention to increase the complexity of the child's thinking, so that he does not rest on the mere expression of opinion but uses language in an exploratory way.
> (DES, 1975, p. 145)

The next section of this chapter will look at some examples of how planning and organising classrooms for talk can develop pupils' language, learning and cognition and increase the complexity of their thinking.

Planning structured group work

What follows is a description of an activity which might be undertaken by a mixed-ability year 9 or year 10 group who are studying Shakespeare's *Henry V*.

The class has reached Act 1V, scene vii, the point in the play when Henry is handed the two lists of those who have died in the battle of Agincourt. The first is the list of the slaughtered French; the second gives the number of the English dead. The two parts, the King and the herald, are first read aloud by volunteers:

King. Now, herald, are the dead numb'red?
Her.   Here is the number of the slaught'red French. . .
King. This note doth tell me of ten thousand French   1
       That in the field lie slain; of princes, in this number,
       And nobles bearing banners, there lie dead
       One hundred twenty-six; added to these,
       Of knights, esquires, and gallant gentlemen,   5

Eight thousand and four hundred; of the which
Five hundred were but yesterday dubb'd knights.
So that, in these ten thousand they have lost,
There are but sixteen hundred mercenaries;
The rest are princes, barons, lords, knights, squires,   10
And gentlemen of blood and quality.
The names of those their nobles that lie dead:
Charles Delabreth, High Constable of France;
Jacques of Chatillon, Admiral of France;
The master of the cross-bows, Lord Rambures;   15
Great Master of France, the brave Sir Guichard Dolphin:
John Duke of Alencon; Antony Duke of Brabant,
The brother to the Duke of Burgundy;
And Edward Duke of Bar. Of lusty earls,
Grandpre and Roussi, Fauconbridge and Foix,   20
Beaumont and Marle, Vaudemont and Lestrake.
Here was a royal fellowship of death!
Where is the number of our English dead?
(*Herald presents another paper*)
Edward the Duke of York, the Earl of Suffolk,
Sir Richard Kikely, Davy Gam, Esquire;   25
None else of name; and of all other men
But five and twenty. O God, thy arm was here!
(*Henry V*, Act IV, scene 7)

Even for adults the speech is difficult to read aloud with feeling straight
away. For pupils it is likely to prove even more so. The activity which follows is designed to encourage closer study of the language with a view to
being able to reread the speech, speaking the words with greater intensity
and emotion. The activity is structured to create maximum opportunities
for purposeful talk which will involve everybody and extend their thinking and understanding.

1. The class of thirty pupils is divided into six groups of five. In the
    groups pupils are labelled A, B, C, D and E. The groups are told that
    they are members of different stonemasons' workshops in France at
    the time when the play is set. They have been given the possibility of
    a contract to create stone memorials to the French dead after the
    battle of Agincourt. The list has arrived at their workshop just as it is
    in the King's speech up to line 22. Their task is to put in a bid for the
    contract. Every group member should keep their own record of the
    results of their discussions.
2. Groups should work their way through the list in the King's speech
    to establish the facts, e.g. about who has died, their names (if known),
    what their rank or position was.
3. Groups should then consider what type(s) of memorial might be

appropriate: should there be just one or should there be several different ones? Why? Where should the memorials be erected?

4. One member of the group (A) should sketch out on an overhead projector transparency what their memorials might look like. The group should consider what should be carved on them and discuss why. They should instruct A in how they want the OHT to look.

5. During these discussions the teacher moves from group to group asking one pupil in each group (B) for an interim explanation of the group's findings, suggestions, decisions.

6. Once all groups have completed this first stage, an envoy (C) is sent from each group to the next group to try out their group's ideas on another audience. The remainder of each group listens to the ideas of the envoy and notes any similarities with, or differences from, their own.

7. Envoys return to their own groups where one person (D) fills them in on what they have missed while they have been away. The group's ideas are adjusted as necessary in the light of anything that has been learnt from the envoys.

8. Each group then sends a representative (E) to the front of the class with the OHT of their plans to summarise briefly to the rest of the class what their ideas are, using the OHT as a visual aid to support their talk. Class members may wish to question or comment on their plans.

9. Finally a decision can be made (perhaps by a representative group from each workshop, e.g. all the A's) as to which stonemasons' workshop should receive the contract and why.

10. Then, of course, the speech can be put back into its context within *Henry V* to be reread or dramatised in the light of understandings which the activity, if successful, will have generated.

One criticism sometimes levelled at this kind of work is that it may take pupils rather a long way from the context of the original speech. You can decide for yourself what you think by going back to the stated learning objectives for the activity, namely: 'to encourage closer study of the language with a view to being able to re-read the speech, speaking the words with greater intensity and emotion'; and 'to create maximum opportunities for purposeful talk which will involve everybody and extend their thinking and understanding.'

When the speech is finally reread and the study of the play itself is resumed, consider what difference the work might have made to the pupils' understanding of the significance of this deceptively awkward speech. A group of student teachers who tried out the activity for themselves found that it led them quickly into discussions about vocabulary (mercenaries, dubb'd), rank (barons, lords, knights), attitudes to warfare (volunteers, paid soldiers), word forms and functions (use of adjectives – gallant, brave, lusty), punctuation (commas to signal words or phrases in

TASK 5.4   ANALYSIS OF TEACHER'S AND PUPILS' ROLES

The purpose of this task is to analyse the roles of pupils and teacher in the *Henry V* activity. If you are able to try out or adapt the task for yourself before analysing it, so much the better.

1. Draw two columns on a sheet of paper, labelling one 'Teacher' and the other 'Pupils'. Work your way through each section of the activity making brief but precise notes about what the teacher and the pupils are doing in terms of speaking and listening.

Teacher	Pupils
1. Explains task	1. Listen to find out nature of task
2. Issues instructions	2. Listen in order to act on instructions

2. Discuss with other student teachers some or all of the following issues:
   a) Involvement. From your experience of reading or working your way through the activity, and from the notes you have made, assess what proportion of the class have been actively involved in purposeful speaking and listening.
   b) Differentiation. Are there noticeable differences between the speaking and listening tasks performed by A, B, C, D and E? If so, can you rank them in order of difficulty? Could the structure of the groups and labelling of group members be prepared by the teacher in advance so as to differentiate between the pupils in the class?
   c) Equal opportunities. How is the activity organised to try to pre-empt any individuals taking an unduly dominant role and to give space to those who are inclined to hold back? Is the subject matter likely to diminish girls' motivation to participate fully? Is the subject matter accessible to all pupils whatever their cultural background, or might the teacher need to provide some support materials, e.g. illustrations of the forms which memorials can take in a variety of cultural contexts?
   d) Envoys. Using envoys is one of a range of ways of organising group work which can successfully promote speaking and listening in the classroom. Can you analyse why it is usually successful? Find out from teachers with whom you are working what some other commonly used methods for grouping and regrouping pupils are and note the differences between them.

TASK 5.5   COLLABORATIVE POETRY WRITING

The purpose is to discover the extent to which the collaborative use of IT relies on and encourages particular kinds of speaking and listening.

Find two other people to work with you. Two of you collaborate, writing a poem on screen; the third person observes the speaking and listening which takes place between the two writers. The first task involves poetry writing and using IT to draft and edit, moving text around on the screen, deleting and inserting as necessary.

A   What the writers do

1. Using a picture as a stimulus, list on screen, one beneath the other, five things which you can see in the picture.
2. Add a verb and an adjective to each line of the list.
3. Underneath, type a list which consists of:

   - four colours you can see;
   - four textures;
   - four sounds you might hear;
   - four similes or metaphors which the picture suggests.

Your screen might now look like this:

```
1. woman
   table
   chair
   doors
   wallpaper

2. old woman looking sad
   table set out for tea
   straight-backed chair standing in the background
   wooden doors painted orange
   old-fashioned patterned wallpaper peeling off the walls

3.
•  orange brown rust yellow
•  smooth rough scratchy glossy
•  woman breathing, clink of tea cups, muffled murmuring,
   wind outside
•  single button like a buttercup; hair like unspun cotton; little
   jug like a fairy's mirror; scarf knotted like a tulip
```

4. Now that initial ideas have been gathered, reassemble them using operations like insert, delete, cut and paste, so that they

form a poem of at least four lines in length. Each line should
have a specified number of syllables to give it a regular rhythm.

5. When you are happy with the poem, read it aloud or print it out.

Here is how two student teachers, working from a reproduction
of *Mrs Mounter* by Harold Gilman (1917) which hangs in the
Walker Art Gallery in Liverpool, turned their notes into a poem.

Mrs Mounter

Dejected lonely. Hair like unspun cotton,
Sits rough and pink by table set out for tea,
Woman's old breathing and muffled murmuring,
The clink of tea cups and turquoise wind outside.

Yet an ethereal mirror before her,
Dazzles with images of a buttercup
Of smooth surfaces ripe as a young woman,
Of rich, full, scarlet tulips ready to burst.

Dejected lonely. Sits in contemplation,
Her scratchy thoughts scouring her mind clean away
To happier times of orange and olive.
Straight backed and hopeless but her life not yet dead.

B   What the observer does

Make a note of all the different kinds of speaking and listening
you observe while the poem is being written. Here is a list that
you could photocopy and use as a checklist, adding to it as well,
where necessary:

- listening to instructions;
- interpreting instructions;
- giving instructions;
- seeking clarification;
- questioning, e.g. meanings of words;
- disagreeing;
- negotiating a consensus;
- discussing, e.g. layout, word choices, spelling, punctuation;
- reading aloud;
- explaining;
- thinking aloud;
- dictating;
- asking direct questions;
- answering questions;

- commenting on sounds of poetic words;
- modifying others' suggestions;
- talking oneself into understanding;
- rephrasing ideas;
- hypothesising.

TASK 5.6 EDITING A NEWSPAPER ARTICLE

The second IT task involves editing a newspaper article, locating particularly emotive words and changing them so as to alter the bias of the piece in some way. Work in pairs with an observer in order to assess the effectiveness of the activity in encouraging speaking and listening.

You will need a short newspaper article which has been retyped and copied into two columns so that the two versions can be viewed side by side on screen.

Fen tiger spotted at scene days before
SWAN KILLED IN SAVAGE ATTACK
By Suzanna Chambers

ANIMAL welfare experts were investigating today after the headless body of a full-grown swan was discovered.

The grisly find at a park and ride site used by hundreds of commuters each day heightened local fears that the bird may have been the victim of the Fen Tiger.

The swan had been dragged from the lake, probably last night, and mauled to death by a large animal.

It was found lying by the side of a lake in the Madingley Road park and ride early this morning.

Derek Neville, a car park attendant at the site, said: 'I saw it this morning and I thought it was a white paper bag. There were feathers everywhere and its head had been bitten off.'

1. Read through the article to see what it is about and whether it is biased in any particular direction.
2. Read through the article again to identify any emotive words which are contributing to the bias of the piece.
3. Highlight each emotive word, as it occurs, in the version in the right-hand column and discuss a replacement for it which will help to bias the article in a different direction.

Fen tiger spotted at scene days before SWAN KILLED IN SAVAGE ATTACK By Suzanna Chambers	Fen tiger spotted at scene days before SWAN KILLED IN *SURPRISE* ATTACK By Suzanna Chambers

ANIMAL welfare experts were investigating today after the headless body of a full-grown swan was discovered.
  The grisly find at a park and ride site used by hundreds of commuters each day heightened local fears that the bird may have been the victim of the Fen Tiger. . .
	ANIMAL welfare experts were investigating today after the headless body of a full-grown swan was discovered.
	  The *unusual* find at a park and ride site used by hundreds of commuters each day *supported* local *theories* that the bird may have been the victim of the Fen Tiger. . .

apposition; semi-colons to separate the individuals listed). That they were in role as stonemasons bidding for a contract led also to thinking about ordinary people's attitudes to remembering those who die in battle and how those attitudes might be swayed by financial considerations. The student teachers differed in their views about whether the activity impeded or enhanced the emotive qualities of the speech. But they were not in doubt about the extent to which it promoted valuable focused discussion.

SPEAKING AND LISTENING AND IT

Observation of speaking and listening undertaken when pupils are working collaboratively using IT will have shown you how extensive and how varied their talk can be. Tasks 5.5 and 5.6 are two tasks which you may wish to try for yourself before exploring them with pupils.

These two tasks, like most of the activities described in this chapter, show how different elements of the English curriculum may be integrated: poetry, language study, writing, IT, speaking and listening, media studies. There will be occasions when, as a teacher, you want to put speaking and listening under the spotlight, to teach specifically about an aspect of oral work which you want your pupils to develop. Much of the time, however, the richest and most fruitful speaking and listening will occur when the complexity of the activity demands it and when classrooms and resources are organised so as to maximise pupils' opportunities for purposeful talk.

PROGRESSION AND ASSESSMENT IN SPEAKING AND LISTENING

You have now been introduced to a number of classroom ideas for encouraging speaking and listening. However, it is also necessary to think about how pupils make, and can be helped to make, progress in oral work. There are several things which need to be considered simultaneously:

- how will the task set engage pupils in speaking and listening and make appropriate demands of them?
- to what extent will the learning objectives for the lesson be focused on learning through talk or learning about talk?
- how will pupils' oral records influence the setting up of the task and the pupils' involvement?
- are there any aspects of speaking and listening within the task which need *teaching*, e.g. the difference between asking each other open and closed questions when trying to elicit information; explanations of concepts such as register or dialect?
- how will pupils' contributions be recorded? Will they be taped or summarised by the pupil and commented on by the teacher on a speaking and listening record sheet?
- what criteria will you use to assess their involvement?
- are pupils aware of the criteria by which they will be assessed?

As these questions suggest, progression involves a cycle of planning, teaching, task-setting, pupil activity, recording, assessing against criteria, pupil review, teacher reflection and evaluation. You will need to find out how speaking and listening is recorded across the age range in your department and to familiarise yourself with whatever systems are in place for ensuring continuity of pupil records from year to year. When you are preparing to teach a lesson or unit of work which involves speaking and listening activities and assessment, you will need to look back at pupils' oral records in order to plan for progression and continuity. It is worth discovering early on what technology is available to enable audio–visual recording of speaking and listening, and how to use it.

SUMMARY AND KEY POINTS

Pupils need opportunities to speak and listen in a wide variety of contexts and for a wide range of purposes, in order to increase the complexity of their thinking, to develop their powers of communication and to provide

TASK 5.7　SETTING TARGETS

This task is designed to help you develop your ability to plan for progression in speaking and listening, taking into account a pupil's prior learning and achievements across a range of oral activities and making use of given criteria.

Look at the following speaking and listening record sheet for a pupil in year 10 (Figure 5.2). The teacher has commented on the pupil's performance in four different activities. A target has been set after Activity 1, but not after the other three activities.

Activity 1 Debate about animal rights – pupils in role　　　　　　　　　2 Oct. 1995

You worked hard to put a strong case from the floor. You listened to others' points of view but you seldom challenged any of the points raised even though they conflicted with those you had made earlier. You chose to be in role as a character rather like yourself – you were convincing in role, but you didn't really have to adjust your language to any significant degree, as you would have done if you had been role playing someone very different.
Target: To follow through an argument in a debate or discussion, rather than just to present it. To role play a character who holds different views to your own and who is likely to speak rather formally in a debate or discussion.

Activity 2 Talk on karate　　　　　　　　　　　　　　　　　　　　12 Dec. 1995

Your talk was clearly delivered. It engaged the attention of your listeners, especially when you used video clips to illustrate a point. You responded well to questions asked afterwards. For example, when you were asked what people think about girls doing karate you gave two points of view, making both clear but indicating which one you supported. ('Some people think . . . but others, including myself, think . . .)
Target:

Activity 3 Small group discussion about short story　　　　　　　　　15 March 1996

You didn't make many comments. You rather relied on others to lead the way. You made a good point, however, when you were asked directly what you thought about the way the writer built up the suspense, namely that he used lots of questions rather than stating facts. Was there a reason why you didn't contribute this observation voluntarily, earlier in the discussion?
Target:

Activity 4 Directing the banquet scene in Macbeth　　　　　　　　　　25 June 1996

You listened carefully to views offered by others in your group. You were able to see quite quickly which to accept and which to reject. You obviously had strong ideas of your own, too, and managed to communicate them to the relevant actors effectively. You gave reasons for your suggestions, e.g. 'Lady Macbeth should smile wickedly because the audience must see the murderous thoughts she's having.' Giving a reason like that lends weight to your point and helps to convince those who are listening to you. Well done!
Target:

1. Look at the GCSE criteria for speaking and listening and try to establish which level description best suits this pupil at the end of Year 10.
2. Drawing on any speaking and listening activities you think would be appropriate and referring to the speaking and listening criteria, set targets for this pupil for activities 2, 3 and 4 which will help her to aim for a higher grade at the end of Year 11.

Figure 5.2　Speaking and listening record sheet

examples of language in use through which to develop their explicit knowledge about speaking and listening.

As a teacher you will need to learn when and how to intervene in pupils' discussions to help them to move on, and when just to listen to what they have to say unprompted.

When considering pupils' progression it is necessary to analyse and reflect on their oral work and to plan subsequent teaching accordingly. Activities often need to be carefully organised and classrooms deliberately arranged to maximise the chance of all pupils being able to participate to the best of their ability. Pupils' achievements need to be communicated to them both in general terms and in relation to specific assessment criteria.

You also need to be able to recognise and to make explicit to pupils their achievements. This can be done by teaching about spoken language and how it differs from written language, as well as by assessment, recording and reporting.

FURTHER READING

DES (1975) *A Language for Life*, London: HMSO.
Commonly referred to as the Bullock Report, this is an important work for anyone wanting to explore ideas raised in this chapter in greater depth. Chapters 4 and 10, on language and learning and oral work respectively, are well worth reading.

Howe, A. (1992) *Making Talk Work*, Sheffield: NATE.
A survey of some of the many different ways in which talk can be employed in the classroom. The book contains a particularly good chapter on the organisation of classrooms and pupil groupings.

Norman, K. (ed.) (1992) *Thinking Voices*, London: Hodder & Stoughton.
A very useful reader which summarises the work of the National Oracy Project and provides an introduction to recent developments in oral work in schools.

There are also several videos available produced by the examination boards and by SCAA. They provide examples of pupils of various ages and abilities engaged in a range of speaking and listening activities. Time spent with other student teachers and with more experienced teachers, analysing the pupils' contributions and trying to assess them against given criteria can be a very valuable way to familiarise yourself with the process of assessing oral work.

ACKNOWLEDGEMENTS

The author would like to thank the many colleagues and students with whom the ideas in this chapter have been developed over the years.

6 Reading

INTRODUCTION

When we teach pupils to read, we enter an area of seemingly awesome responsibility: for we are teaching individuals something which affects so many aspects of personal and social development, and which plays a special role in language development. Through reading, we are able to interpret, comprehend and respond critically to the ideas of others. We learn about the particular ways in which text helps to formulate and express those ideas; we reflect upon the relationship between our own experiences, and those we discover in what we read. Pupils' experience of reading impacts upon their participation in wider learning; it has implications for: personal enrichment; economic viability and employment prospects; social relationships; leisure activities and cultural identity. Reading in the social and cultural context is closely bound up with concepts of citizenship, civilisation and national identity.

There is much at stake for pupils at any stage in their development as readers. Views on what constitutes reading, and what counts as literature worth studying in school, are deeply polarised. It is important to consider the range of views on what reading is *for*, and the differing emphases which will affect your aims and decisions about methods and texts. Consider the following statements:

1. How do we ensure there is a common core to produce citizens? The book must be at the heart of our culture. We must preserve the distinctive culture of this country.

   (Nick Tate, 1996)

2. Children (should be helped) towards a critical understanding of the world and cultural environment in which they live. Children should know about the processes by which meanings are conveyed, and about the ways in which print and other media carry values.

   (DES and Welsh Office, 1989, 2.25)

3. Now that there are more readers than at any time in the past, more books to choose from and new literacies, we must accept that differences among readers and amongst texts are normal. There is no going back to a single text, a single way of reading, a single way of defining 'good readers'.

   (Meek, 1991, p. 36)

What cultural assumptions underlie these three statements? What issues are raised here, to do with the role of reading in British society? What special significance is ascribed to the study of books? What are the implications for the part played by English teachers in cultural development?

The first statement was delivered by Nick Tate, chief executive for the School Curriculum and Assessment Council (SCAA), at its conference on 'Information Technology, Communications and the Future Curriculum' in 1996 (*Times Educational Supplement* 12 July 1996). It reveals some of the factors which lie at the heart of debate about reading, literacy and the selection of appropriate reading material for schools, as they prepare pupils to be readers in the twenty-first century. This statement makes explicit the connections between the books which carry authorised value in our society, and the forging of national identity. Such texts form 'the canon', the collection of literature from the English literary heritage, which has characterised literature courses in schools and universities since the institution of English as an academic subject. Authors include Chaucer, Shakespeare, the Metaphysical Poets, Milton, Pope and Dickens. The centrality of these texts indicates a close connection between 'reading' and 'literature study' as part of a cultural process, aimed at national cohesion. It implies a shared value system, into which pupils may be inducted, and a reading of texts which can be agreed upon as containing values within a common cultural heritage (see Chapter 2).

By contrast, the cultural analysis view, which is acknowledged in *English for Ages 5 to 16* (Cox Report 2) (DES and Welsh Office, 1989), identifies the need to teach pupils to be critically aware as readers. This view asks questions of the cultural heritage model for reading, and seeks to empower pupils by teaching them to examine texts as being culturally produced. It emphasises the way in which readers are positioned in relationship to authorised literature, and helps them to understand that relationship.

The convening of the SCAA conference tells us something about reading which is more complex still, and indicates the current national debate about what constitutes reading and texts. Meek's statement reveals how our understanding of what it is to 'read' has become increasingly diverse. Contemporary society makes demands on its members to acquire an ever-widening repertoire of communication skills. To have studied the entire works of Shakespeare may, in one sense, be an indication of being 'well-read', but this concept of literacy is not likely to prove helpful to someone who needs to 'browse' pages of electronic text in order to find information. The increasing complexity of what it means to be a reader is illustrated in Chapter 9's treatment of teaching media and information technology in English. Reading as literacy today requires pupils to experience texts which variously represent the world through written, aural and visual language which the reader can interpret. Margaret Meek's analysis of contemporary literacies helps us to understand the need for diversity in our choice of texts and ways of reading with pupils.

Peter Benton (1996) reminds us that we can think of literature study as a particular aspect of reading: other aspects feature non-literary, printed information texts, media texts, electronic and audio-visual texts, all of which form a reading culture in which many of our pupils are already highly experienced. This reading culture forms the rich basis from which to develop our objectives for teaching texts within the contemporary classroom:

> Teachers will be at a disadvantage in understanding their students' responses to reading and to literature unless they have at least some understanding of, and interest in, the reading and viewing culture that adolescents are busily constructing and reconstructing in their everyday lives. Official texts are read in the context of a multitude of unofficial texts both literary and visual. There is no reason to believe that such unofficial texts are any less important in shaping students' imaginative capacity and view of the world than those promulgated by the formal demands of the curriculum . . . Texts offered from on high without an understanding of students' own reading and view-ing background are likely to be rejected.
>
> (Benton, in Davies (ed.) 1996, pp. 77–78)

OBJECTIVES

By the end of this chapter you should be able to:

- understand the significance of 'making meaning' for pupils' engage-ment with texts;
- plan for pupils to experience a broad range of texts, both literary and non-literary;
- develop activities which build on pupil difference, to teach reading in the mixed-ability classroom;
- consider ways of creating a reading environment in your classroom;
- consider ways of assessing progress in the reader.

READING IN THE NATIONAL CURRICULUM

It is worth highlighting the concepts of breadth, variety and individual enjoyment of reading, which underpin the opening declaration about the teaching of reading in secondary schools, in the National Curriculum for English. It represents an acknowledgement that, without the pupils' *own* engagement in a text which has meaning *for them*, reading lessons become an empty ritual.

Pupils should be given opportunities to read a wide variety of literature, and to respond to the substance and style of texts. They
should also be encouraged to read widely and independently solely
for enjoyment. Some texts should be studied in detail, but the main
emphasis should be on the encouragement of wider reading in order
to develop independent, responsive and enthusiastic readers.

(DFE, 1995, p. 19)

TASK 6.1 READING THE NATIONAL CURRICULUM

- At this point, try listing the types of texts which you think
  might help to achieve the goals outlined in the above extract.
- Compare your list with another student teacher's, and discuss
  your predictions for how prevalent this type of reading is in
  schools.
- If you are in England or Wales, read pages 19–21 of *English in
  the National Curriculum* (DFE, 1995), which contain the reading requirements for eleven to sixteen-year-olds. What conclusions do you draw about what reading *is* and what reading *is
  for*, as it is presented in the document?

Note down how the guidelines in the document are problematic
in relation to the ways in which reading has been described by
Meek and Benton in the introduction to this chapter.

The revised National Curriculum Orders for English (DFE, 1995) set
out an agenda for what counts as reading, in a way which places high
emphasis on reading as a particular form of *literary* practice. The range
of reading required at Key Stages 3 and 4 is drawn mainly from the traditional heritage of canonised English literature, with specific authors
appearing in an approved list. Demands are made for pupils to study: two
Shakespeare plays, two pre-twentieth century authors, four pre-twentieth
century poets, two-twentieth century authors, four-twentieth century
poets and drama by 'major playwrights'. It offers a culturally exclusive
definition of literature which may qualify as 'high quality', and imposes
set texts from the English national heritage as the foundation for reading
development at KS 3 and 4. The reading of literature from 'other cultures', non-fiction and media texts is marginalised by its summary
appearance (a total of eleven lines out of two pages of guidance). Popular fiction is not required at all.

A teacher wishing to develop a broad experience, and to promote the
individual pleasure of reading, needs to undertake a careful and critical
reading of the document. You will need to acknowledge the diversity of
pupils' experience and preferred texts, and reconcile this with teaching

prescribed literature; you will need to manage the transition from reading at Key Stage 2, which is less prescriptive of reading material, to meeting the requirements at secondary school which lead ultimately to class preparation of 'set' examination texts and core practice questions; you will aim to develop confident personal and critical readings of texts, while inducting pupils into the literary discourse of examinations, with its assumptions that some readings are more acceptable than others. You need to reconcile the broad range of demands made by these versions of reading, in how you organise your schemes of work.

MAKING MEANINGS OUT OF TEXTS

It is easy to lose sight of the readers in the midst of debate concerning appropriate school literature, manageable assessment procedures and differing classroom methods. This chapter is based upon the centrality of the reader in the reading process, and highlights issues of difference in the cultural and social histories which pupils bring to their reading. If we are building upon a popular reading and media culture in which pupils are already immersed, we need to consider how we present *choice of texts*, *range* and *relevance* in ways which encourage *variety*, *breadth* and *critical reading skills* to be developed upon new ground. The diversity of texts encountered outside the English classroom contributes to the continuum of pupils' reading histories: popular fiction, television programmes, videos, computer games, newspapers and magazines, comics and hobby books. Pupils *expect* a text to mean something – this has been their experience in their own choice-led and needs-led encounters with texts outside the classroom, where an unsatisfactory text can be switched off, left unfinished or replaced by readily available alternatives.

What are the aims of reading?

If the starting point is the pupil, then that pupil's experience of culture, gender and social environment will all help to compose her understanding of why any text should be significant: in other words, she has her own *reading position*, her individual perspective from which to interpret what she reads. Our teaching aims need to take account of the pupil's development as a reader over time, and will be relevant beyond the particular text of the moment. Questions to ask yourself before embarking on teaching any text should include:

- what can my pupils already do as readers?
- what can help to develop my pupils as readers?
- what do pupils need to know about this text?

It is easy to assume the existence of a body of uncontested knowledge about a literary text we are about to teach: volumes of 'pass notes' are testimony to the view that knowledge can exist in an uncomplicated way for pupils, which can be handed on by teachers in order to produce standard responses about what a text means, for test purposes. Underneath lies the assumption that the book's meaning is not subject to the reader, whose own individual history will in fact confer an infinite range of significance on that text.

Consider the following possible aims for a scheme of work to teach Charles Dickens's *A Christmas Carol* to a KS 3 class. Make brief notes on what each aim implies about reading development, and how it can be achieved:

- to widen the reading experience of pupils already knowledgeable about ghost stories;
- to develop strategies for pupils to make meaning out of unfamiliar forms of written language;
- to teach characteristic features of Dickens's style.

The first two aims relate to what pupils can *learn* about how to read texts: the last is more concerned about what can be *taught* about the book, and will probably feature in schemes of work which are aimed increasingly towards common exam preparation.

TASK 6.2 CONSTRUCTING A READING AUTOBIOGRAPHY

A reading autobiography charts out your history of reading, and attempts to include your most influential experiences with printed texts, which includes non-fiction. It is useful to divide texts between authorised ones studied at school (and in higher education in your case), and unauthorised reading, chosen entirely for your own pleasure or needs. The autobiography indicates texts which have had a powerful impact on the reader, either positively or through their rejection. It can go back as far as you can remember, to comics and nursery favourites. The important thing is to highlight those moments in your personal reading history which made an impact on your choices and preferences about reading. A simple format for it is suggested below.

Age	Authorised texts	Unauthorised texts
11	*A Midsummer Night's Dream* – we acted it out, abridged version, but I still didn't understand it.	Serial read of Enid Blyton – couldn't put it down. Read the entire Mystery series, and *Malory*.
13	*Tale of Two Cities* – teacher read it out to us with a grim look on her face – she obviously would rather have read something else as well. Took all year.	Don't remember reading anything else that year.

When you have completed your reading autobiography, compare it with another student teacher's. It is very unlikely that you will have a common appreciation of 'the best' literature, and in non-fiction it is probably even harder to find a common text or genre that was powerful for both of you. Differences between you both in terms of age, gender, ethnicity and schooling might make even broader diversity in your reading experiences and responses to texts. Discuss what made those highlighted texts successful or not, and examine the balance between school-taught texts and 'unauthorised' reading choices.

Discuss how you could account for your differing reading histories and what impact your findings make on how you might make decisions about choosing texts in school?

If your aims are to do with the development of enthusiastic, confident and independent readers, you must make explicit for them the unique path which each follows to becoming experienced with text. A good place to start is a conscious examination of your own reading history.

READING STRATEGIES: INDIVIDUAL, GROUP, WHOLE-CLASS

Demands made upon readers today, both in and out of school, are huge, varied and growing. If we aim for pupils to read traditional and contemporary material, including electronic and media texts, and to develop individual preferences as well as awareness of shared cultural ones, then pupils will benefit from learning a variety of ways to read, and from understanding that we treat texts differently for different purposes. Different ways of reading can be incorporated into schemes of work to satisfy the varied demands of pupil difference and curriculum requirements. Not all pupils in the same class will read the same amount of the same types of books: schemes of work throughout a key stage should ensure that the requirements of the National Curriculum can be met, and beyond that, that pupils are able to develop different reading patterns. 'Range' is achieved through the combination of class and group shared texts, and individual reading. Within 'range', in addition to the National Curriculum, you can include popular fiction, comics, picture books, books by pupil-authors, books which ensure an overall balance is achieved in the representation of cultural diversity and gender. Your sources for texts will vary, as will some of the tasks, according to the way you group pupils for reading. The importance of *grouping* pupils for differentiated reading activities cannot be overstated:

it is surely important to ensure that teaching and resources do match the learning needs of pupils . . . Since group reading is very seldom used in many classrooms, and individual reading often lacks the focus needed to produce a fully differentiated diet, it is usually through work based on the class reader that reading is being most consciously developed. Thus overall differentiation in the diet is often inadequate.

(Daw, 1995, p. 15)

Consider how your learning objectives are best matched by the differing models for grouping pupils for reading, offered in Figures 6.1 and 6.2. The rest of the chapter examines teaching based on these three approaches, *independent reading*, *group shared reading* and *whole-class reading*. It considers how you can plan for your pupils in their individual development as readers, and what strategies might best achieve your aims.

Of course, no grouping of pupils has to exclude the treatment of particular texts. You might decide that a small number of pupils would benefit from a shared reading of a further Betsy Byars novel, having studied one as a class, and there will clearly be overlaps in how texts are approached. The important point is that pupils are introduced to texts in

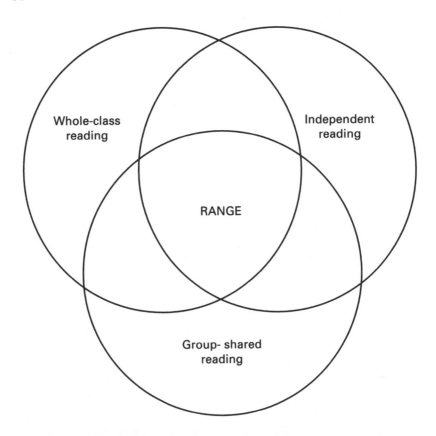

Figure 6.1 The range of reading in the secondary classroom

Independent reading	Group-shared reading	Whole-class reading
school library	book box/class library	thematic schemes of work
pupils' own books from home	small class sets by author	GCSE set texts for exams
peer-swapped texts	small class sets by theme/genre	KS3 SAT texts
book box/class library	playscripts	National Curriculum list of authors
local library	library project loan	literature by visiting writers
school book club	computer-generated/ on-screen texts	Theatre in Education texts

Figure 6.2 Sources for texts

a way which offers structured guidance to meet their individual needs and pleasures as readers.

Individual Reading

Pressure to prepare classes for common examination texts can make it seem a luxury to allow pupils the time to read their own choice of books in English lessons, especially to allow sufficient time for real engagement in such texts. This is allied with concerns about how we know what is being learned – evidence of progression in individual reading can appear elusive at secondary school. Some schools operate a short fixed reading period at the start of English lessons, which has the benefit of guaranteeing time for private reading, but which also emphasises it as something fairly dispensable when the lesson-proper begins, and can lead to it being used chiefly as a tool to achieve quiet; individual reading needs to be accommodated elsewhere as a sustained activity which is not fragmentary.

Private reading is critical to meeting the different needs of pupils, through access to appropriate reading material and tasks tailored to the individual. Special Needs pupils (slow learners – gifted pupils also need to be guided in their individual reading, but not in order to complete it) need to spend time with a text of their choice to be able to *complete* it, and they sometimes receive additional support for reading with a helper or specialist teacher. It is important, however, that they spend time reading with the rest of the class during sustained reading time, if they are to identify themselves as part of a community of readers, and to learn that able readers also experience preferences and difficulties with texts which do not work for them. The organisation of space for all pupils to find a quiet spot to read, and to read sometimes with a teacher, is an important factor in planning for differentiated reading activities. How many of us gain much from reading in an upright position on a hard wooden chair for a ten minute period? Finding appropriate time and space to read is critical. Try to observe a teacher using the library with a class as a *space* to read and respond to books.

In your school, find out about the different strategies used for monitoring and assessing individual reading. These can range from those which stress reading as a private activity, to those which form a bridge

---

TASK 6.3 WHAT MAKES A SUPPORTIVE READING ENVIRONMENT?

Make a detailed observation of an English classroom in your school. Analyse how the following factors send messages about reading to pupils. Consider especially how these factors influence the reading environment for pupils with Special Educational Needs and with English as a second or additional language:

- book displays and class libraries. What types of books count as reading? Literary, non-literary, information, hobby books, picture books, books written in languages other than English, comics?
- what provision is there for 'quick reads' which can give a sense of achievement to slower readers?
- what access is there to material written and printed by pupils, both in English and in the languages of multilingual pupils?
- wall displays. Do pupils read the walls? Is pupils' work presented so that it can be read by others? Are the displays interactive, requiring a response to what is read?
- book boxes. If they exist, what is their intended audience? Again, consider the range of material they contain which counts as 'reading';
- information about school book clubs, sponsored or national reading events, the school library, local library?
- how is space and furniture organised inside/outside the classroom to accommodate individual and group reading?
- how is gender and cultural diversity represented in the books and other materials displayed?
- is information material available in the local community languages?
- how easy is access to information technology texts?
- what types of books are on the teacher's desk – is the teacher seen as a reader too?

Discuss with another student teacher, your mentor or tutor what you think the environment says about what it means to be a reader in that classroom.

with the shared reading activities going on in the class, and so allow for pupils to develop experience of active interrogation of texts with their peers, and ways of responding to literature. The range might include:

- keeping a personal reading diary, with some common criteria to be considered but mostly emphasising the particular significance which a text has for the reader. For pupils with English as a second language, the diary offers scope for reading in a first language to be recorded, and for pupils to develop reflective reading of those texts. First language reading is crucial to developing confidence in the transferability of critical reading skills between texts.
- private reading as a basis for written work, or taped oral response: this means that the teacher needs to recognise that he frequently *does not know as much* as the pupil about the text being used. It confers real power on the reader to *make her own meaning*, within a guided context. Your job is to engage in a dialogue about the text, which helps her to reflect upon its meaning, in a way that can be communicated to a broader audience. She begins to develop awareness that texts can have shared significance for some people, and through a negotiated task, can consider her reading as something which might interest others. Responses might include: designing a book jacket for the text; selecting a key passage for reading onto a tape, and explaining the selection made; designing the advertising materials which would accompany the 'film of the book'; a book review with recommendations.
- pupils also need to share individual reading in a way which looks at common criteria, to establish a foundation of common discourse to which they can have access. An example of this is the group preparation of a 'Book Programme' or Literary Magazine, in which pupils bring together their individual reading, and present it in a format which builds on their familiarity with the language conventions of media presentation. In this way, pupils use their language experience of media texts to couch their exploration of the critical discourse about texts they have chosen to read.

Group-shared reading

This method of reading is suitable for small groups of pupils reading a core text, author or genre, and working on a task, either as a group or individually: pupils show that they have taken account of the responses and views of others in their reading of the text.

Group reading is demanding in terms of class organisation and sufficient resources. It is, however, a critical bridge between individual reading and class set texts, between pupils exercising their own purely personal criteria for responding to a text, and learning about the prevailing literary discourses of examinations, and how to be critical readers. It allows for guided choice, for the teacher to ensure range, while supporting the autonomy in readers. It is a way of keeping a personal dialogue going, and maintaining an individual reading position, while pupils move towards examinations which increasingly prescribe what to read and how to respond.

Group reading is an important way of addressing difference, and requires both the class and support teachers to give guidance and allocate appropriate targets for reading. In the multilingual classroom, shared language groups can read in a first language to develop critical reading skills. Pupils at different stages of reading fluency in English, can be directed to texts which they are ready to try. Areas of study for group reading might include the following examples:

- further texts by an author already introduced as a class reader;
- genre, e.g. horror, with different groups reading Point Horror books, Stephen King, nineteenth-century short horror stories, Mary Shelley's *Frankenstein*, the X-files, Arthur C. Clarke's *Mysterious World* series;
- a study of texts as preparation for a class reader, John Steinbeck's *Of Mice and Men*, to include a library project loan on the Great Depression, atlases of North America, Harper Lee's *To Kill a Mocking Bird* and Mildred Taylor's *Roll of Thunder: Hear my Cry*.

Reading and gender

Much debate about adolescent boys as reluctant readers was sparked by the OFSTED report, *Boys and English*, which expressed concern that 'In all year groups girls read more fiction than boys' (DFE, 1993, p. 3). Adolescent boys' reluctance to read fiction can be seen as part of a broader pattern of under-achievement in English, at a time when the success of girls is increasing. Gender differences in attitudes towards reading are complex, but some generalisable features can be summarised as follows:

- boys and girls can perceive the act of reading itself as a gendered form of behaviour. Much of the reading undertaken in classrooms is performed as a quiet, still, passive, compliant and constrained physical process. This conforms to stereotypical 'feminine' behaviour, at a time when adolescents are increasingly conscious of sexual identities.
- reluctant male readers frequently express a pragmatic perception of what English is *for*. They see it as equipping them with basic literacy skills to get a job – and therefore dismiss the reading of fiction, in particular, as irrelevant to the real world as they see it. It is not seen to be empowering.
- female pupils find compensatory power in the lives of heroines in teenage romance novels, at a time when they are becoming more aware of gender differences in the economic power-roles in society.

- male pupils are often not interested in the main texts which count as reading material, i.e. 'literature', in many classrooms. Their expressed reading preferences are infrequently met beyond occasional private reading opportunities. Factual information books, hobby books, graphic novels and comics are rarely given a high-profile whole-class focus.
- a main emphasis on character study, personal response and empathy as approaches to literature is alienating to many boys, while preferred by girls. Boys in general have expressed greater interest in events and plot development, and analytical ways of writing about literature.

In the light of the points made here, you will need to consider the following questions:

1. How can your planning aim to motivate both boys and girls to develop wider reading habits?
2. How, in particular, can you plan to prevent boys from effectively opting out of reading from age thirteen-plus?
3. Are boys *and* girls encouraged actively to interrogate texts, to change them, rewrite them, talk about them, dramatise them, compare them to their world as they see it?
4. How will you treat the gendered reading of adventure game books and teenage romance?

It is important to explore gender preferences in texts with pupils. As individuals with a reading history, they can learn about why some genres are so important to them at that stage in their lives – to reflect upon their own changing self-perceptions during adolescence. Single-sex group reading is very supportive of this, and of the fact that these texts are often experienced as serial reads. Space should be given for gender preferences to be validated in the classroom. This is not to legitimate a narrow reading experience, but to acknowledge that serial reading is a real need for many pupils, and should be seen as part of a continuum which counts as reading. Pupils need to be able to reflect upon it as part of their reading history in a *conscious* way. Gender groupings can help pupils to explore texts of particular interest to them, and offer opportunities for a critical re-examination of gendered attitudes to reading. Through shared group reading, pupils are particularly enabled to examine their own reading position. Between themselves, they can ask questions about how their attitudes towards reading and their responses to texts have been formed by their social histories. Encourage the broadest definition of what it is to be a reader: this means evaluating the *range* of texts which feature in the curriculum, and the *variety* of methods by which pupils can respond to them.

Class readers

The predominant experience of reading for most pupils in secondary schools is that of a single text, chosen by the teacher or an examination

TASK 6.4 LEARNING ABOUT READING POSITIONS

Learning to be a critical reader means learning about what it means to read. If we want pupils to engage *consciously* in a text, we need to teach about how it positions them as a reader. They need to learn how the text was culturally produced, to treat it as a product of a particular person's experience of culture and history, to demystify its origins and thus its meanings. They need to understand what has influenced their own development as a reader.

Take a short story with a multicultural focus, like *Salt on a Snake's Tail* in *Come to Mecca* (Dhondy, 1978). First read it yourself, and ask yourself the following questions. What is your own experience of:

- the inner-city setting for the story;
- its cultural context;
- the main character-types;
- the family organisation?

What difference does it make to read this story:

- as a member of the Bengali community;
- as a reader from a particular generation – a grandfather, father, teenage son;
- as male or female;
- as a person living in the east end of London, or another inner-city area?

Assess how these factors will influence your own response to this story, and your own desire to read the others in the anthology. Now, consider how important these factors are to pupils' reading of *all* literature. By understanding their own reading position, pupils bring a personal voice to their treatment of texts.

board, which is read with the whole class, usually, therefore, at a common pace, with core aspects of the text focused upon for detailed study and the preparation of examination-type assignments. Class readers, however, are used to achieve specific aims beyond examination preparation. They can:

- provide a common experience which has a part to play in the emotional, social and cultural development of pupils growing up in society. Issues such as racism and the history of slavery are explored in novels like Barbara Smucker's *Underground to Canada*: gender roles and parenting receive an interesting treatment in Anne Fine's *Flour Babies*;

- provide a foundation for an integrated approach to the English curriculum, in which language study is embedded in the exploration of language in use: literary texts provide the *contexts* for meaning, in which pupils can explore their responses to written language;
- be used as a focus for critical reading, in which pupils explore the cultural factors which have influenced a text's construction, and begin to understand that all texts exist within particular social and historical contexts – it is interesting to discuss with pupils *how* their set examination texts came to acquire that privileged status.

Core texts have frequently been used to structure an English curriculum around a theme. Prior to the centralised curriculum development which followed the Education Reform Act (1988), many departments claimed 'we teach English through literature', and this approach is still popular: a common core is established for the class through the teacher's selection of a text, from which springs language study, literary approaches and creative writing. The text is central here to curriculum planning, and is used to embody the concept of a fully integrated approach to English teaching. For example, a scheme of work based on Steinbeck's *Of Mice and Men* might include: a study of accent and dialect in spoken language; a diary written by George; a dramatisation of one scene; an alternative chapter ending and a tracking of events to examine the unities of place and time in the plot development of the novel. Today, a different concept of *core* language experience will often underpin the planning of schemes of work: a film text, drama experience or a study based on language in use could all be used as the foundation for units of English work. A class reader can be seen as one among several core curriculum experiences, all of which will draw on differing areas of pupil expertise and culture.

TASK 6.5 CHOOSING TEXTS

You may be free to select a class reader or you may have to read a text which forms part of a departmental scheme: either way, you need to consider how you 'prepare the ground' for a class reading of a text. Teachers' criteria for choosing texts may be quite different from pupils'! When you are selecting, meet with your tutor or the Head of English to discuss your/their reasons for the choice. Include in your discussion, whether the text is:

- part of a departmental scheme of work;
- a complete set in the book cupboard;
- one which works well with a particular theme;

- personally enjoyed by the teacher;
- recommended by pupils;
- recommended by colleagues;
- a text that the teacher feels will fulfil the needs of a particular class;
- set for an examination.

Will these reasons, and any others, be made explicit to the pupils? They need to understand the circumstances surrounding any text which is chosen for class study, so that a careful appraisal can be made of the status this confers on the text, when they come to make critical responses to it themselves. Some teachers are able to offer pupils the opportunity of choosing class readers, where stock is available: giving a choice depends on your *aims*, which determine whether your scheme of work ties the text very closely to a thematic approach, or is to do with developing experience of text, which can be achieved through a variety of literature.

TASK 6.6 BEGINNING A CLASS READER

Observe the first two lessons where a teacher introduces a new text. Make notes on the following:

- at what stage in the lesson do pupils actually begin to read the text?
- what form of preparation takes place for beginning to read – introduction to themes/issues; reference to other works/authors already familiar to pupils; discussion; group/pair work; improvisation?
- how do pupils establish their own possible relationships with the concerns of the text?
- at what place in the text do pupils begin to read?
- how much does the teacher read in each lesson?
- how are lessons ended in relation to the place that is reached in the text?
- what use is made of writing and speaking and listening in these introductory lessons?

Discuss your observations with the teacher following the lessons. Points made here should help you to formulate ideas for starting reading with your own classes. It would be useful to look at how a different teacher begins reading with a class in another year or Key Stage, and to compare methods.

Now, use your notes based on these principles to start planning your own scheme of work for the text which has been chosen for you to teach.

Reading with the class: some pitfalls

In your observations of pupils reading a class text, you will probably note a range of methods used in different classrooms, which might include: reading undertaken in silence; reading targeted amounts or different sections of text; following the teacher's reading; reading 'around the class', where pupils take turns to read aloud from the set book, and reading some sections of the text for homework.

Many pupils love to read out loud to the class, some with an enthusiasm that is not always matched by competence. The dynamic of the text is quickly lost by just a few minutes of inexperienced, hesitant reading, which frustrates more able readers. Listeners with English as a second language, and less experienced readers, gain little by listening to poor reading. It lacks the necessary pace and inflexion which imparts comprehension. For other pupils, being asked to read aloud is the chief dread of any school day, and holds up an uncompromising public confirmation of what they cannot yet do well. You need to consider the needs of all those who do not raise their hands to read, because they lack confidence, or because of peer pressure. They need a different environment to show what they can do, and to develop skills through constructive and sustained activities. Further disadvantages lie in the use of 'reading around the room' to exact punishment on those 'caught out' not following the text: reading their 'bit' without misadventure becomes the main focus of the exercise, and we impart the notion that once their 'bit' is over, they can relax and switch off again. None of this has very much to do with becoming 'independent, responsive and enthusiastic readers'.

Pupils can, however, develop further competence by reading aloud, and who among us has outgrown the pleasure of listening to someone reading to us, really well? We aim for all our pupils to feel able to read aloud confidently, and this will take place in different contexts. When a whole class is sharing a text, practice in reading can be built into the scheme of work, which gives *everyone* an opportunity to develop reading skills. Variety of reading approach is important. Pupils need to hear good models for reading on a whole-class basis, from the teacher, and from pupils who have a mutual agreement with the teacher about reading aloud sometimes. Much individual progress can be made in group readings of the class text, both in reading competence and in understandings of the text.

All pupils can have an opportunity to read aloud within their group, and to prepare their reading, with support from a teacher if necessary. You will, however, still need to consider whether it is appropriate for every pupil to take part.

The next task pursues the principle that a variety of approaches is important in order to provide a range of opportunities for the range of pupils within a class; in addition, it is important to select an approach which matches the learning objectives of the lesson. The following are examples of ways of reading a core text, having divided pupils into groups:

- reading the dialogue in the roles of speakers and narrator;
- taking the dialogue only, and turning it into a script;
- choosing a section which lends itself to dubbing with sound-effects and background music;
- dividing into narrative sequences, and preparing an individual reading of each one by group members;
- making an abridged reading and performing/taping it;
- selecting passages for choral reading.

You might add to the list of possibilities.

TASK 6.7 CLASS READERS: VARYING THE APPROACH

Find a short story or a chapter from a class reader; decide on your lesson aims and select which of these approaches would be most suitable. Try it out with a group of pupils. Following the readings, discuss with them how they decided to treat the text in order to read it. What have they learned about the way it is written, about the plot, the characters, the style?

SUPPORTING PROGRESSION: READING THE UNFAMILIAR

The 'unfamiliar' might be a new author, a pre-twentieth-century literary text for some pupils, an information text that is packed with specialist terms and which is intended for a particular audience, or a text which is culturally excluding for some pupils: consider the challenges offered by Dickens's *A Christmas Carol* to pupils not of western European Christian origin. What is the significance of 'Bah! Humbug!' in this context? Such a text has become increasingly popular at Key Stage 3, since it meets the requirements to study pre-twentieth-century literature (in a *short* novel), covers an author from the approved list, and suits the desires of many English departments to do seasonal work in the latter part of the autumn term. Whatever the reasons for a text being particularly challenging, active interrogation of it by pupils can develop *progression* in a way which helps them to bring their own language into play. Progression is achieved when pupils can develop language by: practising it upon texts; by hypothesising about meanings; guessing and estimating the intended effects by comparisons with what is already known from other narrative experience; by transposing what they already know to their reading of new or altered versions of it.

Strategies which actively interrogate texts can take many forms; these have been well-documented in summary form in *The English Curriculum: Reading 1 Comprehension*. It includes the following statement in its rationale:

> by providing specific, problem-based but open-ended points of entry to peer-group discussion round a text these activities may

---

TASK 6.8 USING DARTs

For this task, DARTs activities will be considered as a way of reading the following extract from *A Christmas Carol*, in which we learn about its central character, Scrooge.

> Oh! But he was a tight-fisted hand at the grindstone, Scrooge! A squeezing, wrenching, grasping, scraping, clutching, covetous old sinner! Hard and sharp as flint, from which no steel had ever struck out generous fire; secret, and self-contained, and solitary as an oyster. The cold within him froze his old features, nipped his pointed nose, shrivelled his cheek, stiffened his gait; made his eyes red, his thin lips blue; and spoke out shrewdly in his grating voice. A frosty rime was on his head, and on his eyebrows, and his wiry chin. He carried his own temperature always about with him; he iced his office in the dog-days; and didn't thaw it one degree at Christmas.
> (Dickens, 1985, p. 46)

- **Cloze procedure** involves deleting key words prior to pupils' reading. Decide which words or parts of words you would delete to help pupils to explore Scrooge's character, using their own understanding of what a mean person might be like. Would you focus on adjectives, colour, temperature, getting the pupils to complete the similes? Ask them to reflect on how they made their choices.
- **Underlining/highlighting the text** helps pupils to identify the ways in which ideas are structured, and to pool ideas which have a common significance for them; for example the words/phrases which seem to be critical of Scrooge or the

ones which identify the story with a particular season. What you would ask them to highlight would obviously be relevant to the learning objectives.

- Try asking pupils to highlight words about which they would like to find out more; get them to try out predictions for meanings in their pairs/groups, before using a dictionary or asking you.
- **Prediction**. Pupils use their knowledge of other narratives to estimate some of the possible situations and outcomes for this character.
- **Dividing up the text** to explore how meaning develops. Here, appreciating the punctuation is a key to coping with the long sentences. Ask groups to highlight all the punctuation, or use it to cut up the extract, maintaining the sequence. They then use this as a basis for a choral reading. Afterwards, they are ready to talk about the significance of reading punctuation for meaning and emphasis, in texts where the complexity of the language may be new to them.

dispel the inertia that tends to descend on many of us when under instruction in a classroom.

(Simons and Plackett, 1990, p. 82)

This book is well worth reading. It acknowledges the contribution made by the work of Lunzer and Gardner (1979) in their reading research project out of which arose the development of DARTs (Directed Activities Related to Texts). There are many well-tried strategies you can use to match the learning aims which you set for your pupils.

These activities would be particularly valuable for pupils to undertake using word processors (see Chapter 9). The example lesson outline in Figure 6.3 shows how some of these strategies can help to achieve learning aims. The lesson uses the extract as an introduction to the text.

Non-literary texts

Pupils living in the 'age of information' have access to a proliferation of texts which qualify as 'non-literary'. The range is enormous, and is growing constantly: pupils have daily access to materials which make varied reading demands, including newspapers, magazines, leaflets, brochures, instructions, advertisements, timetables, food-packaging, not to mention the whole spectrum of electronic and audio-visual texts.

Informative and persuasive texts pose particular challenges for pupils. Their power lies in their relationship with the 'real' world, being so explicitly a product of it, and having direct bearings upon it. Teaching pupils to read information texts critically involves an evaluation of the sources of the facts which they contain. As with the study of literature, pupils need to learn about the *context* of the text's production, and how the author's intentions will inform the selection of language and form.

Strategies for reading these texts can be particularly helpful in developing pupils' critical awareness of language. Many of the texts are short, serving a pragmatic function as well as contributing to a cultural consciousness of the type of society in which we live. Reading these texts involves learning how to:

- scan;
- sift the relevant from the irrelevant;
- alter text through deletion and substitution;
- collate textual evidence;
- summarise;
- produce alternative text;
- evaluate;
- account for findings.

Information technology has an important role in developing critical reading skills. Access to IT means that pupils can increasingly see themselves as producers of authoritative-looking text: using the language and conventions of 'factual' presentation for themselves is a way of exploring its authority. Meaning can be viewed as something which is subject to the composer of the text: when more than one person is involved in that composing, the pair or group discussion shows what different possibilities for meaning exist within each decision about language and form.

ASSESSMENT

The assessment of reading is as complex as what we mean by reading itself. For assessment to have a purposeful role in the learning process, you will need to consider two main factors:

- how will you *know* what has been learnt?
- how can you *describe* what has been learnt, so that you and your pupils can see the pattern of progression in a way that is motivating, and helps to set new aims for reading?

How will you know what has been learnt?

You need to have assessment objectives in mind when planning your scheme of work around reading. Ask yourself which assessment objectives you are aiming at with your pupils. The following are some examples:

- developing fluency in reading aloud;
- developing reading for pleasure, based on heightened awareness of

Main aims for scheme of work on *A Christmas Carol*:

To broaden the reading experience of pupils; to develop approaches to reading for meaning in texts which contain unfamiliar language.

Lesson objectives:

1. To develop strategies to explore for meaning the extract which introduces Scrooge.
2. To learn about this character through reflecting on the language used here, both by the author and the pupils.

National Curriculum:

ENG AT2   1d 'pupils should be introduced to works published before 1900'. . .Dickens 2a 'pupils should be taught to extract meaning beyond the literal'. . .'explaining how choice of language affects. . .meanings; analyse and discuss unfamiliar vocabulary. . .'

Resources:

Extract in cloze form; text: *A Christmas Carol*

SEN/ESL support:

1. Supplementary sheet with suggestions for cloze procedure to choose from.
2. Glossary for the original text.

Timing	Teacher activity	Pupil activity
5 mins	• register and settle	
5 mins	• explain the aims and objectives to pupils • ask pupils to work in pairs • introduce the reading activity: pupils to read the cloze extract; discuss to complete it	
15 mins	• working around the class • guide individual pupils on use of supplementary support	• pair work on the text • prepare to feedback suggestions to class
5 mins	• respond to small sample of pupil suggestions for cloze exercise • focus on the impact of language choices	• two or three pairs feedback
2–5 mins	• explain next task: pairs are to discuss their language choices, and write a brief statement about their understanding of Scrooge at this point	• pupils discuss and write the statement
10 mins	• support pair work	
5 mins	• distribute the original text • ask pairs to read it out loud to each other • set the task	
15 mins		• pupils read the piece • compare Dickens's language choices with theirs • discuss the language and write a brief statement about how Dickens presents Scrooge
5 mins (70 mins)	• recap what has been learned • close lesson	

Evaluation:

Figure 6.3 Lesson outline: exploring text

what texts can offer;
- developing pupils' comprehension of texts;
- developing skills for reading for information;
- increasing confidence in tackling unfamiliar texts;
- developing a new strand of reading, e.g. graphic novel, pre-twentieth-century literature;
- development of critical reading skills – 'decoding';
- developing proficiency in literary discourse.

All of the above are part of an overriding objective, which is the development of reading for meaning in individual pupils.

Consider how you can gauge progression in your chosen area. The most simple and manageable form of reading assessment is also the most reductive: the comprehension test. It has been resurrected within recent examination reform, and provides a singular perspective on what a pupil has understood in their (usually solitary) reading of disembodied text. It has little to do with the assessment objectives above, which view *meaning* as continually negotiated through language experience in the social environment of the classroom. You will need to consider what appropriate means are available for you to obtain a record of pupils' progression, and to assess it. It might take the form of:

- oral responses to what has been read, either taped or presented to the class;
- dramatisation based on a text;
- visual/graphic accounts of the text;
- written responses, where pupils have been made aware of the *reading* objectives embedded in the task;
- pupils' personal reading journals.

Describing the learning

The following criteria for planning and assessing what pupils can do are not hierarchical. They evolve through the integration of speaking, listening and writing with reading. They indicate areas of development which will correspond at different times to the range of texts and different ways of reading, as in Figure 6.1. Learning here is described in a way which is *formative*. The criteria can form the basis of an ongoing profile of progression in reading, in which both pupils and teacher can map out the reading experiences of a class throughout a year or particular schemes of work.

Making individual meaning: using a reading diary; constructing a reading autobiography; identifying and explaining preferences; identifying emotional responses to events; explaining responses to characters; empathising; identifying a reading position; imaginative and creative manipulation of texts, e.g. adding a chapter or changing an ending; interrogating 'fact' in non-literary text; rewriting texts in different genres; transferring personal responses to imposed texts; learning to examine the cultural context of texts; examining assumptions about gender and race; understanding the individual's relationship with a canonised text.

Broadening reading experience: confirming preferences for types of texts; serial reading; exploring particular genres; exploring an author; rereading texts; developing meaning through peer-discussion; communicating responses to others in oral/written/visual forms; finding that a text's significance is social and cultural as well as individual; learning about the responses of others; learning that texts have a cultural role; learning about writing conventions like plot, structure, character development.

Approaching the unfamiliar: understanding how some texts become canonised; learning about relationships between texts – ('intertextuality'); exploring recurring themes within canonised literature; comparing media and literary texts; using drama improvisation to develop a personal perspective on a text; using DARTs; developing pupils' own questions about written material; learning about literary discourse; exploring new texts through familiar genre and language.

This chapter has raised issues about teaching reading as a classroom activity, while acknowledging that we are engaging in a wider cultural process. What happens with reading in school has implications for the society beyond, and vice versa. The society beyond is complex and continually changing, and you need to respond to that in establishing a rationale for teaching texts.

Mary Hilton has described the teaching of reading in a way which celebrates the relatedness and interdependence of new and traditional texts in contemporary society:

> Through new forms of story *and* through understanding the workings of traditional narrative desire, we get children hooked on books. Through books *and* media texts, through the new and the popular *and* the ancient and traditional, their worlds of cultural possibility are enlarged and enriched. They learn, ideally, to move from one text to the other with intellectual grace and ease.
>
> (Hilton, 1996, p. 191)

Such a view emphasises how this chapter and Chapter 9 need to be read together: together, they examine the spectrum of experiences which constitute 'reading' in the contemporary classroom. The cultural diversity of your pupils is your starting point in planning for broadening and deepening the reading experience.

The *pleasure* and *power* of reading is something which is easily lost or distorted, at a time when texts are screened to meet approval for national testing, and reading development has become synonymous with acquiring basic skills for the world of work. By planning for a range of texts, to be experienced through varied groupings and tasks, you can aim to develop readers who find many sources of *pleasure* and *power* in reading. Power comes with knowing about the different types of reading which are available, and how they are regarded in wider society. An independent, critical reading position is essential if pupils are to appraise the texts which are available today, both in the classroom and in the world beyond school.

FURTHER READING

Meek, M. (1988) *How Texts Teach What Readers Learn*, Stroud: Thimble Press.
This book is short and very readable. It is an excellent way for secondary English student teachers to learn something of how reading can be developed from good practice in the primary years. Margaret Meek explains the significance of intertextuality, which is the way a text's meaning draws on the reader's previous experience of other texts.

Meek, M. (1991) *On Being Literate*, London: Bodley Head.
Meek describes how teaching reading today is bound up with changes in contemporary society. She explains how a modern concept of literacy must embody full recognition of the texts which people actually need and use, and how children develop their reading across a broad spectrum of these texts.

Protherough, R., 'What is a reading curriculum?', and Atkinson, J., 'How do we teach pre-twentieth-century literature?', in Protherough, R. and King, P. (eds) (1995) *The Challenge of English in the National Curriculum*, London: Routledge, pp. 30–64.
Both of these chapters offer practical and detailed suggestions for criteria to assess reading progress and strategies for teaching pre-twentieth-century literature. Appraisal is given of what is required by the National Curriculum, and what it is additionally possible to achieve.

Simons, M. and Plackett, P. (eds) (1990) *The English Curriculum: Reading, 1: Comprehension*, London: English and Media Centre.
This is an invaluable resource for all teachers who are interested in helping pupils to make real meanings out of text, and in helping them to gain access to texts. The book is divided into four sections: the reading process; comprehension; using information books; whole school policies.

See also Pennac, D. (1994) *Reads Like a Novel*, London: Quartet, and Bloome, D. and Stierer, B. (1995) *Reading Words*, Sheffield: NATE.

7 Writing

INTRODUCTION

Some people may tell you that teaching writing is a simple business. They may tell you that when they were at school all pupils were given a title and did one piece of writing each week in their exercise books for their English teacher. They may add that the teacher corrected all the mistakes, which the pupils then wrote out three times. They may reassure themselves that this practice led to effective learning by pointing to all the evidence of hard work which accumulated in those exercise books. However, there are numerous false and dangerous assumptions in these apparently straightforward suggestions.

The assumptions include the ideas that: writing can be usefully isolated from the rest of the English curriculum; producing a large quantity of writing necessarily improves quality; finished pieces of writing can be produced with little preparation; the products of writing tasks are more important than the processes used to create them; school writing consists of exercises, and so presentation and layout can be standardised; the teacher is the audience for school writing; the teacher's main function in assessment is to check technical accuracy; pupils can improve their technical accuracy by mimicking correct forms introduced to them by teachers adopting this copy-editing role.

In this chapter, you will be challenged to question all these assumptions by thinking about: the relationship between writing and other language processes; the development stages which many successful pieces of writing pass through; the ways in which writing makes use of the possibilities and conventions of different genres; the influence of a writer's perception of a real or imagined audience on all aspects of his or her writing, including technical accuracy. A central tenet of the chapter is that, when teaching writing, you will need to support pupils *both* by providing time, opportunities and experiences which allow them to work through a creative, interactive and evaluative process building on their initial ideas *and* by making them aware of the possibilities of the different genres they may choose to adopt and adapt for particular purposes. In other words, to explore the world of writing, pupils need *both* a compass to orientate themselves, plan and follow routes, *and* a map which identifies possible writing destinations.

OBJECTIVES

By the end of this chapter you should understand the importance of the following to the effective teaching of writing:

- the relationships between writing, speaking and listening, and reading;
- the contribution that writing can make to learning;
- the social dynamics of writing in the classroom;
- drafting and the development of pieces of writing;
- writing models, and explorations of genre;
- audiences for writing and publication;
- the formative assessment and evaluation of writing;
- the writer's or writers' experience of making meaning;
- the possibility of developing technical skills through real writing tasks;
- a critical interpretation of the definition of the writing curriculum in *English in the National Curriculum*.

WHAT YOU KNOW ABOUT LEARNING TO WRITE

Writing and language autobiographies

Margaret Meek, one of the most important writers on literacy, asks her readers to find out what they think they don't know about reading by searching their memories for significant moments in their reading autobiographies (Meek, 1988). This activity can usefully be extended to cover other aspects of language development: it draws attention to truths about our own learning experience which we should allow to influence our search for good professional practice.

Here is an example of a story about writing from one teacher's language autobiography:

> One of my earliest memories of infant school is of being taught to use the letters of the alphabet by drawing pictures of things that started with each letter in succession and then writing appropriate accompanying sentences. After each piece of work, the teacher marked our books using a three star marking scale. This practice has stayed in my mind because of the shock I had when I only got two stars for the letter 'v'. The teacher told me it was because the handwriting went downhill. The first discussion I remember ever having about writing was about this surface feature of my work. I corrected the error and continued to the end of the alphabet, having this new idea that 'writing in straight lines makes it perfect', literally rubber stamped. The experience was not in any sense about learning that I

was just beginning to explore the limitless possibilities for making meaning that those twenty-six letters make available to us.

Learning to Write

We had to write a sentence
For each letter: *a, b, c,* . . .
I did all right at first
And got three stars for each
Until we got to *v.*
I drew a van, and wrote:
'This is a van.'

I only got two stars,
And asked the teacher why.
She said; 'It slopes
From left to right.'

My writing's
             gone downhill
                      since then.

    Thirty years later, I wrote this short poem about the incident, at a teachers' training day during which I had been asked to search my language autobiography for significant events. After ten minutes, the course leader asked if anyone would like to read out a piece he or she had written. Since I had finished a draft of the poem, I put my hand up. No one else did. The course leader ignored my hand and used the general response to demonstrate that it is dangerous to make pupils share personal writing with a large audience, especially when they have only had the opportunity to work briefly on a draft. This may be true, but for me, the meaning of the exercise was entirely different: it had enabled me to illustrate, from my own experience, why I think mechanical approaches to the teaching of writing can be dangerously arid. I wanted to share that perception with the other teachers present.

TASK 7.1 YOUR HISTORY AS A WRITER

This story points towards some of the issues about the teaching of writing which this chapter will address. Search your own language autobiography for a significant moment and work out what questions your story, and/or the one quoted above, raise(s) about the teaching and learning of writing. Listen to the stories of some other student teachers. Brainstorm a list of issues to keep in mind while you read the rest of the chapter.

> **Note**
> Exploring your pupils' language biographies always pays dividends, and is especially valuable when you are getting to know them. It provides opportunities for you to learn about where they have come from in terms of their language development and previous English teaching experience. The information can be more useful for planning and target setting than the results of formal reading tests and assessment scores. Work of this kind also raises pupils' reflective awareness of their own language development and enables them to become more usefully self evaluative. It can also provide you with a means of validating pupils' home language or languages in the classroom, whether they are multilingual or experts in a particular regional dialect.

WRITING AND THE PROCESSES OF ENGLISH

One of the central orthodoxies of English teaching is that development in each of the processes of speaking and listening, reading and writing is best promoted by work in which the processes are integrated. It is important to examine the implications of this idea for the teaching of writing.

Talking and reading before writing

The sequence in which the three core language processes are presented in *English in the National Curriculum* (1995) could be seen as suggesting that speaking and listening and reading should precede writing. This impression is strengthened by the fact that the requirements for writing are more concerned with product than process writing. Of course, language development begins with oracy, and there are many human situations in which we choose to talk something through before writing about it. The content of material we read can also be important in stimulating writing, and reading provides models for writing, by suggesting forms, conventions and structures which we can choose to adopt, modify or challenge.

Much classroom practice exploits ways in which speaking, listening and reading can contribute to the development of writing. There are many opportunities for collaborative activities, such as small group brainstorming of ideas about a text, which pupils record to provide ideas for a later writing task. However, individual tasks can also make use of the primacy of speech to develop writing: one example would be provided by a pupil tape recording herself telling a story she knows, which she or a teacher will later transcribe to form the first draft of a written version.

Writing before speaking or reading

While writing is, then, often dependent on the stimulation of speaking and listening or reading, it is important to note that there are also many situations in which writing can support effective speaking, listening and reading. Examples of writing which supports speaking include carefully planned activities such as the preparation of prompt cards to be used in delivering a formal speech or presentation, and much more spontaneous tasks, such as five-minute bursts of silent writing during which pupils are asked to record their first impressions of a text before a class discussion of it. Examples of writing contributing to the development of reading include writing in a particular genre to gain insights into the problems that constructing a particular kind of text presents, which may inform later critical analysis of similar texts.

Analysing talk and texts to support writing

Another important aspect of the relationship between writing and the other core language processes concerns the analysis of talk and texts to support writing. Analysis of the language of speech and of related reading material can help pupils to understand the special character of the language commonly used in writing. For example, pupils who are asked to compare a tape recording of a person being interviewed about an event and the interviewee's written account of the event can be guided to notice organisational features of the writing which the spoken account may lack.

Some of the questions which can be asked when reading any text draw attention to the decisions which writers frequently make, and which pupils will need to make themselves when writing. Examples of such questions include: what do you think the writer's purpose was in producing this text? who do you think the writer imagined reading the text? how has the writer organised the material that has been used in this text? what other texts like this can you think of – what kind of text has the writer chosen to make?

Writing in planning sequences

A fundamental planning issue that arises from these observations concerns the sequencing of activities in teaching. Teachers should be able to explain and justify the function and positioning of writing activities in the sequence of a lesson or scheme of work: often the emphasis is on using speaking, listening or reading to help develop achievement in writing, but writing should be used much more than *English in the National Curriculum* suggests to help develop speaking and listening and reading skills.

TASK 7.2   WRITING TO SUPPORT TALK AND READING

Explore the *English in the National Curriculum* Programmes of Study for Speaking and Listening and Reading for requirements which could be supported by writing activities. Generate a varied list of writing activities which you think would be particularly useful.

WRITING AND LEARNING

English in the National Curriculum (1995, p. 23, 1b) makes a subtle distinction between two purposes for writing. These are: '*to inform others* through instruction, explanation, argument, narration, reportage, description, persuasion and paraphrase' and '*to develop thinking* through review, analysis, hypothesis, recollection and summary'. This distinction, which should be made more explicit in any definition of the writing curriculum, is between writing which conveys the results of learning and writing through which learning takes place.

The distinction is not, of course, watertight: drafting processes, for example, may enable writers to work out what they think about something and then communicate this to an audience. However, some forms of writing are much more concerned with processes of learning than with communication, and their development is much more important than the brief reference to note-making in *English in the National Curriculum* suggests.

Writing to learn: retrospective and prospective writing

There are a number of ways of defining categories of writing to learn. One useful division is between retrospective writing, which has the primary purpose of recording and making sense of experience or material, and prospective writing, which is largely concerned with reorganising and reordering that experience or material for new purposes.

Retrospective writing includes diary and journal writing. In work of this kind, pupils can be given complete freedom over what they select to include, or their attention can be focused in particular directions. A diary could be used to net whatever strikes a writer as memorable or significant, say on a school trip. A reading journal could filter out predetermined categories of information, such as reflections on the characters in a novel. Retrospective writing can be as coherent as a series of reflections on a photograph, written in continuous prose, or as fragmented and architectural as a set of marginal notes and marks on a page of poetry. It can be as personal as a private diary, written with the self as the only intended audience, or as public as notes on the writer's first impressions of a television documentary, written as a contribution to a planned group or class discussion. It can be as unstructured as a commonplace book in which memorable quotations are collected in random order, or as structured as a set of notes on the techniques of newspaper advertising written under headings and gradually compiled from looking at examples.

Prospective writing includes a wide range of ways of planning writing. Some of this may be quite disorganised, like brainstormed lists of ideas and questions, and some may show rudimentary elements of structure, such as schematic plans, columnar or grid-based maps of ideas and spider diagrams, and expressive fragments like those which may become either poems or the opening paragraphs of stories in later drafts.

Writing, thinking and learning

In general, learners often make use of thinking processes such as: reflecting on what is known; connecting what has been understood and what is new; analysing and selecting material and ideas which are relevant to a purpose. Consequently, schemes of work which make use of cycles of related retrospective and prospective writing activities are likely to make powerful contributions to learning. The sequence may start in either mode, but teachers should be conscious of the implications of decisions they make about this. For example, a group working on producing a class newspaper could start by brainstorming ideas and outlining the proposed structure of their paper, or they could start by reviewing the contents of a number of different published papers. There are advantages and disadvantages in both methods. The teacher should know why one method is chosen, or why the class is given a choice.

This discussion has suggested that the writing activities through which learning takes place can vary in the extent to which they are structured and selective. For example, while many teachers believe that writing journals make a particularly useful contribution to learning, they may have very different expectations of the pupils using them. Moreover, some teachers see a journal (for retrospective writing) as something quite different from a planning or drafting book (for prospective writing), but others would expect pupils to carry out both kinds of work in one place.

Some pupil questions which teachers need to be able to answer, and justify their answers, when introducing writing tasks and different kinds of writing include:

- what will I be learning by doing this writing?
- what is the precise nature of the writing I am being expected to produce?
- who will be reading it?
- how is this writing connected to other work I have done or will be doing?
- how much freedom do I have to adapt what I am being asked to do to according to my own priorities and preferences?

Any particular kind of writing raises its own questions. For example, teachers promoting the use of writing journals need to decide, sometimes with their pupils:

- who will have access to the material in the journal (e.g. just the pupil, the pupil and teacher, pupils in the class, parents)?
- to what extent is the journal a place for personal responses to ideas, experiences and material which may not be transformable into 'publishable' writing?
- if the journal is to be a resource for later work, how much guidance (in the form of prompt questions, for example) should pupils have about selecting appropriate material so that their writing is relevant, but so they are not straitjacketed by the teacher's expectations and perceptions of the task?

TASK 7.3   WRITING AND LEARNING ACROSS THE CURRICULUM

Consider what opportunities pupils in your placement school are given to use writing for learning across the curriculum by shadowing a group of pupils for a day and listing the range of writing activities they are asked to engage in. How much of the writing is primarily to aid learning, and how much of it is primarily to show the results of learning?

THE SOCIAL DYNAMICS OF WRITING IN THE CLASSROOM

School writing can sometimes appear a very isolated human activity in which one person, the pupil, independently produces a text, fed by information from one source, the teacher. This work may then be read by the same teacher, not for the purpose of any kind of communication, but for the assessment of this isolated performance. However, important functions of writing in culture and society are clearly dependent on matters such as: the relationship between any piece of writing and what other writers have said or are saying, and the relationship between the writing and the range of actual and potential readers of it. Becoming a writer is partly about learning to see your writing as a contribution to various forms of social and cultural dialogue. It can be argued that pupils are only empowered as writers when they come to recognise their right to participate in this dialogue. To engage meaningfully in what *English in the National Curriculum* (1995) identifies as writing for 'aesthetic and imaginative purposes' and 'to inform others', pupils need a growing awareness of these social and cultural functions of writing.

Some of the teaching which can contribute to the development of this awareness concerns genre and audience, which are discussed later in this chapter, but teachers also need to make use of the microcosm of culture and society that exists as the pupil's world, and to see the social dynamics of the classroom itself as a particularly powerful resource. There are at least four functions which individuals and groups available to pupils inside and outside the classroom can perform in developing an awareness of the social dynamics of writing processes, those of: adviser or information source; co-writer; critical reader, consultant, editor or publisher; and audience. Many of these roles develop the integration of speaking and listening, reading and writing, since they stimulate talk about writing and the reading of writing at numerous different stages before, during and after its composition.

Some of the most interesting teaching of writing takes place when individuals and groups that pupils have access to are placed in specific roles of this kind. For example, younger children (in other classes, feeder primary schools, or siblings) are often used as real audiences for story writing, but this kind of work is further enhanced when these children are also allowed to act as consultants earlier in the process, providing the writers with information about matters such as their likes and dislikes in stories they know.

Some examples of methods which make use of the social dynamics of the classroom to develop writing are as follows. Pupils can provide information sources for each other by conducting and responding to interviews and questionnaires, and by reporting on expert knowledge which they already have (for example, about a hobby), or have researched for a particular purpose. Pupils telling stories that they know to each other can be a particularly powerful resource.

Pairing pupils with writing partners can provide them with temporary or more permanent writing consultants, trusted colleagues who will read their work at different stages and comment on it. Some pupils may need guidance on appropriate responses to the work of others until they have experience in this role, but it is possible to support them by devising prompt sheets with appropriate questions which might be asked. With experience, pupils can become expert at prompting their peers to think about their writing in many different ways, addressing issues such as: the meaning and authenticity of the work (they can be particularly good at talking about what is convincing); the kind of text the writer is producing (especially if they are able to compare it with other texts they like in the same genre); the way in which the writing is organised and whether or not its surface features like spelling and layout enhance its power of communication.

Experience of collaborative writing can enable pupils to learn that contributions to various cultural and social discussions are sometimes more powerful when constructed by groups. In principle, it is easy to see that one of the potential advantages of collaborative writing is that a number of minds working together are able to keep a whole range of considerations about the writing more constantly in view. A disadvantage may be that the increase in the number of possibilities considered leads to an impasse of indecision and total loss of momentum. Strategies which support collaboration include the allocation of different tasks to individuals in a group. For example, pupils working on a class magazine may write different sections and then act as the editors of other contributors' work. Group story writing may benefit from individuals writing first drafts of different chapters after a structure for the whole story has been negotiated. Pupils word processing in pairs or groups may function more effectively if they vary the roles of composer and secretary, one controlling content and the other concentrating on accurate recording of ideas on the screen.

It is very easy to overuse silence in work on writing. While it is important for teachers to create opportunities in which sustained concentration on writing tasks can be developed, it is often appropriate to earmark short periods for intensive silent work which are supported by times in which various forms of consultation with the teacher and other pupils can take place.

TASK 7.4   THE SOCIAL DYNAMICS OF WRITING IN PRACTICE

Devise a scheme of work to develop writing in which you make use of the social dynamics of the classroom to place pupils in one or more of the roles of adviser or information source; co-writer; critical reader, consultant, editor or publisher; and audience.

Drafting and the development of pieces of writing

English in the National Curriculum (1995, p. 23, 2a) makes a brief statement which suggests that the legislation recognises the importance of the processes which contribute to the development of pieces of writing: 'Pupils should be taught to improve and sustain their writing, developing their competence in planning, drafting, redrafting and proofreading their work on paper and on screen.' There is a slight expansion of this statement in the Programme of Study for Key Stage 2, but the previous National Curriculum Orders (1989) gave much more detailed definitions in the Programme of Study for Key Stage 3:

● drafting (getting ideas onto paper or computer screen, regardless of form, organisation or expression);

- redrafting (shaping and structuring the raw material – either on paper or screen – to take account of purpose, audience and form);
- rereading and revising (making alterations that will help the reader, e.g. getting rid of ambiguity, vagueness, incoherence, or irrelevance);
- proof-reading (checking for errors, e.g. omitted or repeated words, mistakes in spelling or punctuation).

This model of the stages of the development of a piece of writing, even when it is presented in the very abbreviated manner of *English in the National Curriculum* (1995), has some merit since it makes explicit the complexity of the processes which pupils often need to use to produce good writing. It also identifies separate activities which teachers can plan for pupils to experience. However, it does not fully represent all the possibilities. For example, earlier in this chapter it was noted that the prospective writing which marks the beginning of the reordering of material or experience, and often precedes attempts to write in a particular genre, can take many forms. Experimental fragments of a text as well as planning diagrams of the overall structure of a piece may both appear in a 'first draft'. In fact, the different processes defined in the 1989 Orders may take place in repeated cycles or other patterns, rather than in a linear sequence, and teachers must be careful not to frustrate pupils by insisting that the development of pieces always follows the same line.

Moreover, whereas the Programme of Study implies that the only function of redrafting and revising is to improve the work, in fact, writers sometimes choose to translate material into a different genre to try something out in a much more experimental way. Classroom teaching can be used to encourage pupils to think flexibly about their own use of different genres by creating tasks in which they learn to translate material which they or others have written in one genre to another.

Drafting processes provide many opportunities for other pupils and teachers to contribute to the development of an individual's work. The role of writing partners and writing groups has already been discussed, but teachers can, of course, also intervene productively in the writing process. In particular, various methods of conferencing are used by many teachers. One method which emphasises pupil ownership of the work while allowing for teacher input involves pupils in making appointments to see the teacher individually during writing sessions, and coming to the meeting with questions about the writing for the teacher. It is possible to draw up lists of sample questions to prompt pupils engaging in this kind of dialogue. Whatever method is used, intervening in the writing process through conferencing enables teachers to examine the decisions which pupils are making as they write, and what they understand about what will help their readers. This is invaluable knowledge for the planning of further work and individual target setting.

It is important to note that GCSE Examination Boards have precise regulations about teachers' involvement in the development of writing which is to be submitted as coursework for examination. Normally, teachers are allowed to comment in ways which might influence redrafting, but absolutely forbidden to act as revisers or proof-readers. Pupils find it helpful if teachers explain the limitations on them, particularly if the regulations cause them to modify their role and behaviour.

English in the National Curriculum (1995, DES and Welsh Office, p. 23, 2a) notes that pupils need to learn 'to judge the extent to which any or all of these processes [i.e. the drafting processes discussed in this section of the chapter] are needed in specific pieces of work', in a paragraph which also indicates that they should learn to write 'when required' with 'speed'. There are numerous situations in which adult writers have to work at speed which can be simulated in the classroom in ways which pupils find challenging and exciting. Some examples include: preparing a press release or writing a radio news bulletin to a tight deadline.

SATs and GCSE examination papers provide all pupils with particular kinds of compulsory writing situations in which writing at speed and without time for drafting is obviously necessary. Many teachers believe that the current emphasis on written examination papers in end of Key Stage assessment forces them to spend an inappropriate proportion of teaching time on this kind of writing. Pupils are sometimes confused by the messages this kind of work gives about writing as a human activity, since they appear to conflict with the lessons they learn through their experiences of collaboration, drafting, choosing genres and writing for particular audiences. This sense of conflict can be reduced if other kinds of speed writing are explored as suggested above, and if examination writing is regarded as a genre which has its own conventions which need to be learnt. It is also important that teachers have the confidence to teach according to the belief that the development of pupils' understanding of texts and of the writing skills which they are required to demonstrate is best supported by a rich experience of a wide range of reading and writing experiences, rather than by excessive practice on

---

TASK 7.5   MAKING DRAFTING PROCESSES EXPLICIT IN THE CLASSROOM

Devise a writing task for a group of pupils you are teaching which gives them good opportunities to make use of the processes of drafting, redrafting, revising and proof-reading. Design a classroom wall poster which includes a flow chart showing these processes and which defines them in language which is accessible and appropriate for your class.

past papers, sample papers, or in other activities which simulate the examination or test.

GENRE

Teaching a range of writing genres

You will find that many books on the teaching of writing emphasise the importance of giving pupils experience of writing in a wide range of genres. Some of the reasons for this are that: each genre is likely to develop different aspects of a pupil's linguistic competence; work in each genre is likely to enable each pupil to demonstrate particular achievements and development needs; working on a variety of genres helps teachers to address a broad range of the aims of the English curriculum. It can also be argued that participation in the various discourses which take place in society is dependent on being able to recognise and manipulate the conventions of particular genres, especially those which are favoured by certain power groups.

English in the National Curriculum (1995, p. 23, 1.c) identifies a number of textual forms or genres which it is suggested that pupils at Key Stages 3 and 4 should learn to write. It is important to notice that the list is illustrative and could easily be extended, for instance, by including sub-genres such as ghost stories, science fiction, romance stories and detective fiction under 'stories'. The list could be extended in other ways: for example, adding e-mail communications or Web pages would acknowledge that new technologies are creating new genres; adding speeches and interviews would place greater emphasis on ways in which the English curriculum can explore the relationships between talk and writing.

A teacher or department's view of English is likely to influence which genres are prioritised in the school curriculum: for example, adherents of the 'cultural heritage' view may give creative writing genres like stories and poetry more space than those who, with an 'adult needs' view of English, emphasise the writing of formal letters and reports. Similarly, a department's view of how writing development occurs may influence which genres are taught most to different year groups: for instance, many pupils are given more opportunities to write stories in Key Stage 3 than Key Stage 4.

TASK 7.6   GENRE IN THE SCHOOL CURRICULUM

Examine the Key Stage 3 and 4 Schemes of Work at your placement school. Which genres are given most curriculum space, when and why? How do SATs and GCSE requirements influence decisions about which genres are emphasised in Years 9–11?

English in the National Curriculum itself pays more attention to the teaching of narrative fiction, poetry, scripts and dialogue than other genres.

Genre and voice

English in the National Curriculum (1995, p. 23, 2.b) suggests that the development of pupils' writing in particular genres should be a consequence of both their exposure to appropriate models and work which develops technique. Only in the paragraph on writing poetry is there a reference to the development of an individual voice and a possible tension between using the conventions of particular genres and writing distinctively: 'pupils should be encouraged to . . . write poetry closely related to the poems they read, in their own distinctive style' (1995, p. 23, 2.b).

In fact, this tension is highly significant in the development of writing. The conventions of a particular genre can be a frustrating straitjacket which limits pupils' opportunities for self-expression, or, if these conventions are unknown or ignored, the writing may be formless and lacking in structure. Many teachers have at one time or another set newspaper writing tasks, for example, and been disappointed by what they have received. Some of the work will have consisted largely of fragmentary, shallow and irrelevant examples of different sections of a paper ('the stars' and football results figuring frequently), and some will have paid lip-service to genre, having perhaps a headline and a page divided into two columns, but the content could equally well have been submitted as a short story. However, with appropriate preparation and support, such as the careful analysis of 'models' and access to desktop publishing packages, teachers find that many pupils are capable of writing newspapers with witty headlines and subheads; catchy lead paragraphs introducing articles which are economically written to a word limit and deadline; appropriately cropped and captioned photographs; the deliberately chosen style of a broadsheet or tabloid. Pupils can learn to do this even if new information is deliberately introduced by the teacher to mimic the conditions in which professional journalists work, making revision necessary during the writing process. In other words, pupils need to understand what kinds of things can be included in particular genres, and to develop a sense of how other writers produce texts in those genres.

In general, writing is often especially successful when the writer has sufficient control of the conventions of a particular genre to be able to use them with some individuality or originality. It follows that immersion in the conventions of genres of the kind described above needs to be balanced in the writing curriculum by opportunities for pupils: to explore ideas for writing without preconceptions about which genre(s) they will adopt; to select the genre which they consider it is most appropriate to use to develop and express a particular set of ideas, and to be free to change their minds about this. Some tasks can be designed which emphasise these choices: for example, pupils engaged in autobiographical writing can be invited to choose which genres to use to tell their stories. Some possibilities which pupils exploit successfully include diary entries, interviews with a relative or friend, school reports, poems and magazine style 'focus' articles. Writing with this kind of attitude to genre can give pupils new insights into their own thinking, by liberating material from the assumptions which are associated with its expression in a particular textual form. Writing activities in which pupils are given opportunities to take material from a text and re-present it in another form can also be liberating in this way. To sum up, the development of a writer's voice is partly about developing confidence in manipulating genre.

TASK 7.7 PLANNING TO EXPLORE GENRE

Plan a sequence of lessons for a class you teach on a teaching placement, in which a primary aim is to enable pupils to use the conventions of particular genre/s to express their own ideas.

Some of the planning questions which the successful teaching of genre writing will often need to address include the following:

- how familiar are pupils with the conventions of the genre(s) the lesson(s) will give them opportunities to adopt?
- what examples/models can be used to reinforce pupil familiarity with the genre(s)?
- how/when will the introduction of these examples/models in the sequence of activities in the lesson(s) best support the pupils' own explorations of the genre(s)?
- how much choice can pupils be given in finding genre(s) which are appropriate for the expression of their ideas?

Some practical activities which could be incorporated in planning include:

- whole class, group and individual reading of texts which provide interesting genre models (including some which challenge conventions) followed by discussion identifying similarities and differences between texts;
- teacher exposition of the stages involved in his or her production of a text in a particular genre (this is especially useful if this is shown to be a messy process including drawing diagrams, false starts, the rejection of material, checking spelling, gaps in composition, rather than a dauntingly smooth linear process);

> - prediction exercises and other DARTs which draw attention to the generic characteristics of a text;
> - pupil brainstorming and compilation of lists of the conventions of particular genres.

The manipulation of genre

It is important to recognise that writers can be manipulated by being forced to use particular genres, and that writers can be empowered by being allowed to manipulate genre.

There are culturally significant ways in which working in particular genres can contribute to the empowerment or disempowerment of pupils. For example, the traditional discursive essay is a specialised genre in which writers are expected to debate issues in an open and balanced way. Since the essay, to some extent, suppresses the expression of committed opinion and has a limited, academic audience, it does not appear to be a particularly empowering form. On the other hand, learning how to write a campaign leaflet, which can in theory be distributed to a wide audience with the specific purpose of presenting the case for an opinion in such a way that others may be influenced to adopt it, gives a writer power in much more obvious ways. One irony, of course, is that access to further educational opportunities is more likely to be achieved through proficiency in writing essays than campaign leaflets.

There are a number of ways in which teaching can empower pupils by enabling them to work flexibly with genres. Teaching some pupils to use difficult genres for their own purposes may be a long-term goal. Writing soap box style opinion pieces can be a staging post towards the production of a discursive essay. Work on descriptive writing or dialogue can anticipate their incorporation in story writing. On the other hand, some pupils can be stretched by being allowed to use the possibilities of more than one genre in a single task: for example, in writing pieces which, like a considerable number of twentieth-century texts, make use of the conventions of several different genres. IT wordprocessing facilities provide a valuable resource for manipulating and experimenting with genre.

Pupils also need opportunities to find an individual voice by making use of the conventions of genres in different ways. For example, whereas some writers of discursive essays will make extensive use of illustrations which are, in effect, short narratives of their own experience, others will make more use of generalisations supported by information gleaned from reference sources. Both approaches may result in convincing argument. When asked to write a science fiction story, some pupils may concentrate on parodying the conventions of the genre, while others will demonstrate its capacity to explore human problems in unexpected ways. Although work on differences in the ways boys and girls use writing to learn and choose to interpret writing tasks is at an early stage, it may be the case that boys and girls tend to manipulate particular genres differently. Certainly, the manipulation of genre is a high order skill, so it is important that writing tasks and the methods which are used to assess them create opportunities for pupils to demonstrate and develop it and to reward their successes.

TASK 7.8   THE VALUE OF WRITING IN DIFFERENT GENRES

A Year 10 pupil's last pieces of written work in English have been a campaign leaflet calling for a lowering of the school leaving age and a postmodern narrative containing elements such as a screenplay and a series of letters to a newspaper. With a partner, role play a discussion between the pupil's teacher and a parent, who is concerned about the appropriateness of this work as preparation for A Level. Discuss the arguments used in your conversation with other student teachers.

AUDIENCE AND PUBLICATION

English in the National Curriculum (1995, p. 23, 1b) indicates that 'Pupils should be given opportunities to write for specific readers, for a large, unknown readership, and for themselves.' There is substantial evidence that writing for real audiences improves the quality of writing that pupils produce. It encourages them to engage in the drafting processes described above, to engage in consultation with other writers and potential readers, and to take care over features of presentation including technical accuracy. It also prompts them to develop their ideas beyond the point where the writing represents a message to themselves (which does not need to be further developed because 'they know what they meant'), or a message to the teacher (which does not need to be developed because the teacher already knows 'the answer'). Writing for real audiences gives pupils real writing purposes and enables them to discover the real power which writers can access.

This chapter's discussion of writing and learning identifies a number of kinds of retrospective writing which pupils can be encouraged to use to make sense of material and experience for themselves, and possibly for future use in writing for an audience in a particular genre. The 'specific readers' available to pupils can usefully be divided into audiences inside and outside the school.

Audiences within the school

The audiences within the school provide one of the most valuable resources available to teachers teaching writing. It is important that teachers planning to use pupils as real audiences think about ways in which the expertise of the pupils doing the writing can be ensured: it is often a writer's sense that he or she, either individually or as a collaborator, has something to say which the reader could not have said and wants to know which gives him or her a sense of purpose and power. Many creative genres, such as poetry, stories, plays and film scripts, clearly allow writers to make unique imaginative statements. However, other genres which communicate information, such as guides, journalistic pieces and prepared oral presentations, can make use of expert knowledge held by writers, and audiences can be found for these within the class or among other groups of pupils in the school.

It is also important to note that there are many modes of publication available in schools, including reading aloud, booklets, wall displays and posters, audio and videotaped presentations, and computer files. Moreover, it is frequently possible to make publication interactive, not only by creating opportunities for other pupils to respond by writing reviews and replies, but also by encouraging writers to produce material which incorporates decision-making roles for the audience, so that the writers have to anticipate choices and plan routes through the material accordingly. Examples of such interactive writing might range from a short play for assembly which is rehearsed with two different endings so the audience can choose one, to a Web page with 'hot words' which allow readers to pursue their own lines of enquiry in reading it.

The value of using pupils as real audiences for writing about reading also needs to be emphasised. Some examples of writing of this kind include: anthologies of poetry and collections of material on a topic with introductions from the editors; classroom displays and presentations on books which have been read as group readers; and files of reviews of books with recommendations, kept in the library. Pupils working towards SATs and GCSE can produce materials on particular aspects of texts to be used as revision aids by other groups within the class.

Audiences beyond the school

Pupils in other schools are often used as audiences for letter exchanges, but the results are often richer when writing in other genres is included so that there is a purposeful exchange of creative endeavour, the results of research, or ideas for and about reading.

Specific groups of adults such as parents and relatives, visitors to the school, figures in the local community, and authors of stories or other texts read by the class can also provide audiences for writing across a range of genres. Using parents as audiences provides an opportunity to develop their understanding of the English curriculum. For example, using them as sources of information on dialect or language change can be followed by the production of booklets containing work which demonstrates the variety of language(s) used by members of any single class of pupils. Published writers and other adults who recognise the value of young people learning to see themselves as writers and as contributors to various social and cultural debates are often prepared to respond to writing sent to them, although it is sometimes useful to check their willingness to do this in advance.

Promoting writing for real audiences is one of the most important means by which teachers can encourage pupils to pay attention to technical and presentational matters such as spelling, punctuation, vocabulary, language register, syntax, paragraphing, discourse structure, layout, and handwriting or choice of font. Having real readers helps pupils to think about the needs those readers will have if communication is to be effective. It reinforces one of the learning points which emerges from learning to write in a range of genres: writers make choices at all levels of textual construction.

TASK 7.9   WRITING FOR A REAL AUDIENCE

Devise, teach and evaluate a scheme of work in which pupils write for a real audience outside the school. Consider ways of incorporating the audience, or a sample of it, in the writing process at an earlier stage.

FORMATIVE ASSESSMENT AND EVALUATION

English in the National Curriculum (1995, 23, 2a) indicates that 'Pupils should be given opportunities to analyse critically their own and others' writing' but does not provide any kind of rationale for this, developmental or otherwise. A number of earlier sections in this chapter have suggested that writers thrive on processes through which they reflect on the development of their writing and share thoughts about it with others, especially, in the school context, teachers and their peer group. The practice in the teaching of writing commended in this chapter will create many opportunities for various sorts of responses to be given to ideas for writing, drafts of writing at different stages in its composition and finished writing.

Both self-evaluation and peer evaluation can be guided by prompt questions established by the teacher, or in negotiation, which draw attention to matters such as the total impression a piece of writing is intended to make on readers, and the effect it actually has; specific strengths in relation to matters such as its use of genre, its selection of content, its appropriateness for its audience and its technical accuracy; general points which the writer could address in redrafting or revising the text; specific changes which the reader thinks particularly important. It is always useful if the teacher can intervene in peer evaluation processes and respond to self-evaluations before the writer takes action, both to provide further advice and to monitor the responses which are being made to writing. Pupils' comments can be highly informative about the writing development of those who make them, and occasionally will need to be counteracted when they make unhelpful suggestions.

Self-evaluation is especially valuable when pupils produce particularly sensitive or personal writing, or when they use genres such as poetry, in which they may invest a great deal of emotion but have difficulty with technical matters. Writers who are asked to discuss what they were trying to achieve and to consider how successful they have been, and to indicate the source of their ideas, can provide a teacher with very important guidance as to what kind of response is appropriate. The self-evaluation forms a kind of objectification of the personal, and the teacher needs to pay attention not only to the quality of the work, but also the extent to which the writer is able to distance him or herself from the content, in deciding how to respond.

Teacher assessment of writing should also draw attention to the issues indicated for peer and self-evaluation. Many teachers begin their responses to writing with comments which indicate their reaction to the way in which the piece has made meanings, and may include emotional responses as well as analytical ones. Many teachers combine these kinds of comments with some form of recognition of the individuality of the writer, at the very least by addressing him or her by name. Positive achievements should always be identified and the teacher should then target a limited and manageable number of areas for further development, if this is appropriate. Sometimes it may not be, because of the content of the piece, or because a pupil needs a simple affirmation for a range of reasons, or because the teacher chooses to respond entirely in relation to the human communication which has taken place.

If areas for development are identified, the advice should be as specific as possible, and it should be clear what opportunity the pupil will have to make use of it in the near future. In other words, the advice is effective when it becomes a form of precise target setting. General advice, like 'Watch spelling!' and more specific advice which does not create such an opportunity, like 'You could have extended the description in the first paragraph' is of little use. Technical and presentational errors should be addressed sensitively, in a way which will support learning. One approach is to to select a limited number of patterns of errors, such as repeated failure to paragraph, or patterns of spelling errors, and to provide information which will help the pupil to learn.

Teachers can fall into tired, repetitive habits of wording, so that every comment always starts 'I enjoyed this, because . . .' followed by the inevitable 'but'. This can be avoided if the teachers' comments form part of an ongoing, open dialogue with pupils about writing. If this is attempted, it is important that the opportunity for pupil response is real. It is no use writing 'See me' on work unless you create the time to do this. If you ask questions in comments, you should acknowledge answers which pupils write later. Some teachers like to carry on this dialogue in writing journals or planning books rather than on or underneath individual writing tasks.

Assessment strategies of the kind described here can be very time-consuming, and teachers need to ensure that they do not miss opportunities to improve their communication with pupils which involve them in writing less. For example, one very valuable marking technique is to read enough examples of pupils' work to predict issues which will arise in the work of the majority of pupils. There is little point in repeating these points in 30 places when making a general note of them can allow you to use them as whole-class teaching points. You can then spend more time responding to the individual achievements of pupils in the written comments you make.

TASK 7.10 EXPLORING DRAFTING AND ASSESSMENT THROUGH YOUR OWN WRITING

Produce a piece of writing which meets the specifications of a task you set for one of your classes. Use this writing in a number of ways. Keep the different drafts of your writing and show them to your pupils on an OHP. Evaluate the impact of this technique on the writings your pupils produce. Ask four different student teachers to write comments on your piece of work, and consider which responses are most helpful to you as a writer and why.

SUMMARY AND KEY POINTS

In this chapter it has been suggested that you should take into account the following points when planning sequences of work which involve writing:

- the relationships between writing, speaking and listening, and reading can be formulated in many different productive ways in teaching;
- writing can make important contributions to learning, both when it is used retrospectively to respond to experience and material, and when it is used prospectively to plan, reorganise and develop material and ideas;
- the social dynamics of writing in the classroom reflect the social functions of writing in society and must be addressed if pupils are to

understand what writing is for;

- pupils benefit from teaching which offers them scope for *both* the drafting and development of pieces of writing *and* the exploration and manipulation of genre;

- writing becomes more purposeful when pupils perceive real audiences and opportunities for publication, and when they see that they have opportunities to make their own meanings;

- pupils pay more attention to the presentation and technical accuracy of purposeful writing;

- the formative assessment and evaluation of writing should take the form of a developmental dialogue between teacher and pupils and among groups of pupils;

- the teaching of writing should be informed by a critical interpretation of the definition of the writing curriculum in *English in the National Curriculum*.

FURTHER READING

Andrews, R. (ed.) (1989) *Narrative and Argument*, Buckingham: Open University Press.

Brindley, S. (ed.) (1994) 'Part IV: Writing' in *Teaching English*, London: Routledge.

Foggin, J. (1992) *Teaching English in the National Curriculum: Real Writing*, London: Hodder & Stoughton.

LINC 'The Process of Writing' and 'The Writing Repertoire' in *Language in the National Curriculum* (unpublished).

Meek, M. (1988) *How Texts Teach What Readers Learn*, Stroud: Thimble Press.

NWP (1990) *Ways of Looking: Issues from the National Writing Project*, London: Nelson). This text provides an overview of issues which can be pursued further in a set of books produced by the project.

Style, M. (1989) *Collaboration and Writing*, Buckingham: Open University Press.

Wilkinson, A. (ed.) (1986) *The Writing of Writing*, Buckingham: Open University Press.

8 Knowledge about language and teaching grammar

INTRODUCTION

The language which pupils use is a key part of their identity. They use language to establish relationships, to understand and interpret their environment and to interact with the world around them. Within English lessons pupils experience language in three different ways.

1. Learning through language. Language is the medium through which much of their learning will take place. Pupils will learn by listening to the teacher and listening to each other. They will learn by reading novels, poems, textbooks, and comments from their teacher and from each other. They will explore and develop their ideas in both speech and writing.
2. Learning to use language. Pupils learn to use language by practising it in a variety of different ways. They practise speaking and writing many different types of text for a range of purposes and to a variety of audiences. They practise reading and listening for many different purposes and in many different contexts.
3. Learning about language. Pupils already know a tremendous amount about language at an implicit level. In every conversation they make sophisticated choices of vocabulary, grammar and emphasis in order to achieve the tone and effect they want. The task of the English teacher is to help pupils to reflect on language and to make their implicit knowledge of language explicit.

Does teaching pupils about language help them to use language better?

Many people believe that teaching pupils *about* language is an effective way of teaching them to use it. Others argue that there is little transfer of knowledge between lessons about language and pupils using language. Surprisingly, there is little clear evidence to support one side or the other.

This issue was addressed by the Cox Report (DES and Welsh Office, 1989). Cox argued that though there was no evidence that teaching pupils about language improved their ability to use language, this was because research had been based on the wrong types of language taught in the wrong way. The research had largely been based on the formal teaching of grammar. If teaching were to focus on language variety rather than on formal grammar, and if language were taught through investigation and in the context of pupils' own reading and writing rather than through exercises, then it was 'very plausible' that learning about language would improve pupils' ability to use language.

Cox went on to give three powerful reasons for teaching children about language.

1. To improve pupils' competence as language users. Cox argued that teaching which focused on language variety, i.e. how the forms of language change according to purpose, audience and situation, was very likely to improve pupils' ability to use language.
2. Language is a key feature of the environment. We teach children about all sorts of other features of the environment as, for example, in science and geography. Language is a particularly important feature because language is a medium through which pupils experience and interact with their environment.
3. To foster tolerance of language. Many adults have strong views about language, but sometimes such views are based on ignorance and intolerance. Children need to be given a secure basis on which to develop their own attitudes to language.

The challenge for teachers is how to implement the Cox ideas in practice. How do you construct a systematic and coherent curriculum for learning about language that is closely related to children's own reading and writing and which builds on their existing knowledge and experience?

This chapter puts forward a three-pronged approach to curriculum planning for knowledge about language. It goes on to analyse the Standard English and Language Study elements of the National Curriculum and to show how these might be developed in practice. The chapter ends by addressing two controversial issues: the teaching of Standard English, and the teaching of grammar.

OBJECTIVES

By the end of this chapter you should:

- have a clear framework for planning knowledge about language work;
- have a variety of ideas that you can explore and develop in your own teaching;
- understand the relationship between Standard English and regional dialects;
- have a variety of ideas about teaching grammar.

KNOWLEDGE ABOUT LANGUAGE

Before looking further at issues and strategies for teaching about language in English lessons, it is important to consider the ideas which you already have about the nature and purpose of language study.

TASK 8.1   PUPILS' ENTITLEMENTS

The purpose of this task is to reflect on what children should be taught about language and why. Think about and then discuss with your mentor or tutor the points (a), (b) and (c) below.

The following list of entitlements was put forward by a working group of English advisers at a conference in 1993:

All children have a right to learn important things about language:

- language changes over time and place;
- language is at the centre of who we are, of all the relationships we make, and of what we are able to become;
- awareness of the systems and patterns of language can help towards more assured and effective communication;
- there are many Englishes;
- as language users, children themselves are language experts.

a) Do you agree with the ideas listed?
b) Are there any ideas you would wish to add or to delete?
c) For each idea, explain why it is important and how it might be developed in the classroom.

TASK 8.2   LANGUAGE AUTOBIOGRAPHY

The purpose of this task is to help you to reflect on your own development as a language user so that you can come to a better understanding of pupils' development as language users.

a) Plan and write your own language autobiography. This should include many of the following: your memories of how you learned to read and write; times when you have felt proud or ashamed of your language; your experiences of Standard English and regional dialects; differences between your home language and school language; learning new languages; your experiences of slang and the language of the playground; your experiences of jargon; words you love; words you hate; circumstances when you feel it easy or difficult to talk or read or write; how you feel when your language is criticised.

b) Share your language autobiography with other student teachers or with your mentor.
c) How do you think your experiences of learning language compare with those of your pupils?
d) What do your experiences of learning and using language suggest to you about how you as a teacher should teach language?
e) What ideas from your autobiography can you adapt and use in your own teaching?

Planning for knowledge about language

The ideas expressed in the Cox Report helped to open out the teaching of knowledge about language from the narrow teaching of formal rules into the breadth and excitement of language exploration. Pupils' existing knowledge and expertise were recognised, valued and exploited. And the concept of language variation gave a clear theoretical framework for teaching which was directly related to the new National Curriculum. But what the Cox Report didn't provide was a strategy for planning work on knowledge about language alongside all the other demands of the new curriculum.

If you follow Cox's ideas and teach knowledge about language in the context of pupils' own reading and writing, the danger is that you will end up with a rather haphazard and disjointed curriculum as each teacher follows the knowledge, experience and interests of each group of pupils. Alternatively, if you set up a systematic framework for teaching knowledge about language, the risk is that you will end up teaching exercises that are unrelated to pupils' experiences of language use.

One strategy for resolving this dilemma is to use a three-pronged approach to developing knowledge about language:

1. through incidental reflection;
2. as a contributory focus;
3. as a main focus.

Developing knowledge about language through incidental reflection

Every English lesson involves pupils in using language in some way. Pupils may be reading the blackboard, notices, textbooks, poems, and notes. They may be writing letters, diaries, advertisements, lists or spells. They may be listening to the teacher or to the television or to each other. They may be speaking to the teacher or to characters within a drama. Throughout this process there are dozens of opportunities for pupils to discuss and reflect on language, provided that their teacher is alert to language issues and willing to encourage questions and comments and discussion:

- Why do you start letters with 'Dear . . .'? Are there other ways of starting letters? What happens in other languages?
- Why isn't there a plural of 'trousers'?
- What's the difference between a list of contents and an index?
- Why do some words sound the same, but have different spellings?
- What's a publisher for?
- Why do newspaper headlines use the present tense to refer to the past?
- What's the point of having a headline?
- Why do people pronounce things differently?

The range and variety of questions and issues is vast. Often children will ask questions which the teacher cannot immediately answer. Questions can lead to research, observation and interviews. Because the discussion of language arises from the language that is already taking place in the classroom, the knowledge about language work is rooted in children's own reading, writing and speech.

Opportunities to explore language through incidental reflection will arise almost every lesson and should be developed in a small way in the majority of lessons.

TASK 8.3   CLASSROOM INCIDENTS

The purpose of this activity is to focus on the opportunities for developing incidental reflection in a real classroom. Observe an English lesson and make notes about the different ways in which the teacher encourages children to discuss and explore language. What other opportunities might have been taken? How did the environment of the classroom support incidental reflection on language?

Developing knowledge about language as a contributory focus

Incidental reflection is an extremely powerful but rather haphazard way of developing pupils' knowledge about language; it needs to be supplemented with more systematic strategies. The first of these is to plan to develop aspects of knowledge about language arising out of existing work.

When many teachers are planning they will have a main focus for their work over a period of several weeks. This may be reading a novel, studying newspapers, organising an advertising campaign or writing poems. A variety of other aspects of English will be developed as contributory focuses supporting the main focus.

Whatever the focus of your English teaching there will be opportunities to plan for knowledge about language as a contributory focus. For example:

- in reading an American novel such as *Huckleberry Finn* or *The Great Gilly Hopkins* you could explore the differences between American English and British English;
- in studying newspapers you could explore the use of rhyme and alliteration in headlines;
- in reading Shakespeare you could explore the ways that English has changed over time;
- in looking at soap operas you could explore the use of regional dialects and English from other countries such as Australia and the United States;
- in writing descriptions you could explore the use of adjectives;
- in writing instructions you could explore the differences between speech and writing.

Planning for knowledge about language as a contributory focus should take place alongside your planning for all other aspects of English within a unit of work. For example, if the main focus of your work is studying a novel you will look for opportunities to develop reading, writing, speaking and listening, drama, media, information technology and knowledge about language during your study of that novel. The time spent on knowledge about language may only be a few lessons within a unit of work, but it will be planned as an integral part of that unit of work.

You will not necessarily wish to develop every aspect of English within every unit of work, but you should anticipate that you will spend time exploring some aspect of knowledge about language as a contributory focus within the majority of units of work.

TASK 8.4   PLANNING A CONTRIBUTORY FOCUS

The purpose of this task is to design, use and evaluate a knowledge about language activity within the context of other English work. Analyse a unit of work that you are planning to use in your teaching practice. In conjunction with your mentor, consider the following:

a)   What is the main focus?
b)   What opportunities are there for:

- reading,
- writing,
- speaking and listening,

- drama,
- media,
- information technology,
- knowledge about language?

c) Choose one aspect of knowledge about language that you wish to develop, and decide when and how you will develop it.
d) Prepare a lesson plan and any support materials you will need.
e) Use and evaluate your plan and materials.

Knowledge about language as a main focus

Just as it is possible to embed your knowledge about language work within other aspects of your English teaching, so it is possible to embed the rest of your English teaching within a project on knowledge about language. So, for example, in a unit of work on local dialect you might have a range of contributory focuses:

Contributory focus	Examples of activities
reading	in regional dialects and in Standard English; poems in dialect; looking at the use of dialect for characterisation in novels
writing	letters to newspapers about the use of dialect; transcribing dialect speech; using dialect for characterisation in stories
speaking and listening	interviewing parents and friends; transcribing speech
drama	acting situations in which dialect speech is more appropriate or less
media	looking at the use of dialect in advertising
information technology	using the Internet to find out about local dialect

You will not wish to develop all of these contributory focuses within every unit of work, but you will need to consider the possibilities in your planning.

You should expect to plan at least one unit of work with knowledge about language as a main focus within the scheme of work for every year group.

What should we teach children about language?

The Cox Report suggested that in the past the emphasis had been too much on formal grammar and too little on language variation. The Language in the National Curriculum Project (LINC) took these ideas further to suggest five possible areas of focus:

1. Language variety:

- differences between speech and writing;
- variety of accents and dialects;
- variety of functions, registers and genres in speech and writing including those of literature;
- differences and connections between languages.

2. Language and society:

   - speaker/listener, reader/writer relationships;
   - interpersonal and mass uses of languages;
   - how social power is constructed and challenged through language.

3. Language acquisition and development:

   - babies learning to talk
   - children learning to read and write
   - a lifelong story of new encounters

4. History of languages:

   - historical change in English
   - historical change in other languages, ancient and contemporary;
   - ephemeral as well as long term change

5. Language as system:

   - vocabulary – connotations, definitions and origins of words
   - grammar – the functions and forms of words in groups
   - phonology
   - graphology (including spelling patterns and scripts)
   - organisation and conventions of layout in texts.

TASK 8.5   PLANNING A KNOWLEDGE ABOUT LANGUAGE PROJECT

The purpose of this task is to design, use and evaluate a unit of work with knowledge about language as its main focus.

a) Consider each of the five areas suggested above. Make notes on how you might develop a unit of work for each area.

b) Choose one of the units of work you have considered and plan it in detail.

   - What will the pupils know already?
   - How can pupils be encouraged to research and investigate?
   - Look closely at opportunities for reading, writing, speaking and listening, drama, media and information technology arising from the language work.

c) Complete the work you have planned as if you were a pupil. If you can, swap the plan and work with another student teacher to explore strengths and weaknesses of the unit of work.

d) Revise your plans and materials on the basis of your own experience of completing the work.

TASK 8.6   KNOWLEDGE ABOUT LANGUAGE AUDIT

The purpose of this task is to reflect on what aspects of the
National Curriculum requirements have been covered in your
teaching. Photocopy the summary below (Figure 8.1) of Standard
English and language study from the National Curriculum.

a)   use a highlighter to pick out any themes or ideas you have
     developed in any units of work you have written yourself, or
     you have seen in any of the lessons you have observed.
b)   use the right hand column to make a note of any ways that you
     could develop any of these themes or ideas in the work you are
     planning for your next teaching practice.

STANDARD ENGLISH AND LANGUAGE STUDY

Within each Attainment Target in the National Curriculum for English,
there is a section on Standard English and language study. This is rather
narrower than the ideas developed in the LINC project or those developed in the Cox Report, and it puts a special emphasis on the teaching of
Standard English. Within the National Curriculum itself the ideas and
issues being considered are rather jumbled together, so they are organised
below under subheadings which make them a little clearer (Figure 8.1).

Speaking and listening	Ideas for development
a) Appropriateness: ● develop fluent, accurate users of Standard English vocabulary and grammar; ● teach the importance of Standard English as the language of public communication; ● teach pupils to adapt their talk to the circumstances; ● develop pupils as confident users of Standard English in formal and informal situations; ● use role play and drama to explore and develop the vocabulary, structures and tone appropriate to different contexts. b) The development of English: ● explore how usage, words and meanings change over time; ● explore how words and parts of words are borrowed from other languages; ● teach about the coinage of new words and the origins of existing words; ● explore current influences on spoken and written language; ● explore attitudes to language use; ● explore the differences between speech and writing; ● teach the vocabulary and grammar of Standard English and explore dialect variations.	

Reading   Ideas for development

a)   Organisations and meaning:

- teach pupils to recognise, analyse and evaluate different types of text;
- consider the effects of organisation and structure;
- explore how author's purposes and intentions are portrayed;
- explore how attitudes, values and meanings are communicated.

b)   Choices and effects:

- explore literary language;
- analyse features of vocabulary and grammar in different types of text;
- analyse and evaluate language in a variety of media, making comparisons;
- explore different genres, including language structure and organisation;
- analyse techniques.

Writing   Ideas for development

a)   Written and spoken language:

- make pupils confident in the use of formal and informal Standard English;
- explore variation in written forms and how these differ from spoken forms and dialects;
- develop opportunities for formal writing;
- teach pupils to distinguish degrees of formality.

b)   Grammar and discourse:

- teach pupils about sentence grammar;
- show pupils how to organise whole texts effectively;
- make opportunities for pupils to analyse their own writing, reflecting on meaning and clarity, and using appropriate terminology;
- teach pupils about phrase, clause and sentence structure;
- analyse words;
- teach pupils about punctuation.

c)   Vocabulary:

- explore the choice of vocabulary and precise use of words;
- explore synonyms and double meanings;
- use dictionaries and thesauri to explore derivations and alternative meanings.

Figure 8.1 National Curriculum requirements for Standard English and language study

What might one expect to find in a 'good' knowledge about language classroom?

A working group of English advisers drew up the following list of qualities at a conference in 1993:

- many and varied opportunities to use language;
- many opportunities to talk about language;
- children asking why words, punctuation, spelling and grammar are like they are, in a spirit of excited curiosity;

- children making comparisons and contrasts between different texts;
- children drawing on their knowledge and experience of language at home, in the media and in the community;
- teachers asking open questions about language to which they do not always know the answers;
- children and teacher asking what would happen if a text were spoken or written differently;
- children and teacher drawing on terminology and specialist words where appropriate;
- a concern for appropriateness and effectiveness rather than mere 'correctness';
- the language of children, their families and the local community treated as a valuable resource: interesting, worth collecting and worth talking about;
- a wide range of sources of English in use: comics, newspapers, magazines, pamphlets, advertisements, poems, stories, instructions, lists, manuals, tapes, language examples from different cultures and times, banks of videos, listening corners with audio tapes;
- many examples of how English has changed and continues to change.

TASK 8.7 THE KNOWLEDGE ABOUT LANGUAGE CLASSROOM

The purpose of this activity is to reflect on what opportunities can be provided for language reflection in the classroom environment. Read through the list of qualities above and consider the following.

1. Which of the qualities could you confidently find in classrooms you have observed?
2. Which of the qualities could be seen in lessons you have taught?
3. Make a list of five simple things you could do to improve your classroom.
4. In conjunction with your mentor, devise an action plan to implement your targets.

Standard English

Standard English is the dominant dialect of English. It is used for almost all writing and for most public or formal communications. As such it has a special place in English teaching and all pupils need to be aware of Standard English and be able to use it alongside their regional dialects as appropriate.

Unlike most other dialects of English, it is spoken by people all over the country, and does not have a regional base (although historically it developed from an East Midlands dialect). Most people in Britain are able to use at least two dialects: Standard English for writing and formal communications, and a regional dialect for informal communications. However, Standard English is also a class dialect: it is used much more consistently by middle- and upper-class people. Like all dialects of English, Standard English has a distinctive vocabulary and grammar; however, unlike most other dialects, Standard English does not have its own accent.

Although a great deal of fuss is made about Standard English in the press and in the National Curriculum, the differences between it and other dialects of English are very slight. The majority of the vocabulary and grammar of English is used in common by all the dialects: there are slight (though very noticeable) differences at the margins.

The Cox Report (DES and Welsh Office, 1989) took pains to identify what Standard English is and to emphasise that it is not what many people take it to be. In particular:

- *Standard English is not the same as 'good' English.*
  Government forms, which are nearly always written in Standard English, may well be overcomplex and full of unnecessary jargon and therefore be very poor at communication. Regional dialect, appropriately used, may be very effective communication.
- *Standard English is not the same as 'correct' English.*
  Although Standard English has a special status among English dialects, its grammar and its vocabulary are no more 'correct' than those of any other dialect.
- *Standard English is not the same as formal English.*
  Standard English can be formal or informal, just as any other dialect. It is perfectly possible (and extremely common!) for people to swear in Standard English. A phrase such as *I'm bloody knackered* uses the vocabulary and grammar of Standard English and yet is extremely informal. A phrase such as *I be very tired* uses a regional dialect form, but yet is much more formal. Which would you prefer in your classroom?
- *Standard English is not the same as logical English.*
  Standard English forms are no more logical than those of any other dialect. For example Standard English uses *themselves* where many regional dialects use the more 'logical' form *theirselves*.
- *Standard English is not the same as Received Pronunciation (RP).*
  Standard English is the one dialect of English that can be spoken in any accent. It is defined by its vocabulary and grammar and not by its pronunciation. Received Pronunciation is an accent which, like Standard English, has a class basis rather than a regional basis, but it is only one of the many acceptable ways of pronouncing Standard English.

How can you teach Standard English effectively?

In the past Standard English was taught in some schools to the exclusion of pupils' regional dialects. Pupils would be corrected and even punished for using regional dialect forms. The effect of this was to drive a wedge between pupils' home and school experiences. Some pupils deliberately spoke less Standard English in order to emphasise their rejection of the school's values. To reject a pupil's home language is to reject an important part of their identity and also to lose a valuable resource for language exploration.

It is not necessary to reject regional dialects in order to teach Standard English: indeed pupils' awareness of regional dialects can improve their use of Standard English. Standard English can be taught through:

- *a focus on writing:* as most writing is in Standard English, a focus on writing is almost inevitably a focus on Standard English;
- *contrasting speech and writing:* looking at the differences between spoken forms and written forms will highlight many features of Standard English;
- *contrasting regional dialects:* contrasting local dialects with Standard English will highlight the Standard English forms and make pupils more aware of the subtle choices which they make subconsciously when they switch between dialects;
- *creating situations where pupils need to use Standard English:* if pupils are put in formal or public situations where they need to use Standard English, this will develop their competence in using it; such situations can be created through drama or by providing adults as an audience for pupils' speech.

TASK 8.8   EXPLORING STANDARD ENGLISH AND REGIONAL DIALECT

The purpose of this activity is to develop an awareness of the local dialect and its differences from Standard English.

1. Find out as much as you can about the local dialect in the area where you are doing your teaching practice. You can achieve this by listening to pupils and making notes; listening to adults; talking to pupils and teachers; recording and transcribing.
2. Ask a class of pupils to find as many differences as they can between their local dialect and Standard English. When they have brainstormed or collected a long list, try to sort them into different words (vocabulary) different patterns and forms (grammar) and different sounds (accent).

> 3. On the basis of your research devise a unit of work which
>   involves pupils investigating Standard English and regional
>   dialects.

TEACHING GRAMMAR

'Traditional' v. 'progressive'

Grammar teaching is often presented as an area of stark conflict
between 'progressive' and 'traditionalist' teachers. In practice there is a
considerable area of common ground. All teachers aim to raise the standards of children's reading, writing and speech. Similarly, there is
agreement that it is appropriate to study grammar as part of developing
children's language abilities. The differences lie only in the approaches
which teachers use to achieve the common end of developing children's
language abilities. Even here there is less difference in practice than in
the rhetoric to be found in the Press (see Chapter 3 and the debates
around the Kingman Report). Most teachers are pragmatists, they will
use whatever seems to work, regardless of the theory behind it. Some
teachers will tend to prefer 'progressive' approaches, others will tend to
prefer 'traditional' approaches, but in practice they will all use some of
each.

So what are the differences?

The main differences are in four areas: the choice of texts, the attitude to
rules, the emphasis on form or function, and the use or avoidance of
exercises.

1. Choice of texts
   'Traditional' approaches use very short snippets of text. Often these
   will have been created in order to demonstrate grammatical features.
   The ideas expressed in these texts are not relevant or significant.
   'Progressive' approaches use longer texts. Texts are chosen because
   they are interesting in themselves as well as to illustrate a grammatical feature. Often they will clearly have been taken from a real
   communication.
2. Attitude to rules
   In 'traditional' approaches grammatical rules are seen as powerful
   formulae from which language can be created. The rules are regarded
   as fixed and any deviation from them is condemned as wrong. In 'progressive' approaches grammatical rules are seen as useful descriptions
   of the patterns of language. However, where people's actual use of

language differs from the supposed 'rule', those differences are explored rather than condemned.

3. Form and function

'Traditional' approaches focus on describing and identifying grammatical forms: *'This is a noun, that is a verb, here is an infinitive used in apposition to a pronoun.'* This is often called 'parsing'. 'Progressive' approaches focus on how grammar contributes to the meaning or effect of a text, its function: *'The writer has chosen to use the present tense here because . . .'*

4. Exercises

'Traditional' approaches develop understanding through exercises rather than through practical uses of language. 'Progressive' approaches teach grammar by helping children to reflect on their own reading and writing.

TASK 8.9   PRINCIPLES FOR GRAMMAR TEACHING

The purpose of this activity is to help you to make your own judgements about key principles in the teaching of grammar. The following principles (Figure 8.2) for grammar teaching are put forward by Elspeth and Richard Bain in *The Grammar Book* (NATE 1996).

a) How far do you agree with the principles stated?
b) Would you describe their ideas as 'progressive' or 'traditionalist' in the terms outlined above?

TASK 8.10   DEVELOPING GRAMMAR ACTIVITIES

The purpose of this task is to design activities to develop the teaching of grammar. Plan two or three lessons in sequence drawing on two of the approaches to grammar from the list above. When you have tried them with a class, evaluate them in conjunction with your mentor or tutor.

SUMMARY AND KEY POINTS

Knowledge about language is not something that should be tacked on to English teaching as an added extra. A fascination with words and meanings and forms and patterns should be a fundamental part of all English teaching, inseparable from the planning, writing, thinking, acting, reading, researching and telling which goes on as a matter of course.

Any approach to grammar for school children should:

- acknowledge and build on what children know already;
- involve children in exploration and investigation;
- be descriptive and not prescriptive;
- address the grammar of informal writing, spoken English and regional dialects in addition to the grammar of formal, written Standard English;
- encourage interest in and respect for all forms of language;
- focus on the functions of grammar in real texts;
- address structures and patterns beyond the level of the sentence;
- be explicitly related to children's own reading and writing;
- relate directly to the issue of how language changes in relation to purpose and audience.

It should not:

- focus predominantly on errors;
- rely on invented sentences out of context;
- ignore or stigmatise regional dialect forms.

Strategies for exploring grammar in texts

Spotting parts of speech:

- pupils identify different parts of speech in their own reading and writing;
- brainstorm lists of nouns, verbs, adjectives and adverbs used in particular contexts.

Finding patterns and rules from a selected list of words:

- analyse a list of nouns to work out the rules for making plurals, using capitals, etc.;
- analyse the different forms and uses of a word, e.g. *shop*: showing it used as a noun, a verb and an adjective, and showing the changes in tense and number;
- make a list of common prefixes and suffixes from a word list; work out how the meaning or form of the stem is changed;
- analyse the patterns of organisation in a range of books: dictionary, yellow pages, recipe book, atlas.

Exploring unexpected uses of language:

- read a story written entirely with nouns in single-word sentences;
- analyse Dickens's use of incomplete sentences, repetition and balance in the opening paragraphs of *Bleak House*;
- explore the ways advertisements break patterns to achieve effect.

Contrasting texts:

- place a group of texts in order from the most formal to the least formal; identify features of formal and informal language;
- contrast similar messages given in speech and writing;
- contrast a series of texts written at different times and for different audiences and purposes, but on the same subject, e.g. a variety of texts about Grace Darling.

Messing about with texts:

- select, change, add and delete nouns, verbs, adjectives and adverbs in a given text or in pupils' own writing.

Exploring features of grammar in texts:

- contrast the use of nouns, verbs, personal pronouns and noun phrases in boys' and girls' comics;
- explore the use of directives, personal pronouns and modal verbs in an examination notice;
- explore the use of rhetorical questions, personal pronouns and modal verbs in 'junk' mail.

Playing games:

- tell stories using different connectives in each sentence;
- build words with prefixes and suffixes.

Exploring children's own writing through drafting:

- pupils check their work for sense and for common errors;
- pupils talk about their work to make their choices explicit;
- pupils mess about with changing and adapting their own writing.

Figure 8.2 Principles for grammar teaching

1. Language is a key feature in pupils' identity and environment. The development of knowledge about language is an entitlement for all pupils.
2. A systematic approach to developing knowledge about language involves three elements:

   - incidental reflection;
   - using knowledge about language as a contributory focus;
   - using knowledge about language as a main focus.

3. Standard English has a special place in our culture as the language of public and formal communication and especially of writing. However, Standard English should be taught alongside rather than at the expense of regional dialects.
4. Grammar is an exciting and interesting aspect of knowledge about language. With planning and imagination it can be taught effectively in the context of pupils' own reading and writing.

FURTHER READING

Bain, R. (1991) *Reflections: Talking about Language*, London: Hodder & Stoughton.
This book gives a clear framework for planning and a wealth of practical suggestions for developing work on knowledge about language.

Bain, E. and R. (1997) *The Grammar Book*, Sheffield: NATE.
This is a book of photocopiable materials for teaching grammar in a secondary school. It provides a range of classroom activities for developing grammar in the context of pupils' own reading and writing.

Crystal, D. (1987) *The Cambridge Encyclopaedia of Language*, Cambridge: Cambridge University Press.
This wonderful book provides entertaining and accessible information about all aspects of language. Browsing through it will give you many ideas for classroom investigations.

Trudgill, P. (1975) *Accent, Dialect and the School*, London: Edward Arnold.
This gives a powerful and succinct account of the issues involved in teaching Standard English.

9 New literacies: media and IT

The school and the family share the responsibility of preparing the young person living in a world of powerful images, words and sounds. Children and adults need to be literate in all three of these symbolic systems, and this will require some reassessment of educational priorities. Such reassessment might well result in an integrated approach to the teaching of language and communication.

(UNESCO Declaration on Media Education, 22 January 1982)

INTRODUCTION

This chapter will explore the ways in which media and information technology (IT) might be seen as central to the teaching of English at the turn of the twenty-first century. Although media and IT are discussed here in a separate chapter, they should not be seen as separate, 'bolt-on' aspects of English. Media and IT work should be seen as central to what might be considered good practice in English teaching. In the same way that all aspects of English are inextricably interlinked in the English classroom, as you read the other chapters – which for the purposes of discussion have focused on key aspects of English teaching separately – you should be looking for opportunities to bring what you learn from this chapter to your practice. The chapter also considers approaches to the teaching of Media Studies examination syllabuses.

The last fifty years have witnessed rapid development in the technology associated with communication in all its forms. It is now commonplace for pupils to have everyday access to desktop computers which are far more powerful than those that, half a century earlier, would have occupied several rooms. Many pupils come to school with experience of not only receiving broadcast materials from radio and television, but also creating and publishing with DTP packages, and communicating via e-mail and the Internet, sometimes with the makers and presenters of radio and television programmes in the act of being broadcast. Mobile telephones have also joined the list of items which should not be brought into public examinations. If teachers are to engage with the notion of literacy in its widest sense, media and IT should be central to the work of the English classroom.

OBJECTIVES

By the end of this chapter you should:

- have an understanding of the key concepts and areas of knowledge of media education;
- understand the difference between media education and Media Studies;
- begin to understand how work on the media may be incorporated into your English teaching;
- have knowledge of the requirements of GCSE and A Level Media Studies syllabuses;
- understand why the use of IT should be central to the teaching of English.

CULTURAL ATTITUDES

Chapter 2 shows not only that there was widespread debate about the nature and purposes of English teaching during the first half of the twentieth century, but also that there was an almost universal antipathy to popular culture. Popular fiction, radio, film and television were regarded with deep hostility and suspicion, because of their perceived detrimental effects upon the minds and behaviour of the young. Latterly, it is possible to see similar attitudes expressed in relation to more modern cultural and technological artefacts, such as videos, computer games and the Internet.

However, both the Newsom Report *Half our Future* (DES, 1963) and the Bullock Report, *A Language for Life* (DES, 1975) recommended that radio, film and television should be studied in their own right. Eight years later in April 1983, the DES published *Popular TV and Schooling*, a report which had been commissioned by Education Secretary, Keith Joseph. The report concluded that television should be put to 'constructive use in the classroom' and that 'all teachers should be involved in examining and discussing television programmes with young people' (DES, 1983). In 1989, Angela Rumbold, Kenneth Baker's junior minister for education, stated that the 'ability to "read" media texts. . .is an important skill for contemporary and future citizens.' As Chapter 3 shows, the first National Curriculum English Order (DES and Welsh Office 1990) directed teachers of English to encompass media texts in their teaching. *English Non-statutory Guidance* contained a section on teaching media and argued that 'by encouraging pupils to reflect upon their own experience as readers and writers of media, teachers will enable them to make their understanding explicit and systematic' (National Curriculum Council, 1990, D4.4).

It was clear, however, that although media education had been located within National Curriculum English, the same tensions about cultural worth were still to be found in the *English Non-statutory Guidance*. The distinction between 'media texts' and 'literary texts'; the mentioning of only one author by name: Shakespeare; and the complete absence of comics in the list of media texts suitable for study, indicated that there were still strong reservations about the worth of popular culture (Davison, 1990). Unsurprisingly, the rewritten Order of 1993 contained almost no mention of the media whatsoever (see Chapter 3). In the ensuing debates, media came to be reintroduced into the 1995 English curriculum – albeit in a lesser form than the Cox Report had envisaged. The *English and Media Magazine*, No. 28 (Summer 1993), contains a very good overview of the debates which followed the 1993 revision.

TASK 9.1   ATTITUDES TO THE MEDIA

Consider the UNESCO statement which opens this chapter and the following statements:

> All media forms are worthy of study. All media texts should be subject to the same scrutiny, whether produced for entertainment, information, as learning resources, or by pupils themselves . . . The most effective media teaching is non-judgmental, rather than about 'good' or 'bad' texts.
>
> (Grahame 1990)

> Is it no wonder that children struggle at school when they are allowed by their parents to spend more time in front of the television than they do in front of the blackboard.
>
> (Patten, 1992)

> Widespread media literacy is essential if all citizens are to wield power, make rational decisions, become effective change agents and have an active involvement with the media. It is in this much wider sense of 'education for democracy' that media education can play the most significant role of all.
>
> (Masterman, 1985)

> What children get from television depends on what children bring to it. Depending on how old they are, how bright they are, how tired they are, what sort of family they belong to, what sort of skills they already have, television will affect them differently. And the same child will react differently to television programmes at different stages of his or her life.
>
> (Messenger Davis, 1989)

> How do you react to these statements? Do you agree with, or
> reject, some of them completely? Are there some statements with
> which you agree/disagree, but have reservations about part of
> their assertions?
>
> Discuss these statements and your reactions to them with
> another student teacher or your tutor/mentor. Keep any notes you
> make. They will be useful when you come to Task 9.2.

MEDIA EDUCATION

What's the difference?

It is not unusual to find the terms 'media education' and 'Media Studies' used as if they are interchangeable. Indeed, the *Times Educational
Supplement* leader on the demise of media in the rewritten 1993 Order
for English does exactly this when it begins: 'So it looks as if media
studies has been cut from the latest version of the national curriculum'
(*TES*, 29 Jan. 1993) and continued throughout to use 'media studies'
when, in fact, it was talking about media education.

Quite simply, media education refers to the development of skills,
knowledge and understanding in relation to the media – what some people have referred to as 'media literacy'. This is the ability to read critically
the range of media artefacts which comprise life at the end of the twentieth
century, whereas, Media Studies (and the capitalisation is deliberate)
refers specifically to courses of study, syllabuses for GCSE, A Level and
degree level focusing on areas of the mass media.

In relation to the English classroom, therefore, the purpose of any
studying of the media should be seen as further developing a pupil's
critical literacy in relation to texts they encounter in their daily lives, be
they printed, televisual or electronic. After all, before the advent of the
printed word, there would have been little purpose in attempting to teach
reading. The printed texts that we believe our pupils should read critically are just products of an earlier technology which today are produced,
manufactured and distributed in the same way as so-called 'media texts'.
The distinction between 'literary text' and 'media text' ignores the fact
that books, newspapers, television programmes, films, commercials,
videos and computer games are all subject to the same economic and
industrial determinants. Such a distinction, of course, is firmly anchored
in beliefs about the respective cultural worth of the artefact. However, a
collection of poetry or a novel does not spring fully-formed from the
writer's brain to the bookshop shelf, but undergoes lengthy negotiation
between author, literary agent, editor, publisher, designer, marketing
department and bookshop among others, before the reader glimpses a

single word. And this is the case whether it be the work of Jane Austen or Jeffrey Archer; Christina Rossetti or Benjamin Zepheniah.

The aims of media education

Media work in the English classroom will enable pupils to develop a range of skills, knowledge and understanding about their lives as critical readers and writers of media texts:

> Media Education aims to enable students to:
>
> - understand the similarities and differences between the many media around us;
> - reflect on their own experiences of media;
> - develop a critical language to describe, categorise and analyse;
> - express themselves in the widest range of media possible.
>
> (Grahame, 1990, p. 10)

While pupils following a Media Studies course may well develop in a similar way, their focus of study is prescribed by the requirements of a syllabus constructed by an examination board. Media Studies pupils in the secondary school will, of course, have the further aim of achieving a qualification at GCSE or A Level. Therefore, while most English teachers find it useful and relatively easy (and enjoyable) to develop the skills and knowledge to engage in media work in the English classroom, as the section on Media Studies later in this chapter shows, teaching Media Studies demands a greater depth of knowledge and understanding of media concepts in relation to examination syllabuses.

KEY ASPECTS OF MEDIA EDUCATION

Because teachers and pupils meet media texts fully formed – the film, comic, television programme or commercial – it is often difficult to know where to begin and how to make the text a manageable object of study. Figure 9.1 provides an invaluable starting point for developing understanding about any text. Indeed, as the Cox Report states: 'the kinds of questions that are routinely asked in media education can fruitfully be applied to literature' (DES and Welsh Office, 1989, 7.23).

In a chapter of this length it would be impossible to explore all the ways in which you might use media work in the English classroom. The Further Reading section at the end of this chapter lists a number of key texts which will support you and help you to develop your skills and knowledge. It is possible, however, to establish some underlying principles and approaches which you might be able to apply to the school context in which you find yourself. As Figure 9.1 indicates, we can develop our understanding of any media text by asking some of the key questions in

WHAT TYPE of text is it?	*Media categories*	Different media (TV, radio, cinema, etc.); forms (documentary, advertising, etc.); genres (sci-fi, soap opera, etc.); other ways of categorising texts; how categorisation relates to understanding.
HOW is it produced?	*Media technologies*	What kinds of technologies are available to whom; how to use them; the differences they make to the production process as well as the final product.
HOW do we know what it means?	*Media languages*	How the media produce meanings; codes and conventions; narrative structures.
WHO is communicating and why?	*Media agencies*	Who produces a text; roles in production process; media institutions; economics and ideology; intentions and results.
How does it PRESENT its subject?	*Media representations*	The relationship between media texts and actual places, people, events, ideas; stereotyping and its consequences.
WHO receives it and what sense do they make of it?	*Media audiences*	How audiences are identified, constructed, addressed and reached; how audiences find, choose, consume and respond to texts.

Figure 9.1 Key questions and aspects of media education
Source: Adapted from DES/BFI (1989)

relation to its production, distribution, exhibition and meanings. Clearly, implicit in this table is a methodology of active interrogation. It does not imply the model of a teacher as the fount of all knowledge about a particular aspect of media. It is salutary to remember that pupils often have sophisticated understandings about their relationship with the media (see for example Buckingham, 1993).

It is likely that your pupils will consume many more media texts – not only in number, but in form also – in any one week than you will. They are likely to have built up a wealth of knowledge and implicit under-standings about the media that impinge upon their lives. A teacher intending to 'tell them all about it' not only smacks of the Leavisite 'inoc-ulation' approach (see Chapter 2), it is also presumptuous. Any attempt to unveil what you believe is cynical manipulation by the promoters of the latest pop music icons is likely to alienate pupils, or to set up confrontation between followers of one pop sensation over another – the rivalries between fans of Oasis and Blur being a prime late 1990s example. Objects of study need to be chosen with care, and it is advisable, not always to opt for the most obvious and current. Examination of texts at a 'distance' can be a useful method of avoiding problems. Distance might be defined in terms of:

- time – for example 1980s pop music; 1970s sitcoms;
- age of target audience – for example comics read by a younger age group, women's magazines;
- cultural hierarchy – for example the 'Three Tenors' and Kiri Ti Kanawa are subject to the same packaging and marketing as any pop group; some factual documentaries use conventions of the Hollywood thriller.

Interrogation of 'distanced' texts can take place, which will enable pupils to ask the same questions of media texts they encounter in their daily lives. Obviously, the texts should not be so rarefied that they are completely remote from pupils' lives and some connection to texts they encounter needs to be made, but you should not attempt always to bring into school the most immediate manifestations of pupils' lives. Pupils need to feel that there are some facets of their out-of-school-lives which are theirs alone.

Media work in the English classroom should be founded upon prac-tical, active investigation of aspects of the media which allows pupils the opportunity to both read and write a range of media texts. Media education can supply the vocabulary which will enable pupils to articulate, to make explicit, their growing knowledge and understanding about the media.

MEDIA IN ENGLISH

If media work is to be central to your English teaching in the classroom, then an obvious way to make it so is to look for opportunities within any current scheme of work. Therefore, it would be useful for you to look at what is offered to pupils in say year 7 in your placement school. Examine any schemes of work or topics which are already in place. It may well be that such opportunities are already present, but if they are not, then the following paragraphs might offer a useful starting point for media work with pupils at the beginning of Key Stage 3.

It is not uncommon for much of the work in year 7 to be autobiographical in nature. It is an obvious way to enable pupils to bring into school that with which they are familiar and to have aspects of their lives valued and celebrated. Similarly, such work enables a teacher quickly to get to know the pupils. Often pupils will write about a variety of facets of their lives: family, friends, likes and dislikes, hobbies, the primary school, favourite teachers, subjects, school journeys, holidays, the neighbourhood and so on. An excellent example of such work is to be found in the *Myself* booklet published by NATE. Such work can provide many opportunities for aspects of media work. Image work which considers representation can be incorporated into 'Myself' work using photography, for instance. Pupils can be invited to provide photographs of 'Me in five places' which are important to them, or which show them at important times of their lives. Pupils can approach representation in this way not only by placing the photograph in context, knowing what occasions are selected as worthy of being photographed, knowing what's been personally important but doesn't have a visual product, but also by examining how the image is constructed, what it 'says' about its subject, etc. This awareness of selection and construction are also ways into discussing narrative in Media Studies and English. A related task could be to take photographs or write about key moments of a school day on cards, and to experiment with the orders in which they could be sequenced. In terms of practicalities, printing out computer pictures taken on a digital camera would be quicker than using a film camera. The two *Eyeopener* books (Bethell, 1983) and *Media Education: An Introduction* (Bazalgette, 1991) offer a variety of useful related work on image analysis.

The local area

The *English Non-statutory Guidance* offers a useful example in its 'The Local Area topic' (National Curriculum Council, 1990, 4.14). Although the Guidance suggests this topic is suitable for KS2, equally, it may be adapted for use in KS3 and form part of a wider unit based upon autobiographical work. Such work offers many opportunities for considering not only how language is used to persuade as well as inform, but also for media work. Media-based work might be anchored in newspapers and advertising and consider: ownership (for example who owns the local press and how this might influence the stance a local newspaper takes upon issues); production and distribution (the high production values of corporate advertising against the more cheaply produced campaigning

Teaching decisions	Planning
	PREPARATORY ACTIVITIES
How will you introduce the activity?	Collect local publications: newspapers, magazines, tourist information, advertisements, local authority information on local services – libraries, parks, etc., publicity for businesses and institutions.
How will you find out what pupils already know?	
How will this knowledge be shared?	**For each publication identify:** • audience; • purpose of publication;
How will you involve pupils in the planning?	• who produced publication; • how publication is produced and distributed; • cost;
How will you maintain pupils' interest?	• design, layout and language used in publication; • use of typefaces, colour, illustrations; • the use of photographs/images and captions;
How will you ensure that pupils are engaged in their own learning?	• the use of quotations – who quoted to what effect? • how the publication represents the local area/institution.
	GROUPWORK
How will pupil groupings be arranged?	Using photographs and captions, groups produce displays of contrasting views of the locality, aimed at different audiences. For example, tourist brochure,
How will you take account of gender issues?	newspaper article on the decline of public services; publication to attract new business; an introduction to the area for children from abroad.
How will you ensure that tasks are matched to ability?	**Planning**
How will you ensure that there are opportunities for learning in groups?	Groups should identify the image of the area they wish to convey, select subjects and locations for photographs. Decide camera angles, framing, lighting.
What opportunities for:	**Production**
• drama? • media work?	Take photographs, noting where plans were changed and why.
• IT work? • cross-curricular links?	**Presentation**
	Groups produce posters, leaflets, articles, etc. and write captions for photographs.
How are pupil experiences recorded and shared?	**REVIEW**
How will these be developed?	Groups review their work in the light of their initial intentions. Did photographs/publications come out as expected? How have other groups interpreted their brief?
What resources will you need?	What choices they made with the photographs and publications and why?
What support might you need and how might it be arranged?	**FOLLOW-UP ACTIVITIES** Look at presentation of localities – in fiction and non-fiction, print and TV or film – and discuss purposes they serve.
What resources might be needed for particular pupils?	Discuss realism and examine how video and TV creates a sense of place. Consider the representation of people, places and issues.

Figure 9.2 The local area

Source: Adapted from 'The Local Area', *English Non-statutory Guidance* (National Curriculum Council, 1990)

literature; representation (of local issues or groups); image work (analysis and construction of photographic images).

Simple image work using 'found' images from magazines or photographs is often a starting point for media work in KS3. Using 'cropping' or 'masking' to change the meanings of images and using captions to 'anchor' the meaning of an image are useful ways of enabling pupils to begin to understand how meaning is constructed in visual terms. Pupils might produce collages of related advertising images of, for example, children, mothers, families and older people, and consider the differences between how these groups are presented in the media and how, in fact, pupils experience such groups in real life. For example, do all families have two children, an older boy and younger girl? Are 'mums' perpetually worried about what to cook for tea or the whiteness of their wash? Do all 'grannies' wear knitted woolly hats, grey overcoats and shuffle along the road? Pupils might also consider the 'absences' from such images. Is the multiracial nature of society represented in advertising? Where are the images of disability? Why are homes always immaculate in advertising images – where is the untidiness and clutter of everyday life?

You can take such work a step further by getting pupils to construct their own images. Getting pupils to construct their own images using photography need not be a difficult task. Many pupils have access to simple fixed-focus cameras of the 'instamatic' kind. Organising pupils into groups and limiting the number of images to be produced – say four or five – will enable you to use only one or two cameras/films to produce the required number of photographs. As well as producing photographs for the work described above, pupils could use their photographs to create their own posters or magazine advertisements for products which more closely reflect their lives. Obviously, such work requires organisation on your part (for example, the need to plan in the time needed for processing and printing of photographs), but it will also develop groupwork skills in your pupils, such as negotiation and co-operation as well as planning.

Two English and Media Centre publications which you will find useful to support image work and work on representation are Grahame's *The English Curriculum: Media 1* (1990) and Stephen's *School* (1990) both of which are available from NATE, (see Further Reading).

The 'Local Area' also provides opportunities for IT. Obviously, leaflets, pamphlets and reports might be produced using word processing or desktop publishing (DTP) software; but there are also database opportunities. Pupils can collect information related, say, to facilities – parks, playgrounds, cinemas, theatres, libraries, fast food outlets – and create a database which gives information about the type, location, cost, quality, etc., of the facility. Such an approach naturally and purposefully integrates the use of a database by pupils in English. The final section of this chapter considers more fully the possibilities for IT in English.

Poetry

Poems are extremely useful for media-based work because, by and large, they tend to be short, complete texts. The practice of storyboarding, or making a video poem, can be one way of beginning to get pupils used to 'writing' with a video camera. A storyboard is the beginning point for all TV, video and film productions (see the two previously mentioned texts for examples). It comprises a number of blank frames on a sheet into which are drawn or pasted approximations of what will appear on screen. Beneath each frame are written details of music, sound effects, dialogue and camera movement. Storyboard work enables pupils to begin to understand how visual images are constructed and how technical and narrative codes and conventions determine the 'look' of TV and film drama.

Working in groups, pupils can produce storyboards of poems they are studying. Details of camera angles, lighting, movement and music and sound effects can be added to the line from the poem which will accompany the image in the frame. For longer narrative or pre-twentieth-century poems, the text might be divided up among groups to storyboard. There will, of course, need to be some discussion by the whole class beforehand related to the tone or mood of the poem and how this will influence the visual style of the storyboard.

Images from magazines and Sunday supplements might be used to create a video poem. Images are pasted on to caption cards, which are then shot on video. Pupils decide whether the image is static and full-frame, or whether different close-up details from the same image might be used; if the camera will pan or zoom, and so on. The text of the poem can be read out as a voice-over at the same time as the image is recorded, or read out to accompany images as they appear on the TV monitor when they are shared with the class. The second approach is often more successful as it limits the number of opportunities for mistakes at the recording stage.

Class readers

When beginning a new class reader it is not unusual to spend some time discussing what we learn about the book from the cover. For example, what clues does the title give about the content of the story? How does the blurb on the back cover raise the reader's expectations? Can the illustration help us to predict what the characters will be like, or what might happen in the story? Media work based on a class reader can include examination of the book cover in media terms in order to make apparent to pupils the industrial nature of a book's production and circulation. For example, what messages are conveyed by the choice of illustration, the nature of the image? How is the cover laid out; what typefaces and font size are used; what use is made of colour? What is the importance of the bar code and ISBN? What does the price tell us about the intended market for the book? Why are sales restricted to certain countries? What do we know about the publisher; what is the importance of logos, imprints and particular series? Such analysis and discussion fits naturally into the type of work that English teachers will do on front covers, but it further develops a pupil's 'media literacy'. Further work related to book covers might include repackaging the book for a new audience. Pupils design a cover aimed at slightly older or younger audience, or, perhaps, as a school text. A range of covers, posters, promotional flyers all reinforce pupils' understandings of the industrial/technological nature of publishing. We return to this topic in the IT section of this chapter.

Storyboarding can also be used when studying class readers. The opening or key scenes are suitable for such work either as a 'free-standing' exercise or as part of a larger media-related topic. Preparatory work should include discussion of what pupils would select as appropriate for visual and sound media such as film and television; more subtle adaptations would consider how non-action but narratively important information like a character's thoughts can be conveyed. Clearly a small extract from a book and its TV or film version would be an invaluable stimulus here. While working on a class reader pupils might make a poster for a TV adaptation, after doing some analytical work on posters – particularly those used to capture the attention of a potential TV audience. Without such preparatory work, pupils might well produce something that looks like a poster with an image and text, but their knowledge and understanding of the conventions of this media text will not have been developed. If you intend to do any media work related to advertising, you will find Grahame's award-winning *Advertising* (1993), available from NATE, an invaluable resource. In 1997 approximately half the English departments in the UK had purchased the pack, so check to see if it is available in your department.

Further related work could involve the pupils in making a two-minute radio commercial for a radio adaptation of the story. Limiting the length of the product and making the focus of the exercise the commercial rather than the adaptation of the whole story is useful in two ways. It clearly constrains the amount of work that pupils have to do and it makes the focus of the exercise media as opposed to literary. Such an exercise involves pupils thinking about: audience (how different might the commercial be on Radio 3 or 4 compared to Radio 5 Live or a commercial station?); technical and narrative conventions of radio drama; purposes and practices of radio advertising. The BBC has a booklet and tape about making radio drama. Equally, older pupils might produce a television trailer for a TV adaptation of the story for Channel 4, Children's BBC or a local cable channel. Once again similar media concepts might be explored. It is but a short step from this type of work to considering promotional campaigns, marketing and merchandising related to TV and films. Many pupils will have tangible proof of the efficacy and ubiquity of such marketing either as part of their collection of toys; their clothing or their pencil cases and lunch boxes they bring to school.

Questions of learning

Finally, when planning media work, remember the point made in the *English Non-statutory Guidance* and build into your English lessons opportunities which allow your pupils to both *read* and *write* in a variety of media. Similarly, before beginning any new media-related topic, you should ask yourself two questions: 'What do I need to know in terms of the media?' and 'What do my pupils need to know in terms of the media?' Remember, getting them to draw a newspaper masthead, a banner headline and dividing the page into two columns for the *Verona Times* or the *Soledad Enquirer* might enable pupils to develop their knowledge of the texts they are studying, but it is not media education unless you have done some preparatory work on, for example, newspaper ownership, distribution, stance, and so on. Similarly, a class magazine is only really a collection of English work unless you have previously explored such areas as: conventions of magazines; audience, etc., to make the work be a valuable experience in terms of media. After media-related work you should, or you should enable your pupils to, make explicit what has been learned in terms of the media. This section of the chapter has been an introduction to some of the practices and processes in which you should engage. The Further Reading section includes key texts which will support your media work in the classroom.

TASK 9.2   WHY STUDY THE MEDIA?

By now you should have a clear idea of the reasons for including media education in the English curriculum. Similarly, you should have developed an awareness of a variety of ways in which media work will underpin your teaching.

Imagine you have to write a letter to parents explaining what happens in the English department in your school in relation to media education. Write a statement on the reasons for and purposes of studying the media in the English classroom. Remember that parents are likely to hold a range of views in relation to the worth of studying media in school.

MEDIA STUDIES

As has been said earlier, Media Studies and media education are separate, if related, disciplines. The first part of this chapter has shown how media education can be located within the work of the English classroom in order to develop pupils' literacy in the widest sense. The focus of this part of the chapter, however, is to consider Media Studies in relation to the preparation of pupils in order to pass public examinations. The general remarks will be predominantly about GCSE and A Level; however, there is mention of AS Level and a brief discussion about GNVQ Media Production and Communication; the section on practical work, for example, outlines the theoretical purpose of production activities, whereas the GNVQ courses naturally have more vocational aims. While following GCSE and A Level syllabuses, unquestionably, pupils will develop skills, understanding and knowledge in relation to the media, it must be remembered that one of the main purposes of this course of study is to achieve an academic qualification. Although teaching Media Studies has historically come to be located within the English department, such teaching requires particular knowledge, skills and understanding to be developed in the teacher, which are in many ways separate from those that a teacher uses in the English classroom.

It is often assumed that because there are some similarities between media and literary texts – for example, in common narrative elements such as plot, themes, character, setting – that 'English' reading skills can be transferred to analysing media texts. Indeed, some learning can take place – there is much rich material in discussing the story, characters and isolated setting of Big Whiskey in *Unforgiven* for instance, or the themes of race and parenthood in *Boyz 'n' The Hood* – but a teacher will not be preparing pupils for the conceptual and theoretical awareness needed for appropriate media analysis required for a good exam grade. Nor will the hopeful intention be that, since you like films, you will be able to base most of the work around film study. Media Studies means just that: a *range* of media forms. While examination boards are fully aware of the lack of formal media training in many teachers, they have to demand appropriate academic standards. The Chief Examiners' reports comment on the good work of teachers in many centres, but annually reiterate the lack of apposite critical media teaching and the limited range of media studied which, consequently, penalises the pupils via their examination results.

> There are too many candidates who have an inadequate grasp of concepts and seem reluctant (or unable) to discuss relevant examples in sufficient depth and detail. There are a few Centres who do not seem to be conscious of the demands of the examination and are not preparing their students as effectively as they might. It is essential to recognise that approaches to the subject matter require theoretical understanding and analytical and discursive skills. Candidates

should also be strongly discouraged from producing answers based almost entirely upon flimsy general knowledge. . .It is worth repeating that Media Studies is a specific subject with its own body of knowledge, theories and debates. . .The best candidates were able to blend theory with apt and imaginatively chosen supporting texts. Answers from these students reflected informed, intelligent appraisals and understanding of concepts and debates.

(UCLES, 1996, p. 4)

If you are keen to teach some Media Studies but have not studied it as an undergraduate, it is best to do so with experienced teachers in an established GCSE and/or A Level course in your placement school. They should, therefore, have units of work based on clear conceptual and theoretical aims and a range of well-focused materials for you to browse through. Should you wish to go on to take up a post which includes Media Studies teaching you need to be aware that the responsibility for further training lies with you. Despite the exhortations for pupils to be prepared for twenty-first-century technology and literacy, training for teaching Media Studies is stumbling through the Dark Ages – partly because since 1992 teacher education has to be provided in National Curriculum subjects.

Not so long ago we were told that education had to be about relevance, providing skills which employers could use, a workforce which could be flexible. Market forces are constantly referred to as central to educational provision, economic awareness and facility with technology are promoted. Media Studies offers all these features in abundance. It is relevant, it promotes a range of flexible skills, building upon basics and encouraging a bridging of the academic/technical divide. It involves group co-operation and knowledge of how business functions.

(Fraser, 1993, p. 19)

If, as a student teacher with little or no Media Studies education, you are offered a post in a school which wants you to start up GCSE or A Level Media Studies that September, you should consider the matter very carefully before you accept. Some schools can be very insistent because Media Studies is a growth area, it thus brings in funding and potentially keeps students who might otherwise leave to do A Levels in the local college. Ideally you might ask them to consider postponing the introduction of the course for a year. You should, though, make it clear to the school that you would like the resources and time (a year) to go on courses, read, collect materials and buy equipment. Without such support, the quality of teaching and the quality of pupil learning will be likely to undermine the purpose of having the course in the first place. If the school is unable to give you such support, you need to be aware of the ramifications on the quality of your professional life. As the HMI report *The New Teacher in School* (OFSTED, 1993) shows, you are likely to be under considerable pressure as an NQT with the physical demands of teaching full-time, learning classroom management with new pupils, handling marking and administration, without undertaking the equivalent of a self-directed undergraduate course in Media Studies in the small hours of the morning.

Even if you do have a degree in Media, you should still be equally cautious. As an NQT you will only have had limited experience of examination teaching and little, if any, experience of managing an examination course. Running GCSE Media Studies could be possible provided you already have teaching resources relevant to the syllabus and are given a budget to buy equipment. However, we would stress that as an NQT you should not have to deal with the responsibility of managing exam board administration, for example being solely responsible for marking coursework, when you have not had the experience of knowing what levels of achievement are appropriate. Indeed, you are no doubt aware that it takes a while to understand the syllabuses themselves. Remember, it is the pupils who pay the price of mismanaged courses. Again, we would suggest being given a year to choose your syllabuses and plan your courses; for A Level in particular there is much which has to be covered and it has to be very tightly managed. Also, the practicalities of organising and monitoring practical work, for instance, are ones learned through classroom management experience.

Short courses

You may be lucky to be on an English course which includes a Media Studies unit, but if you intend to teach Media Studies in school, you will need to become acquainted with the opportunities for short courses and qualifications via part-time courses. Once you have secured a teaching post, contact your local English adviser or the English and Media Centre in London; their courses include one for an accredited qualification which is the Diploma in Media Education. There are also regional Media teaching support groups. The English and Media Centre's *Media Directory* has a list of useful addresses. The British Film Institute Education section can also provide details of regional groups. Specialist institutions such as the British Film Institute (BFI), the Museum of the Moving Image (MOMI) Education, Film Education, Bradford Museum of Photography, Film and Television, NATE and local projects such as video, photography and radio workshops run good quality short courses with professionals. There are independent education companies which provide courses specifically geared to aspects of examination syllabuses. Some of them have Chief Examiners playing a participatory and/or organising role – Alpha Conferences (Len Masterman of the NEAB),

Education Training Cambridge (Pete Fraser of the UCLES), Creative Education (Peter Wall of the SEG and AEB). They offer a range of well-focused workshops and associated material; however course fees vary a great deal and you will have to find out about INSET funding.

Textbooks and readers

There are now some excellent books which offer accessible and succinct explanations of the key media concepts, debates and theories, as well as a range of case studies with good quality visual images. The following books are also worth considering as text books for pupils: for GCSE, *Media Studies: An Introduction* (Dutton and Mundy, 1995), and *GCSE Media Studies* (Wall, 1996); for A Level, *Studying the Media* (O'Sullivan, Dutton and Rayner, 1994) and *The Media Student's Book* (Branston and Stafford, 1996). The last has a comprehensive glossary of key terms. A book which more advanced students may find useful and is certainly useful for you to extend your knowledge and feel that you're more than one step ahead of the students, is *Media Studies* (Price, 1993). *Media Education: An Introduction* is an erudite Open University (1992) distance learning package, written by experienced media teachers, containing activities and opportunities to analyse case studies of media lessons at Key Stages 1, 2 and 3. While it clearly has a media education focus, the teaching and learning skills are sound ones that can be applied to examination courses.

You will also need to read a range of specialist books for particular areas of study; most examination boards have bibliographies printed in their syllabuses or available as support materials. Although targeted at its A Level syllabus, the NEAB's excellent *Media Studies: Teachers' Guide to Studies in Depth* (Masterman, 1995) provides wide-ranging booklists and analytical synopses useful for any media course.

Resources

There are some excellent packs of photocopiable materials which can be used for GCSE, GNVQ and A Level courses. As they are expensive, they should be bought as departmental resources, such as the English and Media Centre's *Advertising Pack* and *News Pack*. Film Education's *Movie Mogul* pack was sent out free to all departments on its mailing list, so try to track one down to photocopy. It is well worth getting on Film Education's mailing list as they organise courses and events around the country and send out free education booklets on current film releases; these are supplemented by TV programmes on BBC2's early morning *The Learning Zone*. Film Education has produced materials focusing on the many film adaptations of literary texts so you can supplement your English resources, too. GNVQ courses have been supported by detailed syllabuses and some materials from the awarding bodies. Major publishers are also now producing books for GNVQ media courses, for example *GNVQ Media: Production and Communication Intermediate* and *GNVQ Media: Production and Communication Advanced* (Longman, 1996). Obtaining catalogues from major academic publishers automatically leads to you being placed on their mailing lists. It is advisable to obtain inspection copies first.

Whether you wish to teach media education and/or Media Studies, you will need your own bank of materials for use in the classroom such as TV listings magazines, music magazines, newspapers (local and national), magazines targeted at men, women and teenagers, comics, film marketing merchandise. Label them and/or keep an inventory which you can check at the end of the lesson. Also encourage pupils to bring in things. Invest in a good VCR at home for film and TV resources.

As you are teaching about contemporary businesses it is important to gain insights from the viewpoints of the practitioners. Obtaining trade magazines such as *Campaign* for the advertising industry, and information about audiences such as BARB figures and press packs, provides active research material for both academic and practical work. *The Media Guide: A Guardian Book* (ed. Peak), annually publishes a list of professional media organisations. One of the stimulations (and demands) of teaching this subject is the need to keep up to date: ownership changes regularly; legislation is amended; new technologies and attendant debates proliferate; there are new spins on old moral panics. You can easily inform yourself via: newspapers such as *Media Guardian, Observer* and *Sunday Times* (the 'Business' sections are particularly useful); radio programmes such as *Medium Wave* and *Today* on Radio 4, *Sight and Sound* magazine and of course television programmes.

Mainstream and alternative

To do the subject justice it is important to tackle alternative media. However, by definition, they are harder to access. The following are some initial suggestions for materials that are easy to obtain. A browse through the shelves of a large high street stationers will reveal a variety of niche market music magazines, as will visiting a specialist music shop. Similarly, you might undertake a case study of alternative press via buying the *Big Issue* – indeed you could set this as a task for the students, if possible, so that they can experience first-hand the alternative exhibition practices of this sector; they could interview sellers to find out the distribution methods. *The News Pack* (NATE, 1996) has a section on Undercurrents an alternative video news organisation; while the London Film and Video Agency (LFDVA) has a video called *11 O'clock High* with an accompanying booklet. The LFDVA is very keen to work with teachers.

Practical skills

The types of practical skills required of both teachers and pupils range from 'low-tech' activities such as the framing exercises outlined above, making cut-and-paste narratives using found images; to technically competent audio mixing, video editing and desktop publishing. Practical work is employed in two ways. Firstly as a teaching method, and all exam boards encourage its use as one of a range of teaching methods. Secondly, as the production of artefacts for examination coursework. There are two types of examination products. They can be integral parts of coursework units for GCSE examinations and thus would be tasks chosen by teacher and pupil as part of a collection of outcomes; and they are compulsory requirements for both GCSE and A Level. The number of compulsory productions varies between the exam boards.

While, if only for obvious practical problems, it is not a requirement of a subject like Business Studies for pupils to make the products of the companies they study, the close reading of individual media texts can only be thorough if the contexts of their economic determinants are understood. Those determinants which most directly affect the finished text are the technology and working practices, the former of which is now available in domestic and semi-professional versions. A significant part of a producers' activities is to explore ideas and meet briefs through experimenting with technology, form and style. It could be argued that pupils undertaking similar processes with similar equipment should gain a more dynamic and comprehensive understanding of the texts they are studying than if they do so in a more detached and passive way. The prime aim in these academic courses, therefore, is to explore conceptual and theoretical issues via practical work; for this reason you will notice that all practical work has to be accompanied by a substantial analytical commentary. Pupils should aim for good quality products and are rewarded for such achievements, though in the interests of academic emphasis there is some leeway for the gap between intention and outcome. You will see that A Level boards like the WJEC, AEB and NEAB integrate practical work more into a written process than the UCLES syllabus. SEG and MEG provide opportunities for teachers to do as much as they wish in their GCSE syllabuses.

As with the academic work, you will have to be resourceful in obtaining training. If you become responsible for choosing a syllabus, the level of your practical skills at that stage should be a consideration. If, at your placement school, there are technically competent media teachers and easily accessible equipment, then ask them to teach you. There should be teachers in other departments who could help you, such as Information Technology, Music and Art – don't be shy! Basic video filming and editing, audio mixing and DTP skills are quite easy to pick up. You will then need to spend time extending your skills to levels needed by the exam board and to make you feel confident teaching pupils. You may be lucky enough to have the support of a technician or Media Resources Officer; however there are obvious professional reasons why you should have some level of competence – not the least of which will be organising the teaching of technical skills to pupils and sorting out the inevitable technological problems that arise when pupils work independently. Practical courses related directly to the exams are less frequent than academic ones, but the English and Media Centre in London, Creative Education and Education Training Cambridge include them in their programmes. Again use local organisations such as video workshops and radio production. There are a steadily increasing number of adult education courses teaching such skills and some universities like Sussex offer short courses.

GNVQ Media Production and Communication

GNVQ media courses are still in their early stages after the initial pilot schemes' development. Currently, the majority of Media Studies courses are run at GCSE and A Level. However, as the Dearing Review strongly advocates vocational courses and changing A Levels to encompass similar approaches, if there is not a GNVQ course in your placement school, it would be worthwhile arranging an observation lesson elsewhere.

You may find the following informal and formal reports from the points of view of students, a teacher and OFSTED useful indicators of what you could encounter teaching such a course. At a workshop during the BFI Media Studies conference 1996, a teacher presented a course review she had asked her GNVQ Advanced students to undertake. In descending order of popularity they liked filming and editing, groupwork, research and planning, individual work and paperwork. In descending order of dislikes: paperwork came first; then assignments and deadlines being set at the same time; disorganisation of their groups; research and planning; Core Skills Maths. Students also wanted more emphasis on practical work.

The teacher's own course review noted the following:

- lack of progress between Intermediate and Advanced levels in tests;
- assignment tasks needed to be more varied;
- similar skills were repeated at different times;
- more hands-on learning of practical skills was needed;
- groups should be kept small (maximum four);
- audio work is quicker to learn and produce;
- avoid over-stressing student evidence, e.g. action planning is not necessary for all tasks;
- deadlines are extremely important for planning; students cannot get a high grade if they are missed.

An OFSTED evaluation of the introduction of GNVQs noted the following key points:

- the delivery of Core Skills Units needed further planning;
- teachers sometimes lacked recent and relevant industrial experience; access to industrial placements is needed;
- some teachers had insufficient understanding of the internal assessment and verification procedures which the awarding bodies require;
- recording and assessment systems were not always satisfactory;
- more emphasis needed to be placed on individual action planning as a basis for planning future targets;
- students needed more guidance on the management of portfolios;
- staff were not always clear on the grading criteria;
- the guidance needs of students entering GNVQ programmes are substantial.

Despite the administrative demands of GNVQ, there are opportunities for constructing a stimulating course which encourages cross-curricular links, for example with Art departments and Business Studies courses, as well as greater pupil autonomy. *GNVQ Media: 1 A Beginner's Guide, 2 Work in Progress* (*English and Media Magazine*, No.32, Summer 1995, pp. 35–39) is a highly informative article by Tricia Jenkins of the LFDVA who has been closely involved in the development of these courses.

GCSE, AS and A Level Media Studies

The examination boards for GCSE are the Southern Examining Group (SEG) and the Midland Examining Group (MEG) which starts its course in 1997. The A Level examination boards are also ones with established courses – the Welsh Joint Education Committee (WJEC) and the University of Cambridge Local Examinations Syndicate (UCLES), and newer courses – the Northern Examination Board (NEAB) and the Associated Examination Board (AEB). It must be noted that some examination boards are in advanced stages of negotiating mergers. The 16–19 curriculum is the latest to undergo review by Sir Ron Dearing's committee (see *The New Qualifications Framework 16–19 Revised Version February 1997*). Therefore, it is important to read the following comments in the light of impending changes to the structures of the courses, the most significant of which is the introduction of the AS Level: 'All A Levels will consist of the AS (Advanced Subsidiary) as the first half of the course, and the second half of the course will be known as A2 . . . so that the two can be taught together' (Dearing, 1997).

You will find that both GCSE and A Level syllabuses state that their overall aims are to engender critical autonomy, conceptual understanding, creative engagement and practical production skills. In order to plan schemes of work to achieve these laudable aims, you need to be very clear about what you want the pupils to learn and why, in terms of knowledge, study and technical skills. You will need to set graduated specific tasks to build up skills and confidence over the two years, or one year in the case of post–16 GCSE. The following suggested list of skills is a general one which you can select or adapt as appropriate to the level or syllabus. Pupils need to be:

- keeping themselves informed about current media issues; collecting materials from their own viewing, reading and listening;
- developing observant, detailed reading of media texts;
- learning and using theories, debates and terminology;
- contributing to class and group discussion;
- writing clear, detailed, succinct notes which can be used for planning practical work, essays and for revision;
- reading independently: selecting relevant information, recording key points in their own words, recording quotations;
- writing well-structured discursive essays in a clear, detailed and succinct style;
- illustrating their arguments with examples, case studies, quotations and references;
- learning technical skills associated with at least two media, for example audio, video and DTP;
- taking responsibility for the organisation of their productions, including research and planning;
- making products to the best of their ability;
- ensuring the products are used to explore media concepts;
- writing clear, succinct critical commentaries which use terminology and are well-focused around theory, concepts and debates;
- participating co-operatively in group work;
- working independently in individual tasks and seeking support when necessary.

There are not necessarily better or worse syllabuses: the choice lies in what suits your educational philosophy, your department's resources, and your school's action plans. You should send off for all of the syllabuses, support and exemplar materials, and past examination papers. When you look at the documentation, elements to consider are:

- the amount of practical work;
- the quality and quantity of support materials;
- what teacher support is offered;
- how supportive is the administration;
- the ratio of exam board/teacher examination marking;
- where there is practical criticism, what is the quality of reproduced materials;
- the clarity of examination questions;

- whether the examination questions reflect the syllabus requirements;
- whether you prefer a linear or modular structure to the course;
- does the GCSE syllabus offer opportunities for a range of activities to be included in the coursework and the examination?

All syllabuses are based around the basic media concepts of Image Analysis/Media Language, Institution, Representation, Genre, Audience as well as others which include Realism, Narrative Structures, Fiction and Non-Fiction. You need to ensure that you cover the range of concepts adequately. You may wish to concentrate on one for an area of study, e.g. Representation in advertising. You can also construct areas of study which explore several concepts: for example, the construction of image in relation to music genres; how audiences are constructed for music artists via other media; representation of gender and race in mainstream and independent music sectors; an institutional comparison of major, independent and alternative record companies.

Your starting point for planning schemes of work should be conceptual, choosing texts which will be fertile ground for such exploration, and which are accessible for the pupils at their examination level. The concepts should be seen as opportunities for exploration rather than as absolutes to be learned. There should be intellectual rigour via a wish to explore complexities rather than succumbing to reductive over-simplification. This approach is applicable to GCSE level, though obviously you will gauge what levels of complexity the pupils can deal with; in the example above of Representation in advertising, learning about stereotypes should include discussion of their positive aspects as well as negative. While it is necessary to establish what 'genre' is, for example via identifying the generic conventions of films and television programmes, this is merely the starting point for exploring how genre is not a descriptive term but a convenient institutional and audience shorthand.

You can use case studies to show how genre is problematic: how would you classify *Blazing Saddles*, *Westworld* or *Posse*? How genre is useful for marketing (look at a range of extracts from film and/or posters, extracts from film review programmes on TV). Look at the relationship of genre to audience and institution, for instance how films are positioned in different genres for different audiences (e.g. *Fargo* was marketed as a thriller in America but as a black comedy in Europe, and *Men Behaving Badly* was transformed for an American audience). How is genre useful for audience expectations and pleasures; how is it useful for production and distribution companies to decide what films, TV programmes or music artists to finance and develop? Such considerations offer a range of learning activities.

Pupils can undertake their own audience research, present and analyse their findings, produce treatments and other planning work. They could be given treatments of proposed films or television programmes and select one they would develop in the light of researching target audience tastes and institutional policies. After finding publicity photographs in magazines of music artists from a range of genres, pupils can annotate them with detailed image and contextual analysis to establish how their images are constructed for target audiences. Research of cinema-going, past and present, could lead to proposals for a new cinema and programming for it.

Outcomes are obviously dictated by syllabus requirements. It is essential to drop the English assumption of outcomes meaning analytical or creative *essays*. Essays are but one of a range of outcomes. SEG embodies this explicitly in the tasks for their examination, as do MEG in their Paper 2 and Coursework options; SEG also implicitly advocates a liberal interpretation of coursework *word* limits as meaning essays, schedules, research findings, artefacts such as extracts from newspapers, magazines and so on. MEG also encourages critical autonomy via preparation for its *Paper 1: Unseen Text*. As you can see, learning through the study of concepts, debates, terminology and practical work, as well as developing knowledge, are the tools of GCSE Media Studies teaching, not just reading written, visual and sound images and then writing about them.

Much of what has been said already in the sections on practical work, general comments and GCSE activities above apply to A Level. The main difference is the increased amount, complexity and depth of knowledge about texts, areas of study, theory, debates and terminology. The Key Stage 4 course allows more time for student-centred activities, whereas the difficulty of some A Level work and, in many places, the steadily increasing class sizes, have considerable implications.

Some argue that, in the attempt to be accepted in the hierarchy of intellectual credibility, the intellectual rigour of A Level Media Studies syllabuses appears much greater than many other courses. The following points are worth considering before you embark on A Level Media teaching. Learning bodies of knowledge, for example about the Hollywood studio system 1930–1959, poses the challenge of how to make that history vibrant. Learning about economic determinants in the record industry threatens to deaden a potentially engaging area of study. Debating the theories of hegemony and pluralism in the news could see off the last vestige of enthusiasm in the most earnest pupil. How are non-Hindi speaking pupils going to engage with a three-hour film with subtitles? How do you make them care what Propp, Todorov or Lévi-Strauss had to say about narrative structure? They should read primary sources, but as the language is often difficult, how do you make it accessible? How do you teach 25 pupils to use the equipment? How do they and you develop their *critical autonomy* (Masterman, 1985).

Teacher-led activities may feature more at A Level, as will the need to engender sound scholarly habits, especially for independent research; however, you should not feel overwhelmed by the need to 'deliver the curriculum' or to just 'explain' apparently difficult theory. Critical autonomy is cultivated by stimulating the pupil's urge to be curious, to find out for him or herself; this is the basis for the analytical level required for a good A Level grade. The range of teaching methods indicated for GCSE should be part of your repertoire for A Level. Collating newspaper front pages or TV news programme running orders invites discussion of news values, target audiences, selection and construction, bias or impartiality, advertisers, representation, narrative construction. Carefully prepared role play with a film production company making pitches to a major and a smaller distribution company; or music artists and their manager discussing the terms of possible contracts with a major and an indie company, give stimulating insights into the economic determinants of those industries.

For the purposes of independent reading, note-making, essay writing, revision and practical work, research, planning and commentaries you can organise role play, research and paperwork. Both the film production and distribution companies form their plans after researching from material provided by you and them, about the current trends in the Hollywood film industry. The film producers attend the meeting with a package containing a treatment, selling points such as proposed stars and director, a draft budget and how their film will appeal to the target audience. The distributors could have a year plan containing research on what film genres are currently popular, whether they want to fund a few blockbusters or several smaller projects, who the 'A-List' stars and directors are, which companies are interested in product placement, possible tie-ins with other companies in the conglomerate, which audiences go to the cinema. The issues raised during the meeting could be recorded in the form of minutes and decisions based on the advantages and disadvantages of each organisation. As half the students will be on one side and half on the other, the documents could be photocopied, or students could feed back to each other their viewpoints. These are just a few ideas to show how you can be imaginative, focused and academic in the aims of your A Level Media Studies teaching.

IS IT ENGLISH?

In its consultation document *Standards for the Award of Qualified Teacher Status* (1997), the Teacher Training Agency proposes :

> a requirement for all new teachers, regardless of phase or subject, to have a sound knowledge of Information Technology (IT) (level 8 of pupils' National Curriculum) and of its contribution to their specialist subject(s).

As a student teacher, therefore, you are required to develop your IT skills in two ways: for personal use and to enable pupil learning. Of course, the

TASK 9.3   IT SKILLS AUDIT

No doubt your ITE course provides opportunities for the
development of your IT skills. It is the Teacher Training Agency's
intention that all student teachers show evidence of progression in
their IT capability, so at whatever level you begin your course you
are expected to improve. The following checklist may be used to
assess your current capability and to create an action plan for
development.

IT skills	Aspects developed Level of knowledge/competence (1 very Good – 3 Basic)	Aspects in need of development	Strategies to enable development
Word processing			
DTP			
Spreadsheet/ database			
CD-ROM			
Curriculum packages			
Electronic mail			
Internet			

When you have completed your audit, discuss with your tutor
or mentor in school opportunities and strategies for
development.

two are inextricably linked. Developing your own word processing or Desk Top Publishing (DTP) skills will not only enable you to produce high quality assignments required by your teacher education course, or to produce a professional looking *curriculum vitae*, but also you will be able to produce interesting and motivating classroom materials to engage your pupils.

IT and the National Curriculum

Since the early 1980s and, in particular, after the introduction of the National Curriculum, IT has developed as part of the curriculum offer of schools. However, in the early days, perhaps more emphasis was placed upon the *technology* as opposed to the *information*, which led to IT work being separated from many subjects. Computer networks tended to be located in the Maths or Business Studies departments, whose pupils tended to have first priority of access. Many teachers of English found it difficult to gain access and, as a consequence, pupils came to regard the use of computers as something out of the ordinary or special, rather than as central to work in English. Obviously, pupils do need to develop keyboard skills, but for your pupils to be fully prepared for the demands of the next century it is clear that emphasis should be placed upon the *information*: that is, computers should be seen as being as much a part of everyday English as is the ball-point pen, the worksheet or textbook, when it comes to working in class. Therefore, as part of the strategies you use for the development of your own IT capability, you should be looking for opportunities for using IT, not only in the preparation and planning of your lessons, but as a part of your ongoing work in the classroom.

IT has much to offer your pupils in the English classroom. IT in English:

- improves the quality of content and form of what pupils produce;
- supports the processes of drafting;
- has much to offer the quality of pupil talk and the nature of discussion;
- offers *real* publishing opportunities;
- enables pupils to operate in a range of genres;
- enables pupils to communicate with a variety of audiences both in school and the wider community (and via e-mail and the Internet, across the country and world);
- benefits those pupils who have problems with writing, as their final drafts will look as good as work produced by any other pupils, thereby increasing their self-esteem.

The rest of this chapter considers some of the ways in which you might begin to use IT as part of your work in the classroom. It takes for granted that you will endeavour to develop your own presentation skills via IT.

Similarly, in a chapter of this length, it would be impossible to cover the whole range of opportunities. Rather, the suggestions here should be seen as the basic minimum. You should seek ways to develop your own knowledge, understanding and skills in IT by referring to the texts recommended at the end of this chapter; through investigation in your school and HEI; through observation and discussion with student teachers, tutors and mentors and by using computer packages every day. The NCET website listed in Further Reading at the end of this chapter is an invaluable source of ideas for use in the English classroom that can be downloaded and printed out.

Writing

> The essential factor . . . is that the writing process changes when we use the computer as a tool . . . Children do not only write more with computers, they write differently . . . Where so many of us misunderstood word processors when they first appeared in the classrooms was seeing them as devices which related to what had gone before, such as the typewriter and the printing press. Word processing is not copy typing followed by printing, but a revising and drafting activity.
>
> (Abbott, 1995, p. 136)

You should not feel that only the most up-to-date package is of use in the classroom, or that only one particular word processing program can be used. It is important to recognise the power of basic facilities which are common to all word processing packages: facilities which allow you to:

- *cut* and *paste* blocks of text;
- insert new text at any point of document;
- *search* and *replace* words or phrases;
- check spelling (and increasingly grammar and style).

Much of the time spent in redrafting handwritten work involves pupils in copying out what was good in the first place: a chore that is unnecessary with a word processor. Now, pupils can move whole blocks of text, reshape and resequence stories using cut and paste. They can search and replace to change the tone, mood and genre of writing; explore issues related to KAL by searching and replacing nouns and adjectives – try using this facility to change the tense of a story, or a character from male to female by replacing *his* with *her* and the anomalies provide a very real context for grammar work. Abbott (1995) notes how some writers have suggested that engaging in the practices of word processing 'alters the thinking processes involved with writing, so that the person involved thinks in blocks of meaning rather than in individual words or ideas'.

Notions of correctness

The debates in the 1960s and 1970s about whether pupils should be allowed to use calculators in maths resurfaced in relation to the use of spellchecking facilities in the English classroom. Somehow these technological aids were seen as 'cheating'. Worries were expressed about pupils' abilities to spell, which would be eroded if pupils used word processing packages. In reality, of course, pupils still do not have unlimited access to computers; but you might want to discuss with your mentor the English department's policy towards word processed homework, or the examination board's regulations related to the number of pieces of word processed coursework which may be submitted. However, you should be aware, and you should make your pupils aware, of the need to proof-read any word processed work as computers are still very 'stupid' things. Spellcheckers do not read work for sense, only for word structure: not even for words, but for 'strings'. Therefore, they will not distinguish between *from* typed instead of *form*, *there* for *their*, *were* for *we're*, *it's* for *its* and so on. Provided a match is found in the software package's dictionary, it will be accepted. And if the word processor's dictionary does not recognise a word at all, it will be unable to suggest alternatives. But even the limitations of the word processor's dictionary can be a useful opportunity for KAL work, as many of them use American English and will suggest substituting, for example *color* or *center* for the UK equivalents. In many ways, therefore, the debate about spellchecking and spelling is a red herring. However, those word processing packages that include a thesaurus can enable pupils to use, search for alternative and replace synonyms in their work with ease and enjoyment.

To begin with, you might wish to introduce year 7 pupils to short, structured pieces of writing, which do not demand much keyboard expertise on their part. The mini saga, a complete story written in exactly fifty words including the title, can be a motivating starting point for pupils new to word processing and develop a number of writing skills. The *word count* facility enables them, and you, quickly to check how close they are to their target.

For poetry work, the haiku or even the limerick can be structured, clearly constrained starting points. Similarly, a file containing the topic sentences of six paragraphs to which pupils add further sentences can be useful for work on paragraphs. Although all pupils have the same starting points, their results can be vey different. Pupils enjoy being able quickly to share the very different outcomes of such 'paragraph work' with their classmates. Similarly, providing them with a short story or news report which they change in mood, location, genre, stance using *search* and *replace* produces excellent results. Such an approach can be used to effect to support work based on *Changing Stories* (NATE/English and Media Centre).

Reading

For reluctant readers, or those who have difficulty reading in KS3, the increasing development of CD-ROM interactive books – the *Living Books* series for example – and the development of word processors with a speech facility for reading text, have real potential for motivating and supporting pupils. Simulation programs provide opportunities for both reading and writing. Perhaps one of the most powerful programs for English teachers is *Developing Tray* (*DevTray*) developed by English teacher Bob Moy and the Inner London Educational Computing Centre in the 1980s. The beauty of *DevTray* is that it is an extremely 'teacher friendly' suite of programs, which provides a skeleton structure into which you can type any text you wish to use with a class. *DevTray* involves pupils in creating the meaning of the partial text in front of them and in getting into the *deep structures* of the text. Using the program to investigate texts which are being read as class readers, or for GCSE or A Level, involve pupils in a detailed, active investigation of the text which is difficult to sustain in any other way. *DevTray* can be used by the teacher with one computer via a large screen monitor (a boon when computer resources are limited) or by individuals, or groups of pupils in a network room. You might wish to see if there is a copy on the program in school and to acquaint yourself with it.

The proliferation of CD-ROM packages has seen the increase in the availability of information packages, in particular encyclopaedias, dictionaries, texts and, more recently, interactive non-fiction texts of the kind produced by Dorling Kindersley, and much more interactive texts based upon GCSE and A Level set texts. These newer texts are more sophisticated, much more interactive, including related video and audio capabilities. As well as allowing pupils to search, cut and paste and save material for research and assignment purposes, they enable pupils to read in a different way. This different form of reading is also typical of reading texts on the Internet, which, like CD-ROMs, allows pupils to read *laterally*,

---

TASK 9.4   TO THE INTERNET AND BEYOND

In preparation for your work in class, with the help of your placement school's network manager, spend some time familiarising yourself with the Internet. Using the *Help* facility of a *search* engine, find out how to search for topics related to English, or aspects of English you might be studying with pupils. Find out how to *bookmark* particular website addresses. You can then save these bookmarks and provide pupils with them to begin their exploration of the Internet. Find out how it is possible to download and print information from any website address.

In relation to e-mail, you will find many schools throughout the world on the Internet. Setting up links with such schools via e-mail will enable your pupils to communicate with and genuinely publish their work to pupils around the world. Pupils also find it interesting to realise that the latest communication they receive from Australia was written while they were asleep, or that the pupils in the US to whom they are writing are sound asleep, while they are in school. Unfortunately, however, the dominance of the English language in e-mail and the Internet, recently taken to task by the French, means that there is little opportunity for pupils whose first language is not English to communicate in their first language except via faxes constructed using multilingual word processing software, such as *Allwrite*. The quality of transmission can also be disappointingly inferior when one compares fax with e-mail print outs.

rather than in a *linear* fashion. By using *hot* words or Hyper Text Media Language (HTML) links, pupils starting at exactly the same points can travel across related topics of interest to create webs of meaning very different from the structure imposed by a printed linear text. Visit the NCET home page (http://www.ncet.org.uk) to see an excellent and comprehensive directory of educational CD-ROM reviews.

Speaking and listening

The computer is an effective catalyst of talk both at the screen and away from it. . .Of particular interest is the talk which takes place at the computer screen, for it can differ significantly from small group talk in other contexts. . .While some aspects of computer-stimulated talk will be recognisable as characteristic of small group talk in any context, others arise as a direct result of the children's response to the resource.

(Kemeny, 1990, p. 7)

The series of case studies reported in *Talking IT Through* (Kemeny, 1990) were a result of research conducted jointly by the National Oracy Project (NOP) and the National Council for Educational Technology (NCET) based in Coventry. The report shows clearly the benefits of using IT in the classroom to promote and enhance the quality of talk in a variety of contexts. 'One consistent and powerful observation . . . is that speaking and listening *arise naturally and purposefully at every stage of learning in the classroom'* (p. 2, emphasis original author's). Earlier in this book Chapter 5 has shown in detail how Speaking and Listening may be approached in the English classroom; you might wish to consider how some of the approaches described in it might be developed further using IT.

However, there are real management questions to raise if you use a computer network room for your IT-related lessons. The first relates to access. Discuss with your mentor the possiblity of gaining access to the computer network room. You need to remember that, to be effective, the use of IT needs to be more than the 'one off' lesson: it should be built into a series of lessons, either on a regular weekly basis, or as part of a sequential block of lessons. Therefore, when planning a scheme of work involving IT, the first thing you need to do is to check availability of the hardware. The second relates to classroom organisation, as it is unlikely that the network room will be laid out in the same manner as an English classroom.

Figure 9.3 shows the traditional layout of the computer network room. Computers tend to be arranged around the walls of the room to be connected to the electrical conduiting and two seats are placed in front of the keyboard. With such a layout, the best you might hope for is paired talk: at worst you will get elbow nudging as the pair of pupils tussle for

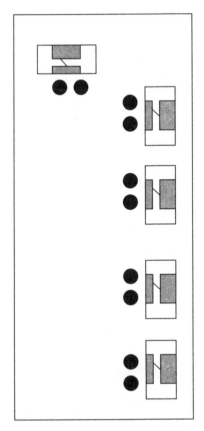

Figure 9.3 Traditional network methodology

Figure 9.4 An English approach

control of the keyboard. Especially in such a situation, if you are placed in a mixed school, you might want to consider having single-sex pairs at the computer. If you are given permission to be more creative in the network room, you should attempt to replicate the kind of seating arrangements you might use for groupwork in the English classroom.

Figure 9.4 shows how this might be achieved by placing another table at ninety degrees to the one bearing the computer. Most computer keyboards are attached by a flex of well over a metre in length which allows it to be placed in the middle of the adjacent table. Placing three seats around the second table allows not only more equal access to the keyboard, but also more closely replicates groupwork in the English classroom. The slightly more distanced screen becomes a focus for discussion, rather than an object of possession. Such an arrangement has the added benefit of allowing more pupils to use fewer machines. Of course, unless the English department has its own dedicated computer room, it does require you to make the necessary arrangements before, and rearrange the room after, any lesson in which you might use this approach. However, the significant improvements in the quality of pupil experience are worth the effort.

SUMMARY AND KEY POINTS

This chapter has explored the ways in which Media and IT work should be seen as central to what might be considered good practice in English teaching. It is clear that pupils come to school from homes which are inextricably linked to all forms of media and technology: radio, television, satellite and cable, e-mail and the Internet, camcorders, personal computers and video games. It is likely that as they grow, they will experience forms of media and communication technology impossible to visualise at present. It is salutary to remember that even Arthur C. Clarke did not forsee fax and e-mail technology in the world of *2001*. English teachers have the dual reponsibility of enabling pupils to develop a sense of their place, to develop a voice in the world in which they find themselves, but also to develop the skills, qualities and attributes which will support them in the culture of the next century.

FURTHER READING

Branston, R. and Stafford, R. (1996) *The Media Student's Book*, London: Routledge.
A key textbook to support the teaching of GCSE Media Studies.

Davison, J. and Grahame, J. (1992) *Media Directory*, Sheffield: NATE/ English and Media Centre.
Although media education publishing has boomed in the past few years, this book contains extensive details of key media texts to support teachers and pupils in all facets of the media. Particularly useful are the details of

seminal texts, which might not be in print, but which can be located in libraries.

Grahame, J. (1990) *The English Curriculum: Media,* Sheffield: NATE/ English and Media Centre.
A comprehensive introduction to media education for English teachers. The book covers a complete range of approaches to support media work at KS3, from ways in which to incorporate media work into established English practice, to ideas for stand-alone media units. The book also includes a list of useful addresses.

Grahame, J. (1993) *Advertising,* Sheffield: NATE/English and Media Centre.
An invaluable award-winning video and pack of photocopiable materials to support work advertising in English and Media Studies from KS3 to A Level. Essential for every English department.

Kemeny, H. (ed.) (1990) *Talking IT Through,* Coventry: NCET.
This publication appeared as a result of a collaboration between NCET and NOP. It considers a range of issues related to supporting talking and learning with IT. Although it is not exclusively limited to a consideration of the English classroom, there is much here that will provide a context for a consideration of IT and Speaking and Listening.

National Centre for Educational Technology (1991) *Language Learning and IT* – a series of four books:
Minns, H. *Primary Practice*; Sealey, A. *Language in Context*; Keith, G. *Knowledge about Language*; Lynch, W. *Planning for Language.*
These books contain a series of case studies of language-related IT work and are a useful introduction to the variety of ways in which IT might be used in the classroom.

You will find the following Websites worth visiting:

English and Media Centre
http://www.rmplc.conk/orgs/emedia/index.html

National Council for Educational Technology (NCET)
http://www.ncet.org.uk/publications/approach/english/intro.html

Scottish Council for Educational Technology (SCET)
http://www.scet.org.uk/scethome.html

10 Drama

INTRODUCTION

If you already know that drama teaching is a distinct and complex skill, that it is possible to train as a specialist drama teacher, and that some secondary schools have separate drama departments, you may wonder why this book contains a chapter on teaching drama. Firstly, it is the case that *English in the National Curriculum* (DFE, 1995) places considerable emphasis on drama: all English teachers have a legal responsibility both to use practical drama methods in a substantial part of their teaching and to stimulate pupils to create and respond to drama texts. Secondly, very much of the drama teaching which goes beyond these requirements is, in practice, undertaken by teachers who have trained primarily as English specialists. Indeed, many English teachers find that the special opportunities of drama both enrich their professional experience, and allow them to challenge and develop their pupils in ways which are excitingly different from those available to them using other parts of their teaching repertoire. It is important that this book should make you aware of both the responsibility that English teachers have to teach drama, and the opportunities that this responsibility gives them. However, this chapter can only be a starting point: the suggestions for further reading at the end of it will point you to a number of important book-length studies which will help you to develop your theoretical and practical knowledge.

OBJECTIVES

By the end of this chapter, you should:

- be able to assess the rationale which underpins the drama teaching in your placement school;
- understand how to create the working conditions for 'risk-taking' drama;
- understand a range of drama teaching methods and their applications.

DRAMA AND THE NATIONAL CURRICULUM FOR ENGLISH

Drama is given considerable emphasis in *English in the National Curriculum* (DFE, 1995). This is particularly noticeable if you compare this document with the old, 1990, National Curriculum Orders. In order to meet the requirements for Speaking and Listening, English teachers now have to provide pupils at Key Stages 3 and 4 with opportunities to take part in a wide range of practical drama activities. Plays are foregrounded in the list of genres to be covered in the Programme of Study for Reading. Scriptwriting is emphasised as much as narrative and poetry in the Writing requirements.

However, *English in the National Curriculum* does not propose a rationale for drama, either as part of the integrated programme of Speaking and Listening, Reading and Writing which is the core requirement of the English Programmes of Study, or as a distinct curriculum subject with its own integrity. If we search the document to establish to what extent work in drama is intended to support the development of other skills and knowledge in English, and to what extent discrete drama skills should be developed, we find very little direction: in fact, drama is not mentioned at all in the General Requirements for English. If we seek guidance on what progression in pupil achievement in drama might be about, we find drama mentioned just once in the Level Descriptions.

Some statements about drama in the Programmes of Study seem to be intended to emphasise ways in which drama should primarily support learning in areas of the English curriculum which are given higher priority: for example, 'In role-play and drama, the vocabulary, structures and tone appropriate to such contexts should be explored' (18, 3a). The *emphasis* here is on using drama to support language study. However, there are some statements which indicate that drama is seen as consisting of a set of activities and conventions worth exploring in their own right: for example, 'In responding to drama, [pupils] should be given opportunities to consider significant features of their own and others' performances' (17, 1d).

Many drama activities can be interpreted so that emphasis is placed either on their function in developing language or on the possibilities of drama as an art form. For example, one teacher might describe 'role play' as an activity in which pupils adopt the attitudes of people with particular roles in society, to consider topics and issues from a number of different perspectives. She might point to the example of some Year 10 pupils who are discussing the rail transportation of nuclear waste. They are working in pairs sitting at their desks with cue cards which describe respectively some of the viewpoints of a Greenpeace activist and a spokesperson for British Nuclear Fuels, and arguing with each other in these roles. The planned outcome is a piece of persuasive writing, such as a pamphlet to be distributed to members of the public.

Another teacher might describe role play as an activity in which pupils explore the tensions between personal identity and public roles through the processes of experimental drama. She might point to the example of Year 7 pupils engaged in a whole-class spontaneous improvisation of a sea voyage in which the vessel is about to be wrecked and there are a limited number of lifeboats. The pupils are exploring roles such as those of captain, ship's cook and child passenger. Within limits imposed by their roles, each pupil is interacting with many other members of the group. This work may lead to the development of a polished improvisation for presentation to another class, in which costume, props and lighting would be used, but it is also possible that the teacher's objectives for the class will be met entirely through the improvisation.

The kind of drama work which it would be appropriate for a student teacher to introduce to these two classes would be very different. A school or individual teacher's rationale for drama, especially as this is represented by the previous experiences of pupils and the resources available, must guide the direction of the drama teaching which a student teacher initially attempts with any particular class. In the next part of this chapter the characteristics of rationales for drama as part of 'integrated English' and 'as a creative art' will be further explored.

A rationale for drama in an integrated English programme

One kind of rationale for drama hinted at in *English in the National Curriculum* is based on recognition of the contribution drama methods make to the development of pupils' skills in each of Speaking and Listening, Reading and Writing. Drama's role in supporting speaking and listening has been long recognised. For example, in *A Language for Life* (DES, 1975, p. 159), it is argued that: 'Drama . . . has the capacity for sensitizing the ear for appropriate registers and responses. It encourages linguistic adaptability, often accustoming the children to unfamiliar modes of language.' Pupils' engagement in the dramatisation of parts of literary texts, whether originally plays or not, is understood to help develop their reading responses, such as their ability to analyse plot and character. In a similar way, it can be argued that improvisation exploring familiar or unfamiliar situations provides a stimulus for writing which is powerful in its capacity to generate vocabulary for dialogue and ideas for narrative. The concept of integrated practice can be extended to incorporate work on the media and using IT. Drama work which allows pupils to make use of the conventions of various media genres, for example, factitious reconstructions, can develop insight into media concepts, such as representation, as well as giving them a structure for the drama itself. Software is now available which stimulates and structures drama experiences and also provides pupils with opportunities to explore some uses of IT in communication. Goodwyn gives some examples of this in *Move Back the Desks* (NATE, 1993).

In much of the best practice linking drama with other parts of the English curriculum, drama does not simply act in a service capacity. Instead, the skills, knowledge and practices of drama are developed together with the core processes of English in dynamic, integrated learning experiences. Where this integration is achieved, pupils who are habitually engaged in making, presenting, remaking and responding to texts in their English lessons learn to use drama as one of the methods available to them for the development and testing of ideas. Pupils engaged in drama activities learn to turn easily to print, media and IT texts for stimuli, and use writing to help explore their ideas for drama with the same confidence. An 'integrated English' rationale for drama emphasises that it develops a wide range of language skills as well as knowledge and understanding of a genre of literary texts. It also implies that progression and continuity will be most sustained when drama is fully integrated in the teaching and learning that takes place in English lessons.

TASK 10.1 DRAMA AND KEY SKILLS

Working in a small group, examine the 'Key Skills' sections of *English in the National Curriculum*'s Key Stage 3 and 4 Programmes of Study and discuss which of the skills identified could be developed using drama and how. Make a list of practical suggestions and share your ideas with other groups. Return to this task when you have read the rest of this chapter and consulted the Further Reading, and see what additions you can make.

A rationale for drama as an arts subject

Partly because of the comparatively low status of drama in the National Curriculum as a whole, and the limited recognition of its possibilities in the first *English in the National Curriculum* (DES and Welsh Office, 1990), the Arts Council published its *Drama in Schools: Arts Council Guidance on Drama Education* in 1992. This document offers a rationale for drama as an arts subject in its own right and also considers ways in which drama can contribute to learning across the curriculum. The guidance acknowledges that English departments carry much responsibility for drama teaching, and recognises that they often use drama primarily to promote language development and enhance literary analysis. However, it insists that effective drama teaching must draw attention to the special character of drama experiences and drama texts. For example, the Guidance argues: 'Making and performing drama . . . is fundamental to drama in schools.' Also, 'It is important that the study of plays as dramatic literature in English at the same time recognises their essential existence as pieces of live theatre' (Arts Council, 1992, paras 5, 8).

Most importantly, *Drama in Schools* proposes a National Curriculum for drama, centred, like the English curriculum, on three core processes. The processes are all primarily concerned with developing pupils' knowledge and experience of the unique characteristics of drama:

Making drama is the ability to generate and shape dramatic forms in order to explore and express ideas;
Performing drama is the ability to engage and communicate with an audience in a dramatic presentation;
Responding to drama is the ability to express understanding, discernment and appreciation of drama in all its forms.

(Arts Council, 1992, para. 8)

These processes are interpreted in Programmes of Study for each Key Stage. At Key Stage 3:

Pupils should be taught to:

- Use increasingly complex drama styles and conventions;
- Respond constructively to direction given by other pupils;
- Use a variety of technical effects;
- Devise and perform plays in different styles;
- Edit and refine their work in the light of constructive criticism
- Develop voice and movement skills, including mime;
- Understand drama from different cultures and times;
- Analyse and evaluate performances with an understanding of style and purpose.

Pupils should be given opportunities to:

- Develop themes from other curriculum areas in drama;
- Read and perform plays from different cultures and times;
- Take part in plays as actors or technicians;
- Learn how drama has developed through the ages;
- See a range of professional performances;
- Evaluate performances using appropriate specialist vocabulary.

(Arts Council, 1992, para. 20)

This Programme of Study affirms: that drama has its own skills, conventions and language; that, as a creative art, it stimulates the development of personal, social, cultural and aesthetic understandings which are vital to the wellbeing of a mature individual; that it makes reference to an historically rich and culturally diverse body of texts and practices; and that its explorations require access to appropriate working spaces and technical resources, such as studios equipped with stage lighting. The Programme of Study also implies that progression and continuity will be most sustained when substantial dedicated curriculum time and resources are available.

Determining a school's rationale for drama

Before you begin to teach drama in a placement school, it is very important for you to establish what kind of rationale underpins its drama teaching, and how this will have influenced pupil expectations and perceptions of drama work. You may find evidence of a rationale which is similar to one of those described above, or which combines elements of both of these, or you may find entirely different thinking.

Some examples of perceptions of drama you may encounter are as follows. A school with an 'adult needs' view of drama will tend to justify the drama curriculum in terms of its development of skills which are transferable to the world of work. As *English for Ages 5 to 16* (DES and Welsh Office, 1989, 8.13) put it: 'Drama provides a discipline for the development of co-ordination, concentration, commitment, organisation and decision-making that depends upon self and group awareness, observation, imagination and co-operation.' Very many teachers see drama's development of these skills as of at least equal importance to its role in developing language or aesthetic understanding.

In a school with a 'cross-curricular' view of drama, teachers in a range of subjects may use role play and other activities to support subject learning, and/or to explore moral, personal and social issues. Pupils may make frequent use of drama in activities such as year group assemblies. In a school with an integrated arts policy, drama may be incorporated in the curriculum time made available for 'expressive arts' or 'performing arts', and pupils may be particularly confident about creating multi-discipline art events.

TASK 10.2   A RATIONALE FOR DRAMA

Establish what kind of rationale underpins the teaching of drama in your placement school. Watch some drama lessons and use the questions which follow as a starting point in your discussions with teachers.

- Is there a scheme of work for drama at Key Stage 3 either within the English department or across the curriculum?
- Is drama taught as a separate subject, as part of an integrated arts programme, or within English?
- Are drama methods used by teachers across the curriculum?
- What resources and how much curriculum time are available for drama?

- What examination courses in drama are available to pupils?
- Are there regular school drama events, and if so, are these, for example, 'cultural heritage' school plays presented by élite casts, or experimental works and festivals involving large numbers of pupils across the age and ability range?

Although teachers' aims in educational drama are sufficiently diverse to allow for the very different interpretations of role play discussed earlier, in the next part of this chapter it will be argued that drama teachers should always work to provide a classroom environment and atmosphere, teaching strategies and lesson structures which make possible what may be called 'risk-taking' drama.

WORKING CONDITIONS FOR RISK-TAKING DRAMA

Anyone who makes a dramatic gesture takes a risk. The risk involves a person in exposing part of his or her understanding of and response to something, and in exploring or projecting this, with commitment, through an act of pretence. This act makes the actor extremely vulnerable to the responses of others, who, whether participants in the drama or observers of it, may reject what is offered because of what they consider to be poor understanding, poor projection or both. However, risk-taking is essential to any kind of educational drama which is not going to settle for superficial work such as the endless re-presentation of tired stereotypes in unchallenging exercises. All drama lessons should be planned to support the risk-taking that is expected of pupils. Some of the practical considerations which need to be taken into account to make risk-taking drama possible are as follows.

The classroom and resources

In a well-equipped drama studio, stage lighting, costume, props and stage blocks may be used to create the atmosphere of many different locations and so support pupils who are being asked to risk behaving other than as themselves in some other world than their own. These resources can and should be used to support drama development processes, as well as to contribute to the multi-sensory impact of performance work. In an ordinary classroom, it is usually possible at least to create an open working space by placing the desks against the four walls with the chairs in front of them, so making an inward facing rectangle. In these more difficult conditions, it is all the more important for the teacher to provide video clips, pictures, music, artefacts, documents or indications of costume, like hats, to help create the idea of the drama.

Such strategies can meaningfully compensate for the lack of more substantial resources. However, this is not to say that drama teachers should ever simply make do with poor accommodation. There are a number of severely limiting problems that teachers may encounter using ordinary classrooms for drama, including: insufficient space for movement, or for groups to work far enough apart to hear themselves; a 'fishbowl' effect during the presentation and sharing of work which may inhibit performers who have the sense of a large, very close audience. For these reasons, it is always important to make a case for the best room available, even if this is only the largest room in the English department suite.

Expectations and signals

Pupils gain confidence from knowing how their risk-taking will be supported by the teacher and the group. Expectations need to be discussed and sometimes negotiated openly, with their purposes being made explicit, although they need not all be introduced to a class new to drama at once. One important expectation is that all pupils in a group will be prepared to work with all others. This can usually be achieved with a new class if pupils have plenty of experience of changing partners and groups frequently for several lessons so that mutual trust is established before the expectation is explicitly defined. Another vital expectation is that pupils will respect each other's work when it is shared, both by listening and watching attentively and by offering constructive criticism when appropriate. It is important for teachers to ensure that sharing serves a useful purpose in the development of the whole group's work, so that attentiveness is encouraged, and that their own observations about shared work build from the identification of praiseworthy features. It is rarely useful to share all the work produced in a lesson: this can be repetitive and always counteracts momentum, so another expectation should be that all pupils will get opportunities to share their work, but on a longer timescale.

A clear set of signals for controlling the lesson and moving the drama on also contributes to the confidence necessary for risk-taking. Signals help the teacher to maintain pupil concentration by allowing rapid movement from one activity to another. This avoids lengthy, disruptive delays in which concentration is broken while pupils work out that something new is expected of them. A signal for silence is vital: the word 'freeze' which means 'stop immediately and hold whatever position you are now in' is useful because it gives teachers a number of options for continuing the work. For example, short pieces of new information can be added before all the 'frozen' pupils are asked to carry on an improvisation at the point at which it was left off. Alternatively, using the technique known as 'spotlighting', one group can be asked to carry on its improvisation while the rest of the class is invited to 'relax' and observe. 'Freeze' is valuable because it is more than a control word: it can be used to introduce pupils to the idea of the 'freeze frame', 'still photograph' or 'statue' which has many applications in drama. These include the identification of key moments in scenes, and the examination of the physical representation of the relationships between characters in a drama.

Drama routines

In general, the human capacity for risk-taking is enhanced when we have a strong sense of security. In drama, routines can make a powerful contribution to the establishment of a sense of security, as well as developing concentration through each pupil's association of a particular set of repeated actions with drama lessons. We must always remember that the expectations of drama are usually very different from those of the lesson pupils have just come from; drama routines help them to make the adjustment. For example, many teachers like to begin and end drama lessons with pupils sitting in a circle. Circles are useful for the democratic sharing of ideas: every member of the group can see and hear all the others, and everyone is in the front row. A number of warm-up activities and drama games use circles, which means that it is very easy to make transitions from discussion to activity. A circle can also provide a focused acting space. One use of it in the development of pupils' confidence about sharing work involves devising a flexible drama situation, set perhaps in a public space, which different characters can easily enter and leave. A rule is established that only three members of the class can be inside the circle at any one time, but with this constraint, pupils are allowed to enter or leave the circle at any time.

Group dynamics and the difficulty of the work

Although it is important for pupils to learn to work flexibly with all other members of the group, it is also important for the teacher to recognise that some of the confidence necessary to risk-taking comes from a person's trust in his or her working partners and audience, and that this will be affected by the difficulty and sensitivity of the work. For some activities it will be appropriate for pupils to work individually, following guidance or instructions from the teacher: for example, pupils who are unused to mime might follow a sequence of actions 'narrated' by the teacher, and concentrate more effectively without the self-consciousness which may be induced by apparently having an audience. Friendship pairs and small groups also provide pupils with security, and it can be a very big developmental step for some pupils to change to working in random groups or to kinds of drama which involve interacting with the whole class, at least for activities which are sustained for any length of time. Similarly, there is a big step for some pupils between, say, showing their pair work to another pair of pupils, and being able to present it to the whole class.

Sharing and reflection

Regularly stepping out of a situation in order to evaluate its progress and direction is another means by which human beings can develop the sense of security they need to be able to take risks within that situation. Some of the most valuable techniques for sharing and reflection in drama teaching provide security by generating ideas for the next stage of the development of the work. For example, 'hotseating', a technique in which actors are interviewed in role about their characters' motivation, intentions and relationships, provides a form of reflection on the drama which an actor can use to develop greater subtlety of characterisation.

TASK 10.3   OBSERVING DRAMA STRATEGIES

Observe some drama lessons and note how the teacher uses the classroom, resources, expectations, signals, drama routines, pupil groups, sharing and reflection to provide the foundations for risk-taking drama. After a lesson, ask the teacher to discuss with you the reasons behind the strategies you have observed.

The next part of this chapter is concerned with some of the working methods available to drama teachers. Rather than attempting to provide a handbook or index of working methods, it aims to consider some of the issues involved in choosing to use methods which appear to be primarily concerned either with developing drama techniques or with engaging pupils in making meaning through drama. Games, movement and mime exercises are discussed as an example of the former, and improvisation as an example of the latter.

DRAMA GAMES

If risk-taking drama is dependent on security, that security is partly dependent on trusting others. A Year 7 pupil who mimes passing a cup of tea to his or her partner trusts in that partner's acceptance of the dramatic gesture which has been made, and on the concentration which has made possible its recognition. Trust is partly about being able to take the risk of pretence with confidence in the capacity of others to concentrate and accept the pretence for what it is. Concentration depends on sensory alertness and attention, watching what other actors do, and listening to what they say. Acceptance makes the continuation of the drama possible.

Writers on drama games frequently make use of at least part of the argument of the last paragraph, maintaining that games contribute to the development of some of the essential drama skills of looking, listening, trust, attention and concentration. In her book *Drama Guidelines* (1977), Cecily O'Neill points out some other benefits: 'many games provide secure frameworks within which communication can easily be established. They are also a means of releasing tension, giving enjoyment, establishing relationships, and increasing the group's level of self-control.' However, when making use of games there are two very important considerations: one concerns the appropriateness of the games chosen, the second the relationship between the games and the rest of the drama work.

Clive Barker's book, *Theatre Games* (1977) provides a thorough and convincing rationale for the use of games in drama, and includes much useful discussion about the purposes of different games, and their influence on the work of a drama group. He stresses the need for the teacher or leader to choose games which match the developmental level of the group. This is important not least because some trust exercises in particular could be very dangerous if attempted by pupils with poor concentration. For example, a number of exercises require pupils to support each other physically or take responsibility for the safety of blindfolded partners. When leading a partner as a school pupil myself, I completely forgot he was blindfolded and walked him into a brick wall with rather bloody results.

The games which contribute most to learning will often be linked by the teacher to the topic of the drama lesson or scheme of work. One example of this from my own practice occurred when I made use of a simple cat and mouse game to develop some movement ideas for work on the story of Theseus and the Minotaur with some Year 7 pupils. In the game, the class forms a grid, and individual pupils join hands to form rows or columns, alternating on the instruction 'change', while one pupil as cat pursues another as mouse through the grid. The game clearly develops listening, watching and concentration skills. Playing it in slow motion and talking about how it works suggested how the class could work on using bodies to represent the Minotaur's labyrinth, and exposed some of the central themes of the story for them: power, fear, frustration, the subconscious, brain against brawn. You might now wish to plan a drama lesson in which you use games or exercises to introduce a topic in such a way that the games establish, develop or extend learning which is integral to your teaching and learning objectives.

MOVEMENT AND MIME EXERCISES

Movement and mime exercises can help pupils to develop an awareness of the physical resources available to them, and also provide them with a drama vocabulary to describe the quality of particular effects they have observed or are attempting to achieve. Progression can be achieved through the experience of increasingly subtle and complex exercises, but movement work, like games, is enriched by opportunities to make meanings.

Many teachers make use of a technical vocabulary to describe physical positions, which has as its starting point the word 'freeze' discussed above. When half a class is 'frozen', the others can be invited to describe the physical positions which their classmates have taken up, and the value of some shared terminology soon becomes apparent. A basic vocabulary might describe a physical position using the term 'level'. In a 'high level' freeze, part of the body will be in a position above head height; in a 'middle level' freeze, the most expressive part of the body will be between standing head height and standing waist height; in a 'low level' freeze, most of the body will be in a position below standing waist height.

If we want to progress from describing physical positions to movements, Bronwen Nicholls demonstrates in *Move* (1974) how pupils can be equipped with an increasingly sophisticated vocabulary. With an inexperienced class, you might begin by defining the pace and quality of movement respectively as 'fast' or 'slow' and 'smooth' or 'jerky'. This already creates the combinations, 'fast and jerky', 'fast and smooth', 'slow and jerky' and 'slow and smooth' and opens up the possibility of describing movements along two continuums (*Move*, 1974 pp. 10, 30).

With a more experienced class, it is possible to suggest an extended vocabulary for describing quality of movement, such as the following part of the Laban analysis (Figure 10.1):

It is possible to devise sequences of activities which explore quality of movement in a manner which is abstracted from any dramatic context, which makes use of pupils' interest in exploring space and in comparing

---

MOVEMENT		
THROUGH SPACE	can be DIRECT	or FLEXIBLE
IN TIME	can be FAST	or SLOW
WITH GRAVITY AWARENESS	can be STRONG/WEIGHTY	or LIGHT

Putting these three elements of movement together gives 8 EFFORT–ACTIONS:

Direct–slow–weighty	PRESS
Direct–fast–strong	KICK/PUNCH
Flexible–slow–weighty	WRING
Flexible–fast–strong	SLASH
Direct–fast–light	DAB
Flexible–fast–light	FLICK
Direct–slow–light	GLIDE
Flexible–slow–light	FLOAT

Figure 10.1 Qualities of movement
Source: adapted from Laban, 1948

and contrasting ways of using their bodies to achieve different kinds of dramatic effect. However, many pupils would benefit more from exploring fewer categories of movement in ways which related them to the exploration of a dramatic theme. For example, gliding movement could be developed in an exercise centred on the experience of weightlessness, as part of the preparation for improvisation work on space voyages. Thus, a technical vocabulary for an aspect of drama can be a source of ideas for teaching, even when not all of this language is shared with pupils.

Work on mime can lead to further progression in pupils' use of movement because it extends the range of dramatic gestures which it is possible to make using the body alone. Mime can provide a useful means of developing the physicality of any drama work, especially with pupils whose previous drama experience has focused on the verbal. Pupils with limited experience of movement work will sometimes show this by taking chairs with them and conducting any task they possibly can sitting down. When asked to develop a mime, they may also respond by miming a conversation. You might consider doing some work on mime with a class you observe behaving in this way.

Some books on educational drama argue that mime is limited in its capacity for character development and draws pupils towards atrocious stereotyping, and it is true that the knees-bending policeman is not dead. However, miming social experiences which already have powerful physical dimensions or ritualistic elements, such as home decorating, discos and weddings, can teach pupils to express the relationships between different characters and to develop narrative direction using an entirely physical language.

There is a technical vocabulary for mime which teachers can use, and teach pupils to help them describe their work. Some key terms are defined by Kay Hamblin, in *Mime* (1978), a book which is careful to present exercises in which technical understanding is developed in contexts which make use of imagined situations. Some examples include: 'snap', a sudden precise movement with a clear start and finish; 'neutral', a balanced position from which movements originate; and 'mask', a face which can be 'snapped into' from neutral. All of these concepts and techniques can also be incorporated in forms of drama in which speech and props are used.

Isolating different aspects of technique in drama can give pupils more control of later work in which they have more freedom and choice, because it gives them a repertoire of techniques to choose from. However, work on technique is likely to be most effective when it makes use of situations in which pupils can begin to make meaning. The next time you take drama, devise a lesson in which you incorporate some work which deliberately focuses on technique and extends pupils' vocabulary for talking about drama, but which also enables them to use the newly learned technique to make meaning.

IMPROVISATION

In contrast to drama games or movement and mime work, improvisation seems to be much more directly concerned with making meaning. Many drama teachers place improvisation at the heart of their practice for reasons which are closely linked to this. Improvisation is seen as fundamentally democratic, because it involves pupils in developing and using a range of negotiation and co-operation skills. It is also seen as empowering because it allows pupils to focus on the exploration and communication of their own ideas, by freeing them from subjection to the constraints involved in responding to texts or developing particular formal techniques.

However, these freedoms are dependent on the teacher providing strong support for the work. The key tasks of the teacher are: to provide pupils with a structure which supports the processes of negotiation and experimentation through which progress is made; to direct pupils to stimulating topics and ideas, for exploration through their drama; to guide the development of the work as drama, by alerting pupils to techniques they can make use of, and forms they can adopt and adapt.

When planning improvisation lessons, a key decision the teacher needs to make concerns the extent to which the work will be based on contexts which are familiar to the pupils. Pupils' own personal, social and cultural experiences are one very important source of ideas, not least because accessing these immediately gives them the role of experts and considerable control over the direction and outcome of the work. There are many methods by which teachers may help pupils to access these experiences, including discussion and writing tasks which stimulate memory, as well as through work which is more directly dramatic in character, such as bringing to life a real or imaginary photograph. Drama will nearly always require pupils to interpret even their most familiar experience in new ways, because the act of dramatisation will make them focus on the experience of characters other than themselves. However, pupils can be challenged to build the unfamiliar out of the familiar in numerous other ways. For example, known fictional characters may be placed in new situations, or drama may explore gaps in texts to account for what happens between two appearances of a character in a play. A further step is to create drama from situations which make few references to what pupils already know, using historical events, situations from different cultures, or pure fantasy. The further the work moves in this direction the more the teacher will have to do to provide contextualising information or some resources in which pupils can find it.

A second responsibility of the teacher is to provide guidance on the shaping of the drama. Such guidance may include some specific work on matters of technique which are important in all dramatic forms, for example: effective beginnings and endings; establishing the motivation for movement which takes place in the drama and communicating its meaning to an audience; making entrances and exits dramatically effective. It may also include work on the many dramatic forms and conventions pupils can adopt other than soap opera realism. For example, pupils working on comic plays could be introduced to some of the conventions of Shakespearean comedy, such as overhearings, disguise, confusions of identity, misplaced letters and malapropism.

It will sometimes be more appropriate to focus work on character development rather than dramatic structure. Security and confidence in character building can be supported by the use of role play exercises which establish attributes, qualities or habits in structured contexts. For example, in improvised interviews, pupils can experiment with the need for a character to speak and behave in a manner which is appropriate to the situation and yet 'in character'. The discoveries which are made can be fed into work which places the character in less structured situations. Another method of developing character is based on work on 'stock characters'. These may be contemporary stereotypes, which are often introduced by classes to their drama lessons, but there is value in exploring the stock characters of other historical periods and theatre styles such as Restoration comedy, and *commedia dell'arte*. When the typical behaviour of the stock characters has been explored by pupils, character can be enriched by the addition of information which undermines stereotyping: for example, the pupil working on the role of an aggressively dressing teenager is told the character spends his weekends looking after his grandmother. Work on movement of the kind described above can be used to help pupils make choices about the physical presence of characters. Similarly, the power of props and clothing in helping to establish characters physically should not be overlooked: these items are sometimes only added to enhance performance, and may well fail to do so if actors have not become accustomed to working with them.

Spontaneous and prepared improvisation

Many teachers include opportunities for pupils to engage in both spontaneous and prepared improvisation work at different times in the course of a sequence of lessons. It is important to be clear about the opportunities and limitations of each method in relation to the development of the drama work of a class.

In some definitions of spontaneous improvisation, only work in which the teacher calls for an immediate response to a stimulus is included. However, other practitioners would extend the definition to include group work with limited preparation time. This would be a few minutes to establish some ideas about the location, characters who will be needed, and the order in which they will arrive, so that the drama can establish itself without too many people trying to define its direction at once.

In all cases, spontaneous improvisation work is concerned with the processes of interaction achieved by members of the group. In particular, pupils need to learn 'acceptance skills', the willingness to perceive and respond appropriately and creatively to the ideas of others. This willingness contributes to the seeking of 'slow solutions', the ability to continue dramatic situations long enough to explore the ideas and feelings they contain, and often, also, long enough to avoid heightening confrontation in the drama without adequate preparation. Good spontaneous improvisation experiences which make use of these skills will encourage pupils to explore their ideas for prepared improvisation by acting them out, rather than through discussion.

Prepared improvisation challenges participants to develop their understanding of the situation the drama is concerned with by giving it dramatic form and structure. This involves them in making use of their imagination, their understanding of dramatic shape, and in working collectively to develop character, perhaps using some of the methods indicated above, as well as discussion, research and spontaneous improvisation. Very often success is dependent on the teacher providing an appropriate balance of choice and constraint in relation to both form and content: pupils can be overwhelmed by excessive choice and frustrated by too closely defined tasks. Prepared improvisation work can be extended to incorporate the development and appropriate use of presentation skills, which will initially need to be defined for pupils. Effective communication with the audience, by means ranging from audible speech to appropriate costumes and set for a rehearsed improvised play, should be gradually developed, and represented in the assessment criteria for the work at a corresponding rate.

Opportunities for discussion and reflection need to be built into the development of the work. Group members need to feel strong commitment to the work, not least because there is often a period of difficulty between the establishment of a group's perception of the dramatic potential of an idea they are working on and the emergence of confidence about its realisation. Pupils will sometimes press to start on a new idea when they reach a difficulty which blocks the development of the work. The teacher's job is often to suggest techniques and methods, such as some of those for exploring structure or character described above, to help move the drama on, if there appears to be a shortage of ideas. If the group has too many different ideas, and is unable to make decisions for this reason, it can be helpful to provide them with a sequence of limited tasks which will allow a number of options to be attempted before a decision is made. Since work on prepared improvisation often spreads over a number of lessons, teachers need to be prepared to help groups to continue their work when members are absent, by identifying ways of moving forward which the group sees as appropriate.

This section of the chapter has suggested that just as games, movement and other work which obviously focuses on technique should be adapted into meaning-making activities, so meaning-making activities like improvisation need the support of some explicit work developing both pupils' repertoire of dramatic technique and their collaborative working skills.

TASK 10.4   RESEARCHING DRAMA METHODS

Research a range of drama teaching methods in the books listed in Further Reading. Consider how much emphasis there is on developing technique and the making of meaning in the methods you read about. Design and teach some lessons in which you offer pupils an appropriate sequence of work combining the development of technique and opportunities to use drama to make meaning.

WORKING WITH TEXTS

It is important to approach work on drama texts with the understanding that playwrights expect their work to be interpreted by a group of actors in a production. Most playscripts concentrate on the words which are to be spoken, but it is understood that actors will supply the movement, gesture and intonation which will communicate an interpretation of the script. Actors develop this interpretation through rehearsal methods. When working with plays in school, it follows that it is very beneficial for pupils to explore texts in ways similar to those used by actors. Although there are clearly other ways of working productively with playtexts, experiences which reinforce pupils' perception of them as drama are essential. National assessments including the Key Stage 3 SATs and GCSE English Literature examinations increasingly ask questions which reflect an expectation that plays will be studied in this way.

Exploring character

Many actors work by trying to develop a coherent (or incoherent and paradoxical) characterisation from the fragmentary information presented in a drama text. This involves asking questions about what happens to the character during off stage periods, and sometimes in extending this way of thinking by considering everything that has happened before the character first appears on stage. This work requires an actor to make use of clues about characters in the text, including its margins and omissions, and to develop his or her thinking about these clues by making reference to research, his or her own life experience, and other resources. This thinking is brought to bear on the improvisation of events such as those which are only referred to in the text, or which will enable the actors to explore relationships which are only briefly represented in it. It can also be useful to make use of techniques which help an actor to see a character objectively or through the eyes of other characters in the drama, for example by exchanging roles temporarily, or describing the character's thoughts, feelings and motivation at particular points in the action in the third person. These activities, which develop forms of empathetic and analytical understanding of character, are respectively related to the dramatic theories of Stanislavski and Brecht, and are as useful in preparing pupils to write empathetic and analytical essays as they are in rehearsing a stage performance.

Exploring contexts

It is useful to research the societies and cultures in which a play is set. This research may involve referring to historical and sociological texts, but drama methods can be used to make the full significance of the information which is discovered clear. Improvisation can explore the daily lives of the characters in a play which is being studied, outside of the situation with which it is primarily concerned, or, in other words, it can establish what the 'normality' is from which the events in the play dramatically deviate. A closer focus can be established by working on offstage events, both those which are reported in the text and those which are implied, by for example, the opening lines of scenes which show that the text joins conversations and events after they have begun. Improvisation work exploring these events can explore questions about the reliability of the reporters who describe events, and what the dramatist has found it most important to represent.

Exploring the languages of drama

One way of making connections between the idea of drama as a specialised kind of language study and the idea of drama as a performance art, is to search the verbal language of a text for ideas and images which can be translated into the language of theatrical performance. For example, the imagery of clothing and blood in *Macbeth* can be re-presented through design ideas for set, costume and lighting. Rehearsal methods and the process of putting on a production of a play or part of a play may be the best way of exploring such relationships between text and performance, but there are many aspects of this process which can be isolated in classroom work, including the design and preparation of posters and programmes, producing designs for set, costumes or lighting, producing director's staging notes, finding or producing music and sound effects for particular scenes, tape recording readings of scenes, creating tableaux, working on choric readings of soliloquies, or improvising key situations from the play having transferred them to different contexts.

TASK 10.5 PRODUCER'S NOTES

Working either individually on paper or using rehearsal methods in a group, produce director's notes on a scene from a play which you plan to teach in school. Cover as many aspects of production as you can, including instructions for the actors, costume and lighting notes. Use your notes as a source of ideas for the lesson or sequence of lessons in which you will teach the scene.

WORKING METHODS IN DRAMA TEACHING

Drama teachers can choose the methods and combinations of methods they use from a wide range of possibilities. If you watch a number of different drama teachers you will see how the repertoire of methods they use contributes to their personal teaching style. There is only scope in this chapter to consider two of the many areas where choice is available: methods of introducing the drama, and methods of supporting the development of the drama.

Storytelling and the provision of focusing material are two methods which can be used to provide an initial stimulus for drama which can give pupils varying degrees of control and responsibility for the development of the work. For example, very controlled individual work can be achieved if the teacher tells a story which pupils 'follow' through solo mime. Alternatively, the teacher can gradually pass control to groups of pupils by telling them part of a story, allowing them to improvise the next stage and report what happened to the whole class. The discussion can be used to generate ideas for the further development of the work. Providing focusing material is one strategy for providing some narrative guidance while allowing pupils to construct their own story. For example, a map of a journey to an interesting destination such as a treasure island could be 'found' in the classroom along with a manual describing the crew needed to sail the *Hispaniola*. This method could stimulate the development of a whole-class improvisation.

If we consider how the teacher might support the development of an improvisation of this kind, again a range of methods is available. One method would be to start by supporting groups of characters in developing their sense of what their role in the drama will be. For example, groups of ships' officers, crew and passengers would work separately on matters such as their reasons for being on the voyage, their living conditions, their interactions with members of other groups. Discussion, writing, drawing, items of clothing, pictures, and/or research information from books and other stimuli could be used to help each group develop its idea of itself. The role of the teacher, once the improvisation began, would be that of an observer who is able to steer the drama from the outside, by occasionally stopping it and holding discussions.

It would be possible for this role to be disguised as that of the ship's chronicler, who needs to find out information for his or her reports. This method of involving the teacher in the drama is known as 'teacher in role'. It would be possible to develop the same kind of improvisation entirely by using the 'teacher-in-role' method, if, for example, the teacher took the role of ship's captain and explained what the rules of the ship are for officers, crew and passengers rather than allowing groups to work this out by the method described above. This role would also make it easy for the teacher to intervene by, for example, calling for 'all hands on deck' when the drama needed a steer. When pupils are used to 'teacher-in-role' methods of working, it is possible for the teacher to take less powerful roles and so give the pupils more autonomy. The role of information provider, in this case of ship's navigator, for example, would allow the teacher to give the drama some structure without appearing to make decisions. The role of an apparently powerless person like a very sick passenger could also be used with an experienced class, because the pupils would recognise that they were required to make decisions which would affect this character's situation.

All these variations of the development of the work give pupils different degrees of control of the work and are related to different expectations of them. It is important for the rules of different working methods to be made explicit to pupils when they are introduced, so that the number of drama 'genres' they can work confidently in is gradually extended. When using a drama method which is unfamiliar, it will often take time for the whole class to become committed to the work, and some pupils may be very slow to become involved. Some pupils may challenge the drama. The teacher's awareness of this will affect things like the number of times the work is interrupted for the purposes of discussion and the provision of additional stimuli and ideas. It is also helpful if the teacher is prepared to accept and put to positive use remarks and contributions which do not take the drama seriously. This sense of commitment and seriousness helps to give whole-class work momentum in the early stages. It may involve the acceptance of ideas from pupils which take the work in unexpected directions, or which are based on a misunderstanding of factual matters which needs to be corrected later.

Of course, it is possible for whole-class work to combine the strategies described here, and to link them with others. This flexibility allows a teacher working with an experienced class to focus on particular aspects of a story in detail, and to represent others more economically: for example, a series of group photographs could represent a long sea journey where the drama is primarily concerned with events on arrival at a destination, like discovering the treasure.

STRUCTURING DRAMA LESSONS

When beginning to plan drama lessons, you may find it helpful to adopt the following outline structure:

1. Teacher-centred activity with whole class working together as individuals

   reflection/discussion

2. A series of activities in pairs (activities make increasing demands)

   reflection/discussion

3. A series of activities in small groups (activities make increasing demands)

   reflection/discussion

4. An activity with whole class/large groups working together

   reflection/discussion

This sequence could take place in a double lesson, but it may take months to progress from stage 1 to stage 4 with some classes. Of course, some lessons will omit some of the stages suggested here, and, as your confidence and skills develop, you are likely to want to try other approaches.

Examples

1. Teacher-centred activity with whole class working together or as individuals:

   teacher in role introduces topic of drama; teacher organises drama games related to topic; teacher tells a story or uses artifact as stimulus (e.g. photographs, music, costume, document); teacher leads individual mime or acting sequence; teacher leads improvisation work in circle.

2. A series of activities in pairs (activities make increasing demands):

   students work with friends, teacher supplies detailed ideas, closed familiar situations and roles *at first*; improvisation work preceded by lengthy discussion, or e.g. use of piece of drama text or video.

3. A series of activities in small group (activities make increasing demands):

   e.g. students work in random mixed groups, teacher supplies limited stimulus; open, unfamiliar situations and roles <u>later</u>.

4. An activity with whole class/large groups working together:

   teacher in role (later a supportive rather than dominant role) establishes situation and provides structure for groups to see the need for interaction with other groups in the drama.

5. Reflection/discussion stages:

   teacher/pupils interview others in role (hotseating); after sharing or spotlighting of work of several groups with same task, pupils discuss what if felt like to play certain roles; pupils keep journal of drama experiences or write letters following up improvised events.

SUMMARY AND KEY POINTS

Many drama activities can be interpreted so that emphasis is placed either on their function in developing language or on the possibilities of drama as an art form. As a student teacher you may use drama both as 'integrated English' in the same way as you might incorporate elements of media education or IT into classroom activities and 'as a creative art', in which your focus is on drama forms and processes as an end in itself. Both approaches are underpinned by a clear rationale. Within your placement school and in your future department, you should develop a clear understanding of the rationale which underpins the use of drama. Similarly, you should develop a realistic sense of the constraints and possibilities for drama work within the particular context in which you are working. In order to enable your pupils to develop their creativity, imagination and language skills, in spoken or written form, you should look for opportunities to include drama as part of your teaching.

FURTHER READING

Arts Council (1992) *Drama in Schools: Arts Council Guidance on Drama Education*, London: Arts Council.

Barker, C. (1977) *Theatre Games*, London: Methuen.

Bolton, G. (1992) *New Perspectives on Classroom Drama*, New York: Simon & Schuster.

Burgess, R. and Gaudry, P. (1985) *Time for Drama*, Buckingham: Open University Press.

Byron, K. (1986) *Drama in the English Classroom*, London: Methuen.

Hamblin, K. (1978) *Mime*, London: Lutterworth.

Hodgson, J. and Richards, E. (1974) *Improvisation*, London: Methuen.

Laban, R. (1948) *Modern Educational Dance*.

NATE (1993) *Move Back the Desks*, Sheffield: NATE.

Neelands, J. (1984) *Making Sense of Drama*, London: Heinemann.

Neelands, J. (1992) *Learning through Imagined Experience*, London: Hodder & Stoughton.

Neelands, J. (1993) *Structuring Drama Work*, London: Cambridge University Press.

Nicholls, B. (1974) *Move*, London: Heinemann.

O'Neill, C. (1977) *Drama Guidelines*, London: Heinemann.

Rawlins, G. and Rich, J. (1985) *Look, Listen and Trust*.

11 Approaching Shakespeare

INTRODUCTION

Shakespeare is prescribed reading at Key Stages 3 and 4 and on GCE A Level syllabuses. Approaching the Shakespeare play, therefore, provides a means of considering continuity and progression throughout the secondary English curriculum. The approaches to reading and responding to Shakespeare discussed here can, of course, be applied to any text. The compulsory study of Shakespeare also crystallises many of the debates within teaching English, such as: the privileging of the cultural heritage and skills models of English teaching over cultural analysis and personal growth in *English in the National Curriculum* (1995) (see Chapter 2); the impact of assessment by external examination and tiered papers; the lists of prescribed authors and prescribed plays. English teachers are conscious of the correlation between Shakespeare in school, particularly Shakespeare for examination, and a person's future relationship with Shakespeare. The significance of this relationship is that because Shakespeare continues to be used as an emblem of high culture and synonymously British cultural identity, a person's relationship with Shakespeare determines an individual's, and social or ethnic group's, *affection for* or *alienation from* British culture. Consequently, teachers find themselves torn between aiming for the greatest access to Shakespeare texts for all pupils and resisting the force-feeding of Shakespeare. The implications for a class-ridden pluralistic society are keen. As David Hornbook puts it:

> The unavoidable identification of Shakespeare with the examination system is seen as in itself alienating and prohibitive of creative growth. Furthermore, Shakespeare for most children is inescapably associated with social snobbery . . . outside the school, a routine dismissal of his plays as part of an inaccessible middle-class ritual of 'theatre-going' further strengthens this sense of alienation.
>
> (Hornbrook, 1988, p. 146)

Another tension for the teacher is the increasing gap between the cultural studies approach to English studies in Higher Education courses and the focus on language skills required for assessment in the school curriculum. Teachers are also sensitive to the implicit perception that by studying the same text at the same time, young people will become dutiful citizens; the assumption goes like this: *force the same text on all children and we will once again become a unified society; give them Shakespeare, and children, like Caliban through learning Prospero's language, will become tame and subservient.* The paradox is that, on account of its demands in terms of language competence, maturity of experience and conceptual thinking, instead of becoming an instrument of social unity, the Shakespeare play is the means by which social divisions are endorsed, as registered in a tiered examination system where the Shakespeare play is often used to 'sort out' ability groupings. In order to dissociate Shakespeare from the exclusive world of the adult upper- or middle-class theatre-goers, teachers want to bring the theatre into the classroom through drama activities and through pupils acting out parts of the plays themselves. These approaches help them to 'own' the plays, and by association the culture they represent, as well as to understand them.

OBJECTIVES

By the end of the chapter you should have:

- considered the attitude towards studying Shakespeare by pupils of different abilities and cultural identities;
- become familiar with the curriculum requirements for teaching Shakespeare at Key Stages 3 and 4 and GCE A Level;
- explored a range of strategies for teaching a Shakespeare text (and other texts) for coursework and for examination.

BACKGROUND TO THE TEACHING OF SHAKESPEARE IN SCHOOL

Before the 1988 Education Reform Act and the 1989 (Cox) *English in the National Curriculum*, the study of Shakespeare was not compulsory but was common practice in secondary schools and in some measure, albeit often in the form of an introduction to the theatre, life and works of Shakespeare, in primary schools. Changing selections of plays were set for GCE O and A Level exams; the introduction of GCSE changed assessment to coursework and assessing Shakespeare by coursework also became common at A Level. Schools and teachers could choose the texts according to their enthusiasms, what was in the stock cupboard, which productions were on locally or being offered by Theatre in Education groups. The 1989 National Curriculum simply prescribed one Shakespeare play at KS3. Brian Cox envisaged that achievement would be measured by teacher assessment which would have allowed for the continuation of successful practices. These included a variety of 'ways in' to the plays, an emphasis on role play, recreative work and thematic approaches. These were common starting points for study of the language and structure of the plays in coursework GCSE syllabuses and to some extent at A Level.

The first Standard Assessment Tasks (SATs), however, introduced the controversial anthology with differentiated demands for each of three tiers of ability. One major difference between the bottom tier and the top two tiers was that the compulsory Shakespeare element was one speech – 'All the world's a stage' from *As You Like It* – whereas the other tiers could enjoy a whole play (but *As You Like It* was not prescribed so there was little chance of mixed-ability teaching). The tiered papers and rigid comprehension questions were severely criticised and teachers objected to the suggestion that Shakespeare was not deemed suitable for low attainers. These 1993 SATs were boycotted. Sir Ron Dearing's draft proposals for the revised Orders, however, maintained the tiered papers – reduced now to a standard and extension tier – and a compulsory Shakespeare text (Paper 2) but the plays were the same for all children – a choice of *Romeo and Juliet*, *A Midsummer Night's Dream* and *Julius Caesar*. The 1995 Order, therefore, keeps Shakespeare compulsory for pupils working for level 4 and above at Key Stages 3 and 4.

The current KS3 examination consists of a choice of two predetermined scenes from each play with quite open questions about character, meaning and response. The assessment objectives also allocate marks for handwriting, spelling, grammar and style. The pressure to achieve good examination results because of reporting to parents and league tables has enforced setting in many departments, so that pupils thought capable of the extension tier (Paper 1) can be tutored for it. There will inevitably be a self-fulfilling prophecy concerning achievement. In the national survey, *The Real Cost of SATs* (LATE, 1995), Heads of English reporting on the SAT results in 1995, reflect that the Year 9 curriculum has become 'SAT driven' and dominated by the Shakespeare play. They have tried to maintain good practice in teaching Shakespeare and resent reverting to the type of approach which is alienating – flogging one prescribed scene of one prescribed play – and to using the threat of examination performance as a stick:

We did quite an extensive preparation of the Shakespeare texts. This took a large amount of curriculum time and was quite prescriptive. I think teachers should have a choice whether to teach Shakespeare at this age. The class found *Romeo and Juliet* difficult even though we did pupil-friendly activities to do with text. I found that the students became more demotivated as the SATs test loomed near and they had to do 'practice' tasks . . . A far better, educationally worthwhile assessment procedure is one based on teacher assessment, especially at this age.

(Head of English, Enfield, LATE, 1995, p. 31)

The prescription of texts and the nature of the SATs revived the debate over the position and politics of Shakespeare. During the *Shakespeare in Schools Project* (Royal Society of Arts, 1992–4), teachers expressed their anxiety about being able to sustain stimulating approaches to the themes and language of Shakespeare's plays while meeting the assessment requirements of the National Curriculum. Similar anxieties were expressed at the TES *Shakespeare in the Curriculum* conference in December 1992. The implications of prescribed plays and tiered examinations were articulated from several perspectives: academics saw it as social engineering; Theatre in Education groups were concerned that they would be squeezed out by curriculum demands – they were already being squeezed out by lack of funding; actors talked about being condemned to perform *Romeo and Juliet*, *A Midsummer Night's Dream* and *Julius Caesar* relentlessly in order to attract school audiences; inspectors spoke of the threat to widespread good practice; Heads of Department told of stock cupboards bursting with *The Tempest* or *The Merchant of Venice* while having to purchase literally hundreds of copies of *Romeo and Juliet*; classroom teachers talked of being forced to return to dull teaching methods. Most teachers' resistance, therefore, is not to teaching the plays, but to the ways in which assessment prohibits any flexibility in making them relevant or providing experiences which will foster an enthusiasm in pupils to read and watch the plays for themselves, in both the short and long term.

TASK 11.1 PREJUDICES AND EXPECTATIONS ABOUT SHAKESPEARE IN THE CLASSROOM

A. Personal history

It is likely that your own experiences of school Shakespeare have influenced your interest in continuing to read or watch Shakespeare's plays. In discussion with another student teacher or your tutor, consider the following questions to identify negative and positive influences upon your engagement with Shakespeare.

1. What was your first experience of seeing or watching a Shakespeare play? To what extent did it influence your perception of Shakespeare?
2. What were your experiences of reading and viewing Shakespeare plays at school, at university or on your own?
3. How have you been examined on Shakespeare? How well did you do?
4. Do you have preferences concerning plays? On what are these based?
5. What is your response to the following article: 'Was Shakespeare a Tory?' David Lister (*Independent on Sunday*, January 1993)?

Was Shakespeare a Tory?
The Bard is now a subject of political controversy
DAVID LISTER reports

SHAKESPEARE, anarchist or Tory, upholder of traditional values or subversive? The struggle for the Bard's soul is being fought in the world of academia.

Lining up on either side of the argument are some of the country's most respected Shakespeare scholars, and on one thing they all agree: his works are undergoing a fundamental reappraisal.

Michael Bogdanov, founder and artistic director of the English Shakespeare Company, says that schools should not teach Shakespeare for 20 years and neither should any of his work be performed, while a rethink takes place. To get things going, he has decided that he will not direct a Shakespeare play for five years.

Others, including Lord Lawson, the former chancellor of the exchequer, argue that some of the plays were written from a Tory standpoint and that Shakespeare was a strong royalist.

Mr Bogdanov, who is currently rehearsing *Romeo and Juliet*, says: 'The only way Romeo's and Juliet's parents can measure the worth of their children is in gold. Look at Romeo's speech to the apothecary: "There is thy gold, worse poison to men's souls,/Doing more murders in this loathsome world/Than these poor com- pounds that thou mayst not sell:/I sell thee poison, thou hast sold me none." He is saying that money is the real poison in the world. This nice, romantic wimp gives a whole social and political comment on the value of money.' Not perhaps how this play – one of the Government's prescribed three texts for 14-year-olds – will generally be taught. But that, says Bogdanov, illustrates the problem.

In fact, he says, Shakespeare is full of 'invisible bullets', the elements that are potentially embarrassing and are often ignored or cut by those who want to see the plays as 'shoring up the system with its class divisions and government by divine right'.

'We must reclaim Shakespeare for the anarchists,' Bogdanov goes on. 'He was a challenge to society, but this is not the Shakespeare that is taught or, on the whole, performed. Shakespeare is never used as a social and political dramatist. He is used as a moral dramatist.'

Lord Lawson does not see Shakespeare as an anarchist. He said in an interview that 'Shakespeare was a Tory without any doubt', adding that Coriolanus, espousing 'the Roman virtues, the Tory virtues', was 'written from a Tory point of view.'

Brian John, an English teacher at King Edward VI Grammar School in Chelmsford, adopts a similar approach to literary criticism, showing that the Lawson philosophy continues down the line into the classroom. He told a recent conference: 'Shakespeare was a great enthusiast of royalty and a true Conservative.'

Elaborating on this, he explained to me: 'I do feel that he must be generally a Conservative in asserting the basic principle of the desire for stability and order. Just look at the 'degree speech' in Troilus and Cressida. Take his whole philosophy of history. He has a low opinion of rebellion: look at the Jack Cade example in Henry VI Part Two. And as a person he knew how to handle his finances and was upwardly mobile.'

The dispassionate Shakespeare Institute in Stratford-upon-Avon, an academic centre for the furtherance of understanding of the Bard, recognises that the battle lines over Shakespeare are changing.

Its director, Professor Stanley Wells, says: 'There is an academic conflict over Shakespeare. A lot of critics of the cultural materialism school are arguing that the plays contain elements of subversion which haven't been adequately recognised in the past.'

Alan Sinfield, of Sussex University's English department, ought to be a leader of the Young Turks preaching cultural materialism. He has just written a book entitled *Fault Lines: cultural materialism and the politics of dissident reading* and claims cohorts at several universities outside Oxbridge.

'Cultural materialism,' he explains, 'is materialism as opposed to idealism. Idealism says there's an ideal conception of a Shakespeare play, a reading that transcends all performances. Materialism says it is located in a political and historical context, his context but also ours.

'In the old days the thing you were meant to do with a literary text was to point out how whole and complete it was. The trick now is to do the opposite, to look for the gaps and silences and stress and pressure points.

'As you start looking for the fault lines, the text reveals its project. If you look at Desdemona, for example, she starts off incredibly spunky. She tells the Senate she wants to go off and have sex with her husband. Later she has turned into a nagging wife. Then she lies back and says 'I've done wrong but don't kill me yet'. It's not really a continuous character, it's a series of stereotypes and the play is deploying those stereotypes as a political representation to explore gender politics.'

(David Lister, *Independent on Sunday, 3* Jan, 1993)

B. Questionnaire

Based on the above questions, devise a questionnaire in conjunction with your tutor or mentor. Interview a range of pupils, preferably across the whole age range, of differing abilities and of different cultural identities. To what extent are gender, class, age, race and past experiences relevant to pupils' attitudes to Shakespeare? Find out their experiences of watching plays and films as well as of reading the texts. Make a note of the reasons why pupils may be hostile to studying a Shakespeare play.

WHY SHAKESPEARE?

Addressing initial hostility can be the experience of teachers who have to tell adolescent pupils that Shakespeare is compulsory, that they have to 'do' a scene or a play for an exam for, or after, which they are likely to be setted. At the same time, pupils often have a sense of pride and achievement when they have acted out a piece from one of the plays or know titles, quotations or the stories. Recurring objections to the plays are that they are too 'difficult', 'irrelevant' or 'elitist'. These may be based on a child's experiences but are often grounded in hearsay. Rather than be instantly defensive, the teacher can find out the prior experiences of pupils. The Royal Society of Arts initiative, the *Shakespeare in Schools Project*, aimed to give opportunities for working on and through Shakespeare throughout and across the curriculum. In interviews, pupils and teachers in primary and secondary schools expressed how their prejudices against the plays before the project had been changed:

> 'People think that Shakespeare is posh and serious, but when we did it, it was fun' (John, aged 9).

> 'Students were excited by their ability to understand something called Shakespeare which had primarily seemed alien to them and their lives'.
> (Teacher, Market Bosworth High School)
> (Gilmour, 1994, frontispiece; p. 26)

The *Shakespeare in Schools Project* culminated in quality presentations which involved all pupils in a class. The presentations demonstrated a range of skills from several curricular areas:

> 'Beginning a new project in a way that arouses curiosity and a desire to learn is perhaps the most important art of the process. If effective the students' own enthusiasm usually carries it along and they meet not only the academic demands more readily, but also develop perceptive, artistic and social skills'.
>
> (Teacher, Brookvale High)

'The use of choreographed dance and live improvised music gave the production an exciting edge. The students worked excellently and within six weeks "Lear's Dance of Death" had been created'.

(Teacher, Groby Community College)

(Gilmour, 1994, pp. 31, 33)

The findings of the *Shakespeare in Schools Project* support the following arguments *for* teaching Shakespeare:

1. The plays are entertaining because they work dramatically: they have good stories and interesting characters; they mix comedy and tragedy; they contain conflict and produce mixed feelings in the audience; they require special effects to show magic, shipwrecks or fights; there is plenty of action;
2. The plays are examples of good theatre and suitable for developing critical analysis of drama as a genre;
3. The language provides a valuable model and resource;
4. The characters and situations can be made relevant;
5. All are entitled to have access to the dominant culture;
6. The plays offer alternative ways of perceiving;
7. The stories and themes challenge and therefore extend the imagination, from which can come new ideas;
8. The plays stimulate a range of reading, oral and writing activities;
9. The range of linguistic registers and frames of reference can be liberating not restricting; through reading and analysis pupils develop powers of rhetoric and discourse;
10. A cultural materialist approach to the texts – for example, the analyses of government and authority in the plays – can be empowering;
11. The exploration of identities through universal experiences, like marriage or death, in different cultural contexts can promote cultural exchange, especially through productions of the plays;
12. Like it or not, taking part in the plays engenders a sense of ownership rather than alienation and enhances self-esteem.

Shakespeare *can* therefore promote rather than inhibit personal and social development through opportunities for extending language awareness and usage, through the representations of complex relationships and through the debates explored in the plays; there is plenty of scope for cultural analysis through the study of power systems or the nature and structures of family life and marriage. There are debates about individual responsibility, the concepts of loyalty and duty and the relationship between religious and state laws; the plays depict people falling in love, telling lies and quarrelling. Since Shakespeare is performed across the world the productions can mediate between cultures as any production will reproduce the values and conventions of its social context. This is what Michael Bogdanov also discovered in his project of taking Shakespeare to a Birmingham housing estate (*Shakespeare on the Estate*, BBC 2 Television, 1994): as the plays were appropriated by different groups – a single mothers group worked on scenes with Lady Macduff; sequences were rewritten and performed as rap; one group acted out the Capulet/Montague brawl in a mixture of 'Shakespeare's' and contemporary English, for example – there can be an exchange and understanding of different cultural codes. Progression in teamwork, creativity, commitment and self-confidence, as was demonstrated in *Shakespeare on the Estate* and the *Shakespeare in Schools* projects, is difficult to measure. Consequently, examinations have tended to prioritise accuracy in reading and writing rather than an involvement with the narratives, characters and themes of the plays which can be enjoyed across the ability and social range. Teachers' objections are not to improving pupils' ability to write sentences, write neatly, spell correctly or use quotations, but to limiting these, which yield up possibilities for identifying achievement in many different ways, to the assessment of mechanical skills which can be charted by a rigid mark scheme. In addition, tiered papers endorse a cultural hierarchy with Shakespeare on top; oddly, one argument for studying the plays is to make the so-called British national heritage available to all, but this system of testing is designed to bar the majority from it. The tragic paradox is that the plays, instead of engendering social unity, are exploited to entrench social divisions.

APPROACHES

In the longstanding and continuing debates about teaching literature in schools, the 'why Shakespeare?' question will not and should not go away. The immediate problem for the new and established teacher alike is not only 'why teach Shakespeare?' but also 'how to teach Shakespeare?' One reason why teachers find themselves locked into a hostile situation is because pupils get 'switched off' at the reading stage. The common practice of reading plays in the classroom is to distribute characters to the good readers; as these readers go through their speeches, which are often long and read without understanding, the non-participants become disaffected. There is no simple answer to this problem, but there are different strategies with which you can experiment.

A valuable learning model is that proposed in *Small Group Learning in the Classroom* (Reid, Forrestal and Cook, 1989). This model sets out the stages of learning in the classroom as 'Engagement, Exploration, Transformation, Presentation and Reflection'. There are a variety of activities which are appropriate for each part of the learning process as illustrated in Figure 11.1.

It is assumed that most of these stages can be the same for all pupils. There are possibilities for differentiation by task – with projects of varying difficulty, for example, and at the transformation and presentation

Engagement. The teacher introduces the learning activity. With Shakespeare especially, pupils actually need to know what is happening before they read because comprehension is unlikely at first reading. You need to give enough away to arouse their curiosity and provide guidance about the plot and character development without telling them everything. Consider the following points:

- what pre-reading activities could introduce the central themes and situations of the play or scene (e.g. brainstorm what makes a good crime story before reading *Macbeth*) ?
- how should the reading be managed – whole-class/ groups/ audio tapes?
- how will all the class get to know the play and characters – e.g. through scene summaries, acting out key extracts or 'keeping track' activities like timelines or ongoing character profiles?
- what use can be made of film or television production: (e.g. the *Animated Tales* series on video) before starting the text; watching film sequences in conjunction with reading?

Exploration. The pupils are given opportunities to become involved with the text. Activities might include:

- comprehension questions which demand close reading and individual exploration of the text and which deal with difficulties in vocabulary;
- using film, such as *Shakespeare Shorts* (BBC Education 1996); pupils should script or storyboard passages before viewing alternative productions;
- use of drama conventions and improvisation such as interviews, hotseating, freeze frames;
- guided group discussion or activities: e.g. character profiles;
- projects on social or theatre history: (e.g. marriage customs); researching different productions.

Transformation. At this stage there is a focus on a particular aspect of the work and the understanding gathered so far; tasks could be:

- writing up a project;
- preparing a draft for an essay;
- polishing up a script or improvised piece for performance;
- recreative writing: (e.g. a character's journal or letter); a modern English version; a cartoon strip.

Presentation. The process of feeding back and sharing ideas and information: it gives value to the work achieved and can sharpen critical awareness through the response of a sympathetic but critical audience. Tasks can include:

- exchanging work within a pair, followed by redrafting;
- handing in work to the teacher;
- a wall display;
- talk, performance or presentation to the class;
- word processing a review for a newsheet;
- timed examination practice.

Reflection. The vital stage where teacher and pupils discover what has been learned and what still needs learning. It may take a variety of forms, such as:

- feedback from the teacher after marking work;
- peer response to a presentation;
- whole-class feedback;
- evaluation sheet.

Figure 11.1 Learning model for approaching texts

stages where there may be choice of tasks or essays; presentation and performance tasks can provide opportunities for pupils who are stronger at research or speaking and listening than at writing. Because Shakespeare's plays include debates about complex issues, such as power relations in domestic and national contexts, it is easy for the teacher to jump from the level of narrative, 'What is going on in the passage?', to a highly conceptual question, 'should this character behave in this way?' Work will be accessible to most pupils if there is progression through the levels of thinking, identified as record, report, generalise, speculate/ hypothesise and theorise (Reid, Forrestal and Cook, 1989, p. 9). The questions on the extract from *Romeo and Juliet* in Figure 11.2 illustrate these in practice.

Each of these questions is a process which needs time and varying degrees of support from the teacher, depending on the ability of the pupils: the more structure the better. The practice of structuring exploration of the plays along these lines can help not to lose the pupils who are working at the lower levels and need to be engaged at the level of description and narrative. For this reason, the most able pupils can underachieve if they do not have opportunities to respond to the more

---

The following questions are based on Shakespeare's *Romeo and Juliet*, but the principles of developing progression in thinking can be applied to setting questions on any scene in any play, or a passage in any text.

Read *Romeo and Juliet* Act 111. scene 5. Focus on lines 104–200 and answer these questions:

1. What is the 'joyful news' that Lady Capulet brings to Juliet? (*record*)
2. Discuss with a partner how you would produce Capulet's speech, lines 160–168, for play or film. Describe his facial expressions, volume and tone of voice, movements around the set/stage and body language in relation to the other characters. (*report*)
3. Read Capulet's speech beginning line 176. Sum it up in modern English. Jot down: (a) what you learn of Capulet as a father; (b) whether you think that fathers now behave like Capulet? (*generalise*)
4. Read the rest of the scene. Write the letter which Juliet might have written to Romeo that night. Tell him of the conversations between herself and her parents. What would her feelings be? What will she say to Romeo? (*speculate/hypothesise*)
5. Arranged marriages were common in Shakespeare's time. Look back over this scene and decide whether you think that Shakespeare was suggesting that Juliet should have obeyed her parents. Work out what the reaction of the audience will be at different stages of the scene. Write a paragraph starting: 'I think that Shakespeare wanted us to sympathise with . . . Give reasons by referring to speeches in the play. (*theorise*)

Figure 11.2 Questions to encourage progression in thinking

complex issues of the plays because the teacher does not include the more theoretical approaches for fear of 'losing' other pupils, who may misbehave if the work seems 'above their heads'.

SHAKESPEARE THROUGH THE CURRICULUM

The chart shown in Figure 11.3 is a starting point for considering continuity and progression through the curriculum stages. It is important to build upon prior learning. You may also need to address resistance to studying Shakespeare, caused by prejudices or previous experiences. Photocopy and add in your own observations and ideas.

Figure 11.3 is not exhaustive in identifying the requirements of each curriculum phase and possible teaching strategies. it is intended to illustrate that much work is common all the way through from Key Stage 3 to GCE A Level. Consequently, It is appropriate to use a range of approaches, including acting out and recreative work, at the engagement and exploration stages at all levels. Your observations, however, might find that the more active strategies are usual at Key Stage 3 and below, intermittent at GCSE and invisible at A Level. Assessment requirements do, of course, mean that pupils must have a close knowledge of the text and must practice particular skills at each stage, but a range of approaches enables them to perform well because they have genuinely engaged with the plays; it will also enable them to engage with the texts beyond what is assessed. Any of the approaches, whether acting out or writing a character's diary, will require pupils to look closely at the texts and explore their possible meanings. Looked at this way, you do not have to choose between providing opportunities for pupils *either* to explore the plays for their own development, for cultural analysis and for improving drama techniques, *or* to prepare for assessment; broad learning objectives and the narrow requirements of assessment can be seen to inter-relate. The active exploration of the plays is preparation for responding to assessment tasks and assessment validates the exploration of the plays. The problem is in safeguarding time from being swallowed up by specific exam work.

Shakespeare at Key Stage 3

In spite of pressure from teachers to change the assessment of Shakespeare to coursework, at KS3, a Shakespeare play is examined by the SAT Paper 2. Pupils answer a question on one scene of the selected play. They are required to demonstrate an understanding of the scene on its own and in relation to the rest of the play. They may be asked to comment on character, consider how to produce the scene and explain their decisions or to demonstrate their understanding of some features of production such as 'tension' or 'humour'. They are awarded marks for writing in 'good English'. All the work on the play will obviously feed into their

Curriculum phase	Teaching strategy
Throughout the curriculum Know the play: plot; characters; themes Look at language use and change	Read through the text – whole class; in groups; in conjunction with film/TV/audio adaptation; use 'keeping track' strategies
Possibilities for the text in performance	See productions Role play; interview; hotseating; acting out; scripting film
Write structured essays, using references and quotations	Essay practice
Key Stage 3 Character work Personal response to characters at different stages of the play Understanding of some dramatic functions – e.g. irony – and structures – e.g. tragedy Practice for SAT, paper 2	Group work on different characters with key references and quotations and present to whole class Hotseat or trial characters Transpose into modern equivalents Use productions to record individual responses and how these have been achieved Close study of set scenes Timed essay with open questions
Key Stage 4 (GCSE) Historical and social background Objective analysis of characters Detailed study of productions Comparison of plays Coursework	Project work on different aspects of the times – e.g. marriage; idea of kingship; key laws and events; religious movements Choice of essays, as suggested in the syllabus Empathetic tasks – e.g. diaries, letters, writing in a scene
A Level Ability to interpret a character in two or more ways Explore themes and concepts – e.g. revenge; love; suffering Engage with critical debate Argue a point Write well-structured essay in examination conditions	*As for KS3 and 4, and also:* Students prepare papers on characters, introducing questions for debate Put Shakespeare on trial with a *J'Accuse* type or other TV question-time programme – e.g. of being anti-monarchy or anti-women Give two opposing articles on the play or a production Take a passage for small group discussion Exam practice

Figure 11.3 Teaching approaches across the curriculum

ability to answer the question; to do well, they also need practice in timed examination in order to understand the need to read the question carefully, plan their answers and leave time for checking their writing.

Shakespeare at Key Stage 4

In the 1998 syllabuses, all examining groups assess the Shakespeare play through coursework but prescribe the play. The coursework for English may also be used for the English Literature examination but if so, it needs to meet the specific requirements of the syllabus. Usually, this involves demonstrating awareness of the historical context of the play, in addition to other reading and writing skills. The support material will give guidelines for suitable activities for assessment, such as:

1. Close study of a scene, incorporating analysis of dramatic qualities, language, development of character, reference to the social context of the play;
2. Written assignment on a character;
3. Review of a production, demonstrating the same features as for (1).

Some exam boards invite a variety of forms of assessment, such as a spoken response on tape. Teachers are likely to be cautious over using unorthodox assessment methods until they have experience of the moderation by their examining group.

Shakespeare at GCE A Level

As for Key Stages 3 and 4, A Level candidates are expected to demonstrate a close knowledge of the plays through specific reference and quotation. They are expected to write in good English. In addition, there is emphasis on interpreting the play; they need to demonstrate a more conceptual grasp of themes and characterisation and the possibility of more than one meaning in a particular passage and the play as a whole. Principally, they are required to select material in order to argue a point in answer to a specific question.

TASK 11.2 PREPARING TO TEACH SHAKESPEARE THROUGHOUT THE CURRICULUM

This task will develop your understanding of what is common and what is specific to teaching Shakespeare at each curriculum phase. You will need to get copies of the following documentation for each phase:

Key Stage 3:

- Past SAT question papers;
- Three pupils' scripts across the ability range (e.g. level 4, level 5, level 7);
- *Key Stage 3 English Tests: Mark Scheme for Levels 4–7, Paper 2,* SCAA.

Key Stage 4

- Copy of the relevant GCSE syllabus and support materials – sample questions, marking criteria.

A Level

- Copy of the relevant A Level English Literature syllabus and support material – sample questions, marking criteria.

1. Check out Figure 11.1 against your observations of teaching Shakespeare in schools, and of the requirements for Key Stages 3 and 4 and A Level.
2. Get a past Key Stage 3 question paper 2 and write an answer yourself. Use the marking criteria (SCAA's *Mark Scheme*) and award yourself the appropriate level. Compare yours with actual scripts by pupils. Incidentally, you should try to write 'model' answers for your pupils at all examination levels.
3. Draw up a worksheet to support pupils in a mixed-ability class preparing for examination at Key Stage 3. You will need to identify the skills and processes being rewarded: e.g. awareness of dramatic effectiveness; character studies and personal response; good English and presentation; well-structured essay under timed conditions. You should give guidance on reading the rubric; choosing the answer; reading the questions; planning an answer; writing an answer. Include definitions, explanations and examples of specialist terms, e.g. 'dramatic tension'.
4. Using the learning model and chart of progression in thinking above, under 'Approaches'(Figures 11.1 and 11.2), draw up a scheme of work for approaching a Shakespeare play leading to GCSE coursework. You will need to look at the relevant syllabus. Aim to use a range of strategies and resources. Discuss your scheme of work with your tutor or mentor.

A final note on using productions

Taking pupils to see a play or using a video of a television or film production in the classroom can be disappointing. With any production there is a danger of 'reality referral', especially with film and television, because of their powerful illusionism. There is also a danger of embedding the sense that reading is 'work' and to be avoided, whereas 'watching', particularly watching television, is 'pleasure'. These attitudes are undesirable because they suggest that reading cannot be pleasurable and that watching should not be analytical. In the case of video, if it is used after the text, it becomes the 'carrot' – and the teacher can find herself bribing students with 'settle down; the sooner we get through the text, the sooner you can watch the film'. In addition, as Susan Leach observes,

> if the video is used after the text has been read it tends to become a realism conferring agent, to the extent that students will say things

like 'I didn't know he looked like that', or 'I thought she was older than that', thereby betraying their own subjection to the expectations of realism fostered by television, infinitely powerful in its conditioning of young viewers.

(Leach, 1992, p. 70)

On the other hand, watching a play or screening can enhance the reading process and develop pupils' ability to analyse critically both the text and the particular medium. To this end, Peter Reynolds recommends fracturing the perceived authority of the visual text through breaking it up:

I would argue that to teach Shakespeare on film with the same degree of close analysis that you use in reading a printed text you have to . . . keep your finger continually on the pause button, for the whole thrust of the illusionist convention is to give the impression of continual motion, to avoid breaking up the action, and to drive the viewer inexorably forward in linear progression.

(Reynolds, 1991, p. 201)

This is not so easy in a play, but can be done in the preparation for and reflection on a production.

Strategies for watching a play

Consider suitable preparation, such as:

- pupils decide on how they would produce the play – costumes; setting; actors;
- take the opening of the play and write production notes;
- write their own programme – blurb; plot summary; key points; theatre history;
- show pupils two versions from different folios and they choose which to use. This puts them in the position of producers and editors and helps them to see the text as less 'fixed' or 'sacred'.

Strategies for using film and TV

Viewing should be considered as 'reading' and always be made active in preparation. Experiment with the following:

- choose a passage and ask pupils to script it using film codes – music; length of shots; background;
- use *Shakespeare Shorts* (BBC Education, 1996), or extracts from two adaptations, to illustrate that there are different interpretations and that any production is *a*, not *the*, version;
- vary the order of reading a scene, acting it out and watching the adaptation; watch two if possible to minimise 'reality referral'. While

watching, pupils should be looking out for film narrative, camera manipulation of the audience and for 'differences' between book and production texts and between theirs and the producers' interpretations; this kind of considered scrutiny will enable them to become better acquainted with the text and to be critical viewers.

Resources

There are many texts designed for school use. You will have to use the ones owned by your school, but look at others for your own use or when there is the possibility of buying new ones. The Cambridge School Shakespeare editions are popular but you should compare one or two: look at the way notes, vocabulary, illustrations and scene summaries are used, for example.

There are many commercially published materials to support teaching Shakespeare. Popular ones include:

Broadbent, S. (1994) *Romeo and Juliet: Classroom Material*, London: English and Media Centre.
Garfield, L. (1992) *Shakespeare: The Animated Tales*, London: BBC.
Holding, P. (1992) *Romeo and Juliet*, Text and Performance Series, London: Macmillan.
Jones, P. (1991) *The Shakespeare Workshop*, Rozelle, New South Wales, Australia: St Clair Press.
Orme, D. (1995) *Specials! Romeo and Juliet*, Dunstable: Folens.
Self, D. (1988) *New Guidelines: Romeo and Juliet*, London: Mary Glasgow.
   There are *Guidelines* and *New Guidelines* on several texts.

SUMMARY AND KEY POINTS

There is a sense that in the current school curriculum, the study of Shakespeare is disproportionate to other activities. If nothing else, it takes up time which is needed for other texts and other curriculum areas. Teachers do have to guard against spending too long on a Shakespeare play and rushing through other work, particularly at GCSE level. It is important to plan out carefully the whole scheme of work to gauge the time spent. On the other hand, because the plays make demands on the pupils, they can improve their language competence which can be transferred to other curriculum areas. For example, when working on a play, pupils will be improving their skills in reading, media analysis, role play and drama, understanding of genre, characterisation, language change, speaking and listening, writing in a variety of forms such as diaries, playscripts, posters, letters, news reports, reviews, leaflets and essays. They can develop their thinking, extend their ideas and their moral and emotional understanding. Studying Shakespeare can also develop confidence and self-esteem. Careful planning can prevent the problem of 'overkill' caused by spending too long on a play and prevent the disappointment when pupils respond to a play or film production as 'boring'.

Teachers need to understand their own and their pupils' prejudices and insecurities regarding 'Shakespeare' and find approaches which overcome the difficulty of the language differences in the plays. There are many ideas in circulation and resources available to guide pupils through the processes of learning, from preparation, reading and exploring the plays' meanings to transforming their understanding into specific purposes including examination. The most important principle is that the plays should be experienced as dramas which can be produced in more than one way. Pupils need to be actively involved in constructing meanings of the plays through taking on the roles of producers, actors and reviewers. Preparation for examination is part of this process and also requires the development of specific strategies for taking timed exams.

A Shakespeare play is studied by pupils throughout the curriculum phases; consequently, considering teaching the Shakespeare text includes considering progression and continuity through the curriculum: at KS3, for example, pupils work towards an exam but they are also being prepared for work at KS4 where assessment is by coursework. Active strategies are appropriate throughout the levels to provide the means by which pupils engage with the plays and get to know the text more closely for themselves. The principles which underlie the approaches to studying Shakespeare can be applied to many other areas of the English curriculum.

FURTHER READING

Wells, S. (ed.) (1988) *The Cambridge Companion to Shakespeare Studies*, Cambridge: Cambridge University Press.
This is a collection of essays by contemporary scholars, such as Ingastina Ewbank and Harry Levin, which provides information which you feel that you ought to know and are too ashamed to admit that you don't. The essays cover: Shakespeare's life, times and theatres; the language of the plays; traditions of comedy and tragedy; theatre history and critical history from 1660 to 1980. There is a section on film and television productions and on critical approaches (by Terence Hawkes), but it doesn't include critical theories such as cultural materialism, feminist or postcolonial criticism. It would equip readers for the demands of teaching the plays for the school curriculum.

Leach, S. (1992) *Shakespeare in the Classroom*, Buckingham: Open University Press.
This is an informative and constructive discussion of teaching Shakespeare which successfully combines theory and practice. There are chapters on 'Why Shakespeare?', 'Shakespeare in the National Curriculum' (it

was written before the 1995 version of *English in the National Curriculum*), 'Teachers and Shakespeare', 'Alternative Editions, Alternative Interpretations', 'Shakespeare and Video', 'Race and Gender in Shakespeare', 'Preparing for Classroom Shakespeare', 'Shakespeare in the Secondary Classroom'.

Elsom, J. (ed.) (1992) *Is Shakespeare* Still *Our Contemporary?*, London: Routledge.
This collection came out of a symposium of critics, producers and theatre practitioners who met 'to consider how far the words "universal" and "contemporary" can be sensibly applied to Shakespeare's plays' using themselves as test cases (p. 8). The chapters consist of lively dialogues about longstanding but continuing issues to do with translation, the perceived sexism, colonialism and socially élitist bias of the plays, the barrier of the language – 'Does Shakespeare's verse send you to sleep?'– and adaptations on television. It ends with the question, 'Should Shakespeare be buried or born again?'. It is a particularly valuable book for teachers who feel stale in their own reading of the plays.

12 Possibilities with poetry

INTRODUCTION

Feelings about teaching poetry can vary a great deal. For some it is the most enjoyable aspect of teaching English; for others it is the area about which they are least confident. There are several possible reasons why poetry teaching should give rise to such diverse attitudes. Chief among them is teachers' own experiences of being taught poetry at school or university. Those who enjoy it are often people who were themselves taught by poetry enthusiasts; by teachers who were able to excite a similar enthusiasm in their pupils and develop it through respecting their pupils' responses to poetry and by teaching critical awareness. Those who approach the teaching of poetry with some trepidation may have had less rewarding experiences, finding it difficult, when asked to read or write poetry at school, to see the pleasure or the point.

Of course, a teacher's own enthusiasm for poetry is not enough on its own to ensure that pupils will similarly appreciate it. On the contrary, if that enthusiasm is not reflected upon and tempered for the classroom it may have adverse effects. In his poem 'Them and [uz]' Tony Harrison recalls a former English teacher who would, no doubt, have characterised himself as a poetry enthusiast:

> 4 words only of *mi 'art ache*s and . . . 'Mine's broken,
> you barbarian, T.W.!' *He* was nicely spoken.
> 'Can't have our glorious heritage done to death!'
>
> I played the Drunken Porter in *Macbeth*.
>
> 'Poetry's the speech of kings. You're one of those
> Shakespeare gives the comic bits to: prose!'
> (Harrison, 1984, p. 122)

Poetry revered as 'our glorious heritage' and 'the speech of kings' is likely to end up making many, if not all, feel excluded.

Another reason for conflicting feelings about poetry is the reading challenges it can present. Poetic language may be simple and easy to read, and poems which rhyme, which are funny, which tell a story are often the kind of literature which children most enjoy reading in school. But the syntax, structure, imagery and allusion which some poets employ often require different kinds of reading, and until pupils know that time and effort can yield rewarding pleasures they may not want to persevere. Then their tendency is to dismiss all poetry as 'boring', especially when the challenges are exacerbated in poetry from the past with its sometimes unfamiliar vocabulary and social or cultural references which need explanation.

A third aspect of poetry which can give rise to mixed feelings about teaching is the extent to which it is remembered that poetry has its roots in the oral tradition, and is closely aligned with music, dance and drama. If this lineage is forgotten then poetry can, for many people, be difficult to bring to life. If, however, a priority is to hear poems read or spoken aloud, its rhythms and rhymes can be differently appreciated as these dimensions are brought more clearly into play. The multi-dimensional quality of poetry is, of course, a central concern and challenge for the poet as well as the reader. Sujata Bhatt, in her poem 'The Writer', represents it vividly:

The Writer
The best story, of course,
is the one you can't write,
        you won't write.
It's something that can only live
        in your heart.
not on paper.

Paper is dry, flat.
Where is the soil
for the roots, and how do I lift out
entire trees, a whole forest
from the earth of the spirit
and transplant it on paper
without disturbing the birds?

And what about the mountain
on which this forest grows?
The waterfalls
        making rivers,
rivers with throngs of trees
elbowing each other aside
to have a look
at the fish.

Beneath the fish
        there are clouds.
Here the sky ripples,
the river thunders.
How would things move on paper?

> Now watch   the way
>   the tigers' walking
>   shreds the paper.
>   (Bhatt, in Bhinda [ed.], 1994, p. 3)

If poetry teaching sounds somewhat daunting remember: Tony Harrison has become a popular and widely-respected poet; and Sujata Bhatt's tigers are testament to a writer's success in the struggle to create.

OBJECTIVES

By the end of this chapter you should:

- have begun to develop a rationale for teaching poetry and assessing pupils' work on it;
- have become more familiar with the range of poetry and resources for teaching poetry currently available;
- be aware of the need to justify your selection of poetry, taking into account factors such as pupils' previous reading and work on poetry, and their attitudes towards it;
- be able to explain how lessons you plan will enhance pupils' development as readers, writers and critics of poetry.

THE NEED FOR A RATIONALE

As part of the process of developing a rationale you might find it helpful to explore your own attitudes and possible prejudices concerning the teaching of poetry. One way to do this is to reflect on your experience of being taught poetry and compare it with teachers' and pupils' experiences in school today.

TASK 12.1   POETRY MEMORIES

Discuss with a fellow student or jot down notes on:

- some of your own most vivid memories of being taught poetry in school;
- reasons why they are vivid memories;
- what the balance was between work on poetry through speaking and listening (e.g. hearing it read aloud, reciting or performing it), poetry reading and poetry writing;
- a particular teacher whom you remember teaching you poetry;
- what you think his or her views about teaching poetry were.

In school, find opportunities to:

- talk with different colleagues about teaching poetry and note how attitudes and approaches vary;
- talk with pupils about their views on poetry.

As student teachers embarking on the process of working out your reasons for teaching poetry you will also want to acquaint yourselves with a range of theoretical views which you can use to help you clarify your own ideas and analyse what you observe and learn in the classroom.

Speaking and listening

To start with you could try to discover when, how and why poems are read aloud or performed in class? What might be some of the pleasures and benefits to be gained by pupils who have plenty of opportunities to listen to, as well as read and write, poetry?

It used to be the case that a great deal of oral work on poetry involved pupils learning poems off by heart and then reciting them aloud, together or individually, in class. Because this is not common practice nowadays, it is sometimes assumed that pupils no longer learn poetry by heart at all. It is worth finding out to what extent that is true and exploring whether they do or not and, if they do, what the purpose of doing so is.

Reading

There are different views about why and how poetry is read. For example, what views about teaching poetry, implicit or explicit, emerge from the two extracts below? How far does either of the following two pieces tie in with your own feelings and opinions?

> Clearly there are occasions when a poem needs a comfortable amount of time to be experienced, but poetry works best when it is wanted, not when the timetable decrees it . . . The strength and relevance of the experience within it should engage the pupils' response and thus their willingness to grapple with the language. Some of the best lessons we saw were those where pupils and teacher were enjoying the exchange of opinions on points of vocabulary, attitude, atmosphere and metaphor.
>
> (DES, 1975, p. 136)

Unless we look for them, we apprehend formal patterns subconsciously, if at all. Unless you believe that dissection murders pleasure, some explication of these tacitly apprehended features will make future apprehension more likely and effective. Poetry gives a special chance for this with its habitual re-reading. Early reading gives opportunities to induce the mechanisms; later readings give the chance to recognise them in action and enjoy the satisfactions of formal patterning.

Within current paradigms of teaching literature, mood and content in poems can look after themselves. The structures and processes which realise them need teaching. So while too much teaching and testing suggests that poems are like prose, but the sound features of poetry are well attended to, the urgent need is to foster reading of poems as single, time-free, structured experiences – like gazes at paintings.

(Stibbs, 1995, pp. 14–19)

Writing

Just as there are differing views about poetry reading, so there are various schools of thought about teaching poetry writing. It is, therefore, an area of your work where talking to colleagues and observing them at work in the classroom will prove extremely valuable. You may find that opinions conflict. Some teachers, for example, may view the writing of poetry as a very personal (and perhaps rather private) activity and may, as a result, be reluctant to intervene in the writing process or to assess pupils' writing with as much precision as they might a piece of non-fiction writing. Others, however, may take the view that poetry writing is an art, a craft and skill, elements of which can be taught, practised and refined. These teachers might also hold the view that if pupils' poetry is given the same kind of scrutiny and discussed in the same critical terms as published poets' work, it can enhance pupils' opinions of themselves as writers, rather than just readers of poetry. Where would you place your views within this continuum?

Lavinia Greenlaw, a poet writing in the *Times Educational Supplement*, suggests that the extremes need to be balanced:

Poetry is made of a tension between sense and sensibility. Poets often seem to be those who are scalded by the acuteness of their perceptions while retaining a piece of ice in the heart. Many people find themselves writing poetry for the first time when struggling to articulate some great joy, disturbance or loss. Such poetry can offer catharsis or clarification and this has been the momentum for many great pieces of work. But, without the application of craft, this remains a therapeutic exercise, not a literary one . . . In keeping with its image, poetry is evocative, allusive, startling and mysterious. This is achieved not only through imagination and originality but also rigour and ruthlessness. Every word should count – for its meaning as well as its music.

(Greenlaw, 1996, p. 23)

As you work through this chapter and begin the process of forming a rationale for yourself, you will become aware of the need to make your rationale explicit to others, for example to the Year 9 class who say 'Why do we have to read poetry? Why can't we just read novels and plays?'; to English department colleagues who have to decide between spending limited resources on a class library of fiction or a class library of poetry; to the parents of a Year 10 pupil who ask, at a Parents' Evening, why their son should be spending time on poetry in English when his ambition is to work in a bank. If your rationale can encompass the tension referred to by Greenlaw, it is likely to hold good in a wide range of circumstances.

PLANNING POETRY LESSONS

There are many factors which have to be taken into account when planning poetry lessons. They include:

- formulating learning objectives which are specifically to do with poetry;
- considering pupils' prior knowledge and attainment in relation to reading and writing poetry;
- differentiating between pupils in the same class if necessary;
- ensuring that your plans allow for progression in pupils' knowledge about poetry;
- drawing on your subject knowledge to select poetry and poetry writing activities which will appeal to, interest and challenge pupils;
- drawing on your knowledge of available resources to support your chosen subject matter and approach;
- reflecting on different ways of teaching and learning which will help to achieve the aims and objectives of the lesson(s);
- considering how pupils' learning about poetry can be assessed effectively in order to inform future planning and teaching;
- relating plans to National Curriculum programmes of study or examination syllabus requirements.

These elements will be explored further in the sections which follow.

Poetry reading resources

Work on poetry is often one of the first things that student teachers are asked to undertake in the classroom. The class teacher may ask you to work with a group on a particular poem, or he or she may assume that you would prefer to choose a poem yourself. Explore the English department's stock of poetry texts. Allow time for some lengthy browsing. Look at:

- what sets of poetry anthologies the department has;
- what collections by individual poets they have;

- whether they keep class libraries of poetry books;
- how the department organises poetry stock, e.g. for use with different year groups;
- what else is available in other media, e.g. video, Schools TV programmes, tape recordings, CD-ROM, IT software.

A visit to the school library and resources centre will enable you to ascertain:

- how extensive the poetry stock is;
- whether it caters for all ages, tastes and abilities;
- which poetry books, according to the librarian, are most popular;
- whether they stock periodicals which review poetry publications (e.g. *The School Librarian*) or annotated bibliographies (e.g. *A Guide to Poetry 0–13*).

You could try to find out whether the school publishes pupils' own poetry. If so, are copies of school anthologies available in the library?

Poetry writing resources

Early on in your course you may also find yourself being asked to prepare a poetry writing activity for a particular class. There are many books written about writing poetry. It is worth considering who they are written by and whom they address when deciding which, if any, to use. Many are written by teachers for teachers, or by poets for teachers. (A rare exception is *There's a poet behind you . . .* (Cook and Styles, 1988) which is written by poets for children.)

You may wish to talk to your Head of Department or subject mentor about poetry writing in the English department. Ask:

- which texts or resources they have found most helpful when planning poetry writing activities;
- whether there is any departmental documentation about teaching poetry writing;
- whether the department participates in writers–in–school schemes; encourages pupils to enter poetry writing events; organises workshops and poetry performances.

TASK 12.2   EXPLORING POETRY RESOURCES

This task encourages you to review available poetry resources critically. Browse through the departmental stock of resources. Choose two with which to familiarise yourself further.

- Note one or two activities that you would like to try out in the classroom, and why.
- Read the introductory material to these resources and analyse what views about poetry reading and/or writing they promote.

Selecting poems

Well-judged selecting of poetry is essential to the success of poetry lessons. It is a critical part of the planning process. You need to be able to justify your choice, to be able to say more than 'I think this would be a good poem to do with Year 7'. You need to consider:

- whether the group as a whole is likely to find the poem interesting, both in terms of its subject matter *and* the way it is written;
- how it relates to previous work they have done;
- what the poem will help to teach the group *about poetry*;
- how the poem will *reinforce* what they already know *and develop* their understanding;
- whether it will introduce the group to a familiar or a new poet;
- how your choice affects the balance of poets whose work they are reading;
- whether there are resources available to use when working on this poem, e.g. video or audio recordings; illustrations.

TASK 12.3   MAKING AN INFORMED CHOICE

Select a poem to study with a class you know.

In order to see how fully you are able to justify your choice, ask yourself the above questions. Can you answer them all or do you need to find out more, e.g. about the group and what they have already done, or about available resources?

POETRY ACROSS THE AGE RANGE

The teaching of poetry needs to be as systematic as the teaching of any other area of the English curriculum. There ought to be both differences and continuity between poetry work in, for example, Years 7, 9 and 11. But what might some of those differences be? How is that continuity to be achieved?

One possible framework for thinking about pupils' development as readers, writers and critics of poetry across the secondary age range will now be explored. It is based on a theory of reading outlined by Robert Scholes in *Textual Power*. Briefly, his argument is that three interconnected and recursive elements – reading, interpretation and criticism – need to be actively in play if readers are to realise their full potential. He also argues that students need to be accorded equal status as writers and readers so that they experience their full power as both creators and re-creators of texts.

Recent work on young readers reading picture story books (Meek, 1988; Graham, 1990; Styles and Watson, 1996) has argued that even the youngest readers not only read for pleasure but also respond to texts as interpreters and critics. So the framework is not so much linear as spiral. It is complex and multi-dimensional (Rosenblatt, 1978; Scholes, 1989). Nevertheless, there is a sense in which, with poetry especially, young people will not welcome the effort involved in interpretation and criticism unless they continue to experience the *pleasures* of reading.

EARLY KEY STAGE 3: THE PLEASURES OF POETRY

An important aim for the poetry curriculum in Year 7 might therefore be to extend pupils' enjoyment of reading, writing and performing poetry, introducing them at the same time to more challenging poems, concepts and activities through which they continue to develop their creativity and critical competence. The National Curriculum for English also states that pupils should be 'encouraged to read widely and independently solely for enjoyment'. So how might you make a start?

First find out as much as possible about the pupils you teach. Take every opportunity to discover what they know and what interests them. When it comes to poetry you may find yourself having to follow Polonius's advice and 'by indirections find directions out'. Pupils may not readily inform you that, for example, they are already confident readers and writers of poetry. They may know more poems off by heart than they think they do: playground rhymes and chants; song lyrics; advertising jingles; poems learnt in primary school; their own made-up poems. They may have had poems displayed, read out, or even published in anthologies such as *Words on Water* or *Bossy Parrot* resulting from local or national poetry competitions. Of this they are likely to be proud, but they may be reluctant to tell you about it. You must do the finding out.

While you are getting to know your pupils, you will also be extending your knowledge of what works well in the classroom. In *Continuity in Secondary English* David Jackson writes about pupils in the early years of secondary school having an 'irreverent, humorous world-view . . . a spontaneous wit' often 'revelling in word play for its own sake' (Jackson, 1982). There is certainly a great deal of poetry written and performed in schools by poets such as John Agard, Grace Nichols, Roger McGough, Michael Rosen, Ian McMillan, Jackie Kay and Valerie Bloom which seems to suggest that Jackson is right.

Reading poetry for pleasure

A poem like 'Don' Go Ova Dere' by Valerie Bloom is a good example. Read it, and then consider the suggestions below as ways of encouraging pupils to enjoy reading poetry more widely as well as to pay close attention to how it is written.

Don' Go Ova Dere

Barry madda tell im
But Barry woudn' hear,
Barry fada warn im
But Barry didn' care.
'Don' go ova dere, bwoy,
Don' go ova dere.'

Barry sista beg im
Barry pull her hair,
Barry brother bet im
'You can't go ova dere.'
'I can go ova dere, bwoy,
I can go ova dere.'

Barry get a big bag,
Barry climb de gate,
Barry granny call im
But Barry couldn' wait,
Im wan' get ova dere, bwoy,
Before it get too late.

Barry see de plum tree
Im didn' see de bull,
Barry thinkin' bout de plums
'Gwine get dis big bag full.'
De bull get up an shake, bwoy,
An gi de rope a pull.

De rope slip off de pole
But Barry didn' see,
De bull begin to stretch im foot dem
Barry climb de tree.
Barry start fe eat, bwoy,
Firs' one, den two, den three.

Barry nearly full de bag
An den im hear a soun'
Barry hol' de plum limb tight
An start fe look aroun'
When im see de bull bwoy,
Im nearly tumble down.

Night a come, de bull naw move,
From unda dat plum tree,
Barry madda wonering
Whey Barry coulda be.
Barry getting tired, bwoy,
Of sittin' in dat tree.

An Barry dis realise
Him neva know before,
Sey de tree did full o' black ants
But now in know fe sure.
For some begin fe bite im, bwoy,
Den more, an more, an more.

De bull lay down fe wait it out,
Barry mek a jump,
De bag o' plum drop out de tree
An Barry hear a thump.
By early de nex' mawnin', bwoy,
Dat bull gwine have a lump.

De plum so frighten dat po' bull
Im start fe run too late,
Im gallop afta Barry
But Barry jump de gate.
De bull jus' stamp im foot, bwoy,
Im yeye dem full o' hate.

When Barry ketch a im yard,
What a state im in!
Im los' im bag, im clothes mud up,
An mud deh pon im chin.
An whey de black ants bite im
Feba bull-frog skin.

Barry fada spank im,
Im mada sey im sin,
Barry sista scold im
But Barry only grin,
For Barry brother shake im head
An sey, 'Barry, yuh win!'
        (Bloom in Styles (ed.), 1986, pp. 38–39)

Pupils will probably enjoy the humour and the narrative. They could be encouraged to browse through poetry books and seek out other humorous narrative poems as companions to this one, for example Michael Rosen's poem, 'I share a bedroom with my brother/ and I don't like it' (Rosen, 1974, p. 67).

The style of 'Don' Go Ova Dere' provides the teacher with opportunities to study it as an artefact, not just as a narrative. It has a strong rhythm, rhyme and structure which can be reflected upon and used to discover the extent of pupils' understanding of the poet's craft and to develop that understanding more explicitly.

Because it is written in dialect and includes some dialogue, the poem has a strong sense of voice. It demands to be read aloud. You could read it. Or you could read most of it with volunteer pupils reading the dialogue of different characters. The poem would lend itself well to a group performance with different parts allocated to different voices and choric effects for lines such as 'Firs' one, den two, den three' and 'Den more, an more, an more'.

Writing poetry for pleasure

It was suggested earlier that an important aim for the poetry curriculum in Year 7 might be to extend pupils' enjoyment of writing as well as reading poetry. You might therefore wish to link pupils' poetry writing with work on this poem in several ways. One aim could be for them to experience the pleasures of writing poetry to entertain themselves and others. Another might be to use the characters and narrative of the poem as a basis for poetry writing in another form.

Writing to entertain

Pupils often want their poems to be humorous and to entertain. It is very important to take account of this and to provide opportunities for them to read their poetry aloud to one another for enjoyment and entertainment. In this case, encouraging them to talk about their own experiences of getting into scrapes like Valerie Bloom's Barry may give them plenty of material on which to base the writing of their own poems.

However, it is very hard for pupils to replicate the achievements of experienced poets, and they may need more support to help them to organise their ideas in ways which satisfy them. You might wish to focus their attention on the stanza structure, for example, and how it contributes to the humour; the division of material between stanzas and whether it adds to the humorous effect of the poem; the extent to which the rhythm and rhyme add to the way the poem entertains.

You would need to offer a differentiated structure for pupils to work within. The task, for some pupils, might be to produce a poem written in stanzas of six short lines each. Others might be able to work within the same structure but also try to achieve a regular rhythm. Others still might be able to take on all this and try working out a rhyme scheme as well.

Transforming poetry

There will be pupils for whom the above activity may prove too demanding. They may prefer to write something shorter, more highly structured and not necessarily related structurally or stylistically to the kind of poetry they have just been reading. However, they could use the content of the poem and try transforming it, representing it in a different poetic form. Books for teachers such as *Words Large as Apples* (Hayhoe and

Parker, 1988) will provide you with various good ideas. Writing diamante poems is just one of many which they suggest.

The diamond shape of these poems is determined by particular types of words being allocated to particular lines:

Noun 1

adjective   adjective

-ing   -ing   -ing

synonym 1 synonym 1 : synonym 2 synonym 2

-ing   -ing   -ing

adjective   adjective

Noun 2

Although this kind of approach may at first seem restrictive it is surprising how effective the results can be. As Hayhoe and Parker explain, the structure lends itself well to oppositions and contrasts. Try it for yourself, and see:

Barry

carefree   fearless

daring   running   climbing

explorer   adventurer : watcher   waiter

stamping   snorting   running

frightened   angry

Bull

You can demonstrate to pupils how a diamante is composed by drafting one on the board or overhead projector with contributions from members of the group. It is a good way for them to see how in drafting you record your changing thought-processes, and how poems, like other forms of writing, may go through many versions before they are considered to be finished.

There are, furthermore, exciting possibilities for cross-curricular work here. You could talk, for example, with whoever teaches the group for music, about pupils composing pieces to accompany their diamante poems. You then have another perspective from which to discuss the sounds, rhythms, pace which pupils have built into their writing and which they can replicate in their music.

Assessing work on poetry

Whatever the activity, you need to decide how you are going to assess pupils' work. That will depend on the reasons for your assessment. If you don't know the group very well, your main purpose may be diagnostic assessment, that is finding out what pupils know and can do in relation to poetry and what help they will need from you to rectify weaknesses.

Pupils' progress, however, is likely to be enhanced if they receive some clear, constructive feedback from you as well (formative assessment). You need to decide what form it will take. It could be by written comments from you to which the pupils may respond (e.g. in a profile or record of achievement); verbal feedback to the pupils and written notes for yourself in your mark book; a form of assessment specified by the department. Whatever form it takes, you need to be clear about how assessment relates to learning objectives. Pupils need to be clear, too. The following example shows how that relationship might be formulated.

Linking learning and assessment

1. Learning objective:
   Pupils to develop awareness of the difference between reading poetry silently from the page and a prepared reading of it aloud to an audience.

2. Assessment objectives:
   Pupils demonstrate:
   - attention to features of poetry reading such as intonation, rhythm, pace;
   - ability to suggest ways of speaking different words, phrases, lines;
   - ability to justify their choices;
   - preparedness to contribute to group performance and to realise in practice the group's ideas.

   Written comments for pupil A:

   > Your suggestion that your group should speed up and slow down in your reading of the poem 'Awake and Asleep' was taken up by the others because you made your reasons clear i.e. that it would bring out the difference between the two states. Although at first you didn't want to be in the group performance, you overcame your reluctance and spoke your lines clearly. Having made such a good suggestion it was a pity you didn't quite have the confidence to slow down as much as you intended. It would have added to the contrasts you did achieve in terms of volume: the noisy bustle of the first part; the whispered quietness of the second. Well done!

LATER IN KEY STAGE 3: FOCUSING ON INTERPRETATION

In the preceding section we have foregrounded the importance of the pleasures of poetry. One of the ways in which those pleasures can be extended is by focusing pupils' attention more explicitly on the processes of interpretation. Interpretation has, of course, been involved in the activities described above. But it has been tacit rather than overt. We now move on to explore how developing pupils' consciousness of it might offer them greater understanding and control in their work on poetry without sacrificing the pleasure. From your growing knowledge of what appeals to and seems appropriate for Year 9 pupils, you might wish to consider whether or not you agree that this kind of activity is well suited to them at this stage in their development as readers and writers.

Choosing appropriate texts

'Interpretation' writes Scholes, 'lies on the other side of reading. Its domain is the unsaid.' (Scholes, 1985). If we want pupils to engage in the interpretative process, we need to offer them texts which require it, even force it. A poem by John Mole which begins 'Someone has gone and left the swing . . .' is just such an example. If it is given to pupils without its title, as below, it will instantly generate discussions about what it may mean, and pupils will find themselves automatically involved in the process of interpretation. Some of the pleasures remembered from solving riddles will be in evidence here, but there will also be opportunities for explicit talk about metaphor. (Try guessing the title yourself before turning to the end of the chapter to find out what it is.)*

> Someone has gone and left the swing
> Still swinging, slowly,
> Slower, slow, and now
> It stops, and someone else
> Is coming.
>
> Someone has gone and left the chair
> Still rocking, slowly,
> Slower, slow, and now
> It stops, and there is silence
> In the room.
>   (Mole, 1990, p. 13)

Exploring key concepts

Before proceeding any further, think about a concept such as metaphor which now may be so familiar to you that you take it for granted. Teaching that concept to pupils may prove tricky, so examine your own ideas first. Consider your immediate response to the question 'What is metaphor?' Have you thought how you would define the word metaphor, if you were asked to do so by someone, say, in Year 9?

If words such as 'simile' and 'metaphor' are taught in terms of recognising examples rather than exploring and analysing effects created by them, then the knowledge acquired is merely superficial. Pupils need to understand what metaphor can do so that they can judge for themselves its impact, both in their own and others' poetry. They need to be able to appreciate and create what Jerome Bruner (1986, p. 22) calls the 'atmospheric change' which results from using metaphor, to understand and participate in the way in which metaphor can simultaneously grasp the familiar *and* make it strange, 'rescue it from obviousness' (ibid. p. 24).

'Skills' by Anne Stevenson is a poem which might be used towards the end of Key Stage 3 to explore the concept of metaphor in greater depth and encourage interpretation.

Skills

Like threading a needle by computer, to align
the huge metal-plated tracks of the macadam-spreader
with two frail ramps to the plant-carrier.
Working alone on Sunday overtime,
the driver powers the wheel: forward, reverse, forward
centimetre by centimetre . . . stop!

He leaps from the homely cab like Humphrey Bogart
to check both sides. The digger sits up front
facing backwards at an angle to the flat,
its diplodocus-neck chained to a steel scaffold.
Its head fits neatly in the macadam-spreader's lap.
Satisfying. All of a piece and tightly wrapped.

Before he slams himself, whistling, into his load,
he eyes all six, twelve, eighteen, twenty-four tyres.
Imagine a plane ascending; down on the road,
this clever matchbox-toy that takes apart,
smaller, now smaller still and more compact,
a crawling speck on the unfolding map.

(Stevenson, 1993, p. 23)

What follows is a series of ideas for encouraging active reading and interpretation of the poem. The ideas are intended to provide further concrete examples of some aspects of the planning process, e.g. formulating learning objectives, applying them in practice and linking them to assessment.

Progression and learning objectives

In a mixed ability Year 9 group pupils will have varying degrees of understanding of the concept of metaphor. When planning a lesson or unit of work in which the learning objective is based upon the study of metaphor, you will need to take into account (as with any topic) work they have already done and knowledge they have acquired. Your learning objectives will then be phrased in terms of how you want them to progress.

TASK 12.4   FORMULATING LEARNING OBJECTIVES

This task is intended to help you focus on the process of formulating learning objectives in relation to poetry.

- Imagine that you are to use the poem 'Skills' with a Year 9 group you know. If possible, find out from them or from their teacher, what they have already learnt about metaphor.

- Then use that knowledge to help you formulate up to three learning objectives for a lesson based on 'Skills'. Remember that you are trying to articulate what pupils will *learn*. You are not, at this point in the planning, describing what they will *do*.

Class: Year 9 (mixed ability)

Length of lesson: 75 minutes

Aim: To read and study Anne Stevenson's poem 'Skills'; focusing closely on the poet's use of metaphorical language in order to develop pupils' understanding of the concept of metaphor.

Learning objectives:

1. _____
2. _____
3. _____

Ask another student teacher who has completed this task to compare their learning objectives with yours. Can you both see clearly what it is hoped that pupils will learn?

Turning learning objectives into classroom practice

'Skills' is another poem which forces interpretation particularly through the poet's use of metaphorical language. However, there are two things you want to try to avoid.

The first is simply asking pupils to spot the similes and metaphors without considering what effects and responses are being created. It is a largely pointless exercise and probably fairly devoid of pleasure as well.

The second is taking the idea of interpretation literally and asking pupils to translate the poetic language into prose. This, too, misses the point of a poetry lesson which should preferably be looking towards rather than away from the poetic.

So, what kinds of study activities invite interpretation and enable pupils to remain firmly engaged with the poem? Here are some suggestions.

DARTs

Direct Activities Related to Texts (DARTs) is an idea which arose from the Effective Use of Reading project directed by Lunzer and Gardner. In their report (Lunzer and Gardner, 1979) they offered a definition of 'comprehension' which they formulated as 'the pupil's ability and willingness to reflect on whatever he is reading' and a variety of activities were thus devised to bring about this ability and willingness to reflect. Two examples of DARTs are cloze procedure and sequencing. Both encourage active exploration of a text.

Cloze procedure. Pupils are presented with a poem from which certain words have been deleted. They have to use their understanding of the rest of the text to suggest words to fill the gaps. Comparing the actual words used by the poet may trigger discussion about the effects he or she might have wanted to achieve.

Sequencing. A poem is presented to pupils, not in its original form but divided up into fragments mixed up out of order. The pupils' task is to reconstruct the poem, trying to find the sequence of the original. For this activity pupils may need to identify formal features of the poem such as rhyme or stanza structure. If successful, they will have discovered particular organising principles of the poem for themselves.

Other strategies. Tasks which make visible the processes involved in reflecting on and interpreting poetry include:

- annotating;
- highlighting;
- illustrating;
- drawing diagrams.

The following example of part of a lesson plan illustrates how some of these activities might work in the context of the particular poem, 'Skills'.

Learning objective: To enhance pupils' understanding of how metaphor works by bringing together two ideas which share similarities and differences.

Activity:

- Pupils work in small groups doing a cloze procedure exercise using copies of the poem with the words computer (l. 1), Humphrey Bogart (l. 7), diplodocus (l. 10), matchbox (l. 16) deleted.
- A spokesperson from each group reports on some of their suggestions for words to fill the gaps.
- Pupils then look at the words Anne Stevenson actually wrote and discuss the different effects and resonances created by her chosen words.

- Still in small groups, pupils explore how the metaphors used in the poem connect two ideas that are at the same time similar and different, for example the diplodocus-neck of the digger. At this point it may help if they highlight words or phrases, annotate the text or sketch an illustration.

If you are planning to teach *poetry writing* alongside *poetry reading*, then you might like to use the work pupils do on metaphor in Anne Stevenson's poem as a starting point for them to write their own poems. In your objectives, be clear about what element of poetry writing you want them to be developing. If, as here, it is their use of metaphorical language, their ability to take an element of the ordinary or mundane and 'rescue it from obviousness' then make that clear and plan your lesson accordingly. A poetry writing activity such as 'The Furniture Game' devised by Sandy Brownjohn and described in her book *Does It Have to Rhyme?* could be used or adapted to meet your specific purposes. Requiring pupils, as it does, to think of someone known personally to them and to describe him or her in terms of a piece of furniture, for example, ('she is an old, comfy armchair' or 'he is a stiff, upright, hardbacked chair') or a time of day ('she is the early hours of a warm summer's morning' or 'he is the dark midnight hour') can produce some startling metaphors for pupils then to work into poetic forms.

ENTERING KEY STAGE 4: THE CHALLENGES OF CRITICISM

The third component of the poetry teaching framework which has been outlined in this chapter is criticism. It is, like interpretation, a process in which most if not all readers engage intuitively from an early stage. The suggestion here, however, is that it might be timely, at Key Stage 4, to guide pupils towards a more *explicit* understanding of what the critical process involves. The challenge for teachers is to maintain the pleasure and build on the progress made in Key Stage 3 at the same time as making greater demands on pupils' knowledge, skills and understanding.

In Years 10 and 11 pupils are likely to find themselves increasingly being taught poetry with a view to being able to write about it under exam conditions. Factors such as time pressure or the desire for pupils to achieve the highest possible grades in the exam may, in some cases, lead to what is known as 'teaching to the exam' and thus to a narrowing down of pupils' responses. To what extent do you think that might be the case in the pupil's work which follows?

Vernon Scannell's poem, 'The Fair', has been taught to a Year 10 class.

The Fair
Music and yellow steam, the fizz
Of spinning lights as roundabouts

TASK 12.5 AIMS AND ASSESSMENT OBJECTIVES FOR POETRY AT KEY STAGE 4

- In order to familiarise yourself with the place of poetry in the curriculum for Years 10 and 11, discuss with your Head of Department or subject mentor where and how poetry features in the chosen GCSE syllabuses for English and English Literature. How are the GCSE requirements translated into schemes of work by the department?
- Look at the assessment objectives and grade related criteria for poetry work in GCSE English and English Literature syllabuses. How do they require pupils to demonstrate their achievements as readers, writers and critics of poetry? How adequate do you think they are as the means of summative assessment of pupils' poetry work?

Galloping nowhere whirl and whizz
Through fusillades of squeals and shouts;
The night sniffs rich at pungent spice,
Brandysnap and diesel oil;
The stars like scattered beads of rice
Sparsely fleck the sky's deep soil
Dulled and diminished by these trapped
Melodic meteors below
In whose feigned fever brightly lapped
The innocent excitements flow.
Pocketfuls of simple thrills
Jingle silver, purchasing
A warm and sugared fear that spills
From dizzy car and breathless swing.

So no one hears the honest shriek
From the field beyond the fair,
A single voice becoming weak,
Then dying on the ignorant air.
And not for hours will frightened love
Rise and seek her everywhere,
Then find her, like a fallen glove,
Soiled and crumpled, lying there.

Vernon Scannell, 1971, p. 35

Pupils have read and discussed the poem in small groups. Their attention has been drawn to some of the poetic techniques being used by the poet. Pupils have then completed the following task under test conditions:

Analyse the poem, commenting on subject matter, poetic techniques and your personal response.

Here is what one pupil wrote (transcribed exactly as it was written):

The poem is about a fair. Vernon Scannal gives us a look at one sad night at a fair. He takes us in as if we are walking towards it, first hearing the music then the lights and finally the rides. As we go around the fair we have the fair discribed to us with nice smells of the 'fast food', 'Pungent spice, brandysnap' then a very bad smell of 'diesel oil'. He then discribes the night sky with a picture for our minds to view. 'scattered beads of rice'. the rice being the stars. The fair as a whole is then discribed as being 'melodic meteors' because after we have been looking up we are up in the sky looking down on it and it would look like spinning rock dancing to the music. We now are brought back down on to the ground to feel the atmosphere of the fair. People laugh and scream with delight. Vernon Scannell discribes that the money in the people's pockets is being used to buy sweet thrills 'Pocketfulls of simple thrills, Jingle silver, purchasing a warm and sugared fear that spills. From dizzy car and breathless swing'. also this part of the poem gives us sights at the fair, and the complete look at the fair. Then the poem discribes a horrible sound a scream not a warm enjoyable scream but a 'honest shriek' a scream for real. A person has wandered from the fair and is in great distress. The scream ends. 'dying on the ignorant air'. The atmosphere now has completely reverse the fun and the frill is now cold with horror. Her friends who are at the fair will not notice that she has gone missing, but when they do they search for a long time, but when they discover her they see her lying on the ground 'And not for hours will frightened love Rise and seek her everywhere then find her, like a fallen glove, soiled and crumpled, lying there'. The rape gives us a very negative look to a night fair.

As has been noted earlier, pupils' *development* as critics has much to do with making the processes involved more explicit, so that they engage in critical discussion with deliberate awareness of what they are doing and why.

To be engaged in the critical process, readers need, however briefly, to take a step back from the text and to view it through others' eyes as well as their own. This is something which teachers in school are well placed to foster. After all, they are working with thirty or so individuals who may differ greatly in their outlook and beliefs. Encouraging debate, therefore, is a good way to develop the critical process.

It is important for pupils to know that criticism is not about getting the right answers or finding the correct meaning of a poem. It is about articulating their interpretation and understanding of the text and justifying it in broader terms than just their own idiosyncratic opinion.

Different perspectives from which they might read and comment on a poem could include viewing it in comparison with another poem, perhaps related in theme or structure, or viewing it from different social, cultural,

TASK 12.6 DEVELOPING A CRITICAL RESPONSE TO POETRY

You may initially be slightly distracted by the writer's misspelling of the word 'describe' or by the occasional omission of a capital letter. These are points which should be addressed at an appropriate moment. But it is very important that they should not colour your judgement of the pupil's achievements in terms of completing the task set, in this case analysing and commenting on the poem.

- Using GCSE English Literature grade descriptions for reading, try to decide (as far as is possible on the basis of a single piece of work) what grade best fits this pupil's work.
- If you were marking this essay, what comments would you write at the end to encourage this pupil's development in responding critically to poetry?
- How do you think the pupil has been prepared for writing this task?

historical, political standpoints. This may sound demanding but in many respects criticism *is* more challenging than reading and interpretation. Nevertheless, even if pupils are required to distance themselves somewhat from the text in order to be critical, the process of criticism itself can give pleasure, and the ways of achieving it need not be dry or purely academic.

By the time pupils reach Key Stage 4 there will be significant differences between those who grasp critical concepts with relative ease and those for whom they remain difficult to comprehend. Although the aim of a lesson or unit of work on poetry, for example to develop pupils as critics, and the poetry which is to be read, may be common to all pupils in the class, the teacher's awareness of their differing needs and her expectation of their varied levels of achievement will require the actual work to be differentiated.

Here we will look at how two poems might be used to encourage a mixed-ability group of Key Stage 4 pupils to engage in the process of criticism and, perhaps, to become more consciously aware of what it means to do that.

Meeting at Night

The grey sea and the long black land;
And the yellow half-moon large and low;
And the startled little waves that leap
In fiery ringlets from their sleep,
As I gain the cove with pushing prow,

And quench its speed in the slushy sand.

Then a mile of warm sea-scented beach;
Three miles to cross till a farm appears;
A tap at the pane, the quick sharp scratch
And blue spurt of a lighted match,
And a voice less loud, thro' its joys and fears,
Than the two hearts beating each to each.
    Robert Browning (1812–1889) (from Browning, 1975)

Sonnets from the Portuguese
XIV

If thou must love me, let it be for nought
Except for love's sake only. Do not say,
'I love her for her smile . . . her look . . . her way
Of speaking gently, . . . for a trick of thought
That falls in well with mine, and certes brought
A sense of pleasant ease on such a day' –
For these things in themselves, Beloved, may
Be changed, or change for thee, – and love, so wrought
May be unwrought so. Neither love me for
Thine own dear pity's wiping my cheeks dry, –
A creature might forget to weep, who bore
Thy comfort long, and lose thy love thereby!
But love me for love's sake, that evermore
Thou may'st love on, through love's eternity.
        Elizabeth Barrett Browning (1806–1861) (from
                    Barrett Browning, 1988)

SUMMARY AND KEY POINTS

In order to make a successful start to your teaching of poetry in school you need to be as widely read as possible, especially in the area of contemporary poetry written for young people. There is a great deal of it and much that is of very high quality. Also, think about writing poetry yourself to remind you of the possible challenges and satisfactions involved.

When planning for teaching poetry you need to find out what pupils enjoy, know, and have studied in order to build on their achievements and offer a sense of continuity. Attention needs to be focused on what they are learning about poetry when reading, performing, writing and talking about it. Assessment of their work will enable you to judge their progress and plan ahead.

The teaching of poetry requires a clear rationale which you can begin to develop for yourself by working with pupils, observing poetry lessons,

TASK 12.7   ENGAGING IN THE CRITICAL PROCESS

Look at the following list of activities which are designed to move pupils towards more explicit critical analysis of poetry. The activities are based on the two poems above.

1. a) The teacher reads the two poems with the class without saying who they are by or when they were written. (The pronouns in line 3 of 'If thou must love me . . .' will need to be deleted before copies are handed out.). Pupils discuss in small groups how they imagine the speaker, or persona, in each poem. They refer closely to each text to justify their suggestions. Their speculations might include consideration of gender, historical period, social, cultural and moral issues.

   b) The teacher explains who wrote them and the relationship between the two poets. Alternatively pupils could research this information for themselves. They discuss how this new information affects their rereading of the poems.

2. Pupils are challenged to write a third verse for 'Meeting at Night'. They discuss what they will need to take into account in order to complete this task, for example content, stanza structure, rhyme scheme, type of vocabulary.

3. Pupils imagine they are Elizabeth Barrett Browning writing a diary entry describing an incident which has taken place between her and her lover, prompting her to write this poem. She writes about why she has chosen to communicate with him through poetry (rather than, say, writing a letter).

4. Pupils browse through poetry anthologies to find two twentieth-century love poems, one by a man and one by a woman, which they prefer to these two by the Brownings. They give reasons for their selection based on their reading of all four texts, not just the two new ones they have chosen.

- Consider (perhaps in discussion with a colleague or fellow student) what critical processes each activity involves.
- Decide how and why the different tasks might be suited to pupils of different abilities.

talking with colleagues in school and college and reading what has been written on the subject, linking it with more general theories of reading.

* The title of John Mole's poem on p. 252 is 'Youth and Age'.

FURTHER READING

Bleiman, B. (1995) *The Poetry Pack*, London: English and Media Centre.
This can be used with *The Poetry Video* (1995) compiled by Barbara Bleiman and Michael Simons, also published by the English and Media Centre.

Cook, H. and Styles, M. (1988) *There's a Poet Behind You . . .* , London: A. & C. Black.
Written by poets for children, this book about writing poetry is also an enjoyable and illuminating read for adults.

Hayhoe, M. and Parker, S. (1988) *Words Large as Apples*, Cambridge: Cambridge University Press.
A valuable guide to teaching poetry at secondary level with good practical ideas to use in the classroom. An interesting opening chapter addresses the question, why 'teach' poetry?

Rosenblatt, L. (1978) *The Reader, the Text, the Poem*, Southern Illinois University Press.
An important text for those who want to explore theories of reading poetry in greater depth.

13 Teaching English at 16+: GNVQ and GCE A Level

INTRODUCTION

The number of students who opt to continue their education at 16+ has increased dramatically during the 1980s and 1990s. To both create and respond to this demand for continuing education new courses have been introduced, most notably vocational courses such as the General National Vocational Qualification (GNVQ). Students of a range of varying abilities may be following a range of courses in a sixth form of a secondary school, a sixth form college or college of further education. They may be retaking GCSE English or English Literature. They may be following GNVQ or have opted for A or A/S Level English Language, English Literature or English (a combination of language and literature). Post-16 courses in Theatre and Media Studies also have an English base but demand additional specialised knowledge and skills. (See also Chapter 6.3. in Capel, Leask and Turner, 1995.)

Because students choose to study post-16, there is a different ethos surrounding the sixth form in school and sixth form and further education colleges. Students are given new freedoms: a different dress code; free periods; a less rigid punishment system. These changes are associated with a transition from teacher dependency to independence in learning.

OBJECTIVES

By the end of this chapter you should have:

- considered post-16 teaching in terms of progression from GCSE English, both similarities and differences;
- have some understanding of the requirements of a GNVQ and an A Level syllabus;
- identified a range of strategies for teaching and learning at GCE A Level and GNVQ;
- been introduced to resources to support teaching post-16.

GNVQ

It is likely that every school with a Sixth Form will have a number of students following General National Vocational Qualification (GNVQ) courses. Several factors will determine how many students in a given school are following such courses, but it is certain that the overall popularity of GNVQs is set to rise over the next few years, at least.

What is General National Vocational Qualification?

GNVQ courses are intended as an alternative to GCE A Levels or more GCSE subjects post-16, and it is important to remember that they are equivalent qualifications to those obtainable at GCE A Level and GCSE. Hence, an Advanced GNVQ (Level 3) is equal to two A Level passes at Grades A–E; an Intermediate qualification (Level 2) is equal to four GCSE passes at Grades A*–C. You will also encounter students following Foundation courses (Level 1) which cater for those who are likely to achieve four GCSE passes at Grades D–G.

Built into each course at every level are Key Skills in Communication, Application of Number and IT, which students must pass at the appropriate level or higher to gain full certification. These Key Skills are notated as 1, 2 and 3, rather than Foundation, Intermediate and Advanced.

Communication

Key Skills Communication can be loosely defined as basic English Language skills applied to situations appropriate to the workplace rather than to schools. It is this last phrase which makes the teaching of Communication very different from the teaching of GCSE English, for it is part of a vocational course. It is also administered by Awarding Bodies who do not deal directly with GCSEs although they are affiliated to Exam Boards who do:

- City and Guilds   (C&G);
- Royal Society of Arts   (RSA);
- Business and Technology Education Council   (BTEC).

The end result of this is that the language of GNVQs generally, and of Communication in particular, is very different from that of a GCSE or GCE A Level syllabus.

Communication is divided into four elements:

1. Take part in discussions;
2. Produce written material;
3. Use images;
4. Read and respond to written materials.

(1) Requires skills which are similar to those in the Speaking and Listening component of GCSE English coursework, but with a narrower focus. Most students will fulfil this element through a series of presentations. (2) is closely related to basic writing skills, but is most often presented as a report stemming from the requirements of their GNVQ course (i.e. a vocational unit.). (3) can include images of any sort as long as they support the presentation or written material which they accompany; and (4) has nothing directly to do with comprehension skills. It is information retrieval, from a variety of sources, which forms the basis of the three elements above.

Performance criteria

Within each of the four elements are Performance Criteria (PCs), which give some idea of what is to be assessed. There is nothing novel about these and most of them will be automatically covered by any reasonable piece of work produced by the individual student. There is also some indication of standards, although this is covered in more detail elsewhere.

The PCs for Element 1, for example, at Foundation level (1.1) require the student to:

1. make contributions which are relevant to the subject and purpose;
2. make contributions in a way that is suited to the audience and situation;
3. confirm that s/he has understood the contributions of others;
4. make contributions which maintain the discussion.

The only difference for Intermediate level (2.1) is that the fourth PC reads 'make contributions which *take forward* the discussion'. Advanced level (3.1) differs from Intermediate in that it also requires students to: '(5) Create opportunities for others to contribute'. As far as standards go, this isn't particularly helpful, but there are also differences in the range of coverage for each level.

Range

This is split into four areas: Subject, Purpose, Audience, Situation. It is not necessary to look in detail at each of these, since they are very repetitive (a comment you may find cropping up quite regularly in relation to GNVQs). As an example, Audience will give the best reflection of what is required.

At Level 1 the target audience is: people familiar with the subject who know the student. In a school, this effectively means one of that student's tutors. At Level 2 there is an additional audience of: people familiar with the subject who do not know the student, and for Advanced students, there is the requirement to produce work for: people not familiar with the subject who know the student, and: people not familiar with the subject who do not know the student.

Once again, this is not definitive in terms of standards. This is one of the great differences between a GNVQ and the usual Exam Board syllabus: the latter has to nail down standards very tightly, while GNVQ allows a centre to make recommendations, within common sense limits, as to what meets accepted National Standards. However, the work presented for GNVQ should be of a quality to match that of a student following a GCSE or GCE course at the same level. The easiest of these to assess is at Intermediate level, which aims to be the equivalent of four GCSE passes at Grades A*–C. For practical purposes, this means that if a student produces work which would earn a Grade C at English Language, they are on the right course. You are unlikely to encounter many students on Intermediate courses whose English skills are clearly better than a Grade C. Such students should be actively encouraged to fulfil the requirements of Level 3.

The final part of the requirements placed on the student is the Evidence Indicators.

Evidence Indicators

One example of these should suffice to indicate their nature, but they are the most important piece of information for both student and tutor. At Level 3 students must do the following for Element 1 in order to ensure coverage:

- participate in at least four one-to-one discussions. Two of the discussions should involve people who do not know the student and are unfamiliar with the subject;
- participate in at least four group discussions. Two of these discussions should involve people who do not know the student and are unfamiliar with the subject.

TASK 13.1   PLANNING A LESSON FOR GNVQ

In small groups, using information from the four sections above, devise a one-off situation which would allow an Advanced level GNVQ student to fulfil as many of the requirements of 3.1, 3.2 and 3.3 as possible. You may have only ONE target audience.

Organisation

There are guidelines as to how centres might organise the delivery of Key Skills, but they are left to the centre's own interpretation and you will encounter wide variations in practice. Most centres will adopt one of two broad strategies, however.

The first of these is for Communication to be taught in discrete lessons on a regular basis. If this is the case, you should find that the class in front of you is aiming for the same level, even if they are following different courses.

The second is for students to be given support from a Communication expert within their course lessons on a regular basis. In this scenario, the expert may not necessarily be a member of the English Department. There is also the possibility of finding students working towards different levels within the same classroom.

It might be the policy of a particular centre to make no specific provision for Key Skills teaching within GNVQ. As the Key Skills work should be an integral part of the whole course planning, it is sometimes left to the subject tutors to assess these areas as well as their own course units. This is most often the case with Communication, since it is considered to be the Key Skill most tutors are comfortable with.

If you are to become embroiled in the delivery of Key Skills Communication you will need to work closely with the member of staff responsible for the teaching of each GNVQ course. You must be able to see how opportunities for Communication assessment might arise from the assignments given to the students for their course, and monitor the standards of the work produced. This will require you to become qualified as either a Verifier or an Assessor, or both. Be careful; this is a time-consuming and complicated process.

TASK 13.2   SETTING AN ASSIGNMENT FOR COMMUNICATION SKILLS

Below is an assignment from an Intermediate Business Course. On your own or with one or more student teachers, work out TWO possible methods by which this assignment could be tackled, which would allow for maximum assessment of Communication skills:

Produce an information booklet which explains the job roles of three people within an organisation. The people chosen should be from three different levels of the organisation.

The future of GNVQ

While GNVQ is here to stay, for a while longer at least, its nature will certainly change. There are a number of pilot schemes in the near future, for example, which will almost certainly recommend that Key Skills are assessed by set tasks only, and not just through coursework. These will probably be externally set, but internally marked. The Dearing recommendation on Key Skills for GCE A Levels will also have an impact on the provision that a centre generally makes for Communication delivery throughout the sixth form. It may be several years before a new shape emerges.

A LEVEL

GCE A Level English Literature is the most established and common English course post-16. However, GCE A Level English Language is growing rapidly in popularity and an increasing number of sixth forms offer it to students, where it is becoming a more popular choice than Literature courses. Another option for sixth form students is to choose A/S Levels. These were introduced intending to take half the time of A Levels to deliver, yet to reflect the same standard. In reality, A/S Levels have, as yet, not fulfilled their original purpose. Even schools have mis-understood their existence, using A/S entry for those students they feel will not attain A Level standard or entering students for A/S at the end of Year 12 as some kind of 'gauge' for future A Level performance. For all these reasons, the future of A/S is under debate, educationally and professionally.

In a textbook such as this, it is very difficult to give you specific infor-mation about A Level English. There are so many variables: from the school's own organisation of delivery to choice of board to national changes in the requirements of A Levels. The examining boards for GCE A Level are mostly the same as for GCSE, and, as with GCSE, schools/colleges can select their preference, irrespective of their own geographical area. GCSE and GCE A Level have been subject to the same kinds of changes, too – in 1994, GCSE coursework was reduced from 50 per cent to 20 per cent of the final mark; in 1996, A Levels followed suit. Future developments are for A Level syllabuses to be rewritten again, with probably an even greater emphasis on the so-called cultural heritage, and a call for only one examining board.

Although GCE A Levels still tend to be assessed by terminal examin-ations, there is now the opportunity to choose modular courses. These require students to sit external exams at regular intervals throughout their A Level course, with the possibility of retaking – and improving – their grade if the need arises.

Current debate concerning A Levels focuses on the amount of know-ledge a student should have in relation to her analytical skills. In English, this particularly applies to whether it is more important to develop students' close reading skills, or their understanding of literary texts or language use within their social and historical contexts. There are also issues about: the extent to which A Levels follow on from the programmes of study and assessment requirements of GCSE; how closely they should prepare students for higher education, and therefore introduce students to critical works and to cultural theories such as feminism, New Histori-cism or postcolonialism; how important is it to equip students for the 'world of work' with transferable communication and presentation skills (such as being able to talk and write in a variety of ways).

Teaching A Level: what's the difference?

A common misconception for a student teacher is that A Level will require you to teach all that you have learnt about English during your degree and that students will be immediately ready to employ high-order skills such as sophisticated analysis and eloquent debate. Student teachers and newly qualified teachers are often not given A Level teaching in their first year, as if it is some kind of 'award' that you can attain only when you have taught successfully in the main school. This builds the mystique that A Level is a totally different experience – for the teacher and the students.

TASK 13.3   WHAT IS THE PURPOSE OF STUDYING A LEVEL?

It is likely that students 'stay on' or 'carry on' to the sixth form or college because there is little alternative, because it is expected of them by parents or because their friends are doing so. It can be illuminating to interview some sixth form students about their reasons for studying A Level, their expectations of the courses and their ambitions when they have finished. One criticism of the current A Level syllabuses is that they are too closely geared towards preparing students for higher education courses in the same subject when only a small percentage will study a single-subject course at university. In discussion with some students and/or A Level teachers, try to define the purposes of A Levels in English.

Much about teaching A Level follows on from teaching at Key Stages 3 and 4. You aren't automatically doing anything different: all the teaching strategies you employ at GCSE are relevant and transferable to A Level. Students don't make a magical intellectual leap from the last months of GCSE to their entrance to the sixth form. Don't be tempted into disgorging your own copious notes in sixth form lessons. Having explored the link between GCSE and A Level English, you will also need to consider the aspects of difference.

Developing a student's own responsibility for learning is central to A Level teaching. All examining boards now state that a core aim in English subjects is to reward students who show that they have developed a confident, individual voice which is analytical and perceptive. How you do this involves you achieving a balance in your teaching strategies, between providing students with knowledge of the text and also allowing students to develop their own analytical skills and style independently. For example, to issue students with Toni Morrison's *Beloved* and to ask them to 'read it at home and record your reactions' would be a very daunting task for all but the most able A Level student. Students need guidance on how to read the text; they will need help to see *Beloved*'s account as a rememory of the slave ships and the collective history of black America's past; they will need you to explore with them the Horsemen of the Apocalypse chapter. At the same time, the novel invites close personal analysis; once you have guided students to becoming confident about how the text is working, you can begin to hand over to them the responsibility for responding to its meanings: you would not want to provide all the answers to questions such as 'who or what is *Beloved*?' for them.

There is, quite rightly, an academic edge to A Level which your teaching and learning strategies must address. Students will need to be encouraged to approach texts much more rigorously than at GCSE, but don't assume that you will be working with all A Grade students: as with any set, you will find a remarkable range of ability in the A Level classroom. Even success at GCSE doesn't necessarily indicate a strong A Level candidate. What is more, many schools employ quite wide entrance requirements for A Level, so your students' abilities are likely to be very mixed. You will need, in your teaching approaches, both to reassure students that they will be successful, providing a knowledge base from which they can grow individually, and also to forefront the importance of independence of thought.

Which course and which syllabus?

English Literature A Level

As with GCSE, GCE A Level English Literature syllabuses vary in their specifics quite considerably across boards. The introduction of modular courses further complicates any 'textbook guidelines'. In practice, however, most A Level Literature courses consist of:

- an unseen paper;
- a prepared texts paper (open book);
- a maximum of 20 per cent coursework or a third prepared paper.

Although these areas are discrete and are often taught as separate clearly defined strands, they do all link together. English Literature A Level aims to develop students as autonomous, critical and confident readers. In this sense, whether you are preparing students for an exam or encouraging them to read widely for individual coursework choices, your aim is always the same: to lead each student into close personal analysis of texts and to be able to consider the text in its cultural context.

English Language A Level

As with English Literature, there are specific variations between boards (NEAB produces pre-release material, for example). However, the general format is:

- *Unseen Paper* containing examples from a wide variety of possible sources (e.g. popular and specialist magazines and brochures, advertisements, transcripts, children's writing, textbooks). Students may well be required to 'rewrite' an example in a different form;
- *Prepared Paper* with essay questions on language acquisition, semantics, grammar, sociolinguistic issues such as dialect and political correctness; a compulsory question on the history of language. Essay titles do not of course follow such neat subdivisions as suggested here (although most schools will adopt a thematic approach in Year 12, showing students how the themes cross over later in Year 13);
- *Coursework Option* where students can pursue a language-related study of their own choice, or/and produce some creative writing with an accompanying commentary. This leads to up to 20 per cent of the final A Level result.

GCE A Level 'English' (combined English Language and Literature)

The combined English Language and Literature GCE A Level, like English Language, is relatively new. It is not, however, a straightforward combination of English Literature and Language A Levels. It is very much a 'natural' progression from English at GCSE; so, the A Level Literature section of this chapter will be useful to you, the Language section, less so; that is, you will explore texts as in Literature (although fewer), and the Language element will be grounded firmly on comprehension, summary and creative skills. You will need to lead students into a greater understanding of the purposes of a wide variety of writing, and enable them to acquire analytical skills related to grammar, word choice, structure and semantics. In many ways, the underlying skills you are developing in a combined 'English' A Level are not so very different from their 'single-subject' equivalents. However, the way you do this is different: there is not time to consider English Language under lots of thematic headings; rather, you will use your literature texts to do close language analysis, while developing students' language skills by continuing the emphasis on 'writing for audience' that you began at GCSE.

A/S Levels

If you are required to teach an A/S Level, employ the strategies suggested in this chapter for A Levels. As with all courses, you will need to get to know the syllabus, support material and marking criteria, and plan your work carefully so that you do not spend too much time on one area of the syllabus.

Approaches to teaching at A Level

As with all curriculum areas, our unconsidered approach is likely to reproduce our own experiences; with A Level teaching in particular, there is a convention of a sudden change of teaching strategies which do not take into account the previous experience of the students, principles about effective learning which are considered appropriate at earlier curriculum phases and the range of abilities in the group. The comments of two A Level students at the end of their first term reflect this:

> At the beginning of A Levels it was like being in a different world. We came back and had a strong feeling that teachers expected us to know it all. I did feel as if I'd be the thickest person in the class and everyone would be brainier than me, but they're not.
>
> (Sarah)

> I found GCSE hard but A Level is even harder. You get treated so differently but I haven't changed.
>
> (Yin)

TASK 13.4   CONVENTIONS OF A LEVEL TEACHING

Preferably with a partner or in a group of four, discuss your own experience of English at A Level or equivalent. Consider the following and how these answers might affect your own teaching of A Level?

- the ways you were encouraged to think independently and originally;
- the work you felt was most successful and the circumstances in which this occurred;
- occasions when you were least inspired.

Continuity and progression

English is a spiral curriculum: that is, students keep returning to familiar areas from a more sophisticated viewpoint. Therefore, what works at GCSE works at A Level. Don't exclude those strategies you are using in the GCSE classroom, such as:

- display work;
- brainstorming on to sheets of sugar-paper;
- sequencing/cloze activities;
- use of interactive CD-ROM or research via the Internet;
- group work (and careful planning about the group's make-up, e.g. gender mix, ability, differentiated tasks, etc.);
- 'real' work – for competitions, magazines, school publication.

The above strategies will be welcomed in the A Level classroom, alongside the quieter, more self-consciously analytical seminar approach.

Organisation of the classroom

A major strategy to consider is that of seating. Seating is very important, since, as at GCSE, how you choose to seat your students will profoundly affect the kind of interaction that takes place. A Level groups tend to be smaller (although some schools admit up to twenty per group) so your seating choices can be more flexible than at GCSE. Different learning objectives and teaching styles invite different seating arrangements, so do think about changing seating according to the lesson purpose. Do you want boardroom style so the group can generate opinions easily, or do you want to be the focal point of the lesson? Your decisions about seating will also need to take into account the role of note-taking as this will be affected by your classroom layout.

Note-taking

One of the differences between a Year 11 and a Year 12 class is that the Year 12 students will normally get out paper and pens in the expectation of taking notes as the teacher speaks (but not when each other speaks). If a student is absent he may 'borrow someone's notes': what does this assume about the nature of note-taking and a person's thinking: can learning be transmitted in this way? With reference to your own experiences as a student and to your observations of post-16 teaching, consider your opinion of the role of note-taking at A Level. Do you expect students to note down everything you say, everything everyone says? Nothing? 'The best?' Will you guide them in their note-taking or assume that they are doing it 'right'? How will your approach to note-taking affect your classroom layout? You could interview some students about how they take notes; how confident they are about what they are doing when they make notes; what use they make of their notes.

TASK 13.5 OBSERVATION: ORGANISATION AND AIMS

Observe A Level teaching and note seating arrangements. Consider the link between the seating and the lesson purpose. Which kinds of seating arrangements would suit your own A Level teaching if your purpose is:

- note-taking: you delivering the information;
- whole-class discussion which is teacher-led;
- whole-class discussion which is student-led;
- student(s) present(s) a paper to the class;
- exam practice;
- small group discussions.

Setting assignments

Although individual schools have various approaches, there are some general guidelines to setting writing activities. Again, the advice offered to you at GCSE is directly relevant here. As far as direct exam practice goes, you would use the same style of question as that on the paper set by the examining board. For example, the Associated Examination Board (AEB) at present ask the same question each year for their Shakespeare context question:

> *Remind yourself of this extract from the play. Write a detailed commentary on this extract, paying particular attention to:*

- Shakespeare's presentation of the characters (what they say and the language used);
- the effect of this extract on your thoughts and feelings;
- the importance of the extract in the play as a whole.

It is therefore important that you familiarise students with your own board's particular style – although this obviously does not mean that every writing activity you set on the play needs to be identically worded.

Many A Level writing activities are not specifically for exam purposes but to further develop the students' skills and knowledge in a particular area of the syllabus. At times you may wish to set the same task for the whole group and at others to use the differentiation strategies of GCSE. Tasks which begin with 'discuss' or 'write about' are far too vague and unfocused. Although students should be encouraged to create their own essay titles, these will need to be negotiated with you to make sure that they aren't addressing too general an issue. The key is for titles to encourage analytical exploration of something specific and perhaps the best way to formulate titles is to work closely with the board's marking guidelines beside you. See the following example of the AEB English Literature marking grid (Figure 13.1.)

Another important way to test the success of a task is to have a go at it yourself. This is actually probably one of the best ways of testing out a writing activity's potential for success. Also, when setting tasks, make a list of marking criteria at the same time. This will help you to see if the task is appropriate and manageable; it will also help you to communicate the objectives clearly to the students.

You will need to decide how much support you are going to give students on the task once set. At A Level, the one-to-one tutorial is extremely useful, but it is also time-consuming. You may be able to suspend a lesson in order to see individual students; you might be able to set research topics on aspects of the social context of a text or on characters to be discussed. This would free you to speak to students individually; otherwise, your only option is to see each one in your own time. However,

Level	Marks	Textual grasp and appreciation	Conveying the text (and answering relevantly)	Quality of expression
1	1–3	narrative approach with frequent misreadings.	Mere assertion of points of view. Often irrelevant answer.	Frequent weakness of expression. Excessive, aimless quotation. Misunderstood technical terms.
	4–5	Merely accurate storytelling. Skimpy reading.	Difficulty in engaging with question. Assertive comments largely undeveloped and unsupported.	Simple expression. Flawed but conveying basic ideas. Paraphrase plus lengthy quotation. Unassimilated notes.
2	6–8	Response to surface features of text. Basic and generalised but usually accurate response.	Some awareness of effect of text on selves. An attempt to use specific details to support points made.	Expression generally able to convey ideas. Greater variety of vocabulary and sentence structure. Paraphrase with some embedded ideas. Quotation often overlong. Technical terms or unassimilated notes may be intrusive.
	9–10	Some awareness of implicit meaning. Straightforward approach. Response to obvious contrasts and comparisons	Can explain moods and feelings in text. Becoming aware of effect on reader of scene or events. At least implicit relevance to question.	Adequate expression matching understanding. More sophisticated vocabulary; structure of response can be identified. Quotation probably overlong but sometimes analysed. Fair grasp of technical terms and some ability to use notes.
3	11–15	Beginnings of appreciation of language and style. Secure knowledge and understanding of text. Awareness of subtlety. Closer reading becomes obvious.	Can see alternative interpretations and/or pursue strong personal response. Analysing. Exploring. Clearly aware of effect on reader of scene or event. Coherent, shaped and relevant response.	Expression clear and controlled. Paraphrase rare. Well structured with links between sentences and paragraphs. Wide vocabulary. Neat and purposeful use of short quotation as part of structured argument. Technical terms and assimilated notes become integral part of informed personal response.
4	16–20	*Answers in this category will have some of the following characteristics in addition to all of those in Level 3.*		
		Insight. Conceptualised response. Confident exploration of ideas, language, style. Autonomy as reader.	Overview. Mastery of detail of text. Originality.	Mastery of structure. Confidence in expression. Rarely at a loss for the right word. Skilful use of quotation and close analysis of it. Technical terms and secondary sources enhance response to text.

Figure 13.1 Marking grid: AEB GCE A Level Literature
Source: AEB 0660/0986 English Literature marking grid – Paper 2 (out of 20)

especially when students are working on different tasks, there will be a need to supervise writing in the classroom itself. Although the emphasis at A Level is inevitably on 'the essay', other kinds of assignment will enrich your students' understanding of English at A Level. A Level students do have more time outside the classroom to work on your subject, but many students, especially in Year 12, will benefit if you structure this time for them.

TASK 13.6   SETTING AN ASSIGNMENT

On your own or with another student teacher, choose an A Level text (Literature) or area of study. If you are working with the *Six Women Poets* anthology (Kinsman, 1992), often set at A Level, your 'assignment ideas' might be:

1. Group presentations on particular aspects of the poetry; for example, treatment of motherhood, use of everyday domestic vocabulary; the relationship of these poems to more 'traditional' poetry.
2. Dramatising a poem for radio or television such as 'Letter from a Far Country' and performing the script.
3. Working on a display for the classroom which might be collages aiming at capturing the flavour and themes of each poet.
4. Getting groups to choose a poem from the selection and to work at sympathetic choral reading.

Each of these activities is appropriate to use at any point in the course. They can function as exploratory activities on the text or as revision work. They also serve to develop your students' confidence, as first they share their ideas within a small group, and then present them to a larger audience. On your own or with a partner, devise some similar activities on your chosen text.

Marking strategies

The board's own marking grid (see Figure 13.1.) is obviously your most useful tool when it comes to marking. However, boards don't expect this grid to be restrictive and there is room for good performance to be rewarded even if it doesn't quite fit the mark descriptors. Most schools provide their A Level students with a copy of it; even more so than at GCSE, it is important to involve students in marking procedures – so they can learn from each other and become aware of what makes a 'good' essay. There are numerous ways of doing this:

- by marking each other's work, with reference to the marking grid;
- by attempting the board's own Trial Marking exercise for teachers

(this usually takes place early in the Spring term but there will be a copy of it in school at any time);

- by marking Year 11 work and comparing it with their own.

SPAG

There continues to be a close emphasis on spelling, punctuation and grammar (SPAG) at A Level. The AEB Chief Examiners Report on 1996 English Language exam answers identifies particular areas of concern:

Quality of Language

Assessment Objective 6 requires candidates to communicate clearly the knowledge and insight appropriate to the study of language. It was of great concern therefore to find many whose control of language was such that it intruded on the communication of their ideas. Areas of particular concern were:

- gross spelling errors: *were/where, there/their, are/our*;
- spelling errors in the technical language of their own discipline*: sentance, similie, apostrophie, coma, grammer, Received Pronounciation;*
- no capital letter on English;
- the use of commas at sentence boundaries;
- weakly constructed paragraphs and essay structure;
- convoluted and rambling sentences;
- confusion about when to use *which* and *this* when using subordinate or main clauses;
- a limited range of vocabulary to articulate the effects of texts.

Needless to say such errors were reflected in the assessment of Quality of Language in the marking grid. Students of language, aware of attitudes to correctness, ought to recognise how such errors and the writers of such errors are perceived and the way that mechanical accuracy functions as a gate-keeping device in the educational system. Candidates might be encouraged to carry out an investigation of how employers judge errors and their makers. Focused work in textual analysis and re-casting would help candidates to consider and practise the effects created by different punctuation marks and sentence constructions.

(AEB, 1996)

You will need to work with students on their SPAG skills, as well as developing with them an appropriate A Level essay style (which does not mean that all students write essays following the same 'formula'). One way of raising students' awareness of writing skills is for them to read each other's work and make constructive suggestions for improving their expression, structure and style.

TASK 13.7   MARKING, FEEDBACK AND PROGRESSION

Look at the following opening to a Year 12 student's A Level essay (Figure 13.2). In pairs, discuss what teaching strategies you would employ to aid this student's development of writing skills. How could you adapt strategies you would use at GCSE?

Question: Does Gittings' anthology reveal a rich variety in Keats' poetry? ('negotiated' title)

I have studied all the various themes Keats poems have took, Keats seemed to have the ability to express his thoughts and feelings in many ways, whether it be through rhyme, humour, sonnets or long, story-like poems such as 'Hyperion'.

In Keats early poetic years he seemed to have decided on a formula for his poems. Most of them were in rhyming couplets. Although Keats early poems had a flow and imagery to them it was not until his last days that Keats put emotions and deep feelings into his work.

Keats explored many different aspects of nature and love in his poems, he seemed to be in love with the idea of being a poet and he greatly admired other poets such as Shakespeare. Keats wrote about great works of literature in his poems and gave them high praise. 'On first looking into Chapman's Homer' was one of Keats early poems, in this poem he describes the inspiration and joy he feel from reading this classic text:

> Much have I travelled in the realms of gold,
> And many goodly states and kingdoms seen'.

Keats is saying how he feels he has travelled into another world through literature, he was obviously passionate about exploring the mind's imagination.

Other poems written about literary heroes of Keats include 'On sitting down to read King Lear once again'. This tells of how he is inspired by Shakespeare: 'O Golden tongued Romance, with serene lute!' he seems to want to be as well known and respected as Shakespeare.

Keats wrote many long poems, most of these told stories such as 'Endymion'. This poem was four books long and is based on a great legend:

> From jagged trunks, and overshadoweth
> Eternal whispers, glooms, the birth, life, death.

The poetry was written in rhyme and reflects on the beauty of nature and love.

I feel that when rhyming in poems Keats seems to be limited by having to find rhyming words to express himself. I can see this when 'Endymion' is compared to 'Hyperion', another of Keats long poems. This is about a Greek myth of the defeat of the Titans. In this poem I feel that Keats is far more descriptive. It is full of images and feelings: 'While his bow'd head seem'd list'ning to the earth, His ancient mother, for some comfort yet'. Keats has used a drained sound to depict fear and misery in this line.

Keats has also wrote many humorous poems, most of these in his early days of poetry such as 'On the grasshopper and cricket' which was written as a competition between Keats and a friend to write a sonnet in a set time: 'In summer luxury,- he has never done with his delights; for when tired out with fun He rests at ease beneath some pleasant weed'. Keats wrote many of these poems that seem to be very light at first but he seemed to have a respect for poetry for even in this 'joke' poem he says 'The poetry of earth is never dead'. This shows that he believes poetry comes from the natural world, poetry is found in nature.

Figure 13.2 Student's essay

PREPARING TO TEACH A LEVEL

Building on the general points raised in the previous section on approaches to A Level teaching, this section looks at specific aspects of A Level English and English Language syllabuses.

Knowing the syllabus

As has been indicated already, you need to become familiar with the relevant documentation so that you are clear about how much you have to teach and by when; how is the work assessed: by examination (closed or open book), or coursework? What are the marking criteria? If they have a choice over examining boards, Heads of Department think very carefully about which to use.

TASK 13.8   KNOWING THE CONTEXT

In conjunction with your mentor or Head of Department, find out the following information before you embark on planning your teaching:

1. Which board does the department use – and why have they chosen this particular one? Read the syllabus, syllabus support material, trial marking activities, latest exam paper and examiners' reports to gain a good idea for the board's emphasis and the kinds of tasks set.

2.   Does the department take up the A Level coursework option? If they do, how is this delivered at A Level?

   - Do students make an individual coursework choice or is it teacher selected?
   - Is coursework taught at a particular point in the course or is it threaded through the two years?
   - Is coursework 'taught' differently (e.g. through tutorials, seminars, etc.)?

3.   What kinds of tasks do the department set A Level students? Do all students do the same question/do students formulate their own questions/how frequently do they get set tasks? How much time are students expected to work on English tasks outside of lessons? Do they work on them in lessons?

4.   How is work marked? Many schools will have distributed the board's marking guidelines to their students – but individual schools have their own marking strategies and it will be useful to know these in advance.

5.   What entrance requirements does the school have to the sixth form? Are some students only studying two A Levels, and, if so, why? How 'mixed-ability' is the group?

6.   Where will you be teaching? What kind of seating is available? How is the group 'used' to being seated?

Teaching a set text

Although this section focuses on teaching literature at A Level, much of it transfers to English language teaching. Bear in mind all the approaches and strategies you are employing at GCSE; the main body of this chapter has already led you away from any idea that the lecture situation will be appropriate for your A Level group – other than in small quantities. You should also aim to guide your students to more independence in their thinking by offering alternative ways of responding to their reading. Although boards' requirements differ, no board rewards a student who trots out a practised answer which lacks freshness and does not address the question directly. Remember that one marker will see all the scripts in one group and can easily tell the 'spoon-fed' answers which will resemble each other. It is reassuring to know that boards actually reward fresh analysis, informed by a close knowledge of the text and critical focus in terms of genre and cultural context.

Although you are aiming to encourage your students to become more responsible for their learning, there is quite a lot of preparation you will need to do in advance, even if it doesn't all transform itself to the classroom in several lectures to silent note-taking students. You may be teaching a text with which you are familiar or one which is totally new to you; in either case, you will need to re/read and annotate the text thoroughly. You will need to engage with the critical debates surrounding a writer and the work; these should include up-to-date articles, biographies, critical works and reviews, especially if it isn't a contemporary work. Good starting points are the collections of critical essays in the Macmillan *New Casebook* series. Think about the kinds of teaching strategies you might employ at various points such as: 'ways in' to the text; exploration of themes and concepts during the reading; opportunities for critical debate following reading. Consider setting the students small research projects, which they can present to each other, to explore the background of the text, the literary, historical, social and cultural contexts of its production. Although reference to secondary reading is not included in the criteria, reading two or more reviews, essays or introductions to a text are useful means of demonstrating the areas of debate about the writer and the work and that 'meaning' is not a fixed buried treasure to be unearthed but continues to be made by different kinds of readers. Setting multiple choice questions on a passage or poem where more than one answer can be justified from the text can be a valuable way of exploring how there may be 'meanings' in any text. In addition, find out what video and tape resources exist in relation to the text, such as films, screenplays and interviews with the writer. Consider carefully how these may most profitably be used.

It is common to approach an A Level group with high expectations of debate and discussion, only to find that students 'clam up' and contributions are forced in order to break a silence. As in any context, discussion needs to be structured and works best when individuals have prepared a contribution before the lesson or by working in pairs or groups before reporting back to the larger group. Although there is sometimes a need for lessons to be teacher-centred, especially at first, successful A Level teaching depends upon the extent to which students assume responsibility for reading and responding to texts. On the way to becoming autonomous readers, students will benefit from opportunities to explore the text through recreative work such as pastiche and parody, performance (poetry and drama), hotseating, writing in a scene: in fact, all those strategies suggested at GCSE. For example, if you are to be teaching Margaret Atwood's *The Handmaid's Tale*, you might:

1. Identify various gaps in the text which students could 'fill' by doing a recreative piece – The Ceremony from the viewpoint of the Commander's Wife or another ending after the escape scene.
2. Introduce student to interviews with Margaret Atwood, and critiques of her work (often discovered in a single chapter of a critical text devoted to contemporary women writers); delegate one article to an

individual or pair who read it and report back to the whole group.
3. Show the video of the novel, concentrating on selected sequences. Explore the differences, especially the imposition of a more chronological order and its 'extra scene' at the end.
4. Give students the opportunity to recreate Atwood's style.
5. Set up hotseating of Nick, Ofred's mother or the Commander after the game of scrabble.

Managing the reading

There is no easy answer to managing the initial reading and close textual analysis; although it is universally found to be tedious, it is still common practice to slog through a play line by line. In spite of intentions to try other methods, teachers may resort to this method as the only way of ensuring that students know the text sufficiently well because they cannot be trusted to do it for themselves. Again, strategies used at GCSE are applicable, such as 'keeping track' during the reading and mapping or jigsaw groups working on different aspects of the text afterwards (see, for example, *Wide Sargasso Sea: Teaching a Novel at A Level*, London: English and Media Centre).

TASK.13.9   INTRODUCING A TEXT

Plan three consecutive A Level lessons of 45 minutes each on the opening chapter or scene of a text both you and the students know. (Or you could use *The Handmaid's Tale* if you have no common ground.) Assume the students have already read the chapter/scene through once. Three lessons may seem a lot of time, but beginnings and endings are vitally important to a text; aim to get your group focusing closely on the key features of your text, including language and structure as well as central themes and concepts. Plan to set them a task to explore the text and find out about the context and genre of the text as well as of the writer. For example, make a bibliography of Margaret Atwood's other books; contact the Margaret Atwood society in Canada; find out what 'dystopia' means and other books in this genre.

Unseen work (Literature)

The Unseen Paper requires students to be able to cope with any literary text confidently, to demonstrate close reading skills, to be aware of literary conventions, historical and cultural developments in literature *and* write a clearly structured essay in good English under examination conditions. The area is, in fact, so huge that it can be daunting. At the same time there can be a real opportunity to share your own enthusiasms, availability of text and photocopying rights your only limitations. You do, however, need to guard against concentrating on one genre, such as poetry, because it is your strongest. As a starting point for planning a section of the Unseen preparation, it is useful to look at the set text choices collectively to see if there are any obvious gaps. Unseen papers do not always have extracts from literature; some boards will set non-fiction texts such as travel writing or biography. Unseen work is easiest to approach from a genre rather than a thematic angle because getting students to read closely around, say, Romantic poetry or Theatre of the Absurd or the sonnet across the centuries, will give them a detailed understanding of how writers use and subvert the conventions of genre. Thematic work may not be ruled out completely – Unseen exam papers can include comparative work across genres – but if you have a Year 12 group aim at a sound grounding in the way a genre works.

If you were planning a unit of work which was genre based, you could find examples of the short story, for example; you could include sub-genres such as crime stories, folk tales, science fiction or popular romantic fiction. When studying them with the students you would explore them in a variety of ways but finish with a question in the style of the exam board. A thematic unit of work could be a range of texts about 'War' by historical and contemporary men and women writers across genres and cultures.

Unseen work also offers the opportunity to structure students' own wider reading. Near the start of your teaching experience, you could ask students to report back on a literary text they have recently read and, at the same time, feed in some of your own recommendations. A similar session could be planned for later in your experience, in order to set up an atmosphere that students will always have a book 'on the go'. They need to be answerable for their wider reading by using a 'Reading Log' so that they read different genres, genders, times and cultures.

Coursework

The 20 per cent limit on coursework means that there are two aspects to coursework assignments:

a) coursework assignments ought to develop skills for the exam;
b) students should be given the chance to shine in a way that the exam may not allow them to.

You will, therefore, need to address both (a) and (b) in your teaching of a coursework text. It is a good idea to establish your criteria before you start teaching a text in order to identify skills which are relevant to the knowledge and skills required for the examination and also will not be specifically required, such as recreative writing (i.e. which recreates the story). You will also need to know how a coursework text slots in with other coursework ones – coursework must have a comparative component, for example. As with GCSE, you are likely to teach a coursework text differently, the spirit of coursework being that students have more control over what they write about. At least one A Level board offers an oral assessment option as part of its coursework, so you are not necessarily limited by working towards a written final product.

Preparing to teach a particular aspect of English Language

In order to prepare for this, you will need to do some background reading. All boards provide a comprehensive reading list within the syllabus information, and there is a recommended list of texts which address teaching approaches in the 'Resources' section of this chapter. Some schools may have sets of English Language textbooks from which students can work. Nevertheless, English Language at A Level – as with English Literature – is about nurturing personal response. Students are rewarded for their personal engagement with the subject, shown most clearly in their wealth of personal observations and examples. Although students need to know the theory and major research, these should only be a starting point for students to let examiners know about how this links with their own perceptions of the way English Language is used.

Whatever area of English Language you are teaching, a collection and then analysis of current examples is essential. English Language A Level teaching cannot take place in the classroom alone (although you should, of course, draw on examples of accent, slang, cultural and gender significance as they occur): students need to be actively encouraged to seek out the language of the shopping centre, the nursery, the common room, the assembly. Your best preparation for teaching an area of English Language will therefore be to have collected examples of your own and to have an idea of teaching strategies which will encourage students to collect theirs. For example: if you are looking at spelling, research might include:

1. Scouring each other's essays for common misspellings.
2. Looking at signs on market stalls and outside shops.
3. Considering how spelling is taught in a local school.
4. Examine the purpose of the dictionary (and its history).
5. Collect examples of deliberate misspellings in advertising/products/ news headlines.

You will need to undertake the resource-hunting yourself in order to encourage your own students to work. In order to clarify your objectives for the research and analysis, the board's marking grid will provide you with very useful guidelines when both setting tasks and assessing work. Figure 13.3 gives the marking grid from the Cambridge Examining Board.

Grade	Mark	Criteria
A+	22–25	Excellent work. Original; well informed and argued; fluently and confidently written.
A	16–18	Freshness and originality of view; well-organised presentation; excellent technical accuracy; pertinent and fresh examples; appropriate use of terminology; clarity of perspective and focus.
B	13–15	All-round proficiency: good spelling, punctuation and sentence parsing; sufficient pertinent examples; some control of technical language; good perspective; an answer that satisfied; attempts – perhaps not always successful – to relate language insights to linguistic theory and terminology.
C	13–15	Insights presented which are valid and pertinent; appropriate examples and/or technical analysis; general technical accuracy; answers occasionally lapsing into retelling of the content; an incomplete coverage of the topic, but one showing some sensitivity over language use.
D	10–12	Some comments of value, but entirely in layman's language; an anecdotal approach, with a strong tendency to retell the content of the question material rather than analyse it; noticeably weak technical accuracy; an unordered answer with few examples, containing some comments of value nonetheless. This band should also be used to cover an answer which is good in parts, but is incomplete or too short and has only a minimal number of examples.
E	7–9	Some glimpses of what is being sought in the answer, either in the form of sensitivity to the language use or of appreciation of a point about language, but much more that is unaware of what is at issue; poor technical accuracy; few examples.
N	4–6	Little of value beyond attempting the question.

Figure 13.3 English Language marking grid: Cambridge Examining Board

English Language coursework: creative writing

Although you are very unlikely to be given the responsibility for this during your initial teacher training, you may be working in a school that encourages the creative writing option and, if this is the case, you could be asked to contribute to creative writing lessons. Even if students are not led towards creative writing as coursework, it can be beneficial for all students, since they are to be writing within an already determined genre and to examine its features in relation to their own work will enhance their awareness of language. Ask students to collect examples of the genre they are imitating, get them to share their work, and provide the opportunity for students to employ marking procedures as suggested in this chapter. If you are keen to explore creative writing at A Level, it will always be relevant and welcomed by the school, since the accompanying analysis will benefit the students in the exam itself.

Unseen work (English Language)

As with Literature, this in many ways gives you a totally free hand. Since the Unseen paper could literally reproduce any kind of written text, you could just analyse a different example every lesson. But this wouldn't create any continuity for you – or continuity and progression for the students. Far better to choose a focal point, such as 'the way women are represented in the media' or 'children's fiction: 1900–now'. This way, the class can really focus on specific examples of language use and, at the same time, develop their skills and knowledge for the essay paper. The two papers are inextricably linked; it is the role of the teacher to show how skills are transferable from paper to paper and, if you choose an embracing 'theme' for close analysis, you can combine this with a general essay question on the topic at the end of the unit.

Equipment for A Level English Language

Ideally, English Language A Level needs to be resourced with lots of dictaphones, a video camera, tape recorders and access to television, the Internet and good dictionaries. In reality, this is rarely possible, but do find out what resources would be available to you and then utilise them in your lesson plans. In addition, find out the textbooks which are available in your school or training institution. Recommended texts are given at the end of this chapter.

Teaching A Level 'English' (combined English Language and Literature)

An English A Level 'combines' Language and Literature in the same way that GCSE does. For example, a unit of work based on *I Know Why the Caged Bird Sings* would extend to an exploration of how writers of varied genres (including the media) have expressed issues of racism over the last two centuries. As with all preparation, you would need to make reference to the examining board's syllabus, supporting material and marking criteria.

RESOURCES

There are many valuable support materials available; seek the guidance of your tutor and colleagues in school, as well as student teachers in other schools. Be on the watch for new English education programmes and screenings on television. The following list is a selection of what is available as sources for English Literature and English Language teaching. Remember that it is not the text alone which determines the level of study, but the approach and the requirements of the response.

Barker, V. and Canning, J. (eds.) (no date) *A Level English Language Topics: Authority, Class, Gender*, Somerset: Wessex Publications.

Bleiman, B. (1991) *Activities for A Level English*, London: Longman.

Crystal D. (1995) *The Cambridge Encyclopaedia of the English Language*, Cambridge: Cambridge University Press.

Goddard, A. (1991) *English Language A Level: The Starter Pack*, Lancaster: Framework Press.

Goddard, A. (1993) *Researching Language*, Lancaster: Framework Press.

Lake, C. and Rose, M. (eds.) (1990) *Language and Power*, London: ILEA Afro-Caribbean Language and Literacy Project in Further and Adult Education.

McCulloch, R. (ed.) (1994) *English Literature A Level*, Cambridge: Pearson.

Peet, M. and Robinson, D. (1992) *Leading Questions*, London and Edinburgh: Nelson.

Shepherd, C. and White, C. (1990, 1992) *Essential Articles nos 1–4*, Carlisle: Carel Press.

The Language Awareness Project for KS3 and 4, Lancaster: Framework Press.

Wainwright, J. and Hutton, J. (1992) *In Your Own Words: Advanced Level English Language*, Walton on Thames and Edinburgh: Nelson.

SUMMARY AND KEY POINTS

With the number of students studying at 16+, an English teacher may be required to teach on a range of courses, including GNVQ, GCSE retakes, A or AS Level English or English Language. GNVQ and GCE A Level teaching needs to be seen in the context of continuity and progression within the whole curriculum. Students studying at 16+ will be of a range of ability and consequently differentiation is as much an issue as at earlier curriculum phases; approaches for investigating texts and language study at Key Stage 4 should continue to be applied.

Examining boards provide substantial material concerning the syllabus, marking criteria and sample questions and answers; teachers need to be acquainted with these in order to plan lessons and assess students. They need to consider what is common and what is distinctive about preparing students for examination and for coursework. The main difference between GNVQ, and particularly A Level, and GCSE performance is an independence of enquiry; teachers aim to enable students to develop independence in their thinking through taking responsibility for research, reporting back and responding to their reading. Some students will continue to higher education, but few will follow a single-subject English degree course. Consequently, students need to develop a range of communication and organisation skills; these will not only enable them to make effective use of their time and to do their best in examination at 16, 17 or 18, but to be prepared for both higher education and employment.

FURTHER READING

There is a significant shortage of discussion concerning teaching post-16. The following articles are useful starting points for debating some of the current issues surrounding A Level teaching.

Canwell, S. and Ogborn, J. (1994) 'Balancing the Books: Modes of Assessment in A Level English Literature', in Brindley, S. (1994) pp. 149–153.

Greenwell, B. (1994) 'Alternatives at English A Level, Again', *English and Media Magazine*, Summer 1994, pp. 11–14.

Mitchell, S. (1994) 'Argument in English Literature at A Level and Beyond', *English and Media Magazine*, Summer 1994, pp. 15–20.

14 Teaching English: critical practice

INTRODUCTION

> The vast majority of teachers reported a high level of job satisfaction. Inevitably there were some who found the job unsatisfactory. *Some of these, in particular, had little capacity for self-appraisal and consequently for self-improvement . . . Some . . . had not come to terms with the time commitment of the job. . . .* New teachers who felt that they *could keep abreast of the work, and who were well matched to their posts, found the job rewarding . . . Most were able to evaluate their own work accurately and to identify strengths and weaknesses.*
>
> (OFSTED, 1993, 2.28; 2.29)

The above quotations from an OFSTED survey of Newly Qualified Teachers identify the tension experienced by most at the beginning of their ITE course and work as secondary teachers: teaching their subject and fulfilling the other roles of teaching can be rewarding but there is a cost in terms of time and energy. The statements also identify one key to job satisfaction: self-evaluation. The term 'critical practice' indicates the two factors which are central to successful development as a teacher: the crucial role of school experience and the ability to reflect on that experience. With English teaching it is particularly crucial to develop your own principles by which you can set targets and evaluate yourself in relation to these targets because otherwise you can find yourself driven to please others who may have conflicting criteria; it is this, often unconscious, drive to please or satisfy competing demands which produces the confusion and self-doubt which are common during initial teacher education. For example, you will be wanting to meet the needs and interests of pupils, the differing standards of different parents, the varying ideals and methods of class teachers; the professional tutor in school; the requirements of an OFSTED inspection; college or university directives and guidance; criteria for assignments and the completion of competences. 'Standards' or competences can seem overwhelmingly daunting or unattainable in their requirements of subject knowledge, subject application, class management, ability to assess and record pupils' progress and evidence of professional development (see Capel, Leask and Turner (1995), Appendix 2, pp. 403–405). In addition, if you are sensitive to the political issues, you will realise that school-based ITE encourages an apprenticeship model of training but expects the student teacher to operate as a professional.

Furthermore, the crude statements which are used as criteria for assessing student teacher progress are inadequate for a process where the requisite qualities are always emergent and interrelate. Furlong and Maynard (1995) propose five broad stages of development which student teachers undergo during school experience. These stages are: 'early idealism', 'personal survival', 'dealing with difficulties', 'hitting a plateau' and 'moving on'. Furlong and Maynard are emphatic, however, that these stages are not 'discrete or fixed; rather, they are ... interrelated and mutable' (Furlong and Maynard, 1995, p. 73). Similarly, the writers are keen to stress that progression through these stages should not be viewed in a 'crude or simplistic way':

> We do not suggest that student teachers simply progress along a narrow linear pathway, moving smoothly from stage to stage. This is far from the case. Our research indicates that development from 'novice' to 'professional educator' is dependent on the interaction between individual students, their teacher education programme, and the school context in which they undertake practical experience.
> (Furlong and Maynard, 1995, p. 70)

Development as a student teacher, therefore, can be seen to be the product of, among other things, the complex interactions between the individual, the HEI programme and the school context. These interactions are often perceived as disconnected, and the experience of a partnership course is one of fragmentation; it is difficult, but vital, however, that all parties understand their interdependence. Arthur, Davison and Moss (1997) offer a useful analogy for the process of student teacher development, which they believe takes place in the same way that a photograph develops in a developing tray:

> The image does not develop uniformly from nothing: at one moment a blank sheet; the next a fully-formed, crystal-clear picture. Instead, as the image swims into view, different parts of it emerge simultaneously and independently: a highlight here; a fragment of landscape there; a detail of shadow; now a facial feature, until the complete image emerges. What emerges first and last depends on interactions between information stored in the paper and the chemicals acting upon it. Similarly, the development of the student teacher's practice, knowledge, understandings and beliefs is a *synthesis of experiences*.

There are then no easy answers to the questions of 'what are my goals?', 'how well am I doing?', 'will I make a good English teacher?' What can be said is that you are not expected to demonstrate or achieve all the requirements all at once. If you are unsure about your ability to 'make it' as a teacher, what will be looked for is evidence of progress. Progress will be made, and more significantly, measured, through a process of setting specific targets and, through reflection, identifying achievements and areas for development. According to a survey by HMI, although some newly qualified teachers looked back on their school experience as a time of testing rather than freedom for growth, many appreciated the value of being able to make mistakes and learn from them:

> The teachers particularly valued having a wide range of classes and an opportunity to observe experienced teachers. One teacher referred to teaching practice as a testing ground; another wrote: 'It was a vital part of training. I had to try out ideas, make mistakes, discover weaknesses in myself and start again.'
>
> (OFSTED, 1993, 4.27)

The process of target-setting and realistic self-appraisal cannot happen in isolation; it needs to be done in conjunction with other student teachers, class teachers, the head of department, your tutor and above all, your mentor. You need verbal and written feedback which is constructive and specific. Again, the retrospective comments of a successful NQT endorse the importance of reflection and feedback:

> The staff at my teaching practice school were very supportive – checking lesson plans, making suggestions, observing and giving advice on classroom control. My college tutor was also always available for advice.
>
> (OFSTED, 1993, 4.27)

In what may seem to be a sea of uncertainty, there is a stronghold of consensus that development is complex and takes time. In fearing the censorship of the many masters and mistresses to whom you are answerable, you may find that you are your own severest critic. To some extent this is how it should be; you must be self-critical but realistic and constructive. In order to be neither over-optimistic nor over-critical you need to identify where you are – not where you would like to be (or fear that you might be) – before you can set realistic targets and monitor your progress.

OBJECTIVES

By the end of this chapter you should:

- begin to understand the nature of reflection and the processes of teacher development;
- have an understanding of the qualities, knowledge and skills you bring to teaching;

- be aware of your needs in areas of subject knowledge;
- be aware of the kind of working relationship you wish to develop with your mentor;
- be aware of the importance of the need to develop a wider professional role in the English department and the school as a whole.

MONITORING DEVELOPMENT

Obviously, your overriding aim for the period of your initial teacher education is to develop from a person who is interested in teaching to a confident qualified subject teacher. The difficulty is in how to measure such a development. It has to be acknowledged that 'development' is a complex process and hard to categorise, particularly in terms of a complex role such as that of the teacher; consequently, a profile of competences is bound to be inadequate to describe individual development: 'As yet we have very little detailed understanding of how students develop their own practical professional knowledge in relation to such competences' (Furlong and Maynard, 1995, p. vii). However, Berliner (1994, p. 108) proposes a number of stages in the development of teacher expertise, from the *novice* (student and many first-year teachers) to *expert teacher* ('a small number' of teachers). Indeed, the Teacher Training Agency structure of accreditation for the professional development of teachers relates closely to Berliner's model. However, many are critical of Berliner's 'simplistic' description of the novice which ignores not only the diversity of entrants to teacher education courses, but also the range of knowledge, experience and expertise they bring with them (see for example, Calderhead and Robson, 1991). As Furlong and Maynard (1995, p. 182) observe, it is 'important to recognise that no student teacher enters the classroom as a complete novice – they bring with them a vast array of skills, knowledge and understandings derived from other contexts.' The following task is intended to help you to recognise that you start off with many of the qualities needed for qualified status.

TASK 14.1   INDIVIDUAL STATEMENT

No doubt you have found that the student teachers in your group have had a variety of experiences before they embarked upon a teacher education course: some may be newly graduated in their early twenties, while others may have also studied for a higher degree; some may have had some teaching experience in the UK or abroad; others may have raised families or be embarking upon a second career. Whatever your and their experience may have been, it is clear that you all have different kinds of knowledge and expertise which you will bring to your teaching. Equally, it is important that you are clear in your own mind about your own reasons for teaching. Using the headings given below, write an account of yourself. This will serve as a benchmark against which you will be able to gauge your development at strategic points of your course. When you have completed it, you might wish to share its contents with another student teacher, your tutor or mentor. Keep your Individual Statement as it will be useful at any stage during the year which seeks to review your development.

Individual Statement

Write an account of yourself using the following headings:

Stage of the course
Note the date so that you can monitor development since an earlier point or at a later point of the course.

Reasons for wanting to teach
Describe why/how you have decided to become a teacher.

Me as teacher
What sort of teacher do you wish to become? How would you like to be seen by pupils and colleagues?

Previous experience
Describe any experience you feel is relevant to the course, or to your chosen career.

Personal skills and qualities
Describe any qualities and skills you have which you believe to be appropriate to teaching.

Attitude to the subject
Describe any beliefs or principles you hold about the nature and importance of English as a school subject (see Task 2.1).

Professional concerns
Describe any current issues or problems you are concerned about in relation to teaching.

Any other issues

Having shared your Individual Statement with other student teachers, it will have become apparent that you all have a variety of qualities and experiences which will enhance teaching. To categorise you and your colleagues all as 'novices' ignores the expertise you bring to an ITE course. Postgraduates will have followed markedly different programmes during their time studying for a first degree. No doubt you have discovered the variety of degrees your fellow student teachers have obtained: some may have studied for 'traditional' single-subject degrees in English; others may have followed modular programmes; others still may have studied English and American Studies, Media Studies, Drama, English and Anthropology, for example. Such diversity will enrich your discussions throughout the year. However, it will be equally clear that while you have particular knowledge, skills and qualities related to your work in the classroom, your experiences of English as a subject may mean that there are gaps in relation to National Curriculum English. You should be act-

---

TASK 14.2　SUBJECT REVIEW

Read Chapter 4, 'Working with the National Curriculum'. You will see that National Curriculum English requires teachers to engage with the whole range of aspects of English as a subject. While you may be particularly confident in some areas, there may be gaps in your subject knowledge which need to be filled.

　Photocopy the chart below (Table 14.1). Complete the boxes to identify areas of progression and 'gaps'. The 'action' column should give you goals for your own development. Discuss with your mentor and tutor strategies for developing your knowledge, understanding and experiences through relevant reading, observations in school or training courses.

Table 14.1 Subject knowledge in relation to curriculum areas

Subject area	Confident	Not Confident	Action
Media Studies • analysis of film, TV and journalism • media production			
Drama • conventions such as role play, hotseating • ability to perform drama activities			
Speaking and listening • facilitate group discussion • conventions of formal activities, e.g. debates			
Reading • pre-twentieth-century texts (drama, poetry, novels and short stories) • twentieth-century writers (drama, poetry, novels and short stories) • text from diverse cultures • non-fiction			
Writing • creative writing (to produce or analyse) • formal purposes, e.g. reviews, reports • variety of forms			

Information technology			
• word processing • using specific programs • information retrieval, e.g. library, systems, CD-ROMs			
Language study			
• language varieties • language change • standard English			
Teenage fiction			
• class reader • wider reading			

ively seeking opportunities not only to use your strengths but also to develop your knowledge through reading, attending poetry readings, watching documentary programmes and adaptations, seeing plays and films, debating texts with one another and with colleagues in school.

DEVELOPING ROLES AND RELATIONSHIPS

Working with your mentor

Crucial to 'critical practice' are the relationships between the student teacher, mentor and colleagues within the English department. While most ITE programmes have a teacher designated as a subject mentor, it is highly likely that you will also have the support of the head of department, or of more experienced colleagues whose classes you are teaching. It is most important that you clarify the terms of your relationship with your colleagues very early on in your school experience.

While your mentor will be a knowledgeable, experienced English teacher, who is a good source of ideas and who will engage in discussion

---

TASK 14.3   EXPECTATIONS OF STUDENT TEACHER AND MENTOR

Listed below are a number of words which might describe the many roles of a mentor. In order to clarify how you perceive your needs and expectations, number the words in order of priority (or you could identify your top three):

Colleague	Role model	Critic
Mediator	Motivator	Consultant
Assessor	Counsellor	Provider of materials
Collaborator	Diagnoser	Subject guru
Reviewer	Facilitator	Source of ideas

> Having done so, discuss your expectations with your mentor and ask him to discuss his own views on the mentor's role. Equally, you might invite your mentor to do this exercise separately at the same time as you and then compare your lists. A good starting point for beginning to discuss your needs might be the Initial Statement and Subject Review you produced earlier.

of key issues related to the teaching of English, you should not act simply as a 'sponge' soaking up what is offered. You are expected to be proactive; to take responsibility for your own development; to set agendas; to identify targets.

Central to your relationship should be the notion of openness: 'the ability to ask for, and also be willing to receive, advice' HMI (1993). This openness can be developed once you understand exactly what is the relationship between development and judgement in the work of your mentor. You need to know your mentor's expectations of you and, of course, you need to articulate what expectations you have of your mentor. Such an approach will enable you to engage in productive discussion of your development – your successes, needs and targets for development – during lesson debriefings and review meetings with your mentor.

Collaborative teaching

Much of your time in the first weeks of school experience is likely to be spent observing in an attempt to begin to understand the processes and practices of the English classroom. Some student teachers find this period frustrating. Having made the decision to embark upon a teaching career, they are keen to 'do it for real': to stand alone in front of a class and 'be a real teacher'. Such feelings are understandable, particularly when a student teacher has been observing an accomplished English specialist who makes it all seem so easy. But do not be in too great a hurry. There are other ways in which you will learn as much, if not more, about teaching than from teaching alone. After all, it is sobering to think, that if you enter teaching in your early twenties, you'll have some forty years to teach alone – ample time to perfect the art.

Obviously, observation will take you only so far. However, focused observation in which teacher and mentor have decided on the key aspects for attention, followed by a detailed discussion of the teacher's reasons for certain decisions and actions, can enable you to learn much. Engaging in a dialogue about the mentor's reasons for choosing one course of action, for example, rather than another at a particular point, will identify the multitude of choices that a teacher makes throughout the course of a lesson. Such choices are not only made during a lesson: they will have been made at the planning, preparation and evaluation stages.

Moving on from observation you can ideally negotiate some collaborative teaching. Collaborative teaching will enable you to develop your classroom skills, knowledge and understanding progressively and coherently. By taking responsibility for parts of lessons initially, you will be able to focus upon and develop key aspects of the teaching repertoire: beginning and ending lessons; handling transitions smoothly; instruction and exposition; question-and-answer; story-telling; managing and working with individuals, groups and a whole class. Collaborative teaching with your mentor will help you to develop your classroom teaching skills progressively and it will also enable you to gain access to those choices in relation to all aspects of teaching.

> When a mentor and learner-teacher take joint responsibility for a lesson, plan it together, and each play different parts in the teaching, with the parts played by the learner-teacher being selected to provide focused learning experiences, very nearly ideal conditions can be achieved for practising classroom strategies . . . having to explain to one's planning partner exactly what one's purposes are and the variety of considerations that lead one to choose particular ways of pursuing these purposes can help mentors to make explicit their own planning processes.
>
> (McIntyre and Hagger, 1993, p. 33)

At the heart of collaborative teaching and, indeed, of the working relationship with your mentor, is discussion: discussion which unravels and analyses the reasons for choices made while planning, teaching and evaluating collaboratively-taught lessons. It is the articulation of these reasons for choices which will present the processes and practices of teaching and the values and beliefs about the subject which underpin English teaching.

Collaborative teaching need not necessarily be carried out only with your mentor. There is much to be gained from teaching collaboratively with another teacher or a fellow student teacher. Collaborative teaching does not have to be seen as a one-way process either; classroom teachers who can adjust to co-operative teaching often discover an interchange of ideas, approaches and resources. Again, the survey of NQTs is useful in identifying the areas where teachers learn from others and where the student teacher and NQT can contribute to the department in which they work:

> In their initial plans, the most effective teachers usually identified the structure and content of each lesson. They included the grouping of pupils, the timing of the lesson, the choice of resources and the use of non-teaching support. The survey revealed instances

where some aspects of the new teachers' plans had been adapted by other teachers in the school.

(OFSTED, 1993, 3.17)

Working in the English department

In the early period of their ITE courses many student teachers relate to a model of the teacher which focuses in the main on standing in front of a class. When you listed your skills, qualities and your reasons for teaching in your Initial Statement, it is likely that you used some of the following: 'enthusiasm', 'communication', 'love of subject', 'enjoyment of subject', 'empathy with pupils'. It is precisely these reasons that bring most of us to English teaching, but such attributes focus upon the *act of teaching*: the teacher in a classroom working with pupils. However, once in school it is clear that your working environment goes beyond the four walls of the classroom. While most of your day might be spent engaging with pupils, you will be expected to form positive working relationships with adults, be they mentors, departmental colleagues, other student teachers, support and administrative staff and parents. It is important, therefore, that you see yourself developing professionally in three ways, not only in the classroom, but also in the English department and in the school as a whole. You need to develop your professional role not only as a classroom practitioner, but also as fellow subject professional.

You may find that when you discuss your Individual Statement with other student teachers some hold a 'cultural heritage' view of English (DES and Welsh Office, 1989) and are mainly interested in passing on the humanistic values perceived as being located in literary texts. It may be that they see this approach to be closely linked to transmission, teacher-centred modes of teaching. Conversely, others may hold a 'cultural analysis' view of the subject (DES and Welsh Office, 1989) and are more likely to be interested in how readings of texts are constructed, and in their teaching wish to involve pupils actively in exploring and constructing them. (For further discussion of beliefs about the nature of English as a subject, see Chapters 1–3 in this book.)

Equally, the same diversity of beliefs is true of experienced English teachers. While the English department in which you are placed acts as a cohesive and united team of subject specialists, it is important to realise that in any English department, there will be a wide range of beliefs about the importance of different aspects of the subject; a diversity of opinions on pedagogy; a variety of teaching styles – all of which are informed by the values and beliefs of the members of the departmental team. The shared aims and goals of the English department which are exemplified in collaboratively produced schemes of work, for example, may well be the product of a variety of values, beliefs and attitudes held by different departmental members. There is, of course, no *one* way to teach English.

Indeed, when you observe experienced English teachers, it is likely that you will see them employ a range of styles and approaches with different classes, or, indeed, within the same lesson.

The range of perspectives that teachers of English hold is part of the fabric of the English department. Such a range of perspectives may well be implicit in the day-to-day work of the department, but the differences are likely to be made visible in the discourse of departmental meetings. In such meetings English teachers have to respond to the variety of values, beliefs and attitudes located in the products of many educational discourses: for example, the 'Dearing' National Curriculum English order to be implemented; revised GCSE syllabuses to be planned for and taught; GNVQ initiatives; draft LEA, school and departmental policies tabled for discussion.

Departmental meetings are at the heart of a teacher's working life and are an excellent source for your own professional development. However, initially, they can appear daunting occasions. To be surrounded by confident, experienced subject specialists can make you all too aware of how little you really know about teaching the subject. However, you should attempt to make a contribution to the work of the department beyond your own classroom teaching. Good relationships with your departmental colleagues also mean sharing ideas and resources. It is important, therefore, for you to take as full a part as is appropriate in departmental discussions and decision-making. Many teachers, departments and schools engage in teacher education precisely because student teachers bring a new perspective and fresh ideas. You should display confidence (but not over-confidence) in your knowledge and abilities, but also have a realistic awareness of your needs and the gaps in your knowledge and understanding, which are, for the most part, the result of the limited experience of teaching that you have had hitherto. Above all, you will be expected to ask questions. Such involvement will develop your understandings of how a department is managed, how a school curriculum emerges, and it will highlight the fact that teaching is always a matter of choices. It will deepen your understanding of classroom practice by uncovering the complex interactions between the range of educational discourses with which an English teacher engages both inside and outside the classroom. It is important, therefore, that you discuss with your mentor not only the possibility of your attending departmental meetings but, where appropriate, departmental INSET and parents evenings, at which you will gain further insight into the work of an English teacher.

In relation to examination work – whether or not you are actually teaching GCSE, A Level or vocational groups – it will be extremely valuable to you to attend moderation meetings for two reasons. First, such meetings allow you to begin to become aware of the standards expected of pupils to achieve certain levels in the National Curriculum, or grades in public examinations. Second, discussion at such meetings explores the differences of opinion as to the relative importance of various aspects of English which are exemplified in pupils' work.

Clearly, it is important to recognise that any English department, while working as a united team, with stated aims and policies on a variety of curricular issues, is in fact the sum of a range of values and beliefs related to educational discourses. In order for you to become fully developed as a subject specialist classroom teacher, it is important to participate fully in the life and work of the English department. As Arthur, Davison and Moss (1997) sum up, 'subject teaching should not just be seen in terms of classroom practice; nor should further professional development only be seen in terms of a student teacher's involvement in extra curricular activities and pastoral work: both facets of school experience should be located firmly within the discourses of the subject department.'

REFLECTION

Naturally, in the early days of school experience, like all student teachers, you will be most concerned by approaches to class management. Undoubtedly, one of the key targets at this point of any HEI course is the development of the basic skills of teaching. However, it is equally important to realise that the teaching of a subject is not unproblematic. As Dart and Drake (1996, p. 63) observe: 'a student must possess certain beliefs about the subject, beliefs which are acted out in the way the student teaches, manages the classroom and establishes relationships with pupils.'

Although 'a number of competing models and conceptions of the "reflective practitioner" exist, varying in the meaning which they give to the terminology they use and in the nature of the theoretical articulation of the notion which they offer' (McLaughlin, 1996, p. 30), Calderhead (1989) provides a useful overview of the definitions of reflection which have emerged in the writing related to teaching and teacher education. Reflective practice incorporates a variety of features including: problem setting and solving; the development of analytical skills and attitudes which facilitate reflection, such as self-awareness and self determination; the examination of values, moral principles and ideological and institutional constraints. Such features encompass, and are the foundation of, the process, content, preconditions and product of reflection. To sum up, reflection is 'the mental process of structuring or restructuring an experience, a problem or existing knowledge or insights' (Korthagen and Wubbels, 1995, p. 55).

Frost (1993, p. 140) helpfully summarises the purposes of reflection and how the process enables the student teacher to:

- assess his or her own skills and to improve them;
- evaluate the chosen teaching strategies and materials in terms of their appropriateness;

- question the values embedded in those practices and proceed to challenge the aims and goals for teacher education;
- continue to examine and clarify their personal values and beliefs about society and pedagogy;
- theorise about the context of their pedagogical practice – that is, to try to develop explanations about the pupils, the interactions in the classroom and about the processes of teaching and learning;
- examine the adequacy of theories about pedagogical contexts and processes and develop a critique of them.

The purposes of reflection are much wider, then, than only the acquisition of classroom skills. Reflecting enables you to recognise the aims, values and beliefs which underpin classroom practice and the educational processes of the school. Reflection within an ITE course will enable you to develop practice in the short term, and also begin the development of habitual reflection that will subsequently enable you to continue to improve practice throughout your career. To elaborate: structured, guided reflection on, or analysis of, your own practice, in the light of required reading, or school-based investigations which are part of an ITE course, will begin to develop initial competence in the context of a particular school-experience classroom. This experience will also develop practices of reflection which, as a Newly Qualified Teacher, you may use to facilitate further professional development.

In order to reflect, you need to have a set of terms by which to evaluate how you fulfil your roles as a teacher; a commonly understood set of terms is what is understood by a 'philosophy'. It is common to hear that 'philosophy' or 'theory' are not relevant when learning skills and strategies; you do, however, need a framework of principles by which to evaluate what you are doing and to enable you to make decisions that appear to

---

TASK 14.4   THEORY AND PRACTICE

The following four statements are philosophical in nature. Decide which you agree with most. Explain to your tutor or another student teacher the reasons for your choice.

1. An active involvement with literature enables pupils to share the experiences of others. They will encounter and come to understand a wide range of feelings and relationships by entering vicariously the worlds of others, and in consequence, they are likely to understand more of themselves.

    (DES and Welsh Office, 1989)

2. British education is directed towards the dissemination of certain ideological values, whose preservation will ensure that

the economic inequalities of British society remain unchallenged
. . . As educators, we have a duty to enable our students to
understand the relations between language and society, culture
and economics, knowledge and power. In other words, we must
develop goals, classroom approaches and material which will
transform 'English' into the study of the world and how our
entire culture is produced, sustained, challenged, remade.

(Macdonald, *et al.*, 1989, p. 16)

3. Teaching English at any level needs to be founded on an
    understanding of the nature of language and the way in which it
    is acquired and developed. The teacher must have a clear grasp of
    the range of purposes for which we need and use language. We
    need it for the transactions of our everyday lives. We need it for
    personal and social relationships. We need it for reflecting on and
    understanding our experiences, for responding to the world
    about us, and for understanding and sharing the experience and
    insights of others. We use it to resolve problems, to make
    decisions, to express attitudes. Part of the skill of the teacher is
    to show how the various uses of language illuminate each other:
    how, for example, the language resources used in a poem differ
    from and complement those used in a set of instructions for
    carrying out a process. Good teaching of English, at any level, is
    far more than the inculcation of skills: it is an education of the
    intellect and sensibility.

    (DES, 1984, 3.2, p. 13)

4. [the future agenda for English teaching must be] a curriculum
    which values the whole person, where pupils are taught and learn
    appropriate skills and knowledge, in meaningful, relevant
    contexts. We need to create a situation where pupils learn to
    appreciate others' creativity and develop their own; to construct
    texts and understand how and why texts are produced; to
    appreciate and respond to texts. All this within a context which
    recognises and values cultural diversity and students' own and
    others' heritage. A future where students have the skills necessary
    to function in all aspects of their lives: at work, leisure activities
    and in their personal lives. Ultimately, to help students to take a
    full part in the local community and society at large by exercising
    moral values of honesty, justice, fairness and democracy.

    (Shreeve, 1995, p. 1.)

When you have considered the above statements, try to compose
your own statement about the future agenda for English teaching.

be consistent. A 'philosophy' does not have to be fixed or limiting; instead, it should be dynamic as it responds to experience. It should be developed from combining your reading and analysis of other people's theories with your own ideas and experience. When you apply for a job, your letter of application and your answers to questions in interview will be expected to reflect your personal aims as an English teacher.

SUMMARY AND KEY POINTS

Often, particularly in the early days of school experience, student teachers give little thought to their potential roles as departmental colleagues, or of at some stage being given responsibility for areas of the curriculum in a subject department. This is entirely appropriate as the initial task on which student teachers focus is the ability to motivate and manage pupils in the classroom. However, an approach to school experience which sees it only as a basis for acquiring a set of context- and value-free skills in the English classroom is likely to lead to a relationship with a mentor which might be called an 'apprenticeship'. Such a model of school experience is insufficient. It is not the intention of ITE courses to 'clone' teachers, which would be not only undesirable, but also impossible. Such a model pays insufficient attention to the social dynamics of becoming a teacher. It undervalues the process of developing a personal philosophy which can be articulated and translated into practice through the synthesis of experiences. It does not take account of the varying experiences and skills which each student teacher brings to their initial teacher education.

An open working relationship with your mentor can allow you to begin to probe your own personal theories of teaching and learning – the theories and images of teaching and learning which all student teachers bring to a teacher education course (Calderhead and Robson, 1991) and which develop and change during school experience. Griffiths and Tann (1992) propose that reflection should not be viewed as hierarchical (i.e. practical and critical modes are equally important), rather all student teachers and teachers, who might be considered to be reflective, should engage in all levels in their careers. Therefore a student teacher, or, indeed, an experienced teacher, might engage in the form of reflective practice most appropriate to the context in which they find themselves:

> Everyone has to start somewhere, and no-one can start everywhere. It is being argued that all of the levels are an essential part of reflective practice. At any one time the focus may be on one or another of them, but it is vital that each reflective practitioner should follow all of them at some time.
>
> (Griffiths and Tann, 1992, p. 79)

Mentor and student teacher, by engaging in an articulation of personal experience, by investigating the educational discourses embedded in the descriptions of experience and practice, and by engaging in dialogue, can better understand the contexts in which they are working; in these ways, they will both develop professionally.

FURTHER READING

Arthur, J., Davison, J. and Moss, J. (1997) *Subject Mentoring in the Secondary School*, London: Routledge.
This book looks at the nature of student teacher development in the light of the changes in teacher education since 1992. It examines tendencies in subject mentoring and proposes that 'discursive' mentoring is more likely to promote development. The book also contains case study material relating to observation and collaborative teaching in the English classroom.

Capel, S., Leask, M. and Turner, T. (1995) *Learning to Teach in the Secondary School*, London: Routledge.
The companion volume to this book considers all aspects of school experience from a generic point of view. It supports student teachers whatever their subject.

Dart, L. and Drake, P. (1996) 'Subject Perspectives in Mentoring', in McIntyre, D. and Hagger, H., *Mentors in Schools: Developing the Profession of Teaching*, London: Fulton.
This paper considers in depth aspects of subject mentoring with particular focus on the English classroom.

OFSTED (1993) *The New Teacher in School*, London: HMSO.
This is a report of the third survey by HMI of Newly Qualified Teachers, following others in 1981 and 1987. It includes reference by NQTs to their training and recommendations for improved initial teacher education.

Bibliography

Abbott, C. (1995) 'What use are the new technologies?', in Protherough, R. and King, P. (1995).

Aers, L. and Wheale, N. (1991) *Shakespeare in the Changing Curriculum*, London: Routledge.

Alexander, P. (ed.) (1951) *William Shakespeare: The Complete Works*, London and Glasgow: Collins.

Alvardo, M. and Boyd-Barrett, O. (eds) (1992) *Media Education: An Introduction*, London: BFI/Open University.

Andrews, R. (ed.) (1989) *Narrative and Argument*, Buckingham: Open University Press.

Arnold, M. (1869) *Culture and Anarchy*, London: Penguin (1969 edn).

Arthur, J., Davison, J. and Moss, J. (1997) *Subject Mentoring in the Secondary School*, London: Routledge.

Arts Council (1992) *Drama in Schools: Arts Council Guidance on Drama Education*, London: Arts Council.

Bagnall, N. (ed.) (1973) *New Movements in the Study and Teaching of English*, London: Temple Smith.

Bain, E. and R. (1997) *The Grammar Book*, Sheffield: NATE.

Bain, R. (1991) *Reflections: Talking about Language*, London: Hodder & Stoughton.

Baldick, C. (1983) *The Social Mission of English Criticism*, Oxford: Oxford University Press.

Ball, S. (1985) 'English for the English', in Goodson, I. (ed.) *Social Histories of the Secondary Curriculum*, London: Falmer.

Barker, C. (1977) *Theatre Games*, London: Methuen.

Barker, V. and Canning, J. (eds) (no date) *A Level English Language Topics: Authority, Class, Gender*, Somerset: Wessex Publications.

Barnes, D. (1976) *From Communication to Curriculum*, London: Penguin.

Barnes, D., Britton, J. and Rosen, H., (1969) *Language, the Learner and the School*, Harmondsworth: Penguin.

Barrett Browning, E. (1988) *Selected Poems*, London: Chatto & Windus.

Bazalgette, C. (1991) *Media Education: An Introduction*, London: BFI.

Benton, P. in (1996) 'Children's reading and viewing in the nineties', in Davies, C. (ed.) (1996) *What is English Teaching?*, Milton Keynes: Open University Press, pp.76–104.

Benton, P. and S. (1991, 1990) *Inside Stories 3 and 4*, London: Hodder & Stoughton.

Berliner, D, (1994) 'Teacher Expertise', in Moon, B. and Mayes, A. S., *Teaching and Learning in the Secondary School*, London: Routledge.

Bethell, A. (1983) *Eyeopener*, 1 and 2, London: Cambridge University Press.

Bhatt, S., in Bhinda, M. (ed.) (1994) *Jumping Across Worlds*, Sheffield: NATE.

Black, P. (1992) 'Introduction', in Black, P., *et al.*, *Education: Putting the Record Straight*, Stafford: Network Educational Press.

Blatchford, Roy (ed.) (1986) *The English Teacher's Handbook*, London: Hutchinson.

Bleiman, B. (1991) *Activities for A Level English*, London: Longman.

—— (1995) *The Poetry Pack*, London: English and Media Centre.

Bloom, V., in Styles, M. (ed.) (1986) *You'll Love this Stuff!*, Cambridge: Cambridge University Press.

Bloome, D. and Stierer, B. (1995) *Reading Words*, Sheffield: NATE.

Board of Education (1904) *Elementary Code*, London: HMSO.

—— (1910) *Circular 753*, London: HMSO.

—— (1921) *The Teaching of English in England* (Newbolt Report) London: HMSO.

—— (1926) *Education and the Adolescent* (Hadow Report) London: HMSO.

—— (1938) *Report on Secondary Education* (Spens Report) London: HMSO.

—— (1943) *Curriculum and Examinations in Secondary Schools* (Norwood Report) London: HMSO.

Bogdanov, M. (1994) 'Shakespeare on the Estate', part of the series Bard on the Box, BBC 2 Television.

Bolton, G. (1992) *New Perspectives on Classroom Drama*, New York: Simon & Schuster.

Branston, R. & Stafford, R. (1996) *The Media Student's Book*, London: Routledge.

Brindley, S. (ed.) (1994) 'Part IV: Writing', *Teaching English*, London: Routledge .

Britton, J. (1970) *Language and Learning*, London: Penguin.

—— (1973) 'How we got here', in Bagnall, N. (ed.) *New Movements in the Study and Teaching of English*, London: Temple Smith.

Broadbent, S. (1994) *Romeo and Juliet: Classroom Material*, London: English and Media Centre.

—— (1995) *Key Stage 3 English Units*, London: English and Media Centre.

Browning, R. (1975) *Men and Women and Other Poems*, London: J.M. Dent.

Brownjohn, S. (1980) *Does It Have to Rhyme?*, London: Hodder & Stoughton.

Bruner, J. (1986) *Actual Minds, Possible Worlds*, Cambridge, Mass.: Harvard University Press.

Buckingham, D. (1993) *Children Talking Television*, London: Falmer Press.

Buckley, K., *et al. Exploring Pre-Twentieth-Century Fiction: A Language Approach*, Lancaster: Framework Press.

Burgess, T. (1996) 'English Teaching and its Narratives', *Changing English*, London: Institute of Education, University of London, March 1996, vol. 3, no. 1, pp. 57–77.

Burgess, R. and Gaudry, P. (1985) *Time for Drama*, Buckingham: Open University Press.

Byron, K. (1986) *Drama in the English Classroom*, London: Methuen.

Calderhead, J. (1987) 'The Quality of Reflection in Student Teachers', *European Journal of Teacher Education*, 10, 3, pp. 269–278.

—— (1989) 'Reflective Teaching and Teacher Education', *Teaching and Teacher Education*, 5, 1, pp. 43–51.

Calderhead, J. and Robson, M. (1991) 'Images of Teaching: Student Teachers', *Early Conceptions of Classroom Practice, Teaching and Teacher Education*, 7,1, pp. 1–8.

Canwell, S. and Ogborn, J. (1994) 'Balancing the Books: Modes of Assessment in A Level English Literature', in Brindley, S. (1994), pp. 149–153.

Capel, S., Leask, M. and Turner, T. (1995) *Learning to Teach in the Secondary School*, London: Routledge.

Carter, R. (ed.) (1990) *Knowledge about Language and the Curriculum: the LINC Reader* (London, Hodder & Stoughton).

Cook, H. and Styles, M. (1988) *There's a Poet behind You . . .*, London: A. & C. Black.

Cox, B. (1991) *Cox on Cox - an English Curriculum for the 1990s*, London: Hodder & Stoughton.

—— (1995) *The Battle for the National Curriculum*, London: Hodder & Stoughton.

Crystal, D. (1987) *The Cambridge Encyclopaedia of Language*, Cambridge: CUP.

Daiches, D. (1956) *Critical Approaches to Literature*, London: Longman.

Daly, M., Mathews, S., Middleton, D., Parker, H., Prior, J. and Waters, S. (1989) 'Different Views of the Subject: A PGCE Perspective', *The English Magazine*, 22, pp. 15–17.

Dart, L. and Drake, P. (1996) 'Subject Perspectives in Mentoring', in McIntyre, D. and Hagger, H., *Mentors in Schools: Developing the Profession of Teaching*, London: Fulton.

Davison, J. (1990) 'Uneasy Rider', *Times Educational Supplement*, 21 Oct. 1990.

Davison, J. and Grahame, J. (1992) *Media Directory*, Sheffield: NATE/English and Media Centre.

Daw, P. (1995) 'Differentiation and its Meanings', *English and Media Magazine*, 32, Summer, pp. 11–15.

Dearing, R. *The New Qualifications Framework 16–19*, revised version, London: HMSO.

DES (1963) *Half our Future* (Newsom Report), London: HMSO.

—— (1975) *A Language for Life* [The Bullock Report], London: HMSO.

—— (1983) *Popular TV and Schooling*, London: HMSO.

—— (1984) *English from 5 to 16*, London: HMSO.

—— (1987) *The National Curriculum 5 - 16: A Consultation Document*, London: HMSO.

—— (1988a) *Report of the Committee of Enquiry into the Teaching of English Language* [The Kingman Report], London: HMSO.

—— (1988b) *National Curriculum Task Group on Assessment and Testing: A Report* (TGAT), London: HMSO.

—— (1989) *English for Ages 5-16* [The Cox Report], London: DES.

—— (1990) *English in the National Curriculum (No. 2)*, London: HMSO.

DES and Welsh Office (1989) *English for Ages 5 to 16* (Cox Report 2), London: HMSO.

—— (1990) *The Statutory Order: English in the National Curriculum*, London: HMSO.

—— (1993a) *English 5–16 (1993)*, London: HMSO.

—— (1993b) *The Revised Order: English in the National Curriculum*, London: HMSO.

—— (1995) *English in the National Curriculum* (Dearing), London: HMSO.

DES/BFI (1989) *Primary Media Education: A Curriculum Statement*, London: BFI.

DFE (1993) *Boys and English*, London: HMSO.

—— (1995) *English in the National Curriculum*, London: HMSO; Cardiff, Welsh Office Education Department.

Dhondy, F. (1978) *Come to Mecca*, London: Fontana Lions.

Dickens, C. (1985) 'A Christmas Carol' in *The Christmas Books*, Vol. 1, London: Penguin Classics.

Dixon, J. (1967) *Growth through English*, Oxford: Oxford University Press/NATE.

Dover Wilson, J. (1932) 'Introduction', in Arnold, M. *Culture and Anarchy*, London: Penguin (1969 edn).

Dutton and Mundy (1995) *Media Studies: An Introduction*, London: Longman.

Eagleton, T. (1983) *Literary Theory*, Oxford: Basil Blackwell.

Elsom, J. (ed.) (1992) *Is Shakespeare Still Our Contemporary?*, London: Routledge.

Evening Chronicle (1987) *Bossy Parrot*, Newcastle: Bloodaxe Books.

Foggin, J. (1992) *Teaching English in the National Curriculum: Real Writing*, London: Hodder & Stoughton.

Fraser, P. (1993) 'Chaucer with Chips: Right-wing Discourse about Popular Culture', *English and Media Magazine*, 28, p. 19.

Freire, P. (1987) *Literacy: Reading the Word and the World*, London: Routledge & Kegan Paul.

Frost, D. (1993) 'Reflective Mentoring and the New Partnership', in McIntyre, D., Hagger, H. and Wilkin, M., *Mentoring: Perspectives on School-based Teacher Education*, London: Kogan Page.

Fuller, F. and Bown, O. (1975) in Ryan, K. (ed.) *Teacher Education*, 74th Year Book of the National Society for the Study of Education, Chicago: University of Chicago Press.

Furlong, J. and Maynard, T. (1995) *Mentoring Student Teachers*, London: Routledge.

Garfield, L. (1992) *Shakespeare: The Animated Tales*, London: BBC.

Gibson, R. (1994) 'Teaching Shakespeare in schools', in *Teaching English*, S. Brindley (ed.), London: Routledge, pp. 140-8.

Gilmour, M. (1994) *RSA Shakespeare in Schools Project 1992-4: A Review*, London: RSA Publications.

Goddard, A. (1993) *Researching Language*, Lancaster: Framework Press.

Goodman, S. and Graddol, D. (1997) *Redesigning English: New Texts, New Identities*, London: Routledge.

Goodson, I. (ed.) (1985) *Social Histories of the Secondary Curriculum*, London: Falmer Press.

Goodwyn, A. (1992) 'English Teachers and the Cox Models', *English in Education*, 26 (3), pp. 4–10.

Gordon, L. (1984) *Virginia Woolf: A Writer's Life*, Oxford: Oxford University Press.

Gossman, L. (1981) 'Literature and Education', *New Literary History*, vol. 13.

Graham, J. (1990) *Pictures on the Page*, Sheffield: NATE.

Grahame, J. (1990) *The English Curriculum: Media*, Sheffield: NATE/English and Media Centre.

—— (1993) *Advertising*, Sheffield: NATE/English and Media Centre.

—— (1996) *The News Pack*, London: English and Media Centre/NATE.

Greenlaw, L. (1996) 'Rhyme with Reason', *Times Educational Supplement*, 30 August, p. 23.

Greenwell, B. (1994) 'Alternatives at English A Level, Again', *English and Media Magazine*, Summer 1994, pp. 11–14.

Griffiths, M. and Tann, S. (1992) 'Using Reflective Practice to Link Personal and Public Theories', *Journal of Education for Teaching*, 18, 1, pp. 69–84.

Halliday, M.A.K. (1973) *Explorations in the Functions of Language*, London: Edward Arnold.

Hamblin, K. (1978) *Mime*, London: Lutterworth.

Harrison, T. (1984) *Selected Poems*, Harmondsworth: Penguin.

Hayhoe, M. and Parker S. (1988) *Words Large as Apples*, Cambridge: Cambridge University Press.

Hickman, J. (1995) 'NC English version 3.2: Flawed but Workable', *English and Media Magazine*, 32, Summer 1995, pp. 4–7.

Hilton, M. (ed.) (1996) *Potent Fictions: Children's Literacy and the Challenge of Popular Culture*, London: Routledge.

HMI (1984a) *English from 5 to 16*, London: HMSO.

—— (1984b) *The Curriculum from 5 to 16*, London: HMSO.

—— (1986) *English from 5 to 16: The Responses to Curriculum Matters 1*, London: HMSO.

—— (1993) *The New Teacher in School*, London: HMSO.

Hodgson, J. and Richards, E. (1974) *Improvisation*, London: Methuen.

Holderness, G. (ed.) (1988) *The Shakespeare Myth*, Manchester: Manchester University Press.

Holding, P. (1992) *Romeo and Juliet*, Text and Performance Series, London: Macmillan.

Hornbrook, D. (1988) ' "Go play, boy, play": Shakespeare and Educational drama', in Holderness (1988), pp. 145-159.

Howe, A. (1992) *Making Talk Work*, London: Hodder and Stoughton; reprinted 1997, Sheffield: NATE.

IAAMSS (1952) *The Teaching of English*, Cambridge: Cambridge University Press.

ILEA English Centre (1984) *Changing Stories*, London: English and Media Centre/NATE.

Jackson, D. (1982) *Continuity in Secondary English*, London and New York: Methuen.

Jenkins, T. (1995) 'GNVQ Media: 1 A Beginner's Guide, 2 Work in Progress', in *English and Media Magazine*, 32, Summer 1995, pp. 5–39.

—— (1996) *GNVQ Media: Production and Communication Intermediate*, London: Longman.

—— (1996) *GNVQ Media: Production and Communication Advanced*, London: Longman.

Johnson, J. (1992) ' "Made tongue-tied by authority": the Orders for English', in Norman, K. (ed.) *Thinking Voices*, London: Hodder & Stoughton.

Jones, P. (1991) *The Shakespeare Workshop*, New South Wales: St Clair Press.

Keith, G. (1991) *Knowledge about Language*, Coventry: NCET.

Kemeny, H. (ed.) (1990) *Talking IT Through*, Coventry: NCET.

Kinsman, J. (ed.) (1992) *Six Women Poets*, Oxford: Oxford University Press.

Korthagen, F. and Wubbels, T. (1995) 'Characteristics of Reflective Practitioners: Towards an Operationalisation of the Concept of Reflection', *Teachers and Teaching: Theory and Practice*, 1,1, pp. 51–72.

Kress, G. (1992) *Learning to Write*, London and New York: Routledge.

—— (1995) *Writing the Future: English and the Making of a Culture of Innovation*, Sheffield: NATE.

Laban, R. (1948) *Modern Educational Dance*, London: Macdonald & Evans.

Lake, C. and Rose, M. (eds) (1990) *Language and Power*, London: ILEA Afro-Caribbean Language and Literacy Project in Further and Adult Education.

Leach, S. (1992) *Shakespeare in the Classroom*, Buckingham: Open University Press.

Leavis, F. R. (1948) *The Great Tradition*, London: Chatto and Windus.

Leavis, F.R. and Thompson, D. (1933) *Culture and Environment*, London: Chatto and Windus.

LINC (1992) *Language in the National Curriculum: Materials for Professional Development*, LINC.

—— 'The Process of Writing' and 'The Writing Repertoire', in *Language in the National Curriculum* (unpublished).

Little, R., Redsell, P. and Wilcock, E. (1986) *Contexts*, London and Oxford: Heinemann.

London Association for the Teaching of English (1996) *The Real Cost of SATs: a Report*, London: LATE.

Longhurst, D., (1988) ' "You base football player!": Shakespeare in contemporary popular culture', in Holderness (1988), pp. 59–73.

Lucas, P. (1991) 'Reflection, New Practices and the Need for Flexibility in Supervising Student Teachers', *Journal of Further and Higher Education*, 15,2, pp. 84–93.

Lunzer, E. and Gardner, K. (eds) (1979) *The Effective Use of Reading*, London: Heinemann Educational Books for the Schools Council.

Lynch, W. (1991) *Planning for Language*, Coventry: NCET.

McCulloch, R. (ed.) (1994) *English Literature A Level*, Cambridge: Pearson.

Macdonald, D., *et al.* (1989) 'Different Views of the Subject: A PGCE Perspective', *English and Media Magazine*, Summer, pp. 15–17.

McIntyre, D. and Hagger, H. (1993) 'Teachers' Expertise and Models of Mentoring', in McIntyre, D., Hagger, H. and Wilkin, M. *Mentoring: Perspectives on School-based Teacher Education*, London: Kogan Page.

McIntyre, D. and Hagger, H. (1996) *Mentors in Schools: Developing the Profession of Teaching*, London: Fulton.

McLaughlin, T. (1996) *Beyond the Reflective Teacher*, unpublished paper, Cambridge University Department of Education.

Masterman, L. (1985) *Teaching the Media*, London: Comedia.

Masterman, L. (1995) *Media Studies Teachers' Guide to Studies in Depth*, Manchester: NEAB.

Mathieson, M. (1975) *The Preachers of Culture*, London: Allen & Unwin.

Maybin, J. (1996) 'An English Canon?', in Maybin, J. and Mercer, N., *Using English: From Conversation to Canon*, London: Routledge.

Maybin, J. and Mercer, N. (1996) *Using English: From Conversation to Canon*, London: Routledge.

Meek, M. (1988) *How Texts Teach What Readers Learn*, Stroud: Thimble Press.

—— (1991) *On Being Literate*, London: Bodley Head.

Mercer, N. and Swann, J. (1997) *Learning English: Development and Diversity*, London: Routledge.

Messenger Davis, M. (1989) *Television is Good for Your Kids*, London: Hilary Shipman.

Minns, H. (1991) *Primary Practice*, Coventry: NCET.

Mitchell, S. (1994) 'Argument in English Literature at A Level and Beyond', *English and Media Magazine*, Summer 1994, pp. 15–20.

Mole, J. (1990) *Catching the Spider*, London: Blackie.

National Association for the Teaching of English (1993) *Move Back the Desks*, Sheffield: NATE.

—— (1994) 'GCSE English: The Background to the Current Concerns', *NATE News*, Spring 1994, p. 9.

National Centre for Educational Technology (1991) *Language Learning and IT*, Coventry: NCET.

National Curriculum Council (1990) *English Non-statutory Guidance*, London: NCC.

—— (1993) *National Curriculum in English: The Case for Revising the Order*, London: NCC.

National Oracy Project (1991) *Teaching Talking and Learning at Key Stage 3*, London: NCC/NOP.

—— (1993) *Teaching Talking and Learning at Key Stage 4*, London: NCC/NOP.

National Writing Project (1993) *Responding to and Assessing Writing*, London: Nelson.

Neelands, J. (1984) *Making Sense of Drama*, London: Heinemann.

—— (1992) *Learning through Imagined Experience*, London: Hodder & Stoughton.

—— (1993) *Structuring Drama Work*, London: Cambridge University Press.

Nicholls, B. (1974) *Move*, London: Heinemann.

Norman, K. (ed.) (1992) *Thinking Voices*, London: Hodder & Stoughton.

NWP (1990) *Ways of Looking: Issues from the National Writing Project*, London: Nelson.

OFSTED (1993) *The New Teacher in School*, London, HMSO.

O'Neill, C. (1977) *Drama Guidelines*, London: Heinemann.

Orme, D. (1995) *Specials! Romeo and Juliet*, Dunstable: Folens.

O'Sullivan, Dutton, and Rayner (1994) *Studying the Media*, London: Arnold.

Palmer (1965) *The Rise of English Studies*, Oxford: Oxford University Press.

Patten, J. (1992) Speech to Conservative Party Conference, 7 October 1992, London: Conservative Party Press Office.

Peel, R. and Hargreaves, S. (1995) 'Beliefs about English', *English in Education*, 29 (3), pp. 38–49.

Peet, M. and Robinson, D. (1990, 1992) *Essential Articles nos 1–4*, Carlisle: Carel Press.

—— (1992) *Leading Questions*, London and Edinburgh: Nelson.

Peim, N. (1992) 'Reading and the World of LINC', *English in Education*, 26 (3), pp. 36–39.

Pennac, D. (1994) *Reads Like a Novel*, trans. D. Gunn, London: Quartet.

Perera, K.(1987) *Understanding Language*, Sheffield: NAAE/NATE.

Powling, C. and Styles, M. (1996) *A Guide to Poetry 0 -13*, Reading: Books for Keeps and The Reading and Language Information Centre.

Prain, V. (1996) 'Selves to Discover, Selves to Invent: Rethinking Autobiographical Writing in the English Classroom', *Changing English*, vol. 3, no. 1, London, Institute of Education, University of London, March 1996, pp. 7–19.

Price, S. (1993) *Media Studies*, London: Pitman.

Protherough, R. and King, P. (1995) *The Challenge of English in the National Curriculum*, London: Routledge.

Rawlins, G. and Rich, J. (1985) *Look, Listen and Trust*, London: Macmillan Education.

Reid, J.-A., Forrestal, P. and Cook, J. (1989) *Small Group Learning in the Classroom*, London: Chalkface Press/English and Media Centre.

Reynolds, P. (1991) 'Unlocking the Box: Shakespeare on Film and Video', in Aers and Wheale, pp. 189–203.

Richards, I. A. (1929) *Practical Criticism: A Study of Literary Judgment*, London: Routledge & Kegan Paul.

Richmond, J. (1992) 'Unstable Materials: The LINC Story', *English and Media Magazine*, Spring 1992.

Roberts, A. E. and Barter, A. (1908) *The Teaching of English*, London: Blackie.

Rosen, B. (1988) *And None of It Was Nonsense*, London: Mary Glasgow.

Rosen, M. (1974) *Mind Your Own Business*, London: Andre Deutsch.

Rosenblatt, L. (1978) *The Reader, the Text, the Poem*, Southern Illinois University Press.

Rudduck, J. (1991) 'The Landscape of Consciousness and the Landscape of Action: Tensions in Teacher Education', *British Educational Research Journal*, 17, p. 4.

Sampson, G. (1921) *English for the English*, Cambridge: Cambridge University Press.

SCAA (1994) *English in the National Curriculum: Draft Proposals*, London: SCAA.

—— (1996) *A Guide to the National Curriculum*, London: HMSO.

Scannell, V. (1971) *Selected Poems*, London: Allison and Busby.

Scholes, R. (1985) *Textual Power*, Newhaven and London: Yale University Press.

—— (1989) *Protocols of Reading*, Newhaven and London: Yale University Press.

Schön, D. (1983) *The Reflective Practitioner*, London: Temple Smith.

Schools Inquiry Commission (1868) *The Taunton Report*, London: HMSO.

Sealey, A. (1991) *Language in Context*, Coventry: NCET.

Self, D. (1988) *New Guidelines: Romeo and Juliet*, London: Mary Glasgow.

Shepherd, C. and White, C. (1990, 1992) *Essential Articles nos 1–4*, Carlisle: Carel Press.

—— (1991) *Novel Ideas*, Carlisle: Carel Press.

Shreeve, A. (1995) 'The Future of English', *English in Education*, 29 (2), pp. 1–2.

Simons, M. and Plackett, P. (eds) (1990) *The English Curriculum: Reading 1 Comprehension*, London: English and Media Centre.

Stephens, *et al.* (1990) *School*, London: English and Media Centre/NATE.

Stevenson, A. (1993) *Four and a Half Dancing Men*, Oxford: Oxford University Press.

Stibbs, A. (1995) 'The Specialness of Poetry', *English in Education*, 29 (3), pp. 14–19.

Style, M. (1989) *Collaboration and Writing*, Buckingham: Open University Press.

Styles, M. and Watson, V. (1996) *Talking Pictures*, London: Hodder & Stoughton.

Times Educational Supplement (1915) 'Children and the Cinematograph', 5 January 1915.

Trudgill, P. (1975) *Accent, Dialect and the School*, London: Edward Arnold.

—— (1983) *On Dialect*, Oxford: Blackwell.

Teacher Training Agency (1997) *Training Curriculum and Standards for New Teachers*, London: TTA.

UCLES (1996) *Report on the June 1996 Examination SR21 (UK)*, Cambridge: UCLES.

Vygotsky, L.S. (1978) *Mind in Society*, Cambridge, Mass. and London: Harvard University Press.

—— (1986) *Thought and Language*, Cambridge, Mass. and London: MIT.

Wainwright, J. and Hutton, J. (1992) *In Your Own Words: Advanced Level English Language*, Walton on Thames and Edinburgh: Nelson.

Wall, P. (1996) *GCSE Media Studies*.

Wells, S. (ed.) (1988) *The Cambridge Companion to Shakespeare Studies*, Cambridge: Cambridge University Press.

West, A. and Dickey, A. (1990) *Redbridge High School English Department Handbook*, London: Borough of Redbridge Advisory Service.

Whiting, *et al.* (1996) *Partnership in Initial Teacher Education: A Topography*, London: University of London.

Whitten, W. and Whittaker, F. (1938) *Good and Bad English*, London: Newnes.

Wilkinson, A. (ed.) (1986) *The Writing of Writing*, Buckingham: Open University Press.

Williams, R. (1961) *Culture and Society*, London: Penguin.

Williamson, J. and Woodall, C. (1996) 'A Vision for English: Rethinking the Revised National Curriculum in the Light of Contemporary Critical Theory', *English in Education*, 30 (3) pp. 4–13.

Wood, D., in Norman, K. (ed.) (1992) *Thinking Voices*, London: Hodder & Stoughton.

Young Observer (1987) *Words on Water*, Harmondsworth: Puffin.

Index